A BUSINESS-LIKE APPROACH TO COBOL

A
BUSINESS-LIKE
APPROACH
TO COBOL

HENRY MULLISH
New York University

Thomas Y. Crowell
Harper & Row, Publishers
New York   Hagerstown   Philadelphia   San Francisco   London

Sponsoring Editor: Charlie Dresser
Project Editor: Penelope Schmukler
Designer: Michel Craig
Senior Production Manager: Kewal K. Sharma
Compositor: Kingsport Press
Printer and Binder: The Murray Printing Company
Art Studio: J & R Technical Services, Inc.

A BUSINESS-LIKE APPROACH TO COBOL

Library of Congress Cataloging in Publication Data

Mullish, Henry.
     A business-like approach to COBOL.
     Includes index.
     1. COBOL (Computer program language). I. Title.
QA76.73.C25M83   001.6'424   78–16190
ISBN 0–7002–2506–4

This book is dedicated with deep affection
to the memory of my brother Ben
who derived so much pleasure being a businessman.

CONTENTS

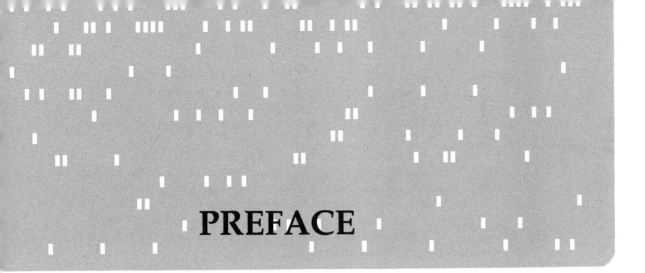

PREFACE

It may be somewhat of a shock to realize that the original version of COBOL was written back in 1960, making it a "contemporary" of the ever popular, scientifically oriented language called FORTRAN. Moreover, COBOL is the most widely used programming language existing today. This will almost certainly be the case also in the year 2000 and perhaps for a long time after that, too.

For pedagogical purposes it is desirable for all students to learn the same standardized language (ANSI* COBOL is used almost exclusively in this text) even though in the real world specialized *dialects* of the language will be used in any given particular shop. But this phenomenon is certainly not new on the educational scene and there is no reason why it should not also apply to the teaching of COBOL.

The approach I have attempted in this book—what I describe as a business-like approach—assumes no prior knowledge of computers, programming languages, or programming techniques; nor for that matter is any familiarity with business procedures assumed. This book is designed as a fully self-contained introduction to the COBOL language, one accompanied by a large number of graduated problems, exercises, COBOL "mysteries," and student examples. It is hoped that after a single, thorough reading of the text the reader will have a solid understanding of the essentials of COBOL programming and will be sufficiently equipped and confident to dare to search for any required additional information in the standard reference manuals, however intimidating they might appear initially.

The major aim is to provide the novice with sufficient information to enable him or her to write a program, however trivial it might be, in

*American National Standards Institute

the shortest possible time. The novice must get involved with structure, flowcharting, keypunching, checking, and debugging from the outset and for this reason there is an abundance of questions and exercises in each chapter. He or she must become totally immersed as soon as possible to achieve the greatest success in the shortest possible time.

This text is designed to cover the essentials of the COBOL language, and care has been taken to provide interesting and pertinent—even entertaining—teaching techniques to enliven the text. In so doing, its aim is to cover a broad scope of material in an acceptable fashion while not in any way doing violence to pedagogical integrity or to the conceptual clarity of the information presented.

Each of the many programs illustrated in the text has been run on an IBM 370/145 computer; to prevent the introduction of printing errors, each program listing has been reproduced directly from the IBM printout, rather than reset for this text. A considerable number of people, for whom a picture is worth "a thousand words," prefer to learn programming by examining a succession of graduated programs rather than by having to read explanatory text. Such students as well as those who also want extended explanations should be content with the manner in which this text is written. The salient principles can be learned either from the descriptive sections or by a careful perusal of the programs—"by inspection," as it were.

The reader is advised that there is a version of COBOL named WATBOL, developed at the University of Waterloo (Ontario), which also developed the well-known student compilers called WATFOR and WATFIV. The WATBOL version of COBOL is rapidly becoming popular in educational institutions; for this reason a special section in this text has been devoted to WATBOL.

This text could be used to advantage in a two semester introductory course at a two-year or four-year college, particularly if COBOL is the student's first exposure to computer languages. The rich selection of questions and exercises should make it ideal for an instructor whose thankless task it is to assign homework problems. It should be pointed out that in the last two years or so several selected New York City high schools have included the teaching of COBOL in their computer science curriculum. Surely this is a trend which will continue in the years to come on a national scale.

Henry Mullish

ACKNOWLEDGMENTS

It is rare that an author himself originates all the ideas that appear in his book. I am deeply indebted to several of my students who served not only as sounding boards for many of the approaches but also in various ways helped to fashion the finished product. Among these I must include the hundreds of students who have sat through my classes in COBOL at New York University. Many of them have since gone out into the business world to reap their rewards. In particular, I would like to thank by name several ex-students who contributed fully and unselfishly: Robert Rosentel for his "Cobolsteries" (COBOL mystery stories), Steve Kochan, John Zachary, Eli Opas, and Peter McKay. It would be unfair not to mention the duplicating button on the keypunch machine without whose aid punching up the programs would have been a far greater chore.

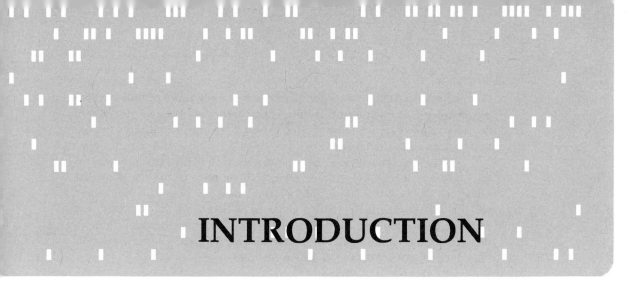

INTRODUCTION

For reasons which may vary all the way from sheer interest to utter economic necessity, millions of people throughout the world have learned, or will have to learn, to program in the most widely used, business-oriented computer language yet devised. That language is COBOL, an acronym for Common Business Oriented Language. The official standardized version of the language is known as ANSI COBOL, where ANSI is an acronym for American National Standards Institute. The COBOL language was written in 1960, although since then it has undergone various changes.

Fortunately, various committees have assumed the responsibility for updating and maintaining the efficiency of the language while retaining its standardization. The purpose is simply to make the COBOL language accessible with little or no modification on any of the existing computers, including those manufactured by International Business Machines (IBM), Control Data Corporation (CDC), Honeywell, and National Cash Register (NCR), to mention just a few manufacturers. To use the current terminology, COBOL is intended to be *machine independent.*

The word "common" (from which the first two letters, CO, are taken to begin the acronym COBOL) is used for several reasons. COBOL is the result of a carefully planned, deliberate, collective, *common* effort undertaken by various branches of the United States government, business representatives, and computer manufacturers, who pooled their efforts back in the late 1950s and designed a language dedicated to the special problems of business and finance. COBOL is a *common* language because it may be run not only on one particular computer but on many. Finally, *common* is appropriate because with the passing of time, COBOL has become the major—and eventually may be the only—business language in use today. In that sense it has become extremely common in commercial establishments. In light of its popularity and in recognition of the irreversible manner in which the business community has become dependent on COBOL to process its mighty workload, it has become increasingly important to master the language.

To the men and women being introduced to COBOL for the first time, we extend a hearty welcome. It might not be easy to master all of the intricacies of COBOL but it is certainly a challenge, and hopefully one which will be met successfully with a sense of satisfaction. In any case, the reader may be assured that of all the programming languages used in the world today, none is in as much demand as COBOL, despite its shortcomings. Indeed, COBOL is a bread-and-butter language.

A
BUSINESS-LIKE
APPROACH
TO COBOL

SOME BASIC COBOL PROGRAMMING CONCEPTS

1.1 THE COBOL COMPILER

> BASIC *is simple*
> PL/ I *is fun*
> FORTRAN *is useful*
> *But* COBOL's *the one.*

The sequence of computer instructions to solve a particular problem is called a program. In the case of a COBOL program, the instructions are usually punched on cards by means of a keypunch machine. COBOL is considered a high level programming language since it is composed of words, phrases, and syntax not entirely dissimilar from written English. Thus COBOL is fairly easy to learn even for people without any programming experience whatsoever.

It would, of course, be very simple if we could present a problem to the computer in the same way that we present a problem to a person, for example, by word of mouth or by writing the instructions down on paper. Unfortunately, the computer, as fast as it is, cannot hear in the way that we human beings can, and in general neither can it read the written word as you are reading these words. What we have to aim at is a compromise solution. In most installations the COBOL instructions are punched on cards which are then "fed" to the computer. You might be surprised if not shocked to learn, however, that even these COBOL instructions are not really "understood" by the computer. The only language a computer is capable of understanding is the so-called *binary* language. This language is composed entirely of 1's and 0's. The binary language is not only very difficult for human beings like ourselves but also is extremely tedious and error prone. For the computer, however, the binary language is ideal, with each 0 and 1 regarded as a tiny switch which is either "on" or "off."

Every computer that is able to accept COBOL as a programming language is equipped with a special set of highly sophisticated programs called the *compiler*. The purpose of the compiler is to scan the COBOL instructions individually and to convert them into their equivalent binary instructions. It is quite possible that one COBOL instruction is translated into 20 or even more machine language (binary) instructions. Once converted into this binary form, the computer is able to follow the instructions with the speed of electricity, or at least at a rate approaching that speed.

This concept of converting from one language to another is probably not unfamiliar to you, particularly if you live in a large metropolitan area. In New York City, for example, when ordering a meal in a luncheonette, one often hears one's order converted to a jargon which seemingly has little or no relation to the original order. For example, a glass of seltzer water is encoded to number "91." A cup of hot chocolate becomes a "51," while a glass of water is converted to "81." A small glass of cola is a "shot" while a large glass is referred to as a "stretch." The number "210" means, believe it or not, that someone is leaving the restaurant without paying. The phrase "check the ice" is the jargon for "take a look at the cute looking girl who just entered the luncheonette." All this may seem rather exotic to the uninitiated. Being a native of Britain, the author takes exception to the jargon which is used for the order "one toasted English muffin." It is none other than "down with the British," or even worse, "one burnt Limey!"

The reason for converting the simple orders into a particular jargon is threefold. First, it lends a certain amount of prestige to the employees of the luncheonette; second, the converted order is generally shorter and less ambiguous; and third, it prevents the possibility of a chef hearing a duplicate order—the one voiced by the customer and that relayed by the waiter.

One might wonder what all of this has to do with COBOL. In a sense, the waiter, when relaying the order from the customer to the chef, acts like a compiler in that he converts the customer's order given in common English to the jargon version which the chef understands and processes.

Once a COBOL program is written and punched on cards (prior to being processed by the computer) the instructions contained in that program must be converted into a form which the computer can handle. This form, as we mentioned earlier, is the binary representation of the instructions. The compiler is composed of a bewilderingly complicated series of routines which examine each of the instructions of the COBOL program and, if after examination they are found to be valid, convert them into the binary form for subsequent execution. Only after the program is executed are the results produced. The compiler is designed to check each program instruction for correct grammatical syntax and the accurate spelling of keywords, and to insure that special reserved words are used properly. What happens if a COBOL instruction is found to be invalid? In that case, a *diagnostic* message is printed along with an attempt at explaining the probable cause of the error. This is reminiscent of the manner in which a medical examiner performs a health checkup on a patient by administering a battery of tests. If the patient passes all of the tests within certain limits, he or she is pronounced in good health. The analogy is not that farfetched since the compiler permits minor infractions to pass with just a printed warning but terminates the program immediately if the error is of a severe nature. Even though a program may contain a series of syntactically correct instructions, they can be put together in such a way that they do not produce the desired results. In other words, there is an error in their logical arrangement. Such an error of logic is often found in everyday life, particularly with respect to children. If a child is told for example, to get dressed and to take a shower, the instructions themselves would be correct, but carrying out the instructions in the order stated would *not* produce the desired results.

Unfortunately, no compiler that has yet been written is so sophisticated that it can correct an error of logic. This kind of error as well as the correcting of any other errors detected by the compiler is the responsibility of the programmer. A printed listing of the program is returned to the programmer together with any computed results. It is pointed out here that it is quite possible for a single error to create a deluge of diagnostic messages. As disappointing as this may be, one should not be too upset by this since correcting the single error will invariably clear up all of the diagnostics. Programmers are sometimes discouraged when, after considerable effort, their programs are returned with more diagnostic messages than instructions. It pays not to be too thin-skinned at this juncture. Everybody makes mistakes, so why not you? With experience and dedication to the task, the number of errors decreases very quickly and correcting them becomes nothing more than a slight inconvenience.

Once the COBOL language program has been converted or translated by the compiler to its equivalent binary program, it is possible to get a copy of this binary program punched on cards. In order to distinguish between these two decks, the original COBOL program is referred to as the *source deck* while the compiled version is spoken of as the *object deck.*

Since one COBOL instruction may produce a great number of machine level instructions, it will become apparent to the reader that programs are hardly ever written in the binary language because it would be much too tedious, time consuming, and too difficult both to amend and to understand. Amending a COBOL program, on the other hand, lightens the burden considerably. Since COBOL programs are so readily understandable and may be amended and updated so easily, United States Government agencies are ordinarily forbidden to purchase a computer unless it comes equipped with a COBOL compiler.

1.2 THE STRUCTURE OF A COBOL PROGRAM

Every COBOL program is divided into four main subgroupings. They are

(a) the Identification Division
(b) the Environment Division
(c) the Data Division
(d) the Procedure Division.

The order of these divisions must be in the order shown so that it would not be a bad idea either to learn the order by heart or else to place a bookmark in this page so that the order can be checked quickly when needed. Remember, this order must be adhered to, "In Every Darned Program." The initial letter of each word, which corresponds to the initial letter of the four divisions, will aid in remembering the order.

When punching a program into the standard 80-column punch-cards, certain rules must be observed. Each of the four divisions mentioned above must be punched on separate cards, but not anywhere on the card. They must be punched beginning in what is called area or margin A, which begins in column 8 and extends to column 11 (see Figure 1). Area or margin B, about which we shall have more to say in a short while, begins in column 12 and extends to column 72. Columns 73–80 are ignored so that they may be used for sequencing, identification, or anything else for that matter.

Columns 1–6 may be used, if desired, for additional sequencing but this is entirely optional. In long programs it would be particularly

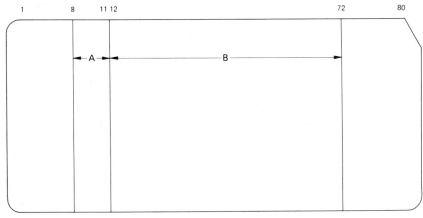

FIGURE 1

useful. Column 7 is used, when necessary, for continuation purposes. But we shall be discussing this feature later on in the text.

THE IDENTIFICATION DIVISION

The Identification Division is indicated by punching these two words in area A, as shown in Figure 2. Although they may be punched beginning in column 8, 9, 10, or 11, we shall always punch them beginning in column 8 and it is suggested the reader do likewise. There must be at least one space between the two words. In COBOL, anywhere that one space is permitted, any number of spaces is also permitted.

The Identification Division header card is the very first entry in any and every COBOL program. It is used, as its name suggests, to identify the program to the computer. The *header card,* as are so many of the remaining cards soon to be described, must be terminated by a period. This card is always followed by another card called the PROGRAM–ID card, again punched in area A and followed by a period. Incidentally, this is always hyphenated by a minus sign between PROGRAM and ID. This is, in turn, followed by a programmer's choice of a name for his program, again ending with a period. When information is punched on the same card following a period, at least one blank space must always separate the two items. Therefore the program name, coming after PROGRAM–ID, must be preceded by at least one blank following the period (see examples on page 6). The rules for constructing PROGRAM–ID names follow.

1. The first character must be an alphabetic letter (A through z).
2. The numerics 0 through 9 may be combined in any order with alphabetics (subject to the first rule mentioned above) and may also contain the hyphen (minus sign), provided the hyphen is

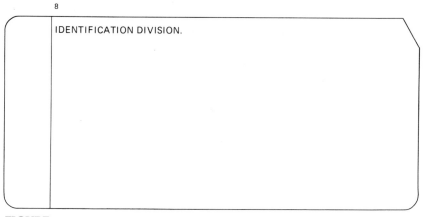

8

IDENTIFICATION DIVISION.

FIGURE 2

neither the initial nor the terminating character. Embedded blanks, that is, included spaces, are not allowed in a name.
3. The length of the name must not exceed 30 characters, but the first eight must be unique to the program since only these initial eight characters are recognized by the compiler.

The reader is cautioned that not all COBOL systems treat PROGRAM–ID names in the same way. On IBM machines the maximum length used by the system (as opposed to the actual PROGRAM–ID name) is eight, whereas on Burroughs machines for example the maximum length used is six only. Now although a dash is permitted within a PROGRAM–ID name, care should be taken not to terminate the name with a hyphen because this is illegal. Ordinarily one would not write a PROGRAM–ID name with a trailing hyphen, but situations can easily arise where the inclusion of hyphens can lead to trouble. For example, the PROGRAM–ID name SALES–N–COMMISSIONS would generate an error on both the IBM and the Burroughs compiler because hyphens appear in the sixth and eighth positions of the name. Furthermore, if a program is named BONDS–AND–STOCKS it would be perfectly valid for an IBM system, but not if transferred to a Burroughs system. Similarly, the name ACCOUNT–STATUS would be fine for a Burroughs system but would create trouble on an IBM machine since the hyphen is in the eighth position.

4. The name selected must not be a reserved word. In COBOL there is a list of several hundred words which are reserved for special purposes. Unless the word is being used for that precise, designated purpose, it must be avoided. The words COMPUTE, INPUT, EXIT, READ, WRITE and VALUE are examples of key words. A complete list of them will be found on page 335, but since it is so long and too difficult to learn by heart, there are two alternatives open to the programmer. Either he can refer to the list everytime he decides upon a name and use it only if it is not one of the reserved words, or he can take advantage of the fact that each of the key words is a regular English word. In selecting a name, therefore, he can make it irregular by, say, prefixing the word with an X. This way he will be sure it is not a key word even though it might closely resemble one.

In any case here are some examples of valid Identification Divisions:

(a) 8
```
IDENTIFICATION DIVISION.
PROGRAM–ID.  FIRST–TRY.
```

(b)
```
IDENTIFICATION DIVISION.
PROGRAM–ID.  HENRY.
```

```
(c) IDENTIFICATION DIVISION.
    PROGRAM-ID.  BILLS-PAID.

(d) IDENTIFICATION DIVISION.
    PROGRAM-ID.  MSTR-FILE.
```

THE ENVIRONMENT DIVISION

The second division is the Environment Division, which is so named because it describes the "computing environment" in which the program is to be processed. That is, it specifies the equipment on which the program is to be run. It allows for the specification of the source computer, that is, the computer on which the COBOL program is to be *compiled,* and the object computer, on which it is to be executed. This section of the Environment Division is called the Configuration Section. For our purposes, we shall assume that both the source computer and the object computer are the IBM 370/145. This being the case, the Configuration Section may be omitted entirely since the IBM COBOL compiler assumes the IBM/370 by default. If it were included, it would look like this:

```
ENVIRONMENT DIVISION.
CONFIGURATION SECTION.
SOURCE-COMPUTER.  IBM-370-145.
OBJECT-COMPUTER.  IBM-370-145.
```

If the computer being used is the IBM 360 (the IBM 370's predecessor) it is suggested that if the model number is 45, for example, the specification should be:

```
IBM-360-45.
```

In the initial programs which follow, we shall simply show the first of the four lines shown above since that is all that is required. However, we shall expand upon this when we deal with input-output devices such as files. But we must learn to walk before learning how to run.

THE DATA DIVISION

To solve a business problem—or any other kind of problem for that matter—one has to start out with data. Indeed, programming may be defined as the art of manipulating data. The kind of data to be used in a COBOL program are specified in the Data Division. We shall have more to say about this division later on. For the present we shall merely include a card punched with the words DATA DIVISION. beginning in margin A, and expand upon the concept at the appropriate time.

THE PROCEDURE DIVISION

Finally we have arrived at the last of the four divisions, the Procedure Division. This is the "action" division, usually the most complicated of

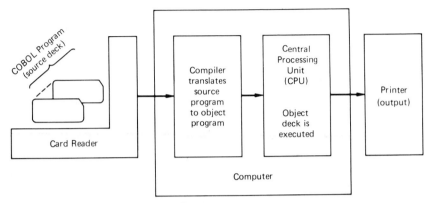

FIGURE 3 **The Flow of a COBOL Program**

the four divisions since it is here that the precise procedure to solve a particular problem must be specified. For the time being we shall concern ourselves with just a simple instruction: the DISPLAY instruction which simply prints out whatever is enclosed between single quotes. For example, to print out "Hi there" we could use the COBOL instruction:

DISPLAY 'HI THERE'.

Such an instruction is punched beginning in column 12, where the B area begins. Indeed, *all* instructions are punched in the B margin. Here is the formalized version of the DISPLAY statement:

$$\text{DISPLAY} \quad \begin{Bmatrix} \text{(data-name-1)} \\ \text{(literal-1)} \end{Bmatrix} \quad \begin{bmatrix} \text{[data-name-2]} \\ \text{[literal-2]} \dots \end{bmatrix}$$

Above is a diagrammatic representation of the flow of a punched COBOL program being processed on a typical computer (Figure 3). Note the double role played by the computer.

Finally, most COBOL programs are terminated by the instruction STOP RUN. and this also appears in margin B. It format is simply STOP RUN.

As our first real, live program, which admittedly doesn't do anything very spectacular, we shall have the computer merely print out the phrase "Hi there." Here is the program and its output. Notice that the header cards for *each* of the four divisions has to appear, even in such an elementary program.

PROGRAM 1
Illustration of DISPLAY

```
00001          IDENTIFICATION DIVISION.
00002          PROGRAM-ID. PROGRAM1.
00003          ENVIRONMENT DIVISION.
00004          DATA DIVISION.
00005          PROCEDURE DIVISION.
00006              DISPLAY 'HI THERE'.
00007              STOP RUN.
```

OUTPUT TO PROGRAM 1*

HI THERE

1.3 THE HIERARCHICAL NATURE OF A
COBOL PROGRAM

Although it is not apparent from the elementary program we have just illustrated, every COBOL program may be broken down into various subordinate parts. We have already seen that each COBOL program is broken up into four divisions. Within each division may be one or more sections. Each section in turn may be written in terms of paragraphs. Each paragraph is composed of individual sentences. Finally, each sentence is constructed of verbs and clauses. This hierarchical nature is represented schematically in Figure 4.

COBB OL MYSTERY #1

It was a quiet rainy afternoon when detective Cobb Ol received the phone call from the American Computer Institute. Mr. Sy Stem, the Institute's manager, hired the world-renowned detective to help solve a baffling problem. The Institute's computer seemed to have been sabotaged. Cobb knew that this case would bring back some nostalgic memories of his college days, when he had learned COBOL programming. He picked up his trench coat and umbrella and headed for the Institute offices.

Cobb Ol met Mr. Stem in the main office. It seemed that the computer

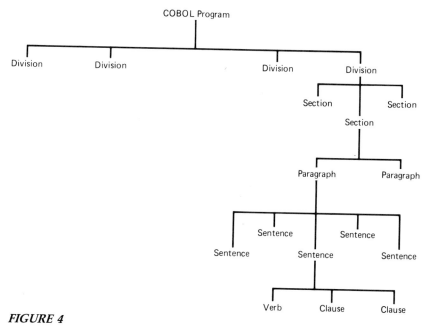

FIGURE 4

* The 5-digit sequence numbers printed to the left of the program instructions are *not* punched by the programmer; they are produced in the listing of the program by the compiler for reference purposes.

would not process a single program even though the engineers couldn't find anything wrong, not even a dented transistor. Millions of dollars of business were being lost each week while the computer was down.

After questioning Mr. Stem about the operations personnel, Ol discovered that only three people could exercise a direct control over the computer's operation. They were his prime suspects.

Katie, the keypunch operator, explained to Ol that it was her responsibility to punch all the COBOL programs onto punch cards and then verify the cards before sending them to the operator for processing. She explained that she often mistakenly punched statements belonging in the A margin in the B margin and vice versa, but she almost always detected these errors herself when she verified the cards.

Oscar, the computer operator, explained how he habitually maintained the utmost care in running each of the programs given to him. He always checked the control cards and made sure that each of the divisions was present.

"What divisions?" asked Cobb.

"Oh, the four divisions which must be present in every COBOL program," Oscar explained, "the Identification, Data, Environment, and Procedure Divisions."

Oscar went back to his card reader, and the detective moved quietly on, gently puffing on his pipe.

Sam, the systems analyst, was very defensive at Cobb's questioning. He himself was puzzled by the apparent malfunction and had checked the compiler system and the library disks and tapes.

"What version of COBOL does this machine use?" asked the detective.

"ANSI," snapped Sam.

Ol wrote in his notebook.

"Look, I don't know what you're doing here but I don't need your help," barked Sam at the detective.

"I'm sorry to have taken up your time," calmly replied Ol as he left the computer room.

"I know who the culprit is," said Ol, as he sat down in an armchair in Stem's office.

"Your saboteur is Oscar, the computer operator, but I wouldn't be too hard on him because it's really just an accident."

"But what did he do?" asked Sy Stem.

"Elementary, sir, he simply took each program deck and put the divisions into what he honestly thought was the correct order—Identification, Data, Environment, and Procedure. Well even the beginning student knows it should be Identification, Environment, Data and Procedure."

"How on earth did you remember that?" asked an astonished Stem.

"When I was a young lad studying COBOL a professor taught us a mnemonic to remember the order of the divisions—

IN EVERY DARNED PROGRAM."

Cobb Ol slid into the easy chair in his study and sipped his evening sherry. "Sabotage," he thought and smiled.

1.4 REVIEW QUESTIONS

1. How does a COBOL source program differ from an object program?
2. What is the name given to the part of the system which converts the COBOL program to the language the computer "understands"?

3. What does the acronym COBOL stand for?
4. The acronym ANSI stands for
    (a) A New Set of Instructions
    (b) All-Purpose Negatively Specified Indicators
    (c) American National Standards Institute
    (d) ANother Silly Invention.
5. COBOL was first written in
    (a) 1984
    (b) 1960
    (c) 200 B.C.
    (d) 1976.
6. The process of translating a COBOL program to machine level language is called
    (a) reformation
    (b) restructuring
    (c) proliferation
    (d) compilation.
7. The term "execution" refers to
    (a) elimination of bugs in a program
    (b) keypunching of original source program
    (c) carrying out the program instructions
    (d) conversion from source program to object program.
8. A "diagnostic" is
    (a) a syntax error in a program
    (b) a questionable path in a program
    (c) a hardware fault in the computer
    (d) a medical term with no relevance to programming.
9. The reason why programs are written in COBOL rather than in machine language is that
    (a) it is more fun
    (b) it is a commercial conspiracy to promote the language
    (c) they satisfy a governmental directive
    (d) it is not only considerably more comprehensible to a nonprogrammer, but it is much easier to write in COBOL since one COBOL instruction could easily translate into dozens of separate machine language instructions.
10. The compiler is so sophisticated that it
    (a) leaves us free to be sloppy
    (b) corrects errors of logic
    (c) permits a mixture of COBOL, FORTRAN, BASIC and ALGOL.
    (d) none of the above.
11. COBOL is such an important language that
    (a) according to law every computer must accept it
    (b) no business procedure is permitted unless it can be written in COBOL
    (c) no government agency may ordinarily purchase a computer which does not have a COBOL compiler
    (d) every department store cashier should know it well.
12. Which, if any, of the following Identification Divisions are free of error?

```
                  Column
      1     8   12

(a)                 IDENTIFICATION DIVISION
                    PROGRAM—ID.  MIKES—FOLLY

(b)             IDENTIFICATION—DIVISION.
                PROGRAM—ID. THIS—IS—IT.
```

Column

```
        1        8   12
(c)     |        |IDENTIFICATION DIVISION.
        |        |PROGRAM–ID. THIS–IS–IT?.

(d)     |        |IDENTIFICATION DIVISION.
        |        |PROGRAM–ID. FINISH–UP

(e)     |        |IDENTIFICATION DIVISION.
        |        |PROGRAM–ID ACCOUNTS.

(f)     |        |IDENTIFICATION DIVISION.
        |        |PROGRAM–ID. THIS–IS–THE–ACCOUNTS–RECEIVABLE.

(g)     |        |IDENTIFICATION DIVISION.
        |        |PROGRAM–ID. 7–8–9–RECORDS.

(h)     |        |IDENTIFICATION DIVISION.
        |        |PROGRAM–ID. MA$$–TRAN$IT.

(i)     |        |IDENTIFICATION DIVISION.
        |        |PROGRAM ID. CLOSING.

(j)     |        |IDENTIFICATION DIVISION.
        |        |PROGRAM–ID. AT–LAST.
```

13. Every COBOL program is composed of four divisions written in a specific order. They are
    (a) ——————————
    (b) ——————————
    (c) ——————————
    (d) ——————————

14. A good COBOL compiler will permit
    (a) a mix-up of the four divisions
    (b) the inclusion of an extra division
    (c) the omission of any one of the four divisions
    (d) none of the above.

15. A margin A COBOL statement may be punched in
    (a) column 1
    (b) columns 1–6 inclusive
    (c) column 8, 9, 10 or 11
    (d) column 8 only
    (e) none of the above.

16. All division headers must be punched in margin A. This means that
    (a) they may begin in column 8
    (b) they may extend to column 80.
    (c) columns 8 through 11 only may be used
    (d) they may begin in columns 8, 9, 10 or 11.

17. COBOL instructions are all punched in area B. This means
    (a) columns 1 through 11 are avoided
    (b) the statement must begin in column 12
    (c) the statement may begin anywhere between columns 12 and 72 inclusive
    (d) anything punched in columns 73–80 will be ignored.

18. Which of the following identification header cards, if any, are valid. Indicate what is wrong with any which are invalid.

(a)
```
1
─────────────────────
IDENTIFICATION DIVISION.
```

(b)
```
7
─────────────────────
IDENTIFICATION DIVISION.
```

(c)
```
8
─────────────────────
IDENTIFICATION DIVISION.
```

(d)
```
12
─────────────────────
IDENTIFICATION DIVISION.
```

19. Which, if any, of the following header card sets is correct. If it is invalid, indicate why.

(a)
```
8
─────────────────────
IDENTIFICATION DIVISION.
ENVIRONMENT DIVISION.
DATADIVISION.
PROCEDURE DIVISION.
```

(b)
```
8
─────────────────────
ID DIVISION.
ENVIRONMENT DIVISION.
DATA    DIVISION.
PROCEDURE DIVISION.
```

(c)
```
8
─────────────────────
IDENTIFICATION DIVISION.
ENVIRONMENT    DIVISION.
DATUM DIVISION.
PROCEDURE DIVISION.
```

(d)
```
8                        23
─────────────────────
IDENTIFICATION   DIVISION.
ENVIRONMENT      DIVISION.
DATA             DIVISION.
PROCEDURE        DIVISION.
```

20. Every identification division has a special paragraph to identify the program to the computer. Which, if any, of the following are valid? Again, indicate why if any are invalid.

8

(a) PROGRAM ID. PROGRAM–NUMBER–1.

(b) PROGRAM–ID.FIRST–TRY.

(c) PROGRAM–ID.
             THIS–IS–IT.

(d) PROGRAM–ID. THIS–IS JUST–GREAT.

21. Write suitable identification division cards (two cards for each) for the programs called:

(a) PROGRAM–TIKVA

(b) THIS–IS–MY–FIRST

(c) TRANSPORTATION

(d) MEDICAL–DATA

22. Which of the following program names is invalid? In each case indicate why.

(a) MATHEMATICS

(b) GASEOUS–DIFFUSION

(c) 1976–INVENTORY

(d) STUDENT–FILE

(e) THIS–IS–THE–GREATEST–PROGRAM–EVER–WRITTEN

(f) H

(g) G–S–A–S–1976

(h) GROSS*

(i) DATA

(j) HEADING

(k) FINAL

23. Which of the following statements are true?
    (a) Every IDENTIFICATION DIVISION must be terminated by a period.
    (b) Every IDENTIFICATION DIVISION must be followed by a PROGRAM–ID card.
    (c) Every PROGRAM–ID must be terminated by a period.
    (d) Every PROGRAM–ID must be followed by a program name which itself must be terminated by a period.
24. What output would you expect to be printed by the following program?

```
IDENTIFICATION DIVISION.

PROGRAM-ID.  QUIZ.

ENVIRONMENT DIVISION.

DATA DIVISION.

PROCEDURE DIVISION.

    DISPLAY 'CONGRATULATIONS, YOU MADE IT.'.
    STOP RUN.
```

25. In the following program are over 20 errors. Circle each one of them and rewrite the program correctly.

```
IDENTFICATION DIVISION.

PROGRAM ID . KOCHAN.

DATA DEVISION.

ENVIROMENT DIVISION ,

CONFIGERATION SEXTION.

SOURCE-COMPUTOR.IBM-370-145.

OBJET-COMPUTOR IBM-370-145.

PROCEEDURE-SECTION.

DISPLAY ". . .'

    HALT-PROGRAM.

END.
```

26. State as precisely as you can what output would be printed by the following program.

```
IDENTIFICATION DIVISION.
PROGRAM-ID. UNE.
ENVIRONMENT DIVISION.
DATA DIVISION.
PROCEDURE DIVISION.
    DISPLAY 'THIS IS THE FIRST LINE'.
    DISPLAY ' '.
    DISPLAY 'AND THIS IS THE SECOND LINE'.
    STOP RUN.
```

2

READING
DATA CARDS
USING ACCEPT
INSTRUCTION

Suppose we were to punch some alphabetic information in the first eight columns of a punch-card. When punching *data* we are not restricted in the same way as we are when punching COBOL instructions. There are no margins in data cards. We are at liberty to use any and all of the columns 1 through 80. Let the card be punched with the eight-character phrase "HI THERE." Figure 5 shows what the data card would look like.

We will now write a COBOL program which *reads in* this data card and does nothing other than print out on paper the contents of the card. This differs from the previous program in that instead of merely printing out a literal message built into the program, this time we want to print

```
 1      8
┌─────────────────────────────────────────────────────────────┐
│ HI  THERE                                                      \
│         ┆                                                       \
│         ┆                                                        │
│         ┆                                                        │
│         ┆                                                        │
│         ┆                                                        │
│         ┆                                                        │
│         ┆                                                        │
│         ┆                                                        │
└─────────────────────────────────────────────────────────────┘
```

FIGURE 5

out the contents of the first eight columns of an *input card.* This we shall do after printing out a suitable phrase with the DISPLAY statement, exactly as was done in Program 1.

There are two implications here. The first is that the data have to be appropriately described in the Data Division. The second is that an appropriate command has to be given to accept the data card. Acceptance of data cards is handled in the "action" division, the Procedure Division.

2.1 DATA DESCRIPTION

One of the subdivisions of the Data Division is called the Working-Storage Section. In the Working-Storage Section one may describe the data associated with the program by means of *level numbers* and appropriate names. The highest level number—and one which must be present—is the 01 level. The reason why it is called the 01 level rather than just the 1 level (even though 1 works just as well, to the surprise of many professional COBOL programmers!) is that lower levels can reach as high as the number 49, which is a two-digit number; for the sake of conformity, levels 1 through 9 are preceded by a zero so that they too will be two-digit numbers.

The question of levels is a very important one and has direct relevance not only to the manner in which business data is normally punched, but also how the individual items of data are related to each other, if at all. For the time being however, since we are considering a somewhat atypical case, let us confine ourselves to the minimum description which is necessary to describe our data card punched with HI THERE. We define the data-item on the 01 level, and 01 is punched in the A margin. Now we assign an arbitrary name to the data-item, say, DATA–NAME. This name is punched in margin B. It is followed by the word PICTURE*, which gives a physical description of the data item in question. After that a statement is made specifying that the data-item is *alphabetic* in character and that there are eight character items involved. This is done by the very brief designation A(8), where the number of characters involved is enclosed within parentheses. Alternatively, it may be written (but usually isn't) AAAAAAAA.

The complete data description in the Working-Storage Section of the Data Division will therefore be

01 DATA-NAME PICTURE A(8).

Here is the complete program to read the data card and to print out its contents. Despite the fact that the program is straightforward, you will notice that the four divisions must nevertheless be present. The

---

* Many COBOL systems permit the use of PIC as an abbreviation for PICTURE.

data card which was used as the sole input to the program is shown in Figure 6.

INPUT CARD TO PROGRAM 2

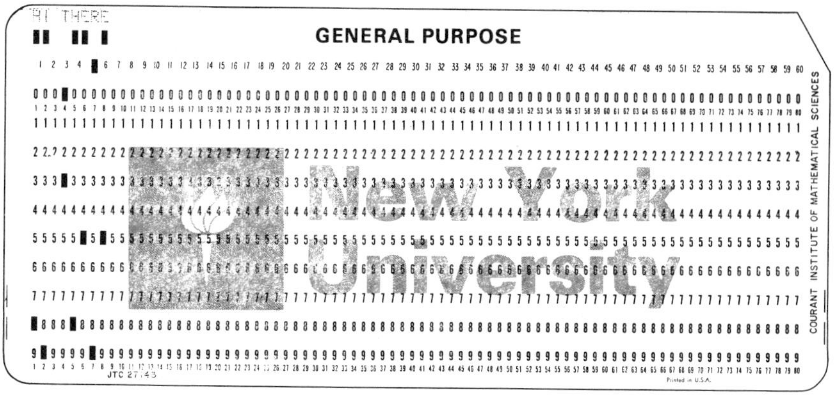

FIGURE 6

2.2 THE ACCEPT INSTRUCTION

In order to read the contents of a punched data card, the ACCEPT statement may be used. Here is the formal representation of the ACCEPT statement:

$$\text{ACCEPT data-name} \left[\underline{\text{FROM}} \left\{ \begin{array}{l} \underline{\text{SYSIN}} \\ \underline{\text{CONSOLE}} \\ \text{mnemonic-name} \end{array} \right\} \right]$$

[For an explanation of the formatting symbols see appendix A]

Since a data card contains 80 columns, the maximum number of characters that can be read by a single ACCEPT instruction is therefore 80. It is the responsibility of the programmer to assign to this data item a name by which it can be referred in the program. We have selected the name DATA–NAME. Since the picture for DATA–NAME is designated A(8), the *first* eight characters punched on the card will be read into the computer's memory. These eight characters can subsequently be referred to in the program by specifying the name DATA–NAME.

PROGRAM 2
Illustration of ACCEPT and DISPLAY

```
00001        IDENTIFICATION DIVISION.
00002        PROGRAM-ID. PROGRAM2.
00003        ENVIRONMENT DIVISION.
00004        DATA DIVISION.
00005        WORKING-STORAGE SECTION.
00006        01   DATA-NAME PICTURE A(8).
00007        PROCEDURE DIVISION.
00008            ACCEPT DATA-NAME.
00009            DISPLAY 'INPUT = ' DATA-NAME.
00010            STOP RUN.
```

OUTPUT TO PROGRAM 2

INPUT = HI THERE

In Program 2 we used the instruction ACCEPT to read a data card and the instruction DISPLAY to print out both a literal text INPUT = and the "value" of the data-item called in the program DATA-NAME, which was HI THERE. Since both these printouts are included in the same DISPLAY statement, they are printed on the same line. It should be stated that the two instructions, ACCEPT and DISPLAY are *not* normally used to read and print information because they are rather slow. When dealing with mass data and when we have volumes of material to read and print, we would ordinarily resort to a much faster method, to be discussed shortly. Nevertheless, both the preceding programs work and they help to illustrate some of the important principles involved in writing COBOL programs.

Here are some more illustrative programs designed to show how the ACCEPT and DISPLAY statements work. In Program 3 the sole input to the program is a data card punched (beginning in column 1) with the 12-character phrase COBOL IS FUN. The program reads in this data card and prints out it contents. After you have studied the program try to anticipate what the output will look like—before looking at the output.

PROGRAM 3
Further Illustration of ACCEPT and DISPLAY

```
00001        IDENTIFICATION DIVISION.
00002        PROGRAM-ID. PROG-3.
00003        ENVIRONMENT DIVISION.
00004        DATA DIVISION.
00005        WORKING-STORAGE SECTION.
00006        01  ITEM-NAME          PICTURE A(12).
00007        PROCEDURE DIVISION.
00008            ACCEPT ITEM-NAME.
00009            DISPLAY 'THIS CARD IS PUNCHED: ', ITEM-NAME.
00010            STOP RUN.
```

OUTPUT TO PROGRAM 3

THIS CARD IS PUNCHED: COBOL IS FUN

In Program 4 three separate data cards are read into the computer's memory using the ACCEPT instruction. They are punched, respectively

card 1 COBOL IS AN ACRONYM
card 2 WHICH STANDS FOR
card 3 COMMON BUSINESS ORIENTED LANGUAGE

Each punched card may be named separately in the program, but this would mean three separate 01 levels in the Working-Storage Section. Rather than resort to this method, another, perhaps better, method would be to assign the *same* name for each one. After each card is read, it could be displayed before the next data card is read. In this way, the second card's contents would occupy the same area in memory as the first card's and subsequently so would the third card's contents. Since each of the three cards contains a varying number of characters (the first is 19, the second 17, and the third 33) we could either assign the maximum length of 33 characters or simply assign the complete 80 columns of the card to the single name selected.

PROGRAM 4

Illustration of ACCEPT and DISPLAY with Several Input Cards

```
00001           IDENTIFICATION DIVISION.
00002           PROGRAM-ID. PRCG-4.
00003           ENVIRONMENT DIVISION.
00004           DATA DIVISION.
00005           WORKING-STORAGE SECTION.
00006           01  CARD-CONTENTS PICTURE A(80).
00007           PROCEDURE DIVISION.
00008               ACCEPT  CARD-CONTENTS.
00009               DISPLAY CARD-CONTENTS.
00010               ACCEPT  CARD-CONTENTS.
00011               DISPLAY CARD-CONTENTS.
00012               ACCEPT  CARD-CONTENTS.
00013               DISPLAY CARD-CONTENTS.
00014               STOP RUN.
```

OUTPUT TO PROGRAM 4

```
COBOL IS AN ACRONYM
WHICH STANDS FOR
COMMON BUSINESS ORIENTED LANGUAGE
```

It is worth contemplating for a moment what would have been the result if the Procedure Division were written:

```
ACCEPT CARD-CONTENTS.
ACCEPT CARD-CONTENTS.
ACCEPT CARD-CONTENTS.
DISPLAY CARD-CONTENTS.
STOP RUN.
```

In this case, the second data card's contents would have erased that of the first's while the third card would have erased that of the second. As a result only the contents of the *last* data card (the third in this case) would have been displayed. Sometimes this kind of logical error is committed by a tired programmer and the most frequent comment heard—especially if the programmer is a novice—is that "the computer made an error!" Of course it didn't; it was the unsuspecting programmer!

For the sake of practice, try answering the following questions. Some of the questions relate to material covered in the previous chapter. Other questions look ahead a little. For the present, be aware that if data is not alphabetic it may be read and printed by the X format rather than the A format, while numeric data is specified by a picture of 9s.

2.3 REVIEW QUESTIONS

1. What is a program?
2. Define a source deck.

3. What is meant by the term "execution" when applied to a program?
4. How many columns are there on the standard punch card?
5. What is always punched in margin A?
6. Where does margin B begin and end?
7. What kind of COBOL statements are punched in margin B?
8. Are columns 73–80 ever used?
9. How is data information transferred to cards?
10. What particular punctuation is used to terminate a COBOL instruction?
11. Name some of the rules for constructing program names.
12. Which division identifies a particular COBOL program?
13. Which division describes the computing environment in which the program is run?
14. If the source computer and the object computer are different, what section card must precede the source and object computer cards?
15. How would you define "programming"?
16. In which of the four divisions is data specified?
17. What is the official name of the "action" division?
18. What instruction will print out a message once it is enclosed by quotes? Are the quotes also printed?
19. In which margin is the DISPLAY instruction punched?
20. What instruction terminates a run?
21. Name an instruction which can read in a data card.
22. Why are all programs and their output shown only in capital letters?
23. What is the maximum number of characters that can be read by a single ACCEPT instruction?
24. In which margin would you expect to see the ACCEPT instruction, if at all?
25. The following program produced the output shown. State precisely how the data were punched, including the columns used and the actual data used in the program.

```
IDENTIFICATION DIVISION.
PROGRAM-ID. TELEPHONE.

ENVIRONMENT DIVISION.

DATA DIVISION.
WORKING-STORAGE SECTION.
01   CARD-SAYS.
     02   GUYS-NAME PICTURE A(5).
     02   FILLER PICTURE X(4).
     02   TEL-NO PICTURE 9(7).
     02   FILLER PICTURE X(5).
     02   SOC-SEC-NO PICTURE 9(9).

PROCEDURE DIVISION.
     ACCEPT CARD-SAYS.
     DISPLAY 'TELEPHONE NUMBER IS ', TEL-NO.
     DISPLAY 'SOCIAL SECURITY NUMBER IS ', SOC-SEC-NO.
     DISPLAY 'GUYS NAME IS ', GUYS-NAME.
     STOP RUN.


TELEPHONE NUMBER IS 4607427
SOCIAL SECURITY NUMBER IS 109282011
GUYS NAME IS HENRY
```

Now try your hand writing the following programs. If you have access to a computer with a COBOL compiler find out from the particular installation what control cards are necessary and run each of the programs. If this is your first exposure to computer programming, it will be a most thrilling experience. Try not to let your excitement interfere with the accuracy of your keypunching!

2.4 EXERCISES

When writing these programs, all input should be read by the ACCEPT verb and all printing done by means of the DISPLAY verb.

1. Write a program which prints out the message I LOVE YOU.
2. Write a program which prints out your name, address and telephone number on three separate lines.
3. Write a program which prints any four-line poem. Here is an example:

    I've always longed for adventure
    To do the things I've never dared
    Now here I am facing adventure
    So why am I so scared?

4. Write a program which accepts as data a card punched (beginning in column 1) with the phrase

    WHERE THERE IS A WILL

    The program should print out this phrase and on the following line the words THERE IS A WAY should be printed.

If you have successfully programmed the four problems above, you are well on the way to becoming a programmer. To be a good programmer will require much patience and perseverance because, depending upon the problem, programming can sometimes become quite complex and even tedious. But it is usually a particularly rewarding experience when the program works the way it was intended to work.

We shall now turn our attention to some other aspects of COBOL which have direct relevance to business problems.

3
AN INTRODUCTION TO FILES

One of the major advantages to COBOL over other programming languages is the ease with which it is able to handle *files*. A file is simply a collection of one or more *records*. We shall shortly explain in detail what is meant by a record but for now we can consider information punched on a single card to be a record. We can also consider the information to be printed out on a single line to be a record.

3.1 USING AN OUTPUT FILE

What we shall now write is a short, elementary program which uses an output file to print out for us on paper the 30-character phrase

THIS IS A PROGRAM USING A FILE

Here is the complete program to do the job and since it involves a few instructions that we have not yet encountered, we shall postpone a discussion of them until after you have had an opportunity to study the program. You will not be expected to fully understand the program, but since you have reached this far in the text, the chances are good that you will have—even without an explanation—a good idea as to what is going on. Here then is the complete program and its printed output. Following it is a detailed description, so perhaps you will want to place a book mark in this page in order to refer back to the program as often as is necessary.

PROGRAM 5
Using an Output File

```
00001        IDENTIFICATION DIVISION.
00002        PROGRAM-ID. PROG-5.
00003        AUTHOR. HENRY MULLISH.
C0004        ENVIRONMENT DIVISION.
00005        INPUT-OUTPUT SECTION.
00006        FILE-CONTROL.
00007            SELECT OUT-LINE-FILE ASSIGN TO UT-S-PRINTER.
C0008        DATA DIVISION.
00009        FILE SECTION.
00010        FD  OUT-LINE-FILE
00011            LABEL RECORDS ARE OMITTED.
00012        01  OUT-LINE-RECORD PICTURE A(30).
00013        PROCEDURE DIVISION.
00014        BEGIN-HERE.
00015            OPEN OUTPUT OUT-LINE-FILE.
00016            MOVE 'THIS IS A PROGRAM USING A FILE' TO OUT-LINE-RECORD.
00017            WRITE OUT-LINE-RECORD.
00018            CLOSE OUT-LINE-FILE.
00019            STOP RUN.
```

OUTPUT TO PROGRAM 5

THIS IS A PROGRAM USING A FILE

Did you guess correctly what the output would be? We hope so. Anyway, we shall now examine each of the four divisions and discuss their contents.

```
IDENTIFICATION DIVISION.
PROGRAM-ID.  PROG-5.
AUTHOR.  HENRY MULLISH.
```

The first question that leaps to the mind concerns the third card, the one beginning with the word AUTHOR. This is one of the optional *paragraphs* permitted in the Identification Division. It provides the author of the program with an opportunity to state his or her name so that credit (or, heaven forbid, criticism) for the program can be properly ascribed to the appropriate individual. Its format is

```
AUTHOR. [comment-entry]  . . .
```

```
ENVIRONMENT DIVISION.
INPUT-OUTPUT SECTION.
FILE-CONTROL.
    SELECT OUT-LINE-FILE ASSIGN TO UT-S-PRINTER.
```

The Environment Division admittedly looks a little confusing at first. It begins with a *section* card named

```
INPUT-OUTPUT SECTION.
```

where the words INPUT and OUTPUT are hyphenated by a minus sign. This is the section reserved for specifying the names of the files which are to be used within the program for both *input*—the reading in of information—and *output*—the printing or writing out of the results. This section header card is always followed by another special, hyphenated, paragraph name called the

FILE-CONTROL.

card. It is within this paragraph that the connection is set up between the arbitrarily assigned names for the input and output files and the physical devices required for their implementation. In our current program we do not have an input file but we *do* have an output file to print out a single line of output. We have to compose a name for the file, so why not pick a name which is literally descriptive of the file, one like OUT-LINE-FILE where the three words are hyphenated together? The rules for composing file names are similar to those for program names, a topic we covered earlier on. This point of creating meaningful names cannot be over-emphasized because by this means COBOL programs become self-documented, enabling almost anyone not familiar with the program to read and understand it. This includes the original programmer, who may have to change the program months or even years after first writing it.

Whatever file-name is chosen, it follows the word

SELECT

The file is assigned to a *hardware* device, according to an abbreviation code indicating that the device is a *u*tility device (hence the abbreviation UT).* It is sequential (therefore the letter S is used) and the device has been arbitrarily but suitably called PRINTER. The complete B margin statement is therefore

SELECT OUT-LINE-FILE ASSIGN TO UT-S-PRINTER.

(This may vary for any particular installation, but by asking the appropriate system adviser one can soon learn the required information.)

If we were using an input file in this program (which we are not), we would have had to compose an additional file name, and assign it to an input device in this same portion of the program. But more about that later.

In the Data Division we have to *describe* the files being used in the program. This is done by a file description which is always written with the initials FD and is *never* spelled out in full, nor are periods used. The letters FD go in the A margin and the name of the file being described (in our case it is named OUT-LINE-FILE) is punched in the B margin. All punched card or printer files must be followed by the clause

LABEL RECORDS ARE OMITTED.

---

* Sometimes one sees the letters UR, which stand for "unit record."

Since this is the end of the description of the output file, it must be terminated by a period.

We now come to the 01 level for the output file record. Why not give this record the self-descriptive name OUT–LINE–RECORD? Once again this will have a PICTURE designating the form of the record—30 alphabetic characters (the spaces are also considered to be alphabetic and therefore must be included in the count), so we write PICTURE A(30). The complete record description now reads

```
01   OUT–LINE–RECORD PICTURE A(30).
```

Finally, we reach the Procedure Division, where the first card is a paragraph name not doing anything in particular other than providing some documentation about where the "action" begins.

The first instruction is one which opens the file in question. Anytime a file is used in a COBOL program it must be opened to enable it to be accessed. This is done by an

```
OPEN
```

clause and is immediately followed by the word INPUT or OUTPUT to indicate the kind of file that is being opened. In our case it is an OUTPUT file. The clause would have little meaning if the name of the file being opened is not mentioned. So the complete statement is

```
OPEN OUTPUT OUT–LINE–FILE.
```

The reader's attention is drawn to the fact that when a file is opened it is *always* the file itself which is opened, not the records associated with that file.

Now, what is it we would like to accomplish in the program? We have to instruct the computer to take the 30-character phrase

```
THIS IS A PROGRAM USING A FILE
```

and place it in the output record called OUT–LINE–RECORD. This is done in COBOL by a verb called

```
MOVE
```

The instruction now becomes self-explanatory:

```
MOVE 'THIS IS A PROGRAM USING A FILE' TO OUT–LINE–RECORD.
```

Once the literal THIS IS A PROGRAM USING A FILE has been moved to OUT–LINE–RECORD, we are in a position to write out this record. This is accomplished by using the COBOL verb WRITE followed by the name of the *record* in question. The generalized form of the WRITE instruction is

WRITE record-name

We therefore write the instruction

WRITE OUT-LINE-RECORD.

You remember that we had to open the file OUT–LINE–FILE before we could use it? Before we terminate the program, we must close it as well. Can you guess the name of the COBOL instruction to close a file? Right, the verb CLOSE. Although when opening a file we had to state whether that file is an input or output file, this is *not* the case when closing it. All we write is

CLOSE OUT-LINE-FILE.

To terminate the program we write, as usual, the words

STOP RUN.

This concludes the detailed description of Program 5.

At first reading there is a great deal to absorb. For this reason it is recommended that the program together with its description be re-read as often as it is necessary for it to become familiar. After all, COBOL is a language and in learning any language—be it a computer or a spoken language—the key to success is repetition.

3.2 USING BOTH AN INPUT AND AN OUTPUT FILE

The time has now come to tackle a problem with both an input and an output file. For our first such program we shall simply read some alphabetic data punched on a data-card and print it out directly. You might be surprised to learn that it is hardly any different from the program we have just discussed. Why don't you take a good hard look at Program 6 before we analyze it in depth? Here it is; the data card is punched with the 50-character statement:

THIS PROGRAM USES BOTH AN INPUT AND AN OUTPUT FILE

PROGRAM 6

Using an Input and an Output File

```
00001          IDENTIFICATION DIVISICN.
00002          PROGRAM-ID. PROG-6.
00003          AUTHOR. HENRY MULLISH.
00004          ENVIRONMENT DIVISION.
00005          INPUT-OUTPUT SECTICN.
00006          FILE-CONTROL.
00007              SELECT IN-FILE ASSIGN TC UT-S-READER.
00008              SELECT CUT-LINE-FILE ASSIGN TO UT-S-PRINTER.
00009          DATA DIVISION.
00010          FILE SECTION.
00011          FD  IN-FILE
00012              LABEL RECORDS ARE OMITTED.
00013          01  CARD-CONTENTS.
00014              05 CARD-RECORD      PICTURE A(50).
00015              05 FILL-UP          PICTURE X(30).
00016          FD  OUT-LINE-FILE
00017              LABEL RECORCS ARE OMITTED.
00018          01  OUTPUT-LINE.
00019              05 OUT-LINE-RECORD  PICTURE A(50).
00020              05 FILL-IT          PICTURE X(82).
00021          PROCEDURE DIVISION.
00022          LETS-GO.
00023              OPEN INPUT IN-FILE.
00024              OPEN OUTPUT OUT-LINE-FILE.
00025              MOVE SPACES TO OUTPUT-LINE.
00026              READ IN-FILE AT END STCP RUN.
00027              MOVE CARD-RECORD TO OUT-LINE-RECORD.
00028              WRITE OUTPUT-LINE.
00029              CLOSE IN-FILE, OUT-LINE-FILE.
00030              STOP RUN.
```

OUTPUT TO PROGRAM 6

```
THIS PROGRAM USES BOTH AN INPUT AND AN OUTPUT FILE
```

The Identification Division again has its PROGRAM–ID paragraph, this time with the program name PROG–6. Incidentally, the PROGRAM–ID paragraph is mandatory and must follow the division header card. There is another optional paragraph name that may follow the AUTHOR paragraph, one called DATE–COMPILED. When the program is punched and run, there is no date written alongside it. Even if there were, it would be ignored by the system. However, when the program is run and a "listing" of the program returned together with the computed output, the listing shows the correct date on which the program was compiled. This can be very helpful because various versions of the program could have been run on different days and the printout could then be used to determine which version was used and when for a particular run.

The Environment Division has its familiar Input-Output Section and accompanying file-control card. Since in this program we are using an input file arbitrarily named IN–FILE, we must have an appropriate SELECT clause connecting this input file to the card reader in the same way that the output file is assigned to the line printer.

In the Data Division we must have the FILE SECTION card. You will recall that it is in this section that the files are described by means of FD's. The 01 level record name of the input file has been arbitrarily named CARD–RECORD. Since the data card—the solitary contents of the input file—

contain a 50-character sentence, the PICTURE specification has been set to A(50), as is the PICTURE for the output record.

It is in the Procedure Division that both the input and the output files have to be opened. The input file must have the word

OPEN

followed by the word INPUT so that the system is aware of the nature of the file about to be opened, just as the word OUTPUT must follow the word OPEN for the opening of the output file.

Notice that the output record called OUTPUT–LINE is composed of 132 characters, 50 of them being taken up by OUT–LINE–RECORD and the remaining 82 positions by FILL–IT. Now, in order to be sure that this area is completely free of extraneous information that might have been left there by a previous user, it may be cleared in one fell swoop by moving spaces to the record. This may be accomplished in COBOL by the single instruction

MOVE SPACES TO OUTPUT–LINE.

We are now ready to read the contents of the input file, naturally in the Procedure Division of the program. You might expect the instruction to read the file to be

READ IN–FILE

The fact of the matter is that there is more to the read instruction than just reading a file. Provision is made in a READ statement to take some definite action in the event that the end of the file has been reached. It is for this reason that the READ statement as shown above is incomplete. Instead one would write

READ IN–FILE AT END . . .

where the three dots indicate the action to be taken if the end of the file has been encountered. If the end of file has *not* been read the AT END clause is simply ignored. In that case the next instruction in line will be executed. Since our data card will have been read and not the end of the file, the next instruction in line, the MOVE, will be the next instruction to be executed.

MOVE is one of the most frequently used verbs in COBOL. It does what it says: it moves an item of information from one place to another, leaving the original intact. In our case we want to move the item we have called CARD-RECORD to the output record (which we have called OUT–

LINE–RECORD) prior to writing it out on paper. What could be more natural than:

MOVE CARD–RECORD TO OUT–LINE–RECORD.

Here is the formalized description of the MOVE instruction just described. Later on we shall be using another form of the MOVE instruction.

$$\underline{\text{MOVE}} \begin{Bmatrix} \text{data-name-1} \\ \text{literal-1} \end{Bmatrix} \underline{\text{TO}} \text{ data-name-2 [data-name-3 . . .]}$$

Once the information has been transmitted to the output area we may write it. As in the previous program we can now say

WRITE OUT–LINE–RECORD.

Having completed our task, we can now exit from the computer with out terminating phrase STOP RUN.

There it is, a complete, working program using an input file for reading the data and an output file for printing out the data. Was it difficult to follow? Of course, the program could be criticized for accomplishing something quite trivial. Perhaps so, but this program contains the seed for all future programs. If you have understood this program, you are ready to proceed. Otherwise it is suggested you review this and the previous chapters, if necessary. If you would like to test yourself, see how you can score on the quiz at the end of this chapter.

3.3 USE OF LEVEL NUMBERS IN DESCRIBING RECORDS

Data punched on a card are always broken down into either group items or elementary items. Every record description entry contains level numbers which reflect whether a particular item is a group or an elementary item. Each record must have an 01 level entry. Level number 01 must be punched in the A margin. Its associated data-name, however, must appear in the B margin. Usually level numbers 02 through 49 are punched in the B margin. At least one space must follow a level number separating it from its data-name. Each entry must have a level number punched to the left of the entry.

The critical level number is the 01. It indicates that the item is a record. It is assigned the level 01 because the record is the most inclusive of the data items. Although a record is usually composed of a series of related elementary items it may, as we have already seen, be itself an elementary level item. Level numbers 02–49 are used for subdividing a

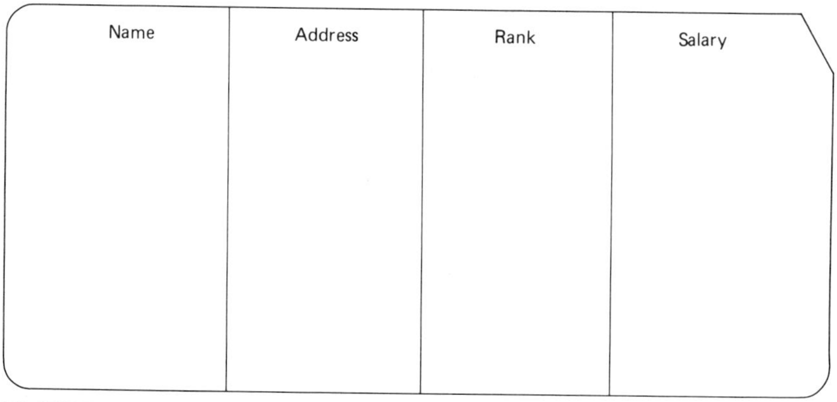

Name	Address	Rank	Salary

FIGURE 7

group item into subsidiary elementary items. The following examples should make this concept clear.

Assume a company's input file is composed of a series of data cards punched with the name, address, rank and salary of the employee, as indicated in Figure 7.

First, we need a general name to describe the whole card. Whatever name we select will be the 01 level name.

```
01 EMPLOYEE-CARD.

   02 EMPLOYEE-NAME
   02 EMPLOYEE-ADDRESS
   02 EMPLOYEE-RANK
   02 EMPLOYEE-SALARY
```

The 02 level items would take PICTURE clauses since they are elementary items, but the 01 level item does not, being a group item. Although the elementary item level numbers are successive—we go from 01 to 02—this does not necessarily have to be the case.

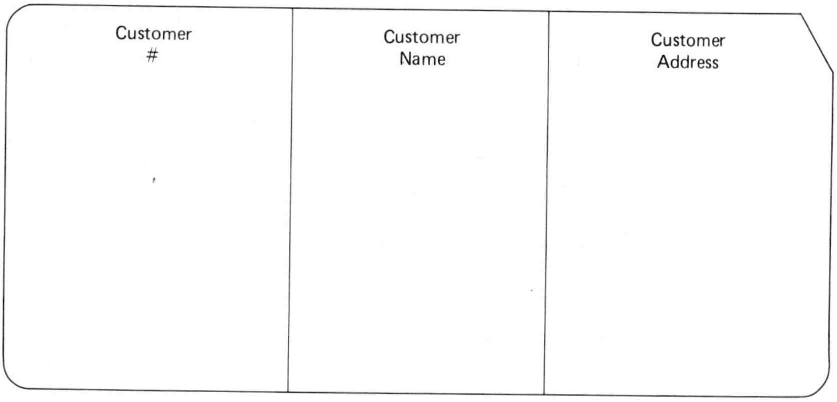

Customer #	Customer Name	Customer Address

```
01 CUSTOMER-CARD.

   05 CUSTOMER-NUMBER
   05 CUSTOMER-NAME
   05 CUSTOMER-ADDRESS
```

Here each of the elementary items have a level number 05.

Salesman Name	Sales-code			Year-to-date Figures		
	Area #	Office #	Id #	Quota	Sales	Comm-ission

```
01 SALESMAN-CARD.

   10 SALESMAN-NAME
   10 SALES-CODE
      15 AREA-NUMBER
      15 OFFICE-NUMBER
      15 ID-NUMBER
   10 YEAR-TO-DATE-FIGURES.
      15 QUOTA
      15 SALES
      15 COMMISSION.
```

In the foregoing example we notice that although SALESMAN–NAME and SALES–CODE each have the level 10, SALES–CODE is broken down to three level 15 elementary items. This, in turn, is followed by another group item, YEAR–TO–DATE–FIGURES, placed also on level 10. It is itself broken down into three subdivisions, each of which has been placed on level 15. Only the elementary items take PICTURE clauses. These would therefore include SALESMAN–NAME, AREA–NUMBER, OFFICE–NUMBER, ID–NUMBER, QUOTA, SALES and COMMISSION, but not SALESMAN–CARD, SALES–CODE, and YEAR–TO–DATE–FIGURES. The size of each group item is determined by adding together the fields occupied by the elementary items of which it is composed.

COBB OL MYSTERY #2

As our detective Cobb Ol, peacefully drove his Bentley down the avenue, he noticed a flashing red light on the car behind him in his rear view mirror. He smoothly pulled over to the curb and stopped.

"What seems to be the trouble, officer?" asked Cobb.

"Are you Mr. Cobb Ol, the world-renowned detective?" asked the police officer.

"Yes, I'm he," politely replied Cobb.

"There seems to be some emergency, sir," reported the policeman. "The commissioner wants you to follow us to headquarters right away."

When they arrived at police headquarters, the detective was quickly briefed.

"There seems to be a fault in our computerized emergency telephone answering system, Mr. Ol," explained the Police Commissioner. "I've been told by Jerry O'Hearn, the lieutenant in charge, that the new program to record and store the endless number of telephone calls is not working. The recording and storage of this information is crucial to the prosecution of almost all our court cases. If this storage system breaks down, hundreds of criminals could never be convicted!" exclaimed the Commissioner.

The thought boggled the mind of the detective. He asked for a glass of water.

Lt. Jerry O'Hearn was very helpful in explaining and showing the system to Cobb OL.

"This computer system is in constant operation, handling all emergency calls, 24 hours a day, seven days a week," Jerry said. "The calls are received, processed, and radioed out to the nearest patrol cars in a matter of seconds. The information for each call must then be keypunched and stored on magnetic tape as a permanent file. This is where our problem is: the new program to read in the cards simply won't work, Mr. Ol. We suspect foul play somewhere."

"You say this system operates constantly?" inquired Ol.

"Sure," replied Jerry. "There is virtually an endless stream of data cards to handle—we get so many emergency calls."

"I see," mused the detective. "Could I see the program?"

The detective quietly paged through the program listing.

"This is the point where the cards are read?" asked Cobb, pointing to the instruction,

    READ CALL-CARDS.

"Yes," replied Lt. O'Hearn. "When all the processing is done it goes back and reads the next card, and so."

"I see the problem Lieutenant," said the detective,

"The AT END clause is missing from the READ statement."

"Nonsense!" snapped Lt. O'Hearn. "I told you that the flow of data cards is virtually endless. We *never* reach the END!"

"Ah, but that is irrelevant, my dear Lieutenant," Cobb responded calmly. "An AT END clause is required in every READ statement in COBOL regardless of whether the end of data is ever reached."

"Oh, that's the problem," mumbled Jerry as the light dawned before his eyes. "But that's a little odd isn't it?"

"Alas," quipped the detective, "COBOL, like life itself, is filled with idiosyncracies."

3.4 REVIEW QUESTIONS AND EXERCISES

1. A file is
   (a) a single record consisting only of numeric data
   (b) one or many records containing either numeric or alphabetic data, or both

    (c) a rough tool used in COBOL

    (d) a list of people with criminal records.

2. A record is

    (a) an unseemly past

    (b) an element of a COBOL file

    (c) a prize-winning program

    (d) a flat platter.

3. The FILE SECTION is part of

    (a) the Identification Division

    (b) the Environment Division

    (c) the Data Division

    (d) the Procedure Division.

4. In COBOL the letters FD stand for

    (a) Fire Department

    (b) Feel Depressed

    (c) File Description

    (d) Full Debit.

5. Which of the following, if any, are correct?

    (a) OPEN A INPUT.

    (b) OPEN INPUT A.

    (c) OPEN OUTPUT-A.

    (d) OPEN OUTPUT A-FILE.

6. Indicate which of the following is valid.

    (a) READ IN-FILE.

    (b) READ A-FILE AT END STOP.

    (c) READ INPUT-FILE AT END STOP RUN.

    (d) READ FILE-IN CAREFULLY AT END STOP RUN.

7. State which of the following is correct.

    (a) MOVE X TO Y.

    (b) MOVE G TO H GENTLY.

    (c) MOVE INPUT TO OUTPUT.

    (d) MOVE RECORD-IN TO RECORD-OUT.

8. Which, if any, of the following is correct?

    (a) CLOSE ALL FILES.

    (b) CLOSE INPUT FILES.

(c) CLOSE OUTPUT FILE.

(d) CLOSE A–FILE.

9. Without looking up the list of reserved words guess which of the following are COBOL reserved words.

(a) SECTION	(e) DIVISION
(b) DATA	(f) PROCEDURE
(c) ENVIRONMENT	(g) FD
(d) CLOSE	(h) FILE

10. Write a record description entry for the four following records. In each case assign an appropriate name to the record.

(a)

Name		Credit Card #	Address	Date		Blanks
	Last Name			Month	Year	
I n i t i a l						

1 2   30 31   –   40 41   –   60 61   62 63   –   66 67   –   80

(b)

Date Enrolled	Advanced Credits	Total Credits	Today's Date			Filler
Month Day Year			Month	Day	Year	

1 2 3 4 5   8 9   10 11   13 14   15 16   17 18   21 22   80

(c)

Salesman's Name	Salesman Code			Year-to-Date Figures			Filler
	Area #	Office #	ID #	Quota	Sales	Comm-ission	

1   30 31   32 33   34 35   36 37   40 41   44 45   48 49

(d)

Low Priced Calculators			Medium Priced Calculators			High Priced Calculators			Filler
Units Sold 1972	Units Sold 1973	Units Sold 1974	1972	1973	1974	1972	1973	1974	

1   4 5   8 9   12 13   16 17   20 21   24 25   28 29   32 33   36 37   80

11. Write a record description entry appropriate to the following data. The record name is MILITARY. Each input card is punched with an ID number in the first eight columns, followed by six spaces. In the next five columns is punched the monthly wage with an implied decimal point separating dollars from cents. A further 15 columns are left blank and the following two columns are punched with the years of service. The remaining columns of the card are blank. Use FILLER to account for any unused portions of the card.

12. Check each of the following statements if it is true. If it is false, give your reasons.
    Every record in a card file must have
    (a) at least 80 characters
    (b) at least five fields
    (c) both numeric and alphabetic data
    (d) at least half a card of data.

13. The name of the COBOL entry to describe blank or non-referred-to fields is

(a) FILLER–UP

(b) FILLED–UP

(c) FILLER

(d) FILL

14. Study the following record description.

```
01 STUDENT–HISTORY.
   05 YEAR–OF–BIRTH                   PICTURE 9(4).
   05 YEAR-GRADUATED–HIGH SCHOOL      PICTURE 9(4).
   05 COLLEGE–CREDITS-EARNED          PICTURE 999.
   05 FILLER                          PICTURE X(69).
```

(a) The record name is _____.
(b) The elementary item names are _____ _____.
(c) The last elementary item is called _____.
(d) The total length of the record is _____.
(e) The number of numeric fields in this record is_____; alphanumeric fields _____.
(f) The largest number of credits that can be recorded is _____.
(g) The year of birth allowed for can be no greater than _____.
(h) The only item which cannot be referenced is _____.
(i) No record can have more than _____ 01 levels entries.

4

MULTIPLE
DATA CARDS

4.1 PRINTING A LISTING FROM CARDS

A less than bright scholar from Doles
Studied COBOL with coffee and rolls
Saw a deck by his teacher
and said, "Gee, you dumb creature
These cards are no good they got holes."

In the last chapter we discussed the method of reading an input record and writing out the contents of that record. In the problem we shall soon tackle, the input file contains many records. Each card of the input file is punched with the name of a company in columns 1–27 and the company's address in columns 30–80. The purpose of the program which we are about to write is to read each of the records of the input file and print a report listing this information, one line for each input card. The input data deck is shown in the top position of Figure 8.

Figure 8 as a whole is a diagramatic representation of the purpose of our next program. What we want to effect is a *transfer* of information from cards to paper with no calculations whatever being done in the process.

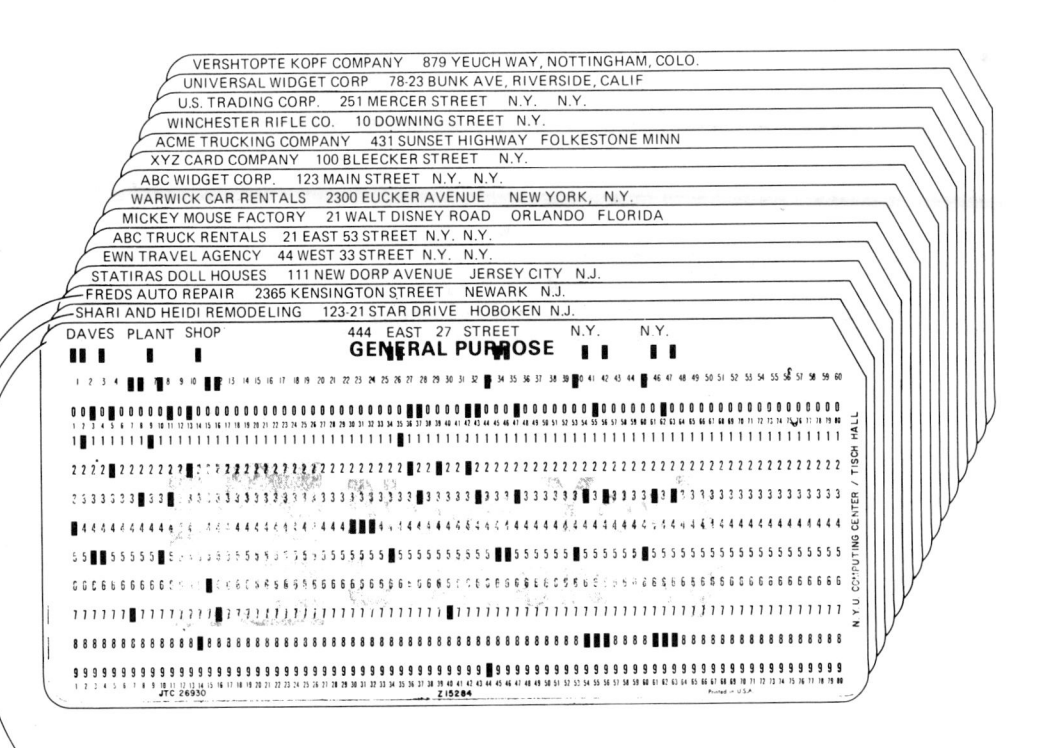

FIGURE 8

PROGRAM 7
Procedure Division

```
00001           IDENTIFICATICN DIVISICN.
CC002           PROGRAM-ID. PRCGO7.
0C003           AUTHOR.  JOHN ZACHARY.
0C004           SECURITY. MANAGEMENT CNLY.
C0005           ENVIRONMENT DIVISICN.
CC006           INPUT-OUTPUT SECTICN.
00007           FILE-CONTROL.
00008               SELECT  IN-FILE     ASSIGN TC UT-S-READER.
00009               SELECT  CUT-FILE    ASSIGN TC UT-S-PRINTER.
00010           DATA DIVISICN.
00011           FILE SECTION.
00012           FD  IN-FILE
00013               LABEL RECCRDS ARE CMITTED.
C0014           01  COMPANY-INFO-RECCRD.
00015               05  COMPANY-NAME      PICTURE X(27).
00016               05  NOTHING           PICTURE X(2).
00017               05  COMPANY-ADDRESS   PICTURE X(51).
CU018           FD  OUT-FILE
00019               LABEL RECCRDS ARE CMITTEC.
00020           01  INFC-CUT-RECORD.
00021               05  CUMPANY-NAME-CUT     PICTURE X(27).
CU022               05  NOTHING-OLT          PICTURE X(10).
00023               05  COMPANY-ADDRESS-ULT  PICTURE X(51).
00024               05  FILL-UP              PICTURE X(44).
C0025           PROCEDURE DIVISICN.
00026           MAIN-LINE.
00027               CPEN INPUT IN-FILE
0C028                    OUTPUT CUT-FILE.
U0029           GET-DATA.
0C030               READ IN-FILE AT END CLOSE IN-FILE, CUT-FILE, SIOP RUN.
00031               MOVE SPACES TO INFC-CLT-RECORD.
00032               MCVE COMPANY-NAME TC CCMPANY-NAME-CUT.
00033               MOVE COMPANY-ADDRESS TC CUMPANY-ADDRESS-CUT.
C0034               WRITE INFC-CUT-RECORD.
00035               GO TC GET-DATA.
```

OUTPUT TO PROGRAM 7

```
DAVES PLANT SHOP              444 EAST 27 STREET     N.Y.   N.Y.
SHARI AND HEIDI REMCDELING    123-21  STAR CRIVE   HOBOKEN N.J.
FREDS AUTO REPAIR             2365 KENSINGTCN STREET      NEWARK N.J.
STATIRAS DOLL HOUSES          111  NEW DCRP AVENUE   JERSEY CITY  N.J.
EWN TRAVEL AGENCY             44 WEST 33 STREET     N.Y.   N.Y.
ABC   TRUCK RENTALS           21 EAST 53 STREET N.Y.     N.Y.
MICKEY MOUSE FACTCRY          21 WALT DISNEY RCAD   CRLANDC FLORIDA
WARWICK CAR RENTALS           2300 EUCKER AVENUE  NEW YCRK, N.Y.
ABC WIDGET CORP.              123 MAIN STREET  N.Y.     N.Y.
XYZ CARD COMPANY              100 BLEECKER STREET     N.Y.
ACME TRUCKING COMPANY         431 SUNSET HIGHWAY    FCLKESTCNE MINN
WINCHESTER RIFLE CO.          1C DCWNING STREET    N.Y.
U.S. TRADING CORP.            251 MERCER STREET     N.Y.     N.Y.
UNIVERSAL WIDGET CORP         78-23 BUNK AVE, RIVERSICE, CALIF
VERSHTOPTE KOPF COMPANY       879 YEUCH WAY, NCTTINGHAM,    CCLC.
```

EXPLANATION OF PROGRAM 7

```
IDENTIFICATION DIVISION.
PROGRAM-ID. PROG 07.
AUTHOR. JOHN ZACHARY.
SECURITY. MANAGEMENT ONLY.
```

The only new feature in the Identification Division is the optional paragraph name SECURITY. This provides for a means to indicate the security measures (if any) to be taken in distributing the output. It might be intended only for top management, or perhaps only for salesmen. This option provides for satisfying precisely this need. It is shown in this program mainly for information purposes and will be omitted from almost all future programs in this text. Remember that even though the listing of the program shows a date for DATE–COMPILED, no date is punched on the card. The system supplies it automatically when the program is run.

```
ENVIRONMENT DIVISION.
INPUT–OUTPUT SECTION.
FILE–CONTROL.
    SELECT IN–FILE ASSIGN TO UT–S–READER.
    SELECT OUT–FILE ASSIGN TO UT–S–PRINTER.
```

The only way in which the Environment Division differs from that of the previous example is the name we have selected for the output file. In Program 6 we arbitrarily named it OUT–LINE–FILE. In Program 7, however, we have changed it to OUT–FILE, a prerogative always open to the programmer.

```
DATA DIVISION.
FILE SECTION.
FD IN–FILE
    LABEL RECORDS ARE OMITTED.
01 COMPANY–INFO–RECORD.
    05 COMPANY–NAME       PICTURE X(27)
    05 NOTHING            PICTURE X(2).
    05 COMPANY–ADDRESS    PICTURE X(51).
```

The names selected for the record in the input file (called IN–FILE) is COMPANY–INFO–RECORD. The 01 level itself does not have a picture this time since it is broken down into three separate fields. The first 27 columns, which contain the company name, is given an 05 level (punched in the B margin) with the name COMPANY–NAME. Its picture is described as X(27). You might wonder why the picture for COMPANY–NAME is described as X(27) rather than A(27). The letter X is used for what is known as *alphanumeric characters.* Although alphabetic information may be described by the A format, a combination of alphabetic numeric and/or special characters such as the period, comma, asterisk, and so on is regarded as alphanumeric and must be described with a picture of X. A close look at the data cards will reveal that some company names contain periods. In order to read a name containing a period, we have no alternative but to read all of the names in alphanumeric format.

Columns 28 and 29 are always blank and so we have given it the name NOTHING with a picture of X(2). The next field occupies the remaining 51 characters of the input card. It contains the company address and is identified again on the 05 level as COMPANY–ADDRESS with a picture of X(51). Once again the alphabetic format would have been quite unsuitable because periods, commas, hyphens, and numbers occur liberally.

The breakdown of the level numbers may be a little perplexing at

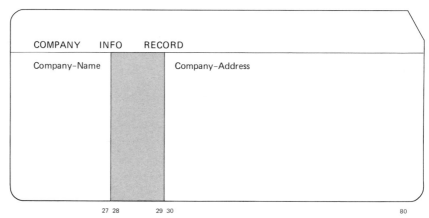

COMPANY   INFO   RECORD

Company-Name   Company-Address

27 28   29 30   80

FIGURE 9

this point. It will become clear, however, if each input card is regarded as shown in Figure 9.

Any level number at all greater than 01 but not greater than 49 could have been selected. Generally, programmers avoid using consecutive level numbers since this minimizes the flexibility of the program.

Now for a description of the records in the output file:

```
FD OUT-FILE
   LABEL RECORDS ARE OMITTED.
01 INFO-OUT-RECORD.
   05 COMPANY-NAME-OUT        PICTURE X(27).
   05 NOTHING-OUT             PICTURE X(10).
   05 COMPANY-ADDRESS-OUT     PICTURE X(51).
   05 FILL-UP                 PICTURE X(44).
```

The name of the output file is OUT–FILE, as defined in its corresponding FD card. The name given to its corresponding record is INFO–OUT–RECORD and, as usual, is given the 01 level number. Provision is made for the 27 alphanumeric characters to be moved to an area called COMPANY–NAME–OUT on the 05 level. This is followed by 10 columns of blanks, which in turn is followed by the field called COMPANY–ADDRESS–OUT, which like its corresponding input field COMPANY–ADDRESS has a picture of X(51). Since the output paper is usually capable of 132 print positions, we have provided for 44 blanks to "fill-up" the line. Each field of a record must be uniquely named and so we cannot use the name NOTHING–OUT again, since this name has already been used in this record. As a matter of fact, COBOL provides us with a special word named FILLER, which can be used as many times as desired so that we don't have to worry about constructing unique names for areas which are never actually addressed. We shall illustrate the use of filler in the Program 8.

4.2 THE CONCEPT OF THE LOOP

Study the following Procedure Division very carefully and pay particular attention to the flow of control. Notice the unconditional transfer to GET–DATA.

```
PROCEDURE DIVISION.
MAIN–LINE.
     OPEN INPUT IN–FILE
          OUTPUT OUT–FILE.
GET–DATA.
     READ IN–FILE AT END CLOSE IN–FILE, OUT–FILE, STOP RUN.
     MOVE SPACES TO INFO–OUT–RECORD.
     MOVE COMPANY–NAME TO COMPANY–NAME–OUT.
     MOVE COMPANY–ADDRESS TO COMPANY–ADDRESS–OUT.
     WRITE INFO–OUT–RECORD.
     GO TO GET–DATA.
```

It is in the Procedure Division, of course, that all the action takes place. After the input and output files have been opened and the first card of IN–FILE is read, the output record INFO–OUT–RECORD is cleared by moving SPACES to this area. SPACE or its alternative SPACES is what is known in COBOL as a *figurative constant.* The instruction MOVE SPACES TO INFO–OUT–RECORD has the effect of moving blank characters into *all* of the fields described by INFO–OUT–RECORD, 132 blanks in total.

When the end of the file IN–FILE is encountered (after all the data cards have been read) the AT END clause closes both files and stops execution of the program as required. Until this point is reached, however, for each data card COMPANY–NAME is moved to COMPANY–NAME–OUT and COMPANY–ADDRESS to COMPANY–ADDRESS–OUT. Having moved these two items of information to their appropriate locations in the output section of memory, we are now in a position to write out the contents of INFO–OUT–RECORD.

The WRITE verb prints out the first line of our output sheet, but our task is not yet completed. We need to read the next input card and repeat each of the moves as outlined above before writing out the new record. This is done by the so-called *unconditional transfer* statement GO TO, followed by an appropriate paragraph name which in this case is GET–DATA. This has the effect of transferring control of program execution directly to the first instruction immediately following the paragraph named GET–DATA.

We have, in fact, set up what in computer programming is known as a *loop,* probably the most important single concept in the whole of computer science. In this case the program loop will repeatedly read and print the contents of data cards until an end of file condition is reached. This is accomplished without having to repeat the instruction cards, which would make for an unwieldy, lengthy program.

What might be apparent from this program is that while we always *read* a *file* we always *write* a *record*. The reason for this will become clear in due course.

4.3 A DIFFERENT APPROACH TO PRODUCING A LISTING

In Program 8, the program we are about to discuss, we are using precisely the same data deck of company names and addresses and are producing precisely the same printed listing as was done in Program 7. You might well wonder what purpose is being served by writing two dissimilar programs to accomplish the same goals. The reason for this is to introduce a new approach to solving this kind of problem. Even while you are yet a novice, you will come to learn that in computer programming there are usually very many different ways of correctly solving a particular problem. The different ways may reflect the individual personality of the programmer and the way he or she views a problem, which might be quite different from that of the next programmer's. Herein lies one of the hidden advantages of this demanding but pleasant discipline. Each programmer is at liberty to solve a problem in accordance with his own particular approach, and yet no single attempt may be any more correct than another.

In Program 8 we have adopted a more interesting approach. The input file together with its associated record is the same as in Program 7, with one small exception. Instead of referring to the two unused columns (28 and 29) of the Company-Info-Record as NOTHING, we have taken advantage of the reserved COBOL word FILLER, which may be used for any field which is never addressed in a program. This relieves the programmer of the need to continually construct different names for such fields. FILLER may be used as often as necessary within a particular record, whereas any other name such as NOTHING or BLANK–SPACE or whatever, would necessarily have to be unique within a record in order to avoid ambiguity. FILLER is considered to be an elementary item and therefore requires a PICTURE clause.

You will notice that the output file has been drastically changed. Whereas in Program 7 the INFO–OUT–RECORD was subdivided into four separate 05 levels, in Program 8 the PRINT–LINE–RECORD associated with OUT–FILE consists of a single 05 level called PRINT–LINE with a picture of X(132). On most computer systems, the maximum number of print positions on the printer is 132. In other words, we may allow for the use of all 132 positions when printing out a given line of information.

The detailed output line itself has now been named RECORD–1 and is placed in an area of memory called WORKING–STORAGE. This is a name given to that section of the Data Division in which records may be prepared prior to being transferred to the output line. Once a record in the WORKING–STORAGE SECTION has been prepared for processing it may be MOVED to the output line to be printed.

You will notice as well that rather than using the acceptable but, nevertheless, bothersome names NOTHING–OUT and FILL–UP to refer to areas which are not addressed, the reserved COBOL word FILLER has been substituted. Remember that this reserved word may be used as often as required within a program or even within the *same* record.

Once the Input and Output files have been opened in the Procedure Division, SPACES are moved to RECORD–1 to clear this area of any and all information that happens to be there. With each reading of the input file, COMPANY–NAME is moved to COMPANY–NAME–OUT and COMPANY–ADDRESS to COMPANY–ADDRESS–OUT. At that point, the whole of RECORD-1 is moved to PRINT–LINE–RECORD prior to reading the next data card. Also worth noticing here is that after the input and output files are opened in the paragraph named MAIN–LINE, SPACES are moved to the RECORD-1 to clear out any previous information stored there. This will ensure that no extraneous information is included in the subsequent printout. If this were not done, the two areas represented by FILLER would have created a minor problem when reading the output sheet.

PROGRAM 8
Another Listing Program

```
00001          IDENTIFICATION DIVISION.
00002          PROGRAM-ID. PROG-8.
00003          AUTHOR. GEORGE STONE.
00004
00005          ENVIRONMENT DIVISION.
00006          INPUT-OUTPUT SECTION.
00007          FILE-CONTROL.
00008              SELECT  IN-FILE ASSIGN TO UR-S-READER.
00009              SELECT OUT-FILE ASSIGN TO UR-S-PRINTER.
00010
00011          DATA DIVISION.
00012          FILE SECTION.
00013          FD  IN-FILE
00014              LABEL RECORDS ARE OMITTED.
00015          01  COMPANY-INFO-RECORD.
00016              05  COMPANY-NAME       PICTURE X(27).
00017              05  FILLER             PICTURE X(2).
00018              05  COMPANY-ADDRESS    PICTURE X(51).
00019
00020          FD  OUT-FILE
00021              LABEL RECORDS ARE OMITTED.
00022          01  PRINT-LINE-RECORD.
00023              05  PRINT-LINE PICTURE X(132).
00024
00025          WORKING-STORAGE SECTION.
00026          01  RECORD-1.
00027              05  COMPANY-NAME-OUT    PICTURE X(27).
00028              05  FILLER              PICTURE X(10).
00029              05  COMPANY-ADDRESS-OUT  PICTURE X(51).
00030              05  FILLER              PICTURE X(44).
00031
00032          PROCEDURE DIVISION.
00033
00034          MAIN-LINE.
00035              OPEN INPUT IN-FILE
00036                  OUTPUT OUT-FILE.
00037
00038          BEGIN.
00039              MOVE SPACES TO RECORD-1.
```

```
C0040            READ IN-FILE AT END CLOSE IN-FILE, OUT-FILE, STOP RUN.
00041            MOVE COMPANY-NAME TO COMPANY-NAME-OUT.
00042            MOVE COMPANY-ADDRESS TO COMPANY-ADDRESS-OUT.
00043            MOVE RECORD-1 TO PRINT-LINE.
00044            WRITE PRINT-LINE-RECORD.
00045            GO TO BEGIN.
```

OUTPUT TO PROGRAM 8

```
DAVES PLANT SHOP              444 EAST 27 STREET       N.Y.    N.Y.
SHARI AND HEIDI REMODELING    123-21  STAR DRIVE    HOBOKEN N.J.
FREDS AUTO REPAIR             2365 KENSINGTON STREET     NEWARK N.J.
STATIRAS DOLL HOUSES          111  NEW DORP AVENUE   JERSEY CITY  N.J.
EWN TRAVEL AGENCY             44 WEST 33 STREET    N.Y.    N.Y.
ABC   TRUCK RENTALS           21 EAST 53 STREET N.Y.    N.Y.
MICKEY MOUSE FACTORY          21 WALT DISNEY ROAD  ORLANDO FLORIDA
WARWICK CAR RENTALS           2300 EUCKER AVENUE  NEW YORK, N.Y.
ABC WIDGET CORP.              123 MAIN STREET  N.Y.    N.Y.
XYZ CARD COMPANY              100 BLEECKER STREET    N.Y.
ACME TRUCKING COMPANY         431 SUNSET HIGHWAY   FOLKESTONE MINN
WINCHESTER RIFLE CO.          10 DOWNING STREET     N.Y.
U.S. TRADING CORP.            251 MERCER STREET    N.Y.    N.Y.
UNIVERSAL WIDGET CORP         78-23 BUNK AVE, RIVERSIDE, CALIF
VERSHTOPTE KOPF COMPANY       879 YEUCH WAY, NOTTINGHAM,  COLO.
```

In their place would, most probably, have appeared some undecipherable nonsense. The reason for this is that although the output line PRINT–LINE is cleared, the contents of RECORD–1 have not all been cleared. As a result when RECORD–1 is moved to PRINT–LINE it contains two FILLER fields which themselves have not been cleared. Whatever information was resident in that part of memory will be passed along to PRINT–LINE and therefore will appear on each output line. It makes for better programming to first move spaces to the 132 line record called RECORD–1. When RECORD–1 is then moved to the output line the entire print line will have been properly cleared.

What might now be apparent is that, in broad principle, a COBOL program requires an input area in memory, an output area, and, if necessary, a Working-Storage Section, in accordance with Figure 10.

Information is read into an input area and transferred to an output area for printing. Sometimes—indeed, most-times—intermediate processing is required and is accomplished using the Working-Storage Section before it is transferred to the output area.

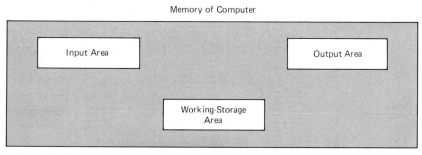

Memory of Computer

Input Area

Output Area

Working-Storage
Area

FIGURE 10

COBB OL MYSTERY # 3

The world-renowned detective sat quietly in his easy chair reading his evening paper and smoothly puffing on his pipe. Cobb Ol was spending a relaxing evening at home after solving another rough case. He soon heard the unexpected chimes of the front door.

"Hello, Uncle Cobb," said the visitor as the detective opened the front door. It was Cobb Ol's nephew Duane.

"I'm sorry to bother you, Uncle," said Duane, "but I'm doing this COBOL program for school and I just can't figure out where I've made a mistake."

"Let me see," said Cobb. "Come in to my study."

"Have a seat, my boy," said Uncle Cobb. "Let's have a look at this."

"I can't figure out where I've made a mistake," said Duane in a tone of despair.

"Look at this part of your program, Duane," said Cobb pointing to the program.

```
02 NAME        PIC A(5).
02 FILL        PIC X(3).
02 RATING      PIC X(5).
02 FILL        PIC A(5).
02 STATUS      PIC X(4).
02 FILL        PIC X(58).
```

"What's wrong with that, Uncle?"

"You meant to have FILLER each time you have FILL, didn't you?" said Cobb.

"Oh, I thought that FILL could be used for FILLER as PIC can be used for PICTURE."

"But, Duane, FILLER is a COBOL reserved word and can't be abbreviated," explained Cobb. "PIC is sort of an exception because it is an accepted abbreviation."

"I'm sorry, uncle," said the nephew. "I should have realized that. I always make such stupid mistakes. I don't think I'll ever learn to program in COBOL."

"Don't worry, nephew," comforted Cobb. "Everybody makes stupid mistakes when learning COBOL. You'll catch on to it soon. Everybody does."

"Thanks, Uncle Cobb, you're a great help."

4.4 WAYS OF IMPROVING A LISTING
PROGRAM

According to some COBOL programmers, even if a problem is solved incorrectly, at least make it look good! Though one cannot advocate this approach, a characteristic of COBOL-produced output is its general attractiveness, perhaps due to the fact that COBOL programmers take pride in their work and the language itself makes it easy to program esthetically pleasing output.

Here, we would like to improve the output of the previous program. For example, we could provide suitable headings for the company name and the company address and perhaps underline both captions. How is it possible to underline, you might well wonder. One way would be to print a string of minus signs directly underneath the literal to be underlined. Another way to improve the output would be to keep a count of the data cards and print out the value of the count with each line of output.

In order to keep a count of the data cards, we would have to assign a suitable name, such as CARD–COUNTER, to that count. Assigning such a name has the effect of reserving storage room for that name in the memory of the computer. Since this item, CARD–COUNTER, is an independent item, that is, one created by the programmer for his own convenience, it is defined in the Working-Storage Section, and is given the special level number of 77.

If we are to keep a count of the cards, we have to start the counter at zero and add 1 to this counter each time a card is read. There is another of those *figurative constants* we spoke about earlier when we discussed the manner of moving SPACES to an area (the words SPACE and SPACES, incidentally, are identical in meaning and produce the same results). In the same way the commonly used figurative constants ZERO— or ZEROS or ZEROES (they are all equivalent)—moves the constant 0 to the pertinent field. In providing for the picture for CARD–COUNTER we, of course, realize that it will assume a numeric value. All numeric data have a picture specified by 9's. Presumably the digit 9 was selected because it begins with the letter "n," for *n*umeric data. A picture of 999 allows for a maximum numeric field of 999, and a picture of 9999 for 9999. Perhaps this is an even better reason for selecting the digit 9 to specify a numeric field.

Professional COBOL programmers seem to prefer setting up records and housekeeping chores in the Working-Storage Section to such an extent that it is often the longest single section of the whole program. There is a very good reason for this. In the Working-Storage Section one can *initialize* numeric, alphabetic, and alphanumeric fields without having to resort to MOVE instructions. They may be set by using the VALUE clause.

For example, the clause

    PICTURE X(5) VALUE 'TABLE'

will fill the five-character space with the literal TABLE.

    PICTURE 999 VALUE 486

will store 486 in the field whose picture is 999, provided the clause appears associated with an elementary level item in the Working-Storage Section of the Data Division.

Notice that the value of an item in question reflects the kind of picture associated with it. A picture of X(5) specifies that the item has a maximum of five alphanumeric characters. Assigning a value clause to such an item is equivalent to moving that value to the specified area. For example,

```
05 COMPANY-NAME PICTURE X(3) VALUE 'IBM'
```

is equivalent to having an entry in the Data Division:

```
05 COMPANY-NAME PICTURE X(3).
```

followed in the Procedure Division by the instruction

```
MOVE 'IBM' TO COMPANY-NAME.
```

The alphanumeric value must be enclosed in single quotes although these quotes are not stored internally by the computer.

By the same token the entry

```
05 NO-OF-DEPENDENTS PICTURE 99 VALUE 3.
```

is equivalent to the Data Division entry

```
05 NO-OF-DEPENDENTS PICTURE 99.
```

and the Procedure Division entry

```
MOVE 3 TO NO-OF-DEPENDENTS
```

There is an important difference in the statements

```
MOVE EMPLOYEE-NAME TO NAME-OUT
```

and

```
MOVE 'EMPLOYEE-NAME' TO NAME-OUT.
```

In the first case the *value* associated with the entry EMPLOYEE-NAME is moved to the area NAME-OUT, while in the second case the entry 'EM-PLOYEE-NAME' itself is moved.

Once a field has been defined by a picture clause, it may be initialized to a succession of any given characters by use of the ALL option.

For example, the clause

```
PICTURE X(7) VALUE ALL '*'
```

will fill the seven-character space with asterisks.

In Program 9, HEADING-1 and HEADING-2 are the record names of the two separate heading lines used to identify the printed output. These lines are printed once only, as distinct from the record named DETAIL-LINE which is printed after each data card is read.

Another point worth mentioning is that in order to improve the clarity of the program listing, a blank card was inserted in the program deck between each of the four divisions.

In the Identification Division is an additional option, namely INSTALLATION. The INSTALLATION option tells anyone reading the compiled listing where the program (job) was run. The name of the installation if punched in the B margin alongside the word INSTALLATION. This option is included in the next program.

Without further ado here is Program 9, which uses the identical data deck as Programs 7 and 8. Do you agree that the output for programming is more appealing?

PROGRAM 9
Yet Another Listing Program with a Card Count

```
00001          IDENTIFICATION DIVISION.
C0002          PROGRAM-ID. PRCG-9.
00003          AUTHOR. STEVE KOCHAN.
00004          DATE-COMPILED. JUL 15,1977.
C0005          INSTALLATION. UNIVERSITY COMPUTER CENTER.
00006
C0007          ENVIRONMENT DIVISION.
C0008          INPUT-OUTPUT SECTION.
00009          FILE-CONTROL.
C0010              SELECT IN-FILE ASSIGN TC UR-S-READER.
00011              SELECT CUT-FILE ASSIGN TC UR-S-PRINTER.
00012          DATA DIVISION.
00013          FILE SECTION.
00014          FD  IN-FILE
00015              LABEL RECORDS ARE CMITTED.
00016          01  COMPANY-INFC-RECCRD.
00017              05  COMPANY-NAME      PICTURE X(27).
00018              05  FILLER           PICTURE X(2).
00019              05  COMPANY-ADDRESS  PICTURE X(51).
C0020          FD  OUT-FILE
C0021              LABEL RECCRDS ARE OMITTED.
00022          01  PRINT-LINE-RECORD.
C0023              05  PRINT-LINE PICTURE X(132).
C0024          WORKING-STORAGE SECTION.
00025          77  CARD-NUMBER  PICTURE 9999 VALUE ZERO.
00026          01  HEADING-1.
C0027              05 FILLER            PICTURE X(6) VALUE SPACES.
00028              05 COMP-NAME-HEADING PICTURE X(15) VALUE 'NAME OF COMPANY'.
00029              05 FILLER            PICTURE X(22) VALUE SPACES.
00030              05 CUST-ADDR-HEADING PICTURE X(16) VALUE 'CUSTOMER ADDRESS'.
00031              05 FILLER            PICTURE X(82) VALUE SPACES.
C0032          01  HEADING-2.
00033              05 FILLER            PICTURE X(6) VALUE SPACES.
00034              05 UNDERLINE-1       PICTURE X(15) VALUE ALL '-'.
C0035              05 FILLER            PICTURE X(22) VALUE SPACES.
00036              05 UNDERLINE-2       PICTURE X(16) VALUE ALL '-'.
00037              05 FILLER            PICTURE X(82) VALUE SPACES.
00038          01  DETAIL-LINE.
00039              05 CARD-NUMBER-OUT   PICTURE 9999.
C0040              05 FILLER            PICTURE X(2) VALUE SPACES.
00041              05 COMPANY-NAME-OUT  PICTURE X(27).
00042              05 FILLER            PICTURE X(10) VALUE SPACES.
C0043              05 COMPANY-ADDRESS-OUT  PICTURE X(51).
00044              05 FILLER            PICTURE X(44) VALUE SPACES.
00045
00046          PROCEDURE DIVISION.
00047          BEGIN-HERE.
00048              OPEN INPUT IN-FILE
00049                  OUTPUT OUT-FILE.
00050              MOVE HEADING-1 TO PRINT-LINE-RECORD.
00051              WRITE PRINT-LINE-RECORD.
00052              MOVE HEADING-2 TO PRINT-LINE-RECORD.
C0053              WRITE PRINT-LINE-RECORD.
00054          MAIN-LINE.
```

```
00055          READ IN-FILE AT END CLOSE IN-FILE, OUT-FILE, STOP RUN.
00056          ADD 1 TO CARD-NUMBER.
00057          MOVE SPACES TO DETAIL-LINE.
00058          MOVE CARD-NUMBER TO CARD-NUMBER-OUT.
00059          MOVE COMPANY-NAME TO COMPANY-NAME-OUT.
00060          MOVE COMPANY-ADDRESS TO COMPANY-ADDRESS-OUT.
00061          MOVE DETAIL-LINE TO PRINT-LINE-RECORD.
00062          WRITE PRINT-LINE-RECORD.
00063          GO TO MAIN-LINE.
```

OUTPUT PROGRAM 9

```
       NAME OF COMPANY                    CUSTOMER ADDRESS
       ---------------                    ----------------
0001   DAVES PLANT SHOP                   444 EAST 27 STREET      N.Y.    N.Y.
0002   SHARI AND HEIDI REMODELING         123-21  STAR DRIVE   HOBOKEN N.J.
0003   FREDS AUTO REPAIR                  2365 KENSINGTON STREET     NEWARK N.J.
0004   STATIKAS DOLL HOUSES               111  NEW DORP AVENUE    JERSEY CITY  N.J.
0005   EWN TRAVEL AGENCY                  44 WEST 33 STREET     N.Y.    N.Y.
0006   ABC  TRUCK RENTALS                 21 EAST 53 STREET N.Y.      N.Y.
0007   MICKEY MOUSE FACTORY               21 WALT DISNEY ROAD  ORLANDO FLORIDA
0008   WARWICK CAR RENTALS                2300 EUCKER AVENUE  NEW YORK, N.Y.
0009   ABC WIDGET CORP.                   123 MAIN STREET  N.Y.     N.Y.
0010   XYZ CARD COMPANY                   100 BLEECKER STREET    N.Y.
0011   ACME TRUCKING COMPANY              431 SUNSET HIGHWAY    FOLKESTONE MINN
0012   WINCHESTER RIFLE CO.               10 DOWNING STREET     N.Y.
0013   U.S. TRADING CORP.                 251 MERCER STREET    N.Y.    N.Y.
0014   UNIVERSAL WIDGET CORP              78-23 BUNK AVE, RIVERSIDE, CALIF
0015   VERSHTOPTE KOPF COMPANY            879 YEUCH WAY, NOTTINGHAM,   COLO.
```

In Program 9, the reader is referred to line 56, where the instruction

ADD 1 TO CARD–NUMBER.

is printed. It would be remiss to gloss over this extremely important instruction, which is self-explanatory. It does precisely what is implied, namely, it adds 1 to the current value of CARD–NUMBER, which initially started out at zero. This is our first instance of an arithmetic operation in the COBOL language. Since we also have to discuss the operations of multiplication, division, and subtraction in all their various forms, we shall treat the whole area of arithmetic manipulation separately in the next chapter.

4.5 REVIEW QUESTIONS AND EXERCISES

1. What disadvantages are associated with the DISPLAY and ACCEPT verbs?

2. Check each of the following independent COBOL statements and, if an error is found, mark it with an X and rewrite it correctly.
   (a) FD OUT–FILE.
   (b) FD RECORD–X LABEL RECORDS ARE OMITTED.
   (c) FD FILE
   (d) OPEN IN–FILE OUT–FILE.
   (e) OPEN INPUT
                  IN–FILE
             OUTPUT
               OUT–FILE.
   (f) MOVE BLANKS TO OUT–FIELD.
   (g) MOVE IN–A–HURRY TO NEW–HOME.

3. According to the following record description of an input data card, identify the card columns containing the indicated fields.
01 RECORD–DETAILS.

15 NAME	PICTURE X(15).
15 FILLER	PICTURE X(2).
15 ADDRES	PICTURE X(20).
15 FILLER	PICTURE X(2).
15 OCCUPATION	PICTURE X(15)
15 FILLER	PICTURE X(2).
15 MARITAL STATUS	PICTURE X(1).
15 FILLER	PICTURE X(23).

4. Write a program which reads a file of input cards as suggested in question 3 and lists (echoes) the information contained on each card onto the printer.

5
BASIC ARITHMETIC OPERATIONS IN COBOL

5.1 ADDITION

We have already encountered, in the previous chapter, the manner in which addition is implemented in COBOL. Essentially, after the verb ADD, a data name (or a data value) is specified and is followed by the reserved word TO. This, in turn, is followed by a data name only. The effect of the instruction is to add the first value to the second, with the result of the addition replacing the contents of the data name specified after the word TO. This might seem somewhat over-formalistic, but it is necessary to point out that there is more in the simple addition than meets the eye. For example, in the instruction

```
ADD A TO B.
```

where A has the value 5 and B is equal to 3, the result of the addition, 8, is stored in B, *destroying the value of 3 previously contained in B.* The further implication of this fact, and one that must be clearly understood, is that a data name *must* appear after the word TO and not a numeric value. We could not, therefore, have an instruction such as

```
ADD 1 TO 2.
```

or even

```
ADD COUNTER TO 1.
```

In order to operate arithmetically on *any* data, it must be resident in the memory and must have been defined with a picture of 9's. Obviously it doesn't make sense to add alphanumeric fields together nor to add a numeric to an alphabetic field for that matter. That would be similar to adding apples and pears.

In order to add A *and* B to C, we could, of course, write the two separate instructions

```
ADD A TO C.
ADD B TO C.
```

which preserve both the values of A and B but overwrites the value of C with the sum of A *and* B *and* C. In COBOL these two instructions may be shortened to the single instruction

```
ADD A, B TO C.
```

The comma separating data names A and B may be omitted provided at least one space is inserted between the two data names. If the comma is used, it must be followed by at least one space. This is a general rule that applies throughout the COBOL language.

The ADD instruction as depicted above may be generalized to add as many items as required to a data name according to the general format

$$\text{ADD} \begin{Bmatrix} \text{data-name-1} \\ \text{constant-1} \end{Bmatrix} \begin{bmatrix} \text{data-name-2} \\ \text{constant-2} \end{bmatrix} \cdots \begin{bmatrix} \text{data-name-k} \\ \text{constant-k} \end{bmatrix} \underline{\text{TO}} \text{ data-name-z.}$$

The convention used throughout COBOL manuals is that all reserved words which are essential are capitalized and underlined. Braces indicate that a choice must be made between the items contained within the braces while the square brackets indicate that use of whatever is contained within them is optional.

COBOL provides for the addition of two numbers such that neither the first nor the second is lost. This involves the use of the GIVING clause as in the following example:

```
ADD A, B GIVING C.
```

This adds the contents of A and B, giving C, in the process replacing any previous contents of C but leaving intact the values of A and B. (The temptation to write ADD A TO B GIVING C is very great but must be resisted since this violates the syntactic rules of COBOL and is flagged as an error.) By the same token, a series of items may be added together as in the following example:

```
ADD A B C D E GIVING F.
```

The following program illustrates the results of adding various numbers using the ADD verb. A careful perusal of the output will show clearly that several of the stated values change during the course of execution.

It will also be noticed that lines 18 and 19, for example, actually represent a single statement. Provided the first card is terminated at an appropriate point, the second card may be continued in margin B without any special continuation indicator being punched.

PROGRAM 10
Adding

```
00001         IDENTIFICATION DIVISION.
00002         PROGRAM-ID. ADDING.
00003         ENVIRONMENT DIVISION.
00004         DATA DIVISION.
00005         WORKING-STORAGE SECTION.
00006         77  A       PICTURE 99  VALUE  17.
00007         77  B       PICTURE 99  VALUE  23.
00008         77  C       PICTURE 99  VALUE  46.
00009         77  D       PICTURE 99  VALUE  68.
00010         77  E       PICTURE 99  VALUE  12.
00011         PROCEDURE DIVISION.
00012         START-HERE.
00013             ADD A TO B.
00014             DISPLAY 'AFTER ADDING A TO B,'.
00015             DISPLAY 'A = ' A ' B = ' B ' C = ' C ' D = ' D ' E = ' E.
00016             DISPLAY ' '.
00017             ADD D, E TO A.
00018             DISPLAY 'AFTER ADDING D AND E TO A,'.
00019             DISPLAY 'A = ' A ' B = ' B ' C = ' C ' D = ' D ' E = ' E.
00020             DISPLAY ' '.
00021             ADD B, C GIVING E.
00022             DISPLAY 'AFTER ADDING B AND C GIVING E,'.
00023             DISPLAY 'A = ' A ' B = ' B ' C = ' C ' D = ' D ' E = ' E.
00024             DISPLAY ' '.
00025             ADD A TO B ON SIZE ERROR DISPLAY 'B PICTURE IS TOO SMALL',
00026             ' B = ', B.
00027             DISPLAY 'A = ' A ' B = ' B ' C = ' C ' D = ' D ' E = ' E.
00028             DISPLAY ' '.
00029             DISPLAY ' '.
00030             STOP RUN.
```

OUTPUT TO PROGRAM 10

```
AFTER ADDING A TO B,
A = 17 B = 40 C = 46 D = 68 E = 12

AFTER ADDING D AND E TO A,
A = 97 B = 40 C = 46 D = 68 E = 12

AFTER ADDING B AND C GIVING E,
A = 97 B = 40 C = 46 D = 68 E = 86

B PICTURE IS TOO SMALL B = 40
A = 97 B = 40 C = 46 D = 68 E = 86
```

Particular attention is drawn to the last addition of A to B. At this point in the program the values of A and B, before the addition is performed, are 97 and 40 respectively. The result of the addition is stored in B, which we notice has a picture of 99. The maximum value that can be stored in a picture of this size is 99, as we have pointed out before. Since the result of the addition is 137, it obviously cannot fit completely into this two-digit field. Whenever a situation of this nature arises in COBOL a wrong answer will result. On most computers as much of the number as possible is stored in the receiving field, beginning with the rightmost digit. That means that the number 137 will be stored in B with the *most* significant digit completely lost. On other computers it is possible that the contents of the field will remain undisturbed. Since this type of occurrence is not considered to be an error in COBOL, an unwitting programmer might see the number 37 (or the number 40, depending upon the computer) printed out rather than 137 and accept this result on its face value. Ignoring this type of error could lead to serious difficulties.

5.1.1. On Size Error

COBOL provides a way of anticipating this type of problem which, in COBOL jargon, is generally referred to as a "size error" meaning that the size of the picture for the receiving field is not wide enough to allow for the full number to be stored. The number is said to have "overflowed." This situation has been deliberately created in the following illustrative program.

PROGRAM 11
SIZE ERROR Program

```
00001          IDENTIFICATION DIVISION.
00002          PROGRAM-ID. SIZE-ERROR-PROBLEM.
00003          ENVIRONMENT DIVISION.
00004          DATA DIVISION.
00005          WORKING-STORAGE SECTION.
00006          77  A PICTURE 99 VALUE 92.
00007          77  B PICTURE 99 VALUE 16.
00008          77  C PICTURE 99 VALUE 12.
00009          PROCEDURE DIVISION.
00010          START-HERE.
00011              ADD B TO C ON SIZE ERROR DISPLAY 'FIELD C IS TOO SMALL'.
00012              ADD A TO B ON SIZE ERROR DISPLAY 'FIELD B IS TOO SMALL'.
00013              DISPLAY 'A = ', A, 'B = ', B, 'C = ', C.
00014              STOP RUN.
```

OUTPUT TO PROGRAM

```
FIELD B IS TOO SMALL
A = 92 B = 16 C = 28
```

In the above program, three data names, A, B and C, each with a picture of 99, have been defined (with a 77 level) to the values 92, 16 and 12 respectively. In the Procedure Division, B is added to C with the proviso that if this overflows, that is, creates a size error, the literal FIELD C IS TOO SMALL should be displayed. Now the value of B is 16 and C is 12. The result of the addition, which is 28, replaces the number 12 stored in C. Since the picture for C is 99, there is no question that the value 28 can be stored in this field. As a result, the ON SIZE ERROR clause is ignored. When we reach the second ADD instruction, the situation changes dramatically. The value of A is 92 while that of B is still 16. The addition of 92 and 16 gives a result of 108, a three-digit number. Ordinarily, this number would be stored in B, which, since it has a picture of 99, would contain 08 rather than 108. However, on this occasion the ON SIZE ERROR option is activated and the literal expression "FIELD B IS TOO SMALL" is now printed. What is clear from the DISPLAY instruction following this addition is that when the ON SIZE ERROR option is invoked, the arithmetic operation itself is *not* completed. The reader will readily see therefore that using the size error option can be of great utility in the writing of sound programs.

Here are two generalized formats for the ADD instruction indicating how the ON SIZE ERROR option may be included.

$$\underline{ADD} \begin{Bmatrix} \text{data-name-1} \\ \text{constant-1} \end{Bmatrix} \begin{bmatrix} \text{data-name-2} \\ \text{constant-2} \end{bmatrix} \ldots$$
$$\underline{TO} \text{ data-name-m [ON \underline{SIZE ERROR} imperative statements]}$$

$$\underline{ADD} \begin{Bmatrix} \text{data-name-1} \\ \text{constant-1} \end{Bmatrix} \begin{bmatrix} \text{data-name-2} \\ \text{constant-2} \end{bmatrix} \ldots$$
$$\underline{GIVING} \text{ data-name-n [ON \underline{SIZE ERROR} imperative statements]}$$

COBB OL MYSTERY #4

Ol relaxed in his armchair, quietly perusing the latest issue of *World News.* Suddenly the phone rang.

"This is the manager of Benchley's Department Store, Mr. Ol," said the excited voice on the other end of the line. "We've got a real problem here, sir, and we need your help desperately."

"What seems to be the trouble?" queried the detective in his characteristically calm voice.

"We have just started using a new program to handle all our credit card transactions on the computer, and it simply refuses to function. With only ten shopping days left until Christmas, too!"

"Hm, you do have a problem, Mr. uh . . ."

"Kaufman."

"Mr. Kaufman," said Ol, "I'll be down there right away."

"Fine," said Mr. Kaufman, "I'll meet you outside my office in the furniture department."

"That will be fine, Mr. Kaufman, but please bring a listing of the new program with you," said Mr. Ol before putting on his coat and heading for his car.

"I'm so glad you could make it, Mr. Ol. Here is the listing you wanted," said Kaufman as Ol entered the furniture department.

"Thank you," replied the detective as he seated himself in a nearby armchair.

There was silence for several minutes while the detective stared at the page.

Finally, Cobb looked up.

"This program must have been written by a novice," said Ol.

"Not at all, Mr. Ol," protested Mr. Kaufman. "I wrote that program myself and I've had extensive training in COBOL."

"Would you please explain this statement to me?" asked Cobb pointing to the instruction,

    ADD A TO 5

"That's simple, Mr. Ol," offered the manager. "The value of A is added to 5."

"And where is the result stored?" asked Ol.

"Why, in A, of course!"

"Ah, but you see, my dear sir, the ADD statement without the GIVING clause causes the result to be stored in the second data name. However, 5 is not a valid data name, therefore the statement is not valid."

"Oh . . .," said Kaufman, somewhat dumbfounded.

"Happy sales to you, Mr. Kaufman," said the detective. "You'll receive my bill in the mail."

As Ol left the store, it began to snow.

5.2 SUBTRACTION

In a manner similar to the addition process, a value may be subtracted from another in COBOL by means of the verb SUBTRACT. In the simplest form of the subtract instruction such as

SUBTRACT A FROM B.

the value of A is subtracted from B, leaving the result in B and replacing whatever previous value was stored in B. Once again, it is the second mentioned data name that is altered. The general format is

$$\underline{\text{SUBTRACT}} \begin{Bmatrix} \text{data-name-1} \\ \text{constant-1} \end{Bmatrix} \begin{bmatrix} \text{data-name-2} \\ \text{constant-2} \end{bmatrix} \cdot \cdot \cdot \begin{bmatrix} \text{data-name-k} \\ \text{constant-k} \end{bmatrix} \underline{\text{FROM}} \begin{bmatrix} \text{data-} \\ \text{name-z} \end{bmatrix}$$

This implies that several items in succession may be subtracted from a given value as, for example,

SUBTRACT A, B, C, D FROM E.

The values of A, B, C and D are individually subtracted from E. Another example might be

SUBTRACT A, 2 FROM B.

in which case the value of B is replaced by the result of subtracting A and 2 from it.

In the instruction

SUBTRACT A FROM B GIVING C.

neither the value A nor B is changed. The value of C assumes the difference of these two values.

In both forms of the subtraction, as indeed with the addition, the ON SIZE ERROR option is permitted.

5.3 MULTIPLICATION

To multiply two values together one may use MULTIPLY:

    MULTIPLY A BY B.

There is a tendency on the part of some programmers, especially novices, to substitute the word BY with the word TIMES. Unfortunately, this is incorrect and will result in a diagnostic message. The word TIMES is a reserved word in COBOL but it is used in an entirely different context as will be seen in due course. In the instruction above, the value A remains unchanged, the product being stored in B, replacing any previous value stored there.

The generalized format is

$$\underline{\text{MULTIPLY}} \begin{Bmatrix} \text{data-name-1} \\ \text{constant-1} \end{Bmatrix} \underline{\text{BY}} \text{ data-name-2}$$

Once again it is the second-named operand which takes the result. It should be mentioned in passing that there are some COBOL compilers which permit an extended version of the MULTIPLY statement. For example, one might be able to write

    MULTIPLY A BY B, C, D

where the product is stored in B, C, and D.

The MULTIPLY verb may also take a giving clause in which case neither of the two multiplicands is changed. Here is such an example:

    MULTIPLY 2 BY C GIVING H.

In this $2 \times c$ is calculated and the result stored in H, replacing whatever contents were in H previously.

The ON SIZE ERROR option is available in conjunction with the MULTIPLY verb.

COBB OL MYSTERY #5

The ad in the *Times* read

> REWARD
> $10,000
> to anyone able
> to discover saboteur
> of newspaper circulation
> computer. Inquire
> *Times* office.

The world-renowned detective Cobb Ol calmly folded his newspaper and headed for the *Times* offices.

"Good morning," said Cobb to the receptionist.

"Good morning, sir, can I help you?"

"Yes, I'm here to answer this advertisement," said the detective, showing her the paper.

"Oh, you want to see Mr. Circuit, the computer system analyst."

"Mr. Ol," said Mr. Circuit, "Am I glad you're here. We made some changes in the program which keeps track of our circulation distribution and now it won't function."

"What do you suspect, Mr. Circuit?" asked Cobb.

"I believe that some rival sabotaged the program when it was fed back into the machine."

"I'd like to see a listing of a program," said Ol.

Ol sat at Circuit's desk and slowly leafed through the 30-page listing.

Finally, the detective looked up.

"The form of the MULTIPLY statement can be very error-prone at times." said the detective.

"What do you mean by that?" inquired the systems analyst.

"Take a look at this statement:

```
MULTIPLY PRICE-PER-LINE TIMES NO-OF-COPIES."
```

"It looks OK to me, Mr. Ol."

"Ah, but look carefully, sir. The word TIMES is incorrect. The MULTIPLY statement always must have the word BY in it. It should read

```
MULTIPLY PRICE-PER-LINE BY NO-OF-COPIES."
```

"Well, I guess you're right, Mr. Ol," said Mr. Circuit, slightly embarrassed. "I guess the word TIMES is a habit around here. "I don't know how to thank you."

"I'll collect my $10,000 at the payroll department on my way out. Good day, Mr. Circuit."

A smile of satisfaction filled the detective's face as he walked out.

5.4 DIVISION

Finally we come to the last of the four arithmetic operations permitted in COBOL—that of the DIVIDE verb. The DIVIDE statement is used whenever a quotient resulting from the division of one data item into another is required. Some typical examples are

```
DIVIDE A INTO B.
```

```
DIVIDE 10 INTO Y.
```

```
DIVIDE 6.2 INTO SUM.
```

In each of the above cases, the first-named item is divided into the second, the latter value being replaced by the result of the division. The generalized format for this DIVIDE instruction is

$$\underline{\text{DIVIDE}} \begin{Bmatrix} \text{data-name-1} \\ \text{constant-1} \end{Bmatrix} \underline{\text{INTO}} \text{ data-name-2}$$

There is a GIVING option which may be used in conjunction with the DIVIDE INTO instruction. A typical example might be

    DIVIDE WEEKLY–TAX INTO ANNUAL–TAX GIVING PROP–TAX.

In this case both WEEKLY–TAX and ANNUAL–TAX are unaltered. In recent years the DIVIDE instruction has been made even more flexible. In the place of the preposition INTO, the word BY may be substituted (as in the MULTIPLY verb). When using the INTO form of the DIVIDE instruction, the GIVING clause may be included or not as the user wishes. What this implies is that the instruction DIVIDE A BY B is unacceptable by the COBOL compiler. An attempt to use it will result in perhaps three lines of diagnostic messages, which may be extremely confusing to the novice. It might help the reader to remember the correct form of the DIVIDE verb by referring to the phrase: One way to succeed in division is BY GIVING.

Upon reflection, it becomes clear why the DIVIDE A BY B instruction should be somewhat controversial. In all of the other arithmetic operations, it was always the second operand which took the result. However, in English, dividing A by B implies that the result will go into A, which would be contrary to the convention adopted by COBOL. Therefore if A is to be divided by B, one is forced to write either DIVIDE A BY B GIVING A, or DIVIDE B into A. The generalized format for this second form of the DIVIDE verb is

$$\underline{\text{DIVIDE}} \begin{Bmatrix} \text{data-name-1} \\ \text{constant-1} \end{Bmatrix} \begin{Bmatrix} \underline{\text{INTO}} \\ \underline{\text{BY}} \end{Bmatrix} \begin{Bmatrix} \text{data-name-2} \\ \text{constant-2} \end{Bmatrix} \underline{\text{GIVING}} \text{ data-name-3}$$

Here are some more examples of valid DIVIDE instructions all of which use the preposition BY and therefore have the GIVING clause appended.

    DIVIDE A BY 2 GIVING B.

    DIVIDE DOLLARS BY UNITS GIVING UNIT–PRICE

    DIVIDE 138 BY 3 GIVING M.

    DIVIDE 358 BY A GIVING B.

In each of the DIVIDE formats discussed above, the ON SIZE ERROR option may be used. A very useful option provided with the DIVIDE instruction is the REMAINDER clause. A remainder is nothing other than that value left after one number is divided by another. For example,

    DIVIDE 14 BY 3 GIVING C REMAINDER D.

has the effect of dividing the 14 by 3, putting the quotient 4 in c and the remainder of 2 into d. The REMAINDER, too, may have the ON SIZE ERROR option attached to it.

5.5 THE COMPUTE STATEMENT

Sometimes it is too cumbersome to perform a particular calculation by means of the four verbs available in COBOL, or the verbs are simply inadequate for the task. For example, if we wanted to raise a number to a non-integer power such as

$$p^{.12}$$

it would be impossible to do so using the operations permitted in what one can describe as "lingo longo," perhaps an affectionate term for the method of specifying an arithmetic calculation by means of the arithmetic verbs. Raising a number to an integer power such as P^8 can be done by a succession of multiplications. This is not possible when the exponent is a fractional quantity.

For such situations COBOL provides the programmer with the COMPUTE statement. A typical example of a COMPUTE statement is:

```
COMPUTE A = B * (C + 1.0 / D) ** E — F.
```

where the word COMPUTE is punched in the B margin. The following points should be noted when using the COMPUTE statement:

1. Multiplication is represented by the symbol *
   Division is represented by the symbol /
   Addition is represented by the symbol +
   Subtraction is represented by the symbol —
   Exponentiation is represented by the double symbol **
   Whenever these arithmetic operators are used they must be preceded and followed by at least one blank.
2. The equals sign must be embedded between blanks and must always appear.
3. In the absence of parentheses, exponentiation takes the highest priority followed by multiplication and division which in turn is followed by addition and subtraction. In the last two cases, where two arithmetic operations are of equal "strength," they are evaluated in a left to right direction. The order of execution may be changed by the programmer by inserting matched parentheses, but the expression within parentheses is executed in accordance with the hierarchy described above. The effect of exe-

cuting the above COMPUTE statement therefore will be to store the value of

$$B(C + \frac{1.0}{D})^E - F$$

into A.

4. The ON SIZE ERROR option is available for the COMPUTEd value.
5. It is mentioned in passing that certain COBOL installations restrict the use of the COMPUTE instruction for reasons associated with program efficiency.
6. The generalized format for the COMPUTE statement is

COMPUTE data-name-1 $\begin{Bmatrix} \text{data-name-2} \\ \text{constant-1} \\ \text{arithmetic expression} \end{Bmatrix}$

[ON SIZE ERROR imperative-statement-1]

5.6 REVIEW QUESTIONS AND EXERCISES

1. Which of the following are valid?
   (a) ADD A TO B.
   (b) ADD B TO A.
   (c) ADD A TO B GIVING C.
   (d) SUBTRACT X FROM Z.
   (e) MULTIPLY A TIMES B.
   (f) MULTIPLY A TIMES B GIVING C.
   (g) MULTIPLY A BY B GIVING C.
   (h) DIVIDE A BY B.
   (i) DIVIDE B BY A.
   (j) DIVIDE AB BY BA.
   (k) DIVIDE C INTO D.
   (l) DIVIDE C INTO D GIVING E.
   (m) DIVIDE A BY A GIVING A.
2. Each of the following algebraic expressions has been converted into COBOL by two different methods. Examine each conversion carefully and indicate whether you agree each conversion has been done correctly.
   (a) $y = ab$ MULTIPLY A BY B GIVING Y.   COMPUTE Y = A * B.
   (b) $f = p - t$ SUBTRACT T FROM P GIVING F.   COMPUTE F = P - T.
   (c) $p = qrt$ MULTIPLY Q, R, T, GIVING P.   COMPUTE P = Q * R * T.
   (d) $r = s/t$ DIVIDE T INTO S GIVING R.   COMPUTE R = S / T.
   (e) $w = \sqrt{y}$ TAKE-ROOT-OF Y GIVING W.   COMPUTE W = Y ** .5.
3. Examine each of the following COBOL instructions and determine which are valid and which are invalid. If you think an instruction is invalid, state your reasons in full. (It is suggested that you have a list of the reserved words readily available).
   (a) ADD ACTUAL TO REAL.
   (b) SUBTRACT EVERY FROM END.
   (c) MULTIPLY DAY BY NIGHT.

(d) DIVIDE WEEK BY DATE.

(e) ADD DATA, SUM, GIVING COLUMN.

(f) SUBTRACT DAY–OF–WEEK FROM MONTH GIVING NEXT.

(g) MULTIPLY PAGE BY PAGE-COUNTER.

(h) ADD FINAL TO LENGTH.

(i) SUBTRACT TOP FROM BOTTOM.

(j) MULTIPLY UP BY DOWN.

(k) DIVIDE DIVIDE BY CHARACTER.

(l) ADD COMPUTE TO CONSTANT.

(m) SUBTRACT ADDRESS FROM AREA.

4. Verify that each of the following algebraic expressions have been correctly converted to their COBOL equivalents.

(a) $b = c^2 d$ COMPUTE B = C ↑ 2 • D.

(b) $c = \dfrac{a+b}{d}$ COMPUTE C = A + B / D.

(c) $d = b^2 - 4ac$ COMPUTE D = B •• 2 − 4 A C.

(d) $e = \dfrac{ab}{cd}$ COMPUTE E = A•B / C•D.

(e) $f = (w^2 + v)^3$ COMPUTE F = (W ••2 + V) ••• 3.

5. Assume an input file called INPUTPHILE, consisting of a number of record cards. The program shown initializes a count called KOUNT to zero and counts the cards, printing the result. However, the program contains a bug. Find it!

```
PROCEDURE DIVISION.
GET–READY.
        OPEN INPUT INPUTPHILE.
        COMPUTE KOUNT = 0.
ON–YOUR–MARK.
        READ INPUTPHILE AT END GO AWAY.
        COMPUTE KOUNT = KOUNT + 1.
        GO TO ON–YOUR–MARK.
AWAY.
        DISPLAY 'THE NUMBER OF CARDS = ' KOUNT.
        CLOSE INPUTPHILE.
        STOP RUN.
```

6. Devise a short program to compute the factorial for any given positive integer (the factorial of 5 for example is $5 \times 4 \times 3 \times 2 \times 1 = 120$)

EDITING

Roses are red
Violets are blue
It sure takes a lot
To print a line or two

You may recall that in section 4.4 we showed two ways of improving a listing program. One of the ways is to print suitable headings above the columns of the printed output. The other way—the one which concerns us in this chapter—is to number each line of output. If you look back at the program on page 54, you will notice that the numbers go from 0001 to 0015. Most people in business would agree that not only should problems be solved accurately and efficiently but also that the output to the project, be it an invoice, an accounts receivable form, a payroll, or just a report—whatever the case—should be clear and easily readable. Referring now to the manner in which the card or line numbers are printed, we notice that each number is preceded by leading zeroes. This format could be criticized for the reason that there is something unnatural to the human eye about printing a number with leading zeroes. COBOL provides methods of "editing out" leading zeroes as well as numerous other changes which may be made to a numeric field to enhance its appearance and to present it in a suitable form. That is the subject of this chapter—the matter of editing output.

6.1 SUPPRESSION OF LEADING ZEROES BY REPLACEMENT WITH BLANK CHARACTERS

In order to replace leading zeroes by blanks—one of the most common of the editing chores one is confronted with in COBOL—the editing symbol z is used. Suppose, for example, that the number 0012 has a picture of 9999 and its leading zeroes are to be suppressed, that is, replaced by blank spaces. We have to set up a picture associated with the receiving field with a suitable number of z's. The source item is now MOVED to the object field. A blank space will now appear in each position where leading zeroes in the source field are matched by z's in the receiving field. In the example shown ƀ means a blank space.

SOURCE ITEM	SOURCE PICTURE	EDITING PICTURE	EDITED ITEM
0012	9999	ZZZ9	ƀƀ12

Thus we see that the result of executing the instruction

    MOVE CARD–NUMBER TO CARD–NUMBER–OUT

is to produce a four character edited item in which the two leading zeroes are replaced by blanks. By the same token, if CARD–NUMBER–OUT had a picture of Z999 instead of ZZZ9 as shown above, the result of the MOVE instruction would have been

    ƀ012

Here are some further examples to illustrate the use of the Z in suppressing leading zeroes. Note that if the symbol Z is used it must precede any character symbol 9.

SOURCE ITEM	SOURCE PICTURE	EDITING PICTURE	EDITED FIELD
01020304	99999999	ZZZ99999	ƀ1020304
004	999	ZZZ	ƀƀ4
976	999	ZZZ	976
2001	9999	ZZZZ	2001
0001	9999	Z999	ƀ001
00200	99999	ZZZ99	ƀƀ200

6.2 INSERTION OF A DECIMAL POINT

All of the examples in the previous table are whole numbers sometimes called *integers*. Although this is the only kind of number which may be punched on a card and subsequently read by a COBOL program, numbers containing *implied* decimal points may nevertheless be handled. The manner in which this is done is a little sneaky. The number is punched on the data card as an ordinary integer without the decimal point. For example, if the number were 23456 one could indicate that the number were to be treated as 234.56 by changing the associated picture from 9(5) to one which stipulates where the implied decimal point is located.

The accountant, for example, uses the columnar accounting sheet, where a vertical line which takes up virtually no space at all indicates precisely where the decimal point belongs. On a blackboard one might be tempted to indicate the position of the implied decimal point by writing

```
        V
    2 3 4 5 6
```

where the carat symbol indicates the position of the decimal point. What could be more natural than to use precisely this shaped symbol in the form of the letter V in the associated picture? The actual picture which would be used in 999V99. The V does not itself physically occupy a position in the memory of the computer so a number expressed with the picture 999V99 occupies only five positions, not six.

Since it is so often desirable for the decimal point to be printed, the decimal point is one of the acceptable editing symbols permitted in COBOL but no picture may contain more than one decimal point. Neither may more than one V appear in a picture for that matter. When a number containing an implied decimal point is moved into an edited field containing a decimal point, the implied decimal point is matched up with the decimal point before any additional editing takes place, as shown in the following examples.

SOURCE ITEM	SOURCE PICTURE	EDITING PICTURE	EDITED FIELD
003ᵥ25	999V99	999.99	003.25
5ᵥ7	9V9	9.9	5.7
52	99	99.99	52.00
005ᵥ876	999V999	999.999	005.876
0123ᵥ0	9999V9	9999.9	0123.0

In the third example shown above the source item 52 is treated as if it were followed by a decimal point. Please note that in COBOL no picture may be terminated by an implied decimal point. The number 52, therefore, is treated as if it had an implied decimal point which is then matched up with the decimal point in the editing picture producing the edited result of 52.00.

The following table illustrates the use of both the decimal point and the Z editing symbols.

SOURCE ITEM	SOURCE PICTURE	EDITING PICTURE	EDITED ITEM
01ᴧ23	99V99	Z9.99	ƀ1.23
2ᴧ345	9V999	Z.999	2.345
0071ᴧ65	9999V99	ZZZZ.ZZ	ƀƀ71.65
ᴧ852	V999	.999	.852
000ᴧ000	999V999	ZZZ.ZZZ	(only blanks appear)

6.3 SUPPRESSION OF LEADING ZEROES BY ASTERISKS

You may have noticed on those happy but all too infrequent occasions when you receive a check that the amount for which the check is drawn is often printed preceded by a string of asterisks. These leading asterisks are printed as protection against forgery. In order to replace leading zeroes by asterisks, the character * is used in much the same way as the editing symbol Z is used to suppress leading zeroes. Here are some examples of asterisks being used for editing purposes.

SOURCE ITEM	SOURCE PICTURE	EDITING PICTURE	EDITED FIELD
00598	99999	***99	**598
000123	999999	*99999	*00123
0005	9999	****	***5
01ᴧ234	99V999	**.***	*1.234
01ᴧ2200	999999	******	*122 00
000	999	***	***

6.4 INSERTION OF COMMAS, SPACES, OR ZEROES

Although it is not permissible in COBOL to insert a comma in a constant to separate off the thousands from the rest of the number as in 636,000 it is nevertheless possible to insert one or more commas in the appropriate positions in the edited field. The same applies to the insertion of a space and also to a zero. Here are some examples where a comma, a space and a zero appear in the edited result by means of the editing symbols comma (,), B, or zero (0), respectively.

SOURCE ITEM	SOURCE PICTURE	EDITING PICTURE	EDITED FIELD
5342	9999	9,999	5,342
0004987	9999999	Z,ZZZ,ZZZ	ƀƀƀƀ4,987
109282011	999999999	999B99B9999	109 28 2011
071655	999999	ZZBZZBZZ	ƀ7 16 55
004876382	999999V999	ZZ9,999.999	ƀƀ4,876.382
387	999	999BB000	387 000
29678	99999	99,999.00	29,678.00
1234	9999	9B9B9B9	1 2 3 4
158	999	999,000	158,000
000345	999999	ZZZ,999	ƀƀƀ345

6.5 INSERTION OF A FIXED CURRENCY SIGN—THE DOLLAR SIGN

When processing business data, it is frequently desirable to precede an amount by a dollar sign ($). This may be accomplished by inserting a single dollar sign as the leftmost character in the appropriate editing field. Combinations of editing symbols may be used with the dollar sign, such as the Z, the period, the comma, and the asterisk, as shown in the next sequence of examples.

SOURCE ITEM	SOURCE PICTURE	EDITING PICTURE	EDITED FIELD
123	999	$999	$123
001ˬ25	999V99	$ZZ9.99	$ᵇᵇ1.25
00015387ˬ26	99999999V99	$****9,999.99	$***15,387.26
086354	999999	$999,999.00	$086,354.00
5ˬ98	9V99	$*.99	$5.98

6.6 INSERTION OF A SIGN INDICATOR: +, −, CR, DB

In describing numeric data, we have confined ourselves thus far to the symbol 9 and to the V for the implied decimal point. If we had no choice but to confine ourselves to these two symbols, all numbers would be treated as unsigned. In the event that the number is positive, no problem would result, but, should the number turn out to be negative, we would be unaware of the fact. In mathematical terminology, we would always be dealing with the *absolute value* of the number in question. If there is even a slim possibility of a value becoming negative as a result of a computation, it is advisable to retain a sign within the associated picture. This is done by prefacing the picture with the letter S (for a signed field). As with the implied decimal point V, the S does not add to the size of the field.

Even if a picture contains the sign symbol S, it is necessary to prepare a special edited field in order that the printed value appears together with the plus or minus sign as appropriate.

For these purposes, +, −, CR (CRedit) and DB (DeBit) are used. In any given picture clause, however, only one of these may be used. Whereas the plus and the minus symbols may be placed either at the extreme left or extreme right of the picture, the CR and DB symbols can appear only at the extreme right and both the CR and DB symbols occupy two positions of the edited field. For most purposes, the plus or minus signs are sufficient, but in accountancy a minus sign can indicate either a credit or a debit, depending upon the particular account. For this reason the CR and DB edit symbols are used. If the item in question is not negative neither the CR nor the DB edit symbols is printed; they are replaced by two blanks. Here are some examples:

SOURCE ITEM	SOURCE PICTURE	EDITING PICTURE	EDITED FIELD
−123	S999	+999	−123
−17890	S99999	99999CR	17890CR
+05876	S99999	−99999	ƀ05876
+083͵759	S999V999	999.999DB	083.759ƀƀ
−000587	S99999	−ZZZZZ9	ƀƀƀƀ587
−12345	S99999	$99,999.00+	$12,345.00−
+9210365	S9999999	ZZZZZZ9−	9210365ƀ
−00424͵55	S99999V99	+$****9.99	−$**424.55
+0689	S9999	9999+	0689+
−783͵52	S999V99	$999.99DB	$738.52DB

The rules of editing may be summarized briefly by two general principles:
1. If the receiving field contains a plus sign, the sign of the number being moved to it, whether it is positive or negative, will always print out.
2. If the receiving field contains a minus sign, it will be printed only if the number being moved to it is negative. Similarly, the CR and DB symbols will be triggered only by a negative number.

6.7 FLOATING EDITING SYMBOLS

In Section 6.3 we discussed the manner by which leading zeroes may be replaced by asterisks. We mentioned that this is an effective security measure in that all the spaces between the dollar sign and the leftmost digit become completely filled with asterisks. An alternative to this approach is to print the dollar sign immediately to the left of the most significant digit. However, it is very rare that we know in advance precisely how large a value is going to be, in order that we may place the dollar sign immediately to the left of it. What is required is some method whereby the dollar sign may "float" to its desired position, that is, immediately to the left of the most significant digit. This is done by inserting in the editing field a *consecutive string* of dollars signs, such that there is *at least one more dollar sign than there are positions in the field*. This extra position is important because one dollar sign will always appear on the printed output and thus it is essential that room be left for it. In this way it is possible to enhance the way printed values appear. The following examples should help to make clear this important concept.

SOURCE ITEM	SOURCE PICTURE	EDITING PICTURE	EDITED ITEM
00058876	999999V99	$$$$$9.99	$588.76
0005	9999	$$$$.00	$5.00
00078	99999	$ZZZZ.00	$ 78.00
34598	999V99	$$$9.99	$345.98
0112	9999	$Z999	$ 112

The plus and minus signs can also be used as floating signs in the same way that the floating dollar sign is used. However, only one may be used in any given picture as a floating insertion symbol.

6.8 BLANK WHEN ZERO

For those situations where the value of an item being printed is zero, the use of editing symbols might lead to confusion. Printing $0.00, for example, would hardly lead to great clarity and for this reason COBOL permits the clause

BLANK WHEN ZERO

to be used for such situations. If the value in question is, in fact, zero, blanks are printed without the editing symbols. The phrase BLANK WHEN ZERO immediately follows the editing field in question.

SOURCE ITEM	SOURCE PICTURE	EDITING PICTURE	EDITED ITEM
0000	99V99	$$$.99	$.00
0000	99V99	$$$.99 BLANK WHEN ZERO	

Here is a table showing all of the permitted symbols which may be used for editing purposes.

SYMBOL	EXPLANATION
A	alphabetic character or space
B	insert blank space
P	decimal position mover for scaling purposes, not included in field count
S	allows for signed numbers and is not included in field count
V	implied decimal point and is not included in field count
X	alphanumeric character
Z	zero suppression character
9	numeric character
0	zero insertion character
,	comma insertion character
.	decimal point or period insertion character
+	plus sign insertion character
—	minus sign insertion character
CR	credit editing symbols
DB	debit editing symbols
*	check protection insertion character (floating)
$	dollar sign insertion character (floating)

6.9 REVIEW QUESTIONS AND EXERCISES

1. One of the most common editing procedures is to print a decimal point in its appropriate location within a number. Assuming the edited picture is 999.999, how will the following numbers appear once they have been moved to this field?

VALUE	EDITED RESULT
12ʌ34	
ʌ9876	
1234	
987ʌ654	

2. Write what you would expect to see when the values indicated are moved to their corresponding pictures.

VALUE	PICTURE	PRINTED RESULT
512ʌ34	99.99	
1234	99.99	
345ʌ678	.9999	
1ʌ2	9(3).9(3)	
45ʌ6	99,999	
987654	9,999,999	
1234ʌ567	9,999.999	
2468135	9,999.999	

3. If the number 1ʌ23 is MOVED to the PICTURE $9.99, it would print out as $1.23. What printed results would you expect from the following:

VALUE	PICTURE	PRINTED RESULT
1ʌ23	$9(4).9(2)	
3ʌ4	$99.9	
56	$$999.99	
ʌ07	$$$$.99	
0	$$$$.99	

THE
MOVE VERB

We have already encountered the MOVE statement in earlier chapters. It was stressed that the MOVE instruction is probably the most frequently used in the whole of the COBOL repertoire. It is so important that we are devoting the whole of this present chapter to a detailed study of the implications of the MOVE statement. Basically, when we tell the computer

```
MOVE A TO B
```

we are actually moving the contents of A into that of B, replacing whatever was stored in B previously. The original value contained in A is retained so that it will perhaps be better to regard the MOVE as moving a copy of the contents of A to B.

7.1 NUMERIC MOVES

When executing the instruction MOVE A TO B we have to consider the pictures applicable to both A and B. If the number 465 with a picture of 999 is moved to another picture of 999, the whole of the number will be retained. If, however, the second picture were 99 rather than 999, truncation would occur—the truncation of the most significant digit, 4. The reason for this is that when numeric data are moved they are always lined up with the decimal point, implied or otherwise. Remember that when no decimal is specified it is assumed to be located at the right of the picture. In this sense, numeric data is said to be *right-adjusted*.

```
                          PICTURE
                          9 9 9
                        ┌───┬───┬───┐
465    moved──→         │ 4 │ 6 │ 5 │
                        └───┴───┴───┘
                          PICTURE
                          9 9
                            ┌───┬───┐
465    moved──→             │ 6 │ 5 │
                            └───┴───┘
```

If, on the other hand, the field into which the number 465 is being moved is 9999, it will appear, when printed out, as 0465. The rule here is that whenever a number is moved to a larger numeric field not only is it lined up with the decimal point but all vacant spaces are filled with zeroes.

```
                          PICTURE
                          9 9 9 9
                        ┌───┬───┬───┬───┐
465    moved──→         │ 0 │ 4 │ 6 │ 5 │
                        └───┴───┴───┴───┘
```

Moving the number 123V45 to a field with a picture of 999V999 has the following effect. First, the implied decimal points are lined up:

```
    123V45
    9999V999
```

Then the remaining places are zero-filled both to the right and to the left, producing the value 0123V450.

In a similar fashion, if the number 123V45 is moved to an editing field such as 9999.999, the edited item becomes 0123.450. In both of the general cases cited above, it is important to remember that the numeric items are always aligned about the decimal point (or the implied decimal point).

Moving the number 9214V63 to a field with a picture of 9999 has important implications in COBOL. As stated above, the decimal points, implied or otherwise, are first lined up. This places the integer part of the number 9214 in the 9999 field, truncating the fractional portion 63 since there is simply no room in the picture to receive it. Incidentally, this is a standard method of truncating a number to its integer portion. To extract the *fractional* portion of the number, all one need to do is to move the original value into a field whose picture is V99; this will, however, produce a warning error message which may be conveniently ignored.

Moving a signed number with a picture of, say, S999 to a field with a picture of 999 has the effect of retaining its *absolute* value only. Here are some examples of numeric moves to illustrate all of the above.

SENDING ITEM	SENDING PICTURE	RECEIVING PICTURE	RECEIVING FIELD
−0987	S9999	9999	0987
12346	99999	99	46
587ᴧ65	999V99	99999V99	00587V65
0123ᴧ28	9999V99	$999999.99	$000123.28
+35	S99	99	35
001	999	99999	00001

If the same item is to be moved to several different receiving fields, it is not necessary to effect each individual move with a separate statement. Instead, one can use a single move instruction, as in the following example:

```
MOVE A TO B, C, D.
```

7.2 ALPHANUMERIC MOVES

Before we discuss what is meant by an alphanumeric move, perhaps we should first define what is meant by alphanumeric data. An alphanumeric field is one that contains *any* valid character which is acceptable by the computer. This includes alphabetic data, numeric data, special characters, or any combination of these three.

If the receiving field of a MOVE statement is alphanumeric (defined by an x field), alphabetic (defined by an A field) or is a group item, the MOVE is considered an alphanumeric move. As opposed to the numeric move, an alphanumeric move has the effect of aligning the MOVEd data to the *leftmost* position of the receiving field.

Assume that a data item (ITEM–OF–DATA) with a picture of xxxxx contains the first-character word PAPER. It is now possible to move another five-character data item such as TAXES into the same field by means of the instruction

```
MOVE 'TAXES' TO ITEM-OF-DATA
```

This will completely replace the previous contents of ITEM–OF–DATA.

If, on the other hand, the receiving field were xxxxxx (a six-character field) rather than xxxxx, the instruction

```
MOVE 'TAXES' TO ITEM-OF-DATA
```

would again have the effect of adjusting the word TAXES to the leftmost position. Unlike moves with numeric data in which excess space is filled with zeroes, any empty room in the receiving field of an alphanumeric item is automatically filled with blanks.

Moving an item into an alphanumeric field of shorter length left-adjusts the item in the receiving field but truncates any excess characters.

7.3 JUSTIFIED RIGHT CLAUSE

It is possible in COBOL to avoid having alphanumeric moves left-adjusted. This is accomplished by resorting to a special phrase JUSTIFIED RIGHT, which is written after the designation of the receiving field. This may be abbreviated to JUST RIGHT or even JUST. This feature is restricted to the Working-Storage Section.

7.4 GROUP MOVES

Whenever a move is made either to or from a group item, that move is defined as a group move. In all such cases, the move is considered an alphanumeric elementary move.

DEVELOPING
A SALES REPORT

8.1 AN ELEMENTARY SALES REPORT

For the purposes of the next problem, let us suppose that a company punches a separate data card for each product sold. In order that these cards may be processed by the computer, they have to be punched in some uniform fashion. Let the format be as shown in Figure 11.

DESCRIPTION OF INPUT CARD

Columns 1–6 are reserved for the product code number which is a six-digit numeric field. When punching the product code care should be taken

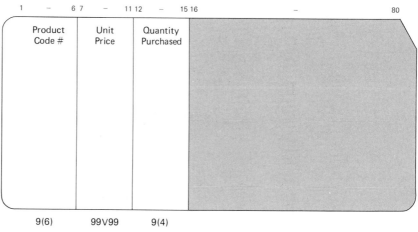

FIGURE 11

that leading zeroes are used, if necessary, to fill out the six columns of the field. Any blank columns left in this field might create serious difficulties for the reason that a blank is not an acceptable numeric character.

Columns 7–11 are reserved for the unit price of the particular product. It is punched in the format 999V99 where an *implied* decimal point is used to separate the dollars portion from the cents. A decimal point is never punched as data in a COBOL program because it simply would be a waste of a column to include it. It should be noted also that in COBOL the decimal point is not a valid numeric character. If the decimal point is imbedded within numeric data it will not be able to be processed. In fact, there is no way to read a decimal point from data cards in COBOL.

In columns 12–15 the quantity purchased is punched. Once again this four column field must be punched right justified with zero fill, if necessary.

Nothing whatever is punched in columns 16–80.

Once all the data for a particular period, say a week or a month has been punched, we would like to prepare a sales report indicating the card number, product code number, unit price, quantity purchased, and the net sales for each product, each of the output fields being edited where appropriate.

INPUT TO PROGRAM 12

```
002452003270999
002325008520532
006542003210523
000052000990945
002384068950635
000017032250145
000215002305246
000333003654230
000035852010366
000001012500250
000002035000200
000222356320553
```

PROGRAM 12
Sales Report

```
00001          IDENTIFICATION DIVISION.
00002          PROGRAM-ID. SALES.
00003
00004          ENVIRONMENT DIVISION.
00005          INPUT-OUTPUT SECTION.
00006          FILE-CONTROL.
00007              SELECT IN-FILE ASSIGN TO UT-S-READER.
00008              SELECT OUT-FILE ASSIGN TO UT-S-PRINTER.
00009
00010          DATA DIVISION.
00011          FILE SECTION.
00012          FD  IN-FILE
00013              LABEL RECORDS ARE OMITTED.
00014          01  SALES-RECORD.
00015              05  PRODUCT-CODE          PICTURE 9(6).
00016              05  UNIT-PRICE            PICTURE 999V99.
00017              05  QUANTITY-PURCHASED    PICTURE 9(4).
00018              05  FILLER                PICTURE X(65).
```

```
00019          FD  OUT-FILE
00020              LABEL RECORDS ARE OMITTED.
00021          01  PRINT-LINE-RECORD.
00022              05  PRINT-LINE PICTURE X(132).
00023
00024          WORKING-STORAGE SECTION.
00025          77  CARD-COUNT              PICTURE 999 VALUE ZERO.
00026          01  HEADER-1.
00027              05  FILLER      PICTURE X(18) VALUE SPACES.
00028              05  FILLER      PICTURE X(24) VALUE 'S A L E S      R E P O R
00029       -  ' T'.
00030              05  FILLER      PICTURE X(90) VALUE SPACES.
00031          01  HEADER-2.
00032              05  FILLER      PICTURE X(18) VALUE SPACES.
00033              05  FILLER      PICTURE X(24) VALUE ALL '*'.
00034              05  FILLER      PICTURE X(90) VALUE SPACES.
00035          01  HEADER-3.
00036              05  FILLER      PICTURE X(21) VALUE SPACES.
00037              05  FILLER      PICTURE X(04) VALUE 'ITEM'.
00038              05  FILLER      PICTURE X(7)  VALUE SPACES.
00039              05  FILLER      PICTURE X(07) VALUE 'PRODUCT'.
00040              05  FILLER      PICTURE X(04) VALUE SPACES.
00041              05  FILLER      PICTURE X(04) VALUE 'UNIT'.
00042              05  FILLER      PICTURE X(08) VALUE SPACES.
00043              05  FILLER      PICTURE X(08) VALUE 'QUANTITY'.
00044              05  FILLER      PICTURE X(08) VALUE SPACES.
00045              05  FILLER      PICTURE X(03) VALUE 'NET'.
00046              05  FILLER      PICTURE X(77) VALUE SPACES.
00047          01  HEADER-4.
00048              05  FILLER      PICTURE X(03) VALUE SPACES.
00049              05  FILLER      PICTURE X(02) VALUE 'NO'.
00050              05  FILLER      PICTURE X(09) VALUE SPACES.
00051              05  FILLER      PICTURE X(04) VALUE 'CODE'.
00052              05  FILLER      PICTURE X(06) VALUE SPACES.
00053              05  FILLER      PICTURE X(05) VALUE 'PRICE'.
00054              05  FILLER      PICTURE X(07) VALUE SPACES.
00055              05  FILLER      PICTURE X(09) VALUE 'PURCHASED'.
00056              05  FILLER      PICTURE X(07) VALUE SPACES.
00057              05  FILLER      PICTURE X(05) VALUE 'SALES'.
00058              05  FILLER      PICTURE X(75) VALUE SPACES.
00059          01  HEADER-5.
00060              05  FILLER      PICTURE X(02) VALUE SPACES.
00061              05  FILLER      PICTURE X(04) VALUE ALL '-'.
00062              05  FILLER      PICTURE X(07) VALUE SPACES.
00063              05  FILLER      PICTURE X(07) VALUE ALL '-'.
00064              05  FILLER      PICTURE X(04) VALUE SPACES.
00065              05  FILLER      PICTURE X(05) VALUE ALL '-'.
00066              05  FILLER      PICTURE X(07) VALUE SPACES.
00067              05  FILLER      PICTURE X(09) VALUE ALL '-'.
00068              05  FILLER      PICTURE X(07) VALUE SPACES.
00069              05  FILLER      PICTURE X(05) VALUE ALL '-'.
00070              05  FILLER      PICTURE X(75) VALUE SPACES.
00071          01  DETAIL-LINE.
00072              05  FILLER            PICTURE X(01) VALUE SPACES.
00073              05  CARD-COUNT-OUT          PICTURE ZZ9.
00074              05  FILLER            PICTURE X(09) VALUE SPACES.
00075              05  PRODUCT-CODE-OUT        PICTURE ZZZZ99.
00076              05  FILLER            PICTURE X(04) VALUE SPACES.
00077              05  UNIT-PRICE-OUT          PICTURE $$$9.99.
00078              05  FILLER            PICTURE X(10) VALUE SPACES.
00079              05  QUANTITY-PURCHASED-OUT  PICTURE Z,ZZ9.
00080              05  FILLER            PICTURE X(01) VALUE SPACES.
00081              05  NET-SALES               PICTURE $$,$$$,$$9.99.
00082              05  FILLER            PICTURE X(73) VALUE SPACES.
00083
00084          PROCEDURE DIVISION.
00085          START-HERE.
00086              OPEN INPUT  IN-FILE.
00087              OPEN OUTPUT OUT-FILE.
00088              MOVE HEADER-1 TO PRINT-LINE-RECORD.
00089              WRITE PRINT-LINE-RECORD.
00090              MOVE HEADER-2 TO PRINT-LINE-RECORD.
00091              WRITE PRINT-LINE-RECORD.
00092              MOVE HEADER-3 TO PRINT-LINE-RECORD.
00093              WRITE PRINT-LINE-RECORD.
00094              MOVE HEADER-4 TO PRINT-LINE-RECORD.
00095              WRITE PRINT-LINE-RECORD.
00096              MOVE HEADER-5 TO PRINT-LINE-RECORD.
00097              WRITE PRINT-LINE-RECORD.
00098
00099          READ-CARD.
00100              READ IN-FILE AT END GO TO FINISH.
00101              ADD 1 TO CARD-COUNT.
00102              MOVE CARD-COUNT TO CARD-COUNT-OUT.
```

```
00103                MOVE PRODUCT-CODE TO PRODUCT-CODE-OUT.
00104                MOVE UNIT-PRICE TO UNIT-PRICE-OUT.
00105                MOVE QUANTITY-PURCHASED TO QUANTITY-PURCHASED-OUT.
00106                MULTIPLY UNIT-PRICE BY QUANTITY-PURCHASED GIVING NET-SALES.
00107                MOVE DETAIL-LINE TO PRINT-LINE-RECORD.
00108                WRITE PRINT-LINE-RECORD.
00109                GO TO READ-CARD.
00110
00111        FINISH.
00112                CLOSE IN-FILE OUT-FILE.
00113                STOP RUN.
```

OUTPUT TO PROGRAM 12

```
                          S A L E S     R E P O R T
                      ****************************
     ITEM        PRODUCT      UNIT        QUANTITY         NET
     NO          CODE         PRICE       PURCHASED        SALES
     ----        -------      -----       ---------        -----
      1            2452       $3.27           999        $3,266.73
      2            2325       $8.52           532        $4,532.64
      3            6542       $3.21           523        $1,676.83
      4              52       $0.99           945          $935.55
      5            2384      $68.95           635       $43,783.25
      6              17      $32.25           145        $4,676.25
      7             215       $2.30         5,246       $12,065.80
      8             333       $3.65         4,230       $15,439.50
      9              35     $852.01           366      $311,835.66
     10              01      $12.50           250        $3,125.00
     11              02      $35.00           200        $7,000.00
     12             222     $356.32           553      $197,044.96
```

As will be seen from the output, a total of five separate lines are set up for the report title and column headings to be printed. Each one of these lines is incorporated into a separate record in Working-Storage and is moved to the output line for subsequent printing as required.

In the Procedure Division, the input file, IN–FILE, and the output file, OUT–FILE, are opened, this time in two separate statements. As each card of the input file is read, 1 is added to the value of CARD–COUNT, which is defined as a 77 level independent item immediately following the WORKING–STORAGE SECTION card. It has a picture of 99 (thus allowing for a maximum of 99 input data cards) and has an initial value of zero.

The detail line is set up by moving CARD–COUNT to CARD–COUNT–OUT, PRODUCT–CODE to PRODUCT–CODE–OUT, UNIT–PRICE to UNIT–PRICE–OUT and QUANTITY–PURCHASED to QUANTITY–PURCHASED–OUT.

In order to compute NET–SALES, UNIT–PRICE is multiplied by QUANTITY–PURCHASED, thus completing all of the needed items for the output record. At this point the record called DETAIL–LINE is moved as a single unit to the PRINT–LINE–RECORD, which is then written in the customary way with the WRITE instruction. An unconditional transfer is then made to READ–CARD, which reads in the next card in sequence. This loop continues reading every single card in the input file until the AT END condition is activated. At this point, control is transferred immediately to the paragraph named FINISH, where instructions are located to close both the input and output files and to stop execution of the program.

As in normal practice in COBOL programming, fields have been edited where appropriate in an attempt to make the output esthetically pleasing and meaningful.

One of the troublesome tasks in COBOL is deciding upon the size of a picture for a computed result. Such a problem, for example, confronts the programmer when he is deciding on the width of the picture to be used for NET–SALES in the program above. The picture for NET–SALES is directly related to the maximum values that UNIT–PRICE and QUANTITY–PURCHASED may assume. UNIT–PRICE has a picture of 999V99 while QUANTITY–PURCHASED has a picture of 9(4). If one multiplies the number 999.99 by 9999 (a pocket calculator is ideal for this purpose) we arrive at the figure 9998900.01. This is an indication of the maximum field-width that the result will occupy. This can be arrived at more directly, even without the assistance of a pocket calculator, by simply adding together the two integer fields (3 for UNIT–PRICE and 4 for QUANTITY–PURCHASED) and adding separately the fractional portions, which in this case are 2 and 0. Therefore, there will be a maximum of seven digits before the decimal point and two after it.

Armed with this information, which gives us full control over the computed result, it is not necessary (or even meaningful) to include the ON SIZE ERROR option into the MULTIPLY statement. The only other point worth mentioning is the card numbered 00030. This is a continuation of the non-numeric literal

```
'S A L E S R E P O R T'
```

Unfortunately, there is not enough room on card 00029 to contain the whole of the literal and so we had to continue it on the next card. A nonnumeric literal is continued by punching a minus sign (hyphen) in column 7 and an apostrophe in column 12. The literal is then continued and terminated by a closing apostrophe. This method of continuing a non-numeric literal is admittedly strange at first sight. The reader is advised, however, that this can be avoided simply by going to another card at any previous point where a blank is to be found, for example, after X(24) or after the word VALUE. If this is done, the remaining part of the statement can be punched in margin B (column 12); no special punch is needed to indicate that this is a continuation card. The following example shows the use of this preferred method:

```
05 FILLER PICTURE X(25) VALUE
   'S A L E S    R E P O R T'.
```

An alternate method is:

```
05 FILLER PICTURE X(9) VALUE 'S A L E S'.
05 FILLER PICTURE X(3) VALUE '   '.
05 FILLER PICTURE X(12) VALUE 'R E P O R T '.
```

Of course, the three spaces dividing the two words may be attached to either one, provided the field is extended accordingly.

8.2 AN IMPROVED SALES REPORT

COBOL, being the world's most popular programming language for processing business data, offers the programmer a rich variety of options and alternatives. Different programmers will select their own alternatives to suit their particular requirements. In an attempt to introduce the reader to some of these additional features, we are going to modify the sales report program from Section 8.1 and write a more sophisticated program using precisely the same input data.

8.2.1 CURRENT-DATE

In many versions of COBOL, there are various special registers in which certain useful information is stored, information which can be of benefit to a diverse group of programmers. One of these registers contains the current date. Having the current date readily accessible in the computer makes the task of printing dated reports, invoices, and even payroll checks that much easier. In the most popular version of COBOL being used today, ANSI 68 COBOL, provision to access the current date has not been provided. However, various manufacturers have extended the 1968 version to allow for accessing the current date. Programmers using the IBM 360 or 370 Series can access the current date simply by moving the reserved word CURRENT-DATE to a suitable eight-character alphanumeric field in which the date is of the form MM/DD/YY, where MM is a two-digit number indicating the month. This is followed by a slash. Next comes a two-digit number indicating the day of the month; this also is followed by a slash. Finally, a two-digit number indicates the year. Therefore, the date December 31, 1976, would appear as

12/31/76 .

8.2.2 Accumulating Totals

The concept of accumulating totals is inherent in almost all COBOL programs. In fact, we have already encountered this concept in keeping a running total of the number of cards read in Program 12, where the card count was printed out on each detail line. If you refer back to that program, you will see that the accumulated count of the number of cards read was maintained by defining a 77 level item called CARD-COUNT. It was given a picture of 99 and *initialized to zero* by means of the clause VALUE ZERO. All data names which are used for totalling must be initialized to zero. If they are not initialized, the program will abort and the programmer will be left to ponder why. In Program 12, before each line of the report was printed, CARD-COUNT was moved to CARD-COUNT-OUT, which has an edited picture of Z9. It is emphasized that once a numeric value has been edited it is impossible to do any arithmetic on it. Any attempt to do so will result in diagnostic messages and the program will be aborted. This therefore precludes the possibility of adding 1 to CARD–COUNT–OUT directly for each card printed.

As mentioned earlier, if a 77 level item is to be used in working storage, it must precede any 01 level entries which may also appear. The reader is cautioned that many managers of COBOL installations prefer the complete exclusion of 77 level items in COBOL programs. They would rather that all such elementary items be included by an 01 level name followed by a lower level number giving the name of the item, followed by a suitable picture and any appropriate initialization information. One advantage of this method is that the programmer does not have to be concerned with the order in which the items in working storage appear. Another advantage to this method is that for some it leads to clearer documentation of the program.

One of the modifications to be illustrated in Program 13 is the means by which we may print at the end of the report the value of the total quantity purchased and under the column NET SALES the value of the total net sales.

8.2.3 The WRITE . . . FROM Option

In each of the programs illustrated so far in which the WRITE statement is used, information to be printed was moved to the output lines before the WRITE statement was executed. This operation may be reduced to a single instruction by using one of the options available with the WRITE instruction. It is possible in COBOL to say, for example,

```
WRITE PRINT–LINE–RECORD FROM DETAIL–LINE.
```

This has the effect of first moving DETAIL–LINE to PRINT–LINE–RECORD before performing the WRITE. In other words, executing the above instruction has the same effect as the two separate instructions

```
MOVE DETAIL–LINE TO PRINT–LINE–RECORD.
WRITE PRINT–LINE–RECORD.
```

The generalized form of the WRITE . . . FROM instruction is

```
WRITE record-name FROM data-name
```

8.2.4 The REMARKS Statement

The REMARKS option is another one of those permissible paragraph names in the Identification Division. It permits the inclusion of relevant information pertaining to the program and therefore serves as further internal documentation for the program. These comments may be composed of one or more sentences, each of which must be punched in margin B and may be terminated with a period. The system determines the end of these remarks when it encounters the Environment Division header card.

PROGRAM 13
Improved Sales Report

```
00001        IDENTIFICATION DIVISION.
00002        PROGRAM-ID. SOPH-SALES.
00003        REMARKS.
00004               THIS IS AN IMPROVED SALES REPORT WHICH
00005               INTRODUCES THE READER TO THE FOLLOWING CONCEPTS:
00006                    1) CURRENT-DATE.
00007                    2) ACCUMULATIVE TOTALS.
00008                    3) THE WRITE...FROM OPTION.
00009                    4) THE REMARKS OPTION.
00010
00011        ENVIRONMENT DIVISION.
00012        INPUT-OUTPUT SECTION.
00013        FILE-CONTROL.
00014             SELECT IN-FILE ASSIGN TO UT-S-READER.
00015             SELECT OUT-FILE ASSIGN TO UT-S-PRINTER.
00016
00017        DATA DIVISION.
00018        FILE SECTION.
00019        FD  IN-FILE
00020            LABEL RECORDS ARE OMITTED.
00021        01  SALES-RECORD.
00022            05  FILLER                    PICTURE X(2).
00023            05  PRODUCT-CODE              PICTURE 9(4).
00024            05  UNIT-PRICE                PICTURE 999V99.
00025            05  QUANTITY-PURCHASED        PICTURE 9(4).
00026            05  FILLER                    PICTURE X(65).
00027        FD  OUT-FILE
00028            LABEL RECORDS ARE OMITTED.
00029        01  PRINT-LINE-RECORD.
00030            05  PRINT-LINE PICTURE X(132).
00031
00032        WORKING-STORAGE SECTION.
00033        77  CARD-COUNT PICTURE 99 VALUE ZERO.
00034        77  NET-SALES PICTURE 9(7)V99.
00035        77  TOTAL-NET-SALES PICTURE 9(12)V99 VALUE ZERO.
00036        77  TOTAL-QUAN-PURCH PICTURE 9(9) VALUE ZERO.
00037        01  HEADER-1.
00038            05  FILLER PICTURE X(12) VALUE SPACES.
00039            05  FILLER PICTURE X(19) VALUE 'SALES REPORT AS OF '.
00040            05  TODAYS-DATE PICTURE X(8).
00041            05  FILLER PICTURE X(93) VALUE SPACES.
00042
00043        01  HEADER-2.
00044            05  FILLER PICTURE X(12) VALUE SPACES.
00045            05  FILLER PICTURE X(27) VALUE ALL '='.
00046            05  FILLER PICTURE X(93) VALUE SPACES.
00047
00048        01  HEADER-3.
00049            05  FILLER       PICTURE X(2)  VALUE SPACES.
00050            05  FILLER       PICTURE X(04) VALUE 'ITEM'.
00051            05  FILLER       PICTURE X(7)  VALUE SPACES.
00052            05  FILLER       PICTURE X(07) VALUE 'PRODUCT'.
00053            05  FILLER       PICTURE X(04) VALUE SPACES.
00054            05  FILLER       PICTURE X(04) VALUE 'UNIT'.
00055            05  FILLER       PICTURE X(08) VALUE SPACES.
00056            05  FILLER       PICTURE X(08) VALUE 'QUANTITY'.
00057            05  FILLER       PICTURE X(08) VALUE SPACES.
00058            05  FILLER       PICTURE X(03) VALUE 'NET'.
00059            05  FILLER       PICTURE X(77) VALUE SPACES.
00060
00061        01  HEADER-4.
00062            05  FILLER       PICTURE X(03) VALUE SPACES.
```

```
00063          05   FILLER          PICTURE X(02) VALUE 'NO'.
00064          05   FILLER          PICTURE X(09) VALUE SPACES.
00065          05   FILLER          PICTURE X(04) VALUE 'CODE'.
00066          05   FILLER          PICTURE X(06) VALUE SPACES.
00067          05   FILLER          PICTURE X(05) VALUE 'PRICE'.
00068          05   FILLER          PICTURE X(07) VALUE SPACES.
00069          05   FILLER          PICTURE X(09) VALUE 'PURCHASED'..
00070          05   FILLER          PICTURE X(07) VALUE SPACES.
00071          05   FILLER          PICTURE X(05) VALUE 'SALES'.
00072          05   FILLER          PICTURE X(75) VALUE SPACES.
00073       01   HEADER-5.
00074          05   FILLER          PICTURE X(02) VALUE SPACES.
00075          05   FILLER          PICTURE X(04) VALUE ALL '-'.
00076          05   FILLER          PICTURE X(07) VALUE SPACES.
00077          05   FILLER          PICTURE X(07) VALUE ALL '-'.
00078          05   FILLER          PICTURE X(04) VALUE SPACES.
00079          05   FILLER          PICTURE X(05) VALUE ALL '-'.
00080          05   FILLER          PICTURE X(07) VALUE SPACES.
00081          05   FILLER          PICTURE X(09) VALUE ALL '-'.
00082          05   FILLER          PICTURE X(03) VALUE SPACES.
00083          05   FILLER          PICTURE X(13) VALUE ALL '-'.
00084          05   FILLER          PICTURE X(80) VALUE SPACES.
00085
00086       01   HEADER-6.
00087          05   FILLER          PICTURE X(36) VALUE SPACES.
00088          05   FILLER          PICTURE X(09) VALUE ALL '-'.
00089          05   FILLER          PICTURE X(03) VALUE SPACES.
00090          05   FILLER          PICTURE X(13) VALUE ALL '-'.
00091          05   FILLER          PICTURE X(71) VALUE SPACES.
00092
00093       01   DETAIL-LINE-1.
00094          05   FILLER          PICTURE X(01) VALUE SPACES.
00095          05   CARD-COUNT-OUT       PICTURE ZZ9.
00096          05   FILLER          PICTURE X(09) VALUE SPACES.
00097          05   PRODUCT-CODE-OUT     PICTURE ZZZZ99.
00098          05   FILLER          PICTURE X(04) VALUE SPACES.
00099          05   UNIT-PRICE-OUT       PICTURE $$$9.99.
00100          05   FILLER          PICTURE X(10) VALUE SPACES.
00101          05   QUANTITY-PURCHASED-OUT PICTURE Z,ZZ9.
00102          05   FILLER          PICTURE X(01) VALUE SPACES.
00103          05   NET-SALES-OUT        PICTURE $$,$$$,$$9.99.
00104          05   FILLER          PICTURE X(73) VALUE SPACES.
00105
00106       01   DETAIL-LINE-2.
00107          05   FILLER PICTURE X(34) VALUE SPACES.
00108          05   TOTAL-QUAN-PURCH-OUT PICTURE ZZZ,ZZZ,ZZZ.
00109          05   TOTAL-NET-SALES-OUT PICTURE $$$,$$$,$$$.99.
00110          05   FILLER PICTURE X(77) VALUE SPACES.
00111       PROCEDURE DIVISION.
00112
00113          OPEN INPUT IN-FILE, OUTPUT OUT-FILE.
00114          MOVE CURRENT-DATE TO TODAYS-DATE.
00115          WRITE PRINT-LINE-RECORD FROM HEADER-1.
00116          WRITE PRINT-LINE-RECORD FROM HEADER-2.
00117          WRITE PRINT-LINE-RECORD FROM HEADER-3.
00118          WRITE PRINT-LINE-RECORD FROM HEADER-4.
00119          WRITE PRINT-LINE-RECORD FROM HEADER-5.
00120
00121       READ-CARD.
00122          READ IN-FILE AT END GO TO PRINT-TOTALS.
00123          ADD 1 TO CARD-COUNT.
00124          MOVE CARD-COUNT TO CARD-COUNT-OUT.
00125          MOVE PRODUCT-CODE TO PRODUCT-CODE-OUT.
00126          MOVE UNIT-PRICE TO UNIT-PRICE-OUT.
00127          MOVE QUANTITY-PURCHASED TO QUANTITY-PURCHASED-OUT.
00128          MULTIPLY UNIT-PRICE BY QUANTITY-PURCHASED GIVING NET-SALES.
00129          MOVE NET-SALES TO NET-SALES-OUT.
00130          ADD NET-SALES TO TOTAL-NET-SALES.
00131          ADD QUANTITY-PURCHASED TO TOTAL-QUAN-PURCH.
00132          WRITE PRINT-LINE-RECORD FROM DETAIL-LINE-1.
00133          GO TO READ-CARD.
00134
00135       PRINT-TOTALS.
00136          WRITE PRINT-LINE-RECORD FROM HEADER-6.
00137          MOVE TOTAL-NET-SALES TO TOTAL-NET-SALES-OUT.
00138          MOVE TOTAL-QUAN-PURCH TO TOTAL-QUAN-PURCH-OUT.
00139          WRITE PRINT-LINE-RECORD FROM DETAIL-LINE-2.
00140          WRITE PRINT-LINE-RECORD FROM HEADER-6.
00141          CLOSE IN-FILE OUT-FILE.
00142          STOP RUN.
```

OUTPUT TO PROGRAM 13

```
          SALES REPORT AS OF 08/04/79
          ============================
ITEM      PRODUCT      UNIT      QUANTITY        NET
NO         CODE        PRICE     PURCHASED      SALES
----      -------      -----     ---------    ----------
 1         2452        $3.27          999     $3,266.73
 2         2325        $8.52          532     $4,532.64
 3         6542        $3.21          523     $1,678.83
 4           52        $0.99          945       $935.55
 5         2384       $68.95          635    $43,783.25
 6           17       $32.25          145     $4,676.25
 7          215        $2.30        5,246    $12,065.80
 8          333        $3.65        4,230    $15,439.50
 9           35      $852.01          366   $311,835.66
10           01       $12.50          250     $3,125.00
11           02       $35.00          200     $7,000.00
12          222      $356.32          553   $197,044.96
                                  ---------   -------------
                                    14,624    $605,384.17
                                  ---------   -------------
```

MAKING
DECISIONS
IN COBOL

In processing large volumes of data, it is usually essential within a program to make certain decisions at various points in the program. As a matter of fact, we have already encountered two situations in which decisions are made automatically. The READ statement, for example, has the clause AT END associated with it. This is simply a succinct way of saying, "If all of the cards of the input file have been read, then execute a predetermined set of instructions." The other situation we have already mentioned is the ON SIZE ERROR option in which we direct the computer to follow a predetermined path if the result of an arithmetic operation is too large to be accommodated in the receiving field.

Both of the above features are extremely useful and are to be found in all professional programs. COBOL would not, however, have reached its high level of popularity if one were confined to these two levels of decision-making only. In COBOL one is provided with an extremely rich selection of decision-making statements, all of which have as their key element the word IF.

We can ask if a data value is equal to that of another, greater than, less than, and so on, and we can ask if a data item being read is alphabetic or numeric in character. Depending upon the result of such a test, we can direct the computer to follow one path if the condition being tested holds, and a completely different path if it does not hold. By placing these IF statements in carefully selected points within a program, the COBOL programmer can design for himself an extremely efficient and highly sophisticated network.

9.1 THE IF STATEMENT

The simplest form of the conditional IF statement is

    IF condition THEN statement-1.

For example, we could write

    IF A IS EQUAL TO B THEN SUBTRACT 1 FROM D.

This is interpreted to mean that if the value contained in A is exactly equal to that contained in B, then 1 is to be subtracted from the value of D. If, on the other hand, the value of A is not equal to B the THEN clause is ignored entirely and execution continued with the next statement in line. A certain amount of flexibility is permitted in writing the IF statement. For example, the word IS may be omitted entirely as indeed may be the words TO and THEN. Here are some other versions of this IF statement, all of which behave in a similar manner:

1. IF A EQUAL B SUBTRACT 1 FROM D.

2. IF A IS EQUAL B SUBTRACT 1 FROM D.

3. IF A EQUAL TO B SUBTRACT 1 FROM D.

4. IF A EQUAL B ADD 1 TO C, DISPLAY 'C = ' C, GO TO PARA–3.

5. IF A IS EQUAL TO B SUBTRACT 1 FROM D.

6. IF A = B SUBTRACT 1 FROM D.

9.2 THE NOT OPERATOR

In the above examples we have confined ourselves to the question of whether A is equal to B. By the same token we can ask whether A is *not* equal to B, as in the following two forms:

1. IF A IS NOT EQUAL TO B THEN SUBTRACT 1 FROM D.

2. IF A NOT = B SUBTRACT 1 FROM D.

The reader is cautioned that despite the strong temptation to write EQUALS instead of EQUAL as in

    IF A EQUALS B THEN . . .

this violates the syntactic rules of the language and will result in a diagnostic if attempted in a COBOL program.

9.3 THE RELATIONAL OR COMPARISON OPERATORS

The flexibility of the IF statement is further increased by the use of other, so-called relational or comparison operators. These relational operators are GREATER THAN ($>$) and LESS THAN ($<$) and are used in an analogous manner to the EQUAL relational operator, as shown in the following examples:

1. IF A IS GREATER THAN B + 1 THEN . . .

2. IF 1.6 IS LESS THAN B THEN . . .

3. IF A-6 IS GREATER B THEN . . .

4. IF A LESS 25 GO TO PARA–2.

5. IF ALPHA $>$ B THEN STOP RUN.

6. IF A ·· 2 + B ·· 2 = C ·· 2 DISPLAY 'PYTHAGOREAN TRIPLET', ADD 1 TO PYTH-TRIPS, GO TO MORE.

7. IF A $<$ B · 2 COMPUTE D = A ·· B.

8. IF A IS $>$ THAN 10 THEN CLOSE IN–FILE.

In all of the above cases, the words IS, THAN and THEN may be omitted. The NOT operator may also be used in conjunction with the relational operators as in the following examples:

1. IF A IS NOT LESS THAN 100 THEN GO TO NYU.

2. IF A NOT GREATER B DISPLAY 'FINISHED'.

3. IF 58 NOT $<$ A THEN GO TO C.

In every case when the symbols $=$, $<$, and $>$ are used, they must be preceded and followed by at least one space.

In order to test whether data-name A is less than or equal to B, for example, one can resort to the use of a logical operator which we shall now describe.

9.4 THE LOGICAL OPERATORS AND AND OR

In certain situations, such as that described above, it is very useful to be able to make two or more tests in a single IF statement. This may be done by means of the logical operators AND and OR, which serve distinctly different functions. For example, to determine if the value A is less than or equal to that of B, we would write

    IF A < B OR A = B THEN . . .

The logical operator OR means that if either one or both of the related conditions hold, then the statement as a whole is true and the THEN clause is executed. If neither of them holds, then the statement is considered false and the THEN clause is ignored. Here are some more valid examples using the logical operator OR:

1. IF (A = B) OR (N < 2 ** T) GO TO QUIT.

2. IF A NOT > C OR D LESS THAN E THEN GO TO PARA-5.

3. IF A < B OR = B THEN . . .

The last example shown illustrates a somewhat unusual feature of computer programming. COBOL permits the subject of a relational operator to be implied in subsequent tests of a compound statement. What this means is that the subject of the first test, A, is tested to see if it is less than B. It is then also tested for equality with B, without having to repeat the subject A for the second test. If either the first test or the second test is met, the expression as a whole is true and the THEN clause is executed. This statement is therefore equivalent to "if A is less than or equal to B."

The second of the two logical operators is AND.

We can in a single IF statement test to see whether one or more conditions hold simultaneously. For example, a certain action might be required only in the event that A is equal to B *at the same time that* C is greater than D. These two conditions are associated together by means of the logical operator AND in the following manner:

    IF A EQUAL B AND C GREATER D THEN . . .

The THEN clause will be executed only if both of the separate conditions hold. If either one of them fails, or if they both fail, the THEN clause is ignored. Here are some more examples of valid compound IF statements:

1. IF A IS EQUAL TO C AND A IS LESS THAN E . . .

2. IF A IS EQUAL TO C AND IS LESS THAN E . . .

3. IF A NOT = B AND > D THEN . . .

4. IF (A − B) / C > D AND < E . . .

5. IF (A = B AND = D) OR (A = E) THEN . . .

The reader is cautioned that some compound IF statements might seem at first blush to simplify the program by shortening it, but in fact compound IF statements tend to complicate programs, often resulting in errors of logic which are sometimes difficult to detect.

9.5 THE IF . . . THEN . . . ELSE . . . STATEMENT

We have already seen how the IF statement may be used in a variety of contexts. The IF statement may be made even more elaborate by using the ELSE (or OTHERWISE) option as in the following example:

```
IF A IS GREATER THAN B THEN ADD 1 TO C
    ELSE SUBTRACT 2 FROM D.
```

Upon execution of this statement, the condition following the word IF is evaluated. If the condition holds, that is, if the value of A is in fact greater than that of B, the THEN clause is executed and 1 is added to the value of C. Whatever appears after the word ELSE is ignored and the next statement in line is executed. If, on the other hand, the condition does not hold, that is, the value of A is not greater than that of B, the THEN clause is ignored and the ELSE clause is executed. This has the effect of subtracting 2 from the value of D. Whichever clause is executed, the THEN clause or the ELSE clause, it is followed by the next sentence in line. The next sentence in line is defined as the statement following the period which terminates the whole of the IF statement. It is therefore critical to ensure that no period appears between the word IF and the end of the IF statement. It is possible in COBOL to have what are known as nests of IF's. That is, it is possible to write an IF statement in the form of

```
IF A = B THEN
    IF G > D THEN GO TO E
        ELSE IF F < G THEN GO TO H.
```

This becomes extremely complicated to follow; the novice programmer is strenuously cautioned against resorting to such nested IF's. Remember, the simpler the program is to follow, the easier it will be to correct and the easier it will be for someone else to follow.

9.6 THE NEXT SENTENCE CLAUSE

It is sometimes convenient to include the clause NEXT SENTENCE within an IF statement.

IF A > B THEN NEXT SENTENCE ELSE ADD 1 TO C.

If, upon testing, A is found to be greater than B, the THEN clause is executed. Since the THEN clause is NEXT SENTENCE, control is sent directly to the next statement in line which is, in fact, the next sentence. If on the other hand, A proves not to be greater than B, 1 is added to C before control is sent to the next statement in line.

The IF statement may be generalized to

9.7 THE SIGN TEST

$$\underline{IF} \text{ condition THEN} \left\{ \begin{array}{l} \underline{\text{NEXT SENTENCE}} \\ \text{imperative} \\ \text{statement(s)} \end{array} \right\} \left\{ \begin{array}{l} \underline{\text{OTHERWISE}} \\ \underline{\text{ELSE}} \end{array} \right\} \left\{ \begin{array}{l} \underline{\text{NEXT SENTENCE}} \\ \text{imperative} \\ \text{statement(s)} \end{array} \right\}$$

We have already encountered the method by which one can test in COBOL whether the value of a numeric operand or even an arithmetic expression is less than zero, equal to zero or greater than zero using the relational operators. COBOL provides yet another way using the words POSITIVE, NEGATIVE and ZERO explicitly. This option is incorporated in the so-called sign test, several examples of which follow:

1. IF A IS POSITIVE GO TO PARA–3.

2. IF B ** 2 − 4 * C NEGATIVE
   THEN DISPLAY 'COMPLEX ROOTS',
       GO TO GET-NEXT-CARD.

3. IF A IS ZERO THEN STOP RUN.

4. IF A IS NOT NEGATIVE GO TO PARA–3.

The reader's attention is drawn to the fact that examples 1 and 4 are not equivalent. Any value which is greater than zero is considered positive while any value less than zero is regarded as negative. Therefore, any value equal to zero or greater than zero satisfies the NOT NEGATIVE condition.

The sign tests may be generalized (read the two following lines of displayed equations as one line):

$$\text{\underline{IF} data-name IS [\underline{NOT}]} \begin{Bmatrix} \underline{POSITIVE} \\ \underline{NEGATIVE} \\ \underline{ZERO} \end{Bmatrix} \text{THEN} \begin{Bmatrix} \text{imperative statement(s)} \\ \underline{NEXT\ SENTENCE} \end{Bmatrix}$$

$$\left[\begin{Bmatrix} \underline{ELSE} \\ \underline{OTHERWISE} \end{Bmatrix} \begin{Bmatrix} \text{imperative statement (s)} \\ \underline{NEXT\ SENTENCE} \end{Bmatrix} \right]$$

9.8 THE CLASS TEST

However careful one might be in punching data, the sad fact remains that whatever diligence we may exert in punching data, errors are bound to occur. One of the most frequent sources of error is the inadvertent punching of alphabetic characters in a numeric field and numeric characters in an alphabetic field. If one were to assume that all of the data have been correctly keypunched and proceeded to operate on the data based on this assumption, the keypunching errors would become apparent only after they had been rejected by the computer and the program aborted. Needless to say, this is not the most efficient way to handle the situation. For this express purpose, COBOL provides yet another test known as the *class test*, in which data can be tested to determine whether they are numeric, that is, contain only the digits 0 through 9 with or without an operational sign, or whether they are alphabetic, meaning that the data contain just alphabetic data or blank spaces. The NOT operator is also permitted as illustrated in the examples which follow:

1. IF A IS ALPHABETIC THEN GO TO FORMAT–1.

2. IF PART-NUMBER NOT NUMERIC GO TO ERR–RTN.

3. IF XYZ NOT ALPHABETIC THEN
         DISPLAY 'INVALID CHARACTER(S) IN XYZ' XYZ
         GO TO PROCESS–NEXT-CARD.

The class tests may be summarized as shown (read both the following lines as one):

$$\text{\underline{IF} data-name IS [\underline{NOT}]} \begin{Bmatrix} \underline{NUMERIC} \\ \underline{ALPHABETIC} \end{Bmatrix} \text{THEN} \begin{Bmatrix} \text{imperative statement(s)} \\ \underline{NEXT\ SENTENCE} \end{Bmatrix}$$

$$\left[\begin{Bmatrix} \underline{ELSE} \\ \underline{OTHERWISE} \end{Bmatrix} \begin{Bmatrix} \text{imperative statement(s)} \\ \underline{NEXT\ SENTENCE} \end{Bmatrix} \right]$$

9.9 THE CONDITION-NAME TEST

When describing level numbers we have used 01 through 49 and also 77 for independent elementary items. COBOL provides another level with a special purpose. It is given the level number 88 and is known as the condition-name. Its use, however, requires some preliminary discussion. Suppose we are reading in a field indicating marital status according to the following code:

1 = single
2 = married
3 = divorced
4 = separated
5 = widowed

If each of these categories is to be treated separately within a program, its particular value can be determined by means of a series of IF statements. such as the following:

```
IF MARITAL-STATUS = 1 GO TO SINGLE-ROUTINE.
IF MARITAL-STATUS = 2 GO TO MARRIED-ROUTINE.
IF MARITAL-STATUS = 3 GO TO DIVORCED-ROUTINE.
IF MARITAL-STATUS = 4 GO TO SEPARATED-ROUTINE.
IF MARITAL-STATUS = 5 GO TO WIDOWED-ROUTINE.
```

The above would work fine but the writers of COBOL decided to provide an alternative to this method. Instead of using a series of IF tests in which the data name being tested is compared with each numeric value in turn, a condition name can be set up to describe any elementary item. Once defined in the normal way, one or more 88 level items may be specified. This may be done in the Data Division, either in the File Section or in Working Storage, as in the following example:

```
FD IN-FILE
    LABEL RECORDS ARE OMITTED.

  01 SURVEY-RECORD.
    05 MARITAL-STATUS PICTURE 9.
      88 SINGLE VALUE 1.
      88 MARRIED VALUE 2.
      88 DIVORCED VALUE 3.
      88 SEPARATED VALUE 4.
      88 WIDOWED VALUE 5.

           ⋮
```

In the Procedure Division one may now write the following instructions in order to determine the marital status of the particular individual:

```
IF SINGLE GO TO SINGLE-ROUTINE.
IF MARRIED GO TO MARRIED-ROUTINE.
IF DIVORCED GO TO DIVORCED-ROUTINE.
IF SEPARATED GO TO SEPARATED-ROUTINE.
IF WIDOWED GO TO WIDOWED-ROUTINE.
```

It is felt that this alternative of using condition-names improves the documentation of the program.

For those situations in which a condition name represents a range of values, say 0 through 100 one may write

```
05 EXAM-RATING PICTURE 999.
   88 A-GRADE VALUE 90 THRU 100.
   88 B-GRADE VALUE 80 THRU  89.
   88 C-GRADE VALUE 70 THRU  79.
   88 D-GRADE VALUE 65 THRU  69.
   88 F-GRADE VALUE  0 THRU  64.
```

and for a grade point average breakdown

```
05 GRADE-POINT-AVERAGE PICTURE 9V99.
   88 HONORS VALUE 3.8 THRU 4.0.
   88 DEANS-LIST VALUE 3.4 THRU 3.79.
   88 AVERAGE VALUE 2.2 THRU 3.39.
   88 PROBATION VALUE 0 THRU 2.19.
```

In all cases in which condition names are used, the reader should note that a condition name never contains a PICTURE. Since this is so, a condition name can never be treated as a regular data name. For example referring to MARITAL-STATUS above, one could not say

```
     IF SINGLE EQUAL 1 . . .
or   MOVE SINGLE TO MARITAL-STATUS-OUT.
```

When MARITAL-STATUS contains a 1, for example, the condition SINGLE is said to exist. Similarly, when MARITAL-STATUS contains a 2, the condition MARRIED is set.

Another option that 88 level items offer is that a series of values may be explicitly specified. For example, one could write

```
88 COND-NAME VALUE 1, 5, 9, 73
```

or its equivalent

```
88 COND-NAME VALUE 1 5 9 73
```

Another option available involves the use of two figurative constants which have not yet been discussed. The constant HIGH-VALUE or HIGH-VALUES is assigned the highest value in the computer's collating sequence. Similarly, LOW-VALUE or LOW-VALUES are both assigned the lowest value in the computer's collating sequence.

One could therefore have an 88 level item which reads

```
88 ERROR-IN-GPA VALUE LOW-VALUE THRU ZERO, 4.01 THRU HIGH-VALUES.
```

There is a further advantage to using condition names, apart from the fact that it renders the program comprehensible to a non-programmer. Suppose for example, it has been decided to code the country of origin of an individual according to the following scheme:

United States $= 1$
Great Britain $= 2$
Israel $\quad = 3$
Ireland $\quad = 4$
Other $\quad \ = 5$

This could be coded in the following way:

```
03  COUNTRY-OF-ORIGIN          PICTURE 9.
    88 UNITED-STATES               VALUE 1.
    88 GREAT-BRITAIN               VALUE 2.
    88 ISRAEL                      VALUE 3.
    88 IRELAND                     VALUE 4.
    88 OTHER                       VALUE 5.
```

Suppose that subsequent to the original writing of the program it is decided to change the coding of the data so that 1 no longer represents the United States but rather OTHER and the code for the United States is changed to the number 5. If condition names are not used, all references to COUNTRY–OF–ORIGIN with codes of 1 and 5 in the Procedure Division of the program will have to be amended. Depending upon the complexity of the program, these amendments could result in a major change in many different parts of the program.

If, on the other hand, advantage is taken of condition names, all that is necessary is for the VALUE clause of the corresponding 88 level items to be changed.

The general format for the IF condition-name test is similar to that for the other already described (read the two following lines as one line).

$$\text{IF } [\underline{\text{NOT}}] \text{ condition-name THEN } \begin{Bmatrix} \text{imperative statement(s)} \\ \underline{\text{NEXT SENTENCE}} \end{Bmatrix}$$
$$\left[\begin{bmatrix} \underline{\text{ELSE}} \\ \underline{\text{OTHERWISE}} \end{bmatrix} \begin{Bmatrix} \text{imperative statement(s)} \\ \underline{\text{NEXT SENTENCE}} \end{Bmatrix} \right]$$

9.10 REVIEW EXERCISES

1. Assume an input file is composed of cards punched in the following format:

    1–12   last name
    14–22 first name
    24–58 address

59–63   zip code
65–69   area code (in parentheses)
70–77   numeric telephone number
79–80   alphabetic school code

Write a program to read each card of the input deck and to print out a listing of the cards. In particular, check that each numeric field is in fact punched with numeric data. If it is not, print a string of 10 asterisks to the right of the listed card. If the percentage of cards with invalid data is greater than 10 percent, print out the correct percentage.

2. Devise a method of determining in COBOL whether a number is odd or even.

SOME ILLUSTRATIVE COMPUTATIONAL PROBLEMS

In this chapter we are going to solve five distinctly different types of problems, each of which teaches some important feature of COBOL besides introducing us to one or two new COBOL instructions. These problems will also reinforce much of the material which has appeared in earlier chapters. Should it be necessary to review the material presented in previous chapters, the reader is urged to do so.

10.1 THE MURDER PROBLEM

As you are probably aware, the use of computers is not confined solely to business establishments. Computers have been particularly useful to the police department in the fight against crime in a great number of varied ways. Perhaps the reader knows to his regret, that automobile license plate numbers, together with any offenses registered against them, are stored in computers by many cities in the United States. This affords police departments instantaneous access to this kind of information when required.

For the purposes of the next program, let us assume that the license plates in a particular state are all of a uniform type, namely, that they are composed of two three-digit numbers separated by a star. A typical license plate would therefore be

$$\boxed{587*633}$$

For each license plate issued, a punched card is filed at police headquarters containing the license plate number, name, address, and telephone number

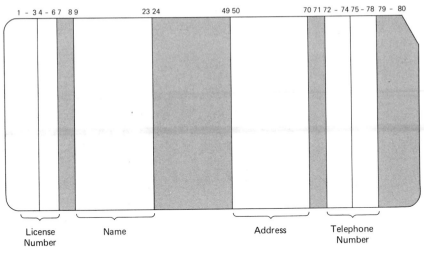

| 1 – 3 4 – 6 7 8 9 | 23 24 | 49 50 | 70 71 72 – 74 75 – 78 79 – 80 |

License Number   Name   Address   Telephone Number

FIGURE 12

of the person assigned that particular license plate. Figure 12 shows a typical input data card.

Subsequent to a murder being committed, a police investigation is undertaken. As a result of the investigation, a witness to the crime is asked to identify the license plate of the automobile in which the perpetrator of the crime was seen to make his escape.

Unfortunately, the best information that the witness can produce is that the first three-digit number on the left of the license plate was *identical* to the three-digit number on the right. Exactly what they were could not be recalled despite strenuous efforts to do so. The exact details of the license plate were lost in the excitement of the moment. In the absence of any further evidence, the detectives working in the computer section have little alternative but to write a program which examines each individual license plate issued, and for each license plate tests whether the first three-digit number is equal to the second three-digit number. It is apparent that there would be no point in writing the program in such a way that as soon as the first occurrence of such a plate is detected the relevant information is printed out and the program terminated. This might seem to make the job of the detectives easier, since they would have a single suspect to apprehend. But such a course of action would be self-defeating since there are probably many, perhaps dozens, even hundreds of license plates on which the first three-digit number is equal to the second three-digit number. It is therefore imperative that *every* such license plate be examined by the computer and a list of suspects printed.

In order to counter a possible question that might be raised in court, the police programmer decides to compute also the percentage of license plates that conform to this pattern. To compute a percentage, it is necessary to keep two separate counts. The first is the total card count while the second is the count for the number of suspects. As each card of the input file is read, CARD–COUNT is updated by 1. Each time LEFT–3, (the left three digits of the license plate number) is equal to RIGHT–3 (the right three digits of the license plate number) 1 is added to NUMBER–OF–SUSPECTS.

10.1.1 MOVE CORRESPONDING

It will be noticed that for the first time in this text data names appearing in one record appear also in another record and are spelled in precisely the same way. In particular, the group names LICENSE–PLATE–NO, PHONE–NUMBER, and the elementary names LEFT–3, RIGHT–3, NAME, ADRESS (sorry, but ADDRESS is a reserved word), FIRST–3, and LAST–4, although unique to each of the records LICENSE–IN and DETAIL–LINE respectively, are nevertheless present in the several records in the same program. This does not violate any COBOL rule since it is perfectly in order for the same data name to be used in different records provided that when they are referenced they are suitably *qualified*.

It is for this reason that the third instruction of the paragraph READ–SUSPECT qualifies both LEFT–3 and RIGHT–3 by use of the word OF. An alternative to OF is IN.

In reader might indeed wonder why this approach is taken in this problem. The reason is simply to illustrate the use of what some COBOL programmers regard as an extremely useful statement, namely the MOVE CORRESPONDING instruction. By means of the MOVE CORRESPONDING option, one can combine many MOVE statements into a single one.

Instead of the four separate instructions

```
MOVE LICENSE-PLATE-NO OF LICENSE-IN TO LICENSE-PLATE-NO OF DETAIL-
  LINE-1.
MOVE NAME OF LICENSE-IN TO LICENSE-PLATE-NO OF DETAIL-LINE-1.
MOVE ADRESS OF LICENSE-IN TO LICENSE-PLATE-NO OF DETAIL-LINE-1.
MOVE PHONE-NUMBER OF LICENSE-IN TO LICENSE-PLATE-NO OF DETAIL-
  LINE-1.
```

the single statement

```
MOVE CORRESPONDING LICENSE-IN TO DETAIL-LINE-1.
```

or its abbreviated form MOVE CORR LICENSE–IN TO DETAIL–LINE–1 accomplishes this same task. The order in which the individual data names appear in the corresponding records do not have to be the same since each data name is handled individually within the computer.

Before one gets carried away with the MOVE CORRESPONDING instruction, a few words of caution are in order. On the surface it would appear that it is a great time saver for the programmer. However, experience has shown that use of MOVE CORRESPONDING can prove to be troublesome, especially for records which in the course of time undergo frequent changes. Moreover, there are some COBOL implementations which provide a somewhat inefficient code for CORRESPONDING statements.

For the sake of completeness, both ADD and SUBTRACT have CORRESPONDING options similar to MOVE CORRESPONDING. Here are their generalized formats.

$$\underline{MOVE} \begin{Bmatrix} \underline{CORRESPONDING} \\ \underline{CORR} \end{Bmatrix} \text{group-data-name-1} \underline{TO} \text{ data-name-2}$$

$$\underline{ADD} \begin{Bmatrix} \underline{CORRESPONDING} \\ \underline{CORR} \end{Bmatrix} \text{group-data-name-1} \underline{TO} \text{ data-name-2 } [\underline{ROUNDED}]$$

$$[\underline{ON} \ \underline{SIZE \ ERROR} \text{ imperative statement(s)}]$$

$$\underline{SUBTRACT} \begin{Bmatrix} \underline{CORRESPONDING} \\ \underline{CORR} \end{Bmatrix} \text{group-data-name-2} \underline{FROM} \text{ data-name-2}$$

$$[\underline{ROUNDED}] \ [\underline{ON} \ \underline{SIZE \ ERROR} \text{ imperative statement(s)}]$$

We return now to the murder problem. Each data card is read and the license plate examined, and the vital details of all the suspect license plates are printed out. After the last data card has been read, control is sent automatically to the paragraph named PRINT–PERCENT, where the percentage of suspects is computed by dividing NUMBER–OF–SUSPECTS by CARD–COUNT and multiplying the result by 100. This percentage is printed from DETAIL–LINE–2, after which the input and output files are closed and the run terminated.

Here is the program and its output, the latter listing each of the suspects and finally the percentage of suspects to the total data cards examined. It will be noticed that in the printout an asterisk has been inserted in the automobile license number so as to render it as similar as possible to the actual license plate. Also the telephone number, which has been read in as a seven-digit number, has been "doctored-up" a little by inserting a hyphen after the first three characters.

PROGRAM 14
The Murder Problem

```
00001        IDENTIFICATION DIVISION.
00002        PROGRAM-ID. MURDER.
00003        ENVIRONMENT DIVISION.
00004        CONFIGURATION SECTION.
00005        SOURCE-COMPUTER. IBM-370-145.
00006        OBJECT-COMPUTER. IBM-370-145.
```

```
00007              INPUT-OUTPUT SECTION.
00008              FILE-CONTROL.
00009                  SELECT IN-FILE ASSIGN TO UT-S-READER.
00010                  SELECT OUT-FILE ASSIGN TO UT-S-PRINTER.
00011              DATA DIVISION.
00012              FILE SECTION.
00013              FD  IN-FILE
00014                  LABEL RECORDS ARE OMITTED.
00015              01  LICENSE-IN.
00016                  05  LICENSE-PLATE-NO.
00017                      10  LEFT-3      PICTURE 999.
00018                      10  RIGHT-3     PICTURE 999.
00019                  05  FILLER          PICTURE X(2).
00020                  05  NAME            PICTURE X(15).
00021                  05  FILLER          PICTURE X(26).
00022                  05  ADRESS          PICTURE X(21).
00023                  05  FILLER          PICTURE X.
00024                  05  PHONE-NUMBER.
00025                      10  FIRST-3     PICTURE XXX.
00026                      10  LAST-4      PICTURE XXXX.
00027                  05  FILLER          PICTURE X(2).
00028              FD  OUT-FILE
00029                  LABEL RECORDS ARE OMITTED.
00030              01  PRINT-LINE-RECORD.
00031                  05  PRINT-LINE     PICTURE X(132).
00032              WORKING-STORAGE SECTION.
00033              77  NUMBER-OF-SUSPECTS      PICTURE 9(5) VALUE ZERO.
00034              77  W-S-CARD-COUNT          PICTURE 9(5) VALUE ZERO.
00035              01  HEADER-1.
00036                  05  FILLER       PICTURE X VALUE SPACES.
00037                  05  FILLER       PICTURE X(11) VALUE 'CARD NUMBER'.
00038                  05  FILLER       PICTURE X(02) VALUE SPACES.
00039                  05  FILLER       PICTURE X(14) VALUE 'LICENSE NUMBER'.
00040                  05  FILLER       PICTURE X(03) VALUE SPACES.
00041                  05  FILLER       PICTURE X(13) VALUE 'NAME OF OWNER'.
00042                  05  FILLER       PICTURE X(13) VALUE SPACES.
00043                  05  FILLER       PICTURE X(07) VALUE 'ADDRESS'.
00044                  05  FILLER       PICTURE X(10) VALUE SPACES.
00045                  05  FILLER       PICTURE X(09) VALUE 'TELEPHONE'.
00046                  05  FILLER       PICTURE X(49) VALUE SPACES.
00047              01  DETAIL-LINE-1.
00048                  05  FILLER       PICTURE X(3) VALUE SPACES.
00049                  05  CARD-COUNT   PICTURE ZZZZ9.
00050                  05  FILLER       PICTURE X(9) VALUE SPACES.
00051                  05  LICENSE-PLATE-NO.
00052                      10  LEFT-3   PICTURE 999.
00053                      10  FILLER   PICTURE X VALUE '*'.
00054                      10  RIGHT-3  PICTURE 999.
00055                  05  FILLER       PICTURE X(6) VALUE SPACES.
00056                  05  NAME         PICTURE X(15).
00057                  05  FILLER       PICTURE X(6) VALUE SPACES.
00058                  05  ADRESS       PICTURE X(21).
00059                  05  FILLER       PICTURE X(2) VALUE SPACES.
00060                  05  PHONE-NUMBER.
00061                      10  FIRST-3  PICTURE XXX.
00062                      10  FILLER   PICTURE X VALUE '-'.
00063                      10  LAST-4   PICTURE XXXX.
00064                  05  FILLER       PICTURE X(28) VALUE SPACES.
00065              01  DETAIL-LINE-2.
00066                  05  FILLER       PICTURE X(30) VALUE SPACES.
00067                  05  FILLER       PICTURE X(22) VALUE
00068                      'PERCENTAGE SUSPECTS = '.
00069                  05  PERCENTAGE-SUSPECT     PICTURE ZZ9.99.
00070                  05  FILLER       PICTURE X(72) VALUE SPACES.
00071              PROCEDURE DIVISION.
00072              BEGIN.
00073                  OPEN INPUT IN-FILE
00074                       OUTPUT OUT-FILE.
00075                  WRITE PRINT-LINE-RECORD FROM HEADER-1.
00076                  MOVE SPACES TO PRINT-LINE-RECORD.
00077                  WRITE PRINT-LINE-RECORD.
00078              READ-SUSPECT.
00079                  READ IN-FILE AT END GO TO PRINT-PERCENT.
00080                  ADD 1 TO W-S-CARD-COUNT.
00081                  IF LEFT-3 OF LICENSE-IN NOT EQUAL RIGHT-3 OF LICENSE-IN
00082                       GO TO READ-SUSPECT.
00083                  ADD 1 TO NUMBER-OF-SUSPECTS.
00084                  MOVE W-S-CARD-COUNT TO CARD-COUNT.
00085                  MOVE CORRESPONDING LICENSE-IN TO DETAIL-LINE-1.
00086                  WRITE PRINT-LINE-RECORD FROM DETAIL-LINE-1.
00087                  GO TO READ-SUSPECT.
00088              PRINT-PERCENT.
00089                  MOVE SPACES TO PRINT-LINE-RECORD.
```

```
00090          WRITE PRINT-LINE-RECORD.
00091          COMPUTE PERCENTAGE-SUSPECT =
C0092              NUMBER-OF-SUSPECTS * 100 / W-S-CARD-COUNT.
00093          WRITE PRINT-LINE-RECORD FROM DETAIL-LINE-2.
00094          CLOSE IN-FILE OUT-FILE.
00095          STOP RUN.
```

OUTPUT TO PROGRAM 14

CARD NUMBER	LICENSE NUMBER	NAME OF OWNER	ADDRESS	TELEPHONE
1	555*555	BILL JONES	245 JAMES STREET	AC2-4963
9	477*477	BILL TUMAS	22 DOWNING STREET	235-6874
14	631*631	RANDY WILLIAMS	14-21 21 AVENUE	RE8-8192
46	232*232	LEROY D NOLE	21 RASPUTIN AVE	546-3214
49	123*123	EILEEN NOONAN	111 BERKSHIRE DRIVE	775-3018
88	449*449	BEATRICE TRICE	233 BROADWAY	925-8960

PERCENTAGE SUSPECTS = 6.66

COBB OL MYSTERY #6

Cobb sat at his desk with the file for his last case in front of him. Quietly, his secretary, Miss Kathy Keypunch, slipped into the office.

"Excuse me, Mr. Ol," she whispered.

"Yes, what is it?" replied Cobb.

"Our audit has detected an error. There is a discrepancy between the total assets and the equity and liabilities of the company," explained Kathy. "We're off by $80,000–and after we switched over to the computer audit system too."

"The program to do the audit is also new, isn't it?" asked Ol.

"Yes, it is," said Kathy.

"I'd like to see the program listing," said the detective.

Kathy returned to Ol's office. "Here's the program, Mr. Ol," said Kathy.

"Thank you, Kathy."

Ol silently perused the listing and puffed on his pipe. "You know, it's very possible that the error is right here," said Cobb pointing to the statement

MOVE CORRESPONDING INREC TO OUTREC.

"That statement looks correct to me," said the secretary.

"The statement is correct, Kathy, but I'll bet the items of the records are not what we think they are."

Cobb looked at the DATA DIVISION.

"Here it is," said Ol. "The item in INREC is called ACCTS–RECEIVABLE and in the OUTREC it is called ACCTS–RECIEVABLE."

"Sure," said Kathy," that's because we want that item in INREC to be moved to OUTREC."

"But it won't be moved, of course," said Ol.

"Why?" queried Kathy.

"Only items with the same name are moved," explained the detective, "exactly the same name. As far as the computer is concerned, ACCTS–RECEIVABLE and ACCTS–RECIEVABLE are not the same name."

"Oh, I see," said Kathy, "the name is misspelled."

"Our programmers are good accountants," replied the detective, "but poor spellers. They should remember the old spelling rule: I before E, except after C."

"Perhaps we should start an annual company spelling bee," quipped Kathy.

The detective smiled.

10.2 THE MANHATTAN ISLAND PROBLEM

As the reader may be aware, legend has it that back in 1627 the island of Manhattan was bought from the Indians for the equivalent of $24 in trinkets. Manhattan island is worth somewhat more than that today.

In the program which follows, each input card contains a year punched in columns 1 through 4, and a fixed rate of interest. The idea is to calculate the final amount that the original $24 invested in 1627 would have become if the $24 had been invested at that rate and compounded annually through whatever year is punched. There are two basic ways in which this can be calculated. In the first, the interest accrued each year can be added to the original $24. In calculating the interest for the following year, the next principle becomes the previous principle plus the accrued interest. This procedure is to be repeated or performed for each successive year until the final year, as punched on the data card, is reached. This approach may be regarded as the brute-force method. A more elegant way to compute the final principle is to resort to the customary compound interest formula, which is

$$S = P(1 + r)^n$$

where P is the original $24

r is the rate of interest (expressed as a percentage)

n is the number of years the investment is compounded annually. In theory, the final values calculated by the brute-force and formula methods should be the same, but in practice these can differ considerably. One of the purposes of presenting this particular problem is to alert the reader to the inconsistencies which can result when working financial problems. These inconsistencies can be minimized by taking advantage of the ROUNDED option. This program also introduces us to the PERFORM statement, whose description follows that of the ROUNDED option.

10.2.1. The ROUNDED Option

As we have seen, any time a value is moved into an area too small to contain that value, truncation occurs. In the case of numeric data, storing the value 1.234 in a field with a picture of 9V99 will result in the quantity 1.23 only being stored. The excess digit 4 is lost. The same would be true if the item 1.234 were the result of some computation or other.

Storing the number 102.128 into a field of 999V99 will result in a truncation of the number to 102.12. For many computational purposes, straight truncation such as we have discussed above is most undesirable. For this reason COBOL provides the programmer with the option to round the result for each of the arithmetic statements. In Program 15 we shall use this ROUNDED option; the reader is urged to compare the result obtained with that in which the ROUNDED option has been omitted. The degree of error which can result when the rounded option is not used will then be clear. Both of these results can then be compared with that obtained using the formula method.

Here are some examples of COBOL statements using the ROUNDED option:

```
ADD A TO B ROUNDED.
ADD A, B GIVING C ROUNDED.
MULTIPLY D BY E ROUNDED.
MULTIPLY D BY E GIVING F ROUNDED.
COMPUTE A ROUNDED = B + C.
```

It is pointed out that if the number to be rounded is negative, the absolute value of the number is rounded first and the result made negative.

10.2.2. The PERFORM Statement

It is probably true that the PERFORM statement is the most powerful instruction in the whole of the COBOL repertoire. The PERFORM statement provides the programmer with a simple way of transferring control to a particular segment of the program. Upon completion of that segment of the program, an automatic return to the statement following the PERFORM is made. In its simplest version it assumes the form

```
PERFORM paragraph-name
```

This has the effect of transferring control to the paragraph name indicated— wherever it is located in the program—and only at the end of that paragraph is control returned.

The next level of sophistication of the PERFORM statement is exemplified by the formalized instruction

```
PERFORM paragraph-name [n TIMES.]
```

This will send control to the paragraph named and perform the instructions within that paragraph n times, where n can be either an integer value or a predefined data item containing an integer value. It is this form of the PERFORM statement which is illustrated in Program 15.

INPUT TO PROGRAM 15

```
177603125
181805000
186409123
170512685
168404875
162810000
170008988
162810000
197601000
```

PROGRAM 15
Manhattan Island Program

```
00001          IDENTIFICATION DIVISION.
00002          PROGRAM-ID. MANHATTAN.
00003          AUTHOR. DANNY SCHWARTZBAUM.
00004
00005          ENVIRONMENT DIVISION.
00006          CONFIGURATION SECTION.
00007          SOURCE-COMPUTER. IBM-370-145.
00008          OBJECT-COMPUTER. IBM-370-145.
00009          INPUT-OUTPUT SECTION.
00010          FILE-CONTROL.
00011              SELECT IN-FILE ASSIGN TO UT-S-READER.
00012              SELECT OUT-FILE ASSIGN TO UT-S-PRINTER.
00013
00014          DATA DIVISION.
00015          FILE SECTION.
00016          FD  IN-FILE
00017              LABEL RECORDS ARE OMITTED.
00018          01  YEAR-CARD.
00019              05  YEAR-OF-MATURITY        PICTURE 9(4).
00020              05  RATE                    PICTURE V99999.
00021              05  FILLER                  PICTURE X(71).
00022          FD  OUT-FILE
00023              LABEL RECORDS ARE OMITTED.
00024          01  PRINT-LINE-RECORD.
00025              05  PRINT-LINE    PICTURE X(132).
00026
00027          WORKING-STORAGE SECTION.
00028          77  CARD-NUMBER             PICTURE 999 VALUE ZERO.
00029          77  ROUNDED-AMOUNT          PICTURE 9(16)V99.
00030          77  UNROUNDED-AMOUNT        PICTURE 9(16)V99.
00031          77  YEAR-DIFFERENCE         PICTURE 9999.
00032          77  FORMULA-AMOUNT          PICTURE 9(16)V99.
00033
00034          01  HEADER-1.
00035              05  FILLER     PICTURE X(2) VALUE SPACES.
00036              05  FILLER     PICTURE X(4) VALUE 'CARD'.
00037              05  FILLER     PICTURE X(5) VALUE SPACES.
00038              05  FILLER     PICTURE X(8) VALUE 'YEAR OF'.
00039              05  FILLER     PICTURE X(4) VALUE SPACES.
00040              05  FILLER     PICTURE X(8) VALUE 'RATE OF'.
00041              05  FILLER     PICTURE X(20) VALUE SPACES.
00042              05  FILLER     PICTURE X(7) VALUE 'FORMULA'.
00043              05  FILLER     PICTURE X(23) VALUE SPACES.
00044              05  FILLER     PICTURE X(7) VALUE 'ROUNDED'.
00045              05  FILLER     PICTURE X(23) VALUE SPACES.
00046              05  FILLER     PICTURE X(9) VALUE 'UNROUNDED'.
00047              05  FILLER     PICTURE X(12) VALUE SPACES.
00048
00049          01  HEADER-2.
00050              05  FILLER     PICTURE X(02) VALUE SPACES.
00051              05  FILLER     PICTURE X(03) VALUE 'NO.'.
00052              05  FILLER     PICTURE X(06) VALUE SPACES.
00053              05  FILLER     PICTURE X(08) VALUE 'MATURITY'.
00054              05  FILLER     PICTURE X(04) VALUE SPACES.
00055              05  FILLER     PICTURE X(08) VALUE 'INTEREST'.
00056              05  FILLER     PICTURE X(101) VALUE SPACES.
00057
00058          01  DETAIL-LINE-1.
00059              05  FILLER     PICTURE X(2) VALUE SPACES.
00060              05  CARD-NUM-OUT  PICTURE ZZZ.
00061              05  FILLER     PICTURE X VALUE '.'.
00062              05  FILLER     PICTURE X(6) VALUE SPACES.
00063              05  YEAR-OF-MATURITY-OUT    PICTURE 9(4).
00064              05  FILLER     PICTURE X(9) VALUE SPACES.
00065              05  RATE-OUT   PICTURE Z9.999.
00066              05  FILLER     PICTURE X(2) VALUE SPACES.
00067              05  FORMULA-AMOUNT-OUT PICTURE $$,$$$,$$$,$$$,$$$,$$9.99.
00068              05  FILLER     PICTURE X(5) VALUE SPACES.
00069              05  ROUNDED-AMOUNT-OUT PICTURE $$,$$$,$$$,$$$,$$$,$$9.99.
00070              05  FILLER     PICTURE X(6) VALUE SPACES.
00071              05  UNROUNDED-AMOUNT-OUT PICTURE $$,$$$,$$$,$$$,$$$,$$9.99.
00072              05  FILLER     PICTURE X(36) VALUE SPACES.
00073
00074          01  DETAIL-LINE-2.
00075              05  FILLER     PICTURE X(2) VALUE SPACES.
00076              05  CARD-NUM-ERROR         PICTURE ZZZ.
00077              05  FILLER     PICTURE X VALUE '.'.
00078              05  FILLER     PICTURE X(6) VALUE SPACES.
00079              05  YEAR-OF-MATURITY-ERROR PICTURE 9(4).
00080              05  FILLER     PICTURE X(3) VALUE SPACES.
```

```
00081                  05  FILLER          PICTURE X(19) VALUE 'ERROR FOUND IN DATE'.
00082                  05  FILLER          PICTURE X(94) VALUE SPACES.
00083
00084          PROCEDURE DIVISION.
00085          BEGIN.
00086              OPEN INPUT IN-FILE
00087                   OUTPUT OUT-FILE.
00088              WRITE PRINT-LINE-RECORD FROM HEADER-1.
00089              WRITE PRINT-LINE-RECORD FROM HEADER-2.
00090
00091          MAIN-LINE.
00092              READ IN-FILE AT END CLOSE IN-FILE, CLOSE OUT-FILE, STOP RUN.
00093              MOVE 24 TO ROUNDED-AMOUNT, UNROUNDED-AMOUNT.
00094              ADD 1 TO CARD-NUMBER.
00095              IF YEAR-OF-MATURITY LESS 1628 THEN
00096                  MOVE CARD-NUMBER TO CARD-NUM-ERROR
00097                  MOVE YEAR-OF-MATURITY TO YEAR-OF-MATURITY-ERROR
00098                  WRITE PRINT-LINE-RECORD FROM DETAIL-LINE-2
00099                  GO TO MAIN-LINE.
00100              SUBTRACT 1627 FROM YEAR-OF-MATURITY GIVING YEAR-DIFFERENCE.
00101              COMPUTE FORMULA-AMOUNT = 24 * (1 + RATE) ** YEAR-DIFFERENCE.
00102              PERFORM BRUTE-FORCE-METHOD YEAR-DIFFERENCE TIMES.
00103              MOVE CARD-NUMBER TO CARD-NUM-OUT.
00104              MOVE YEAR-OF-MATURITY TO YEAR-OF-MATURITY-OUT.
00105              MULTIPLY RATE BY 100 GIVING RATE-OUT.
00106              MOVE FORMULA-AMOUNT TO FORMULA-AMOUNT-OUT.
00107              MOVE ROUNDED-AMOUNT TO ROUNDED-AMOUNT-OUT.
00108              MOVE UNROUNDED-AMOUNT TO UNROUNDED-AMOUNT-OUT.
00109              WRITE PRINT-LINE-RECORD FROM DETAIL-LINE-1.
00110              GO TO MAIN-LINE.
00111
00112          BRUTE-FORCE-METHOD.
00113              COMPUTE ROUNDED-AMOUNT ROUNDED =
00114                  ROUNDED-AMOUNT + ROUNDED-AMOUNT * RATE.
00115              COMPUTE UNROUNDED-AMOUNT =
00116                  UNROUNDED-AMOUNT + UNROUNDED-AMOUNT * RATE.
```

OUTPUT TO PROGRAM 15

ROUNDED	UNROUNDED
$2,352.65	$2,338.14
$267,464.38	$266,591.78
$23,251,413,515.45	$23,194,105,231.43
$266,500.75	$266,059.74
$361.93	$360.53
$26.40	$26.40
$12,846.06	$12,823.99
$26.40	$26.40
$773.44	$758.62

Note in the program a single PERFORM instruction executes the paragraph BRUTE–FORCE–METHOD YEAR–DIFFERENCE times. care has been taken to insure that the instructions to be PERFORMED are placed in the Procedure Division in a location such that they are not executed *inadvertently*. If, for example, this paragraph were placed immediately following the PERFORM instruction, it would first be executed YEAR DIFFERENCE times by the PERFORM instruction. At this point, control "falls through" to the statement following the PERFORM instruction. This has the effect of executing the paragraph an *additional* time and would lead to inaccurate results.

COBB OL MYSTERY #7

"Keep the change," said the detective as he left the taxicab and headed for the airline terminal.

"Good afternoon," said the detective as he reached the reservation counter and handed over his ticket.

"Thank you sir," said the hostess." Oh, Mr. Ol, the air controller has been trying to reach you. There is some sort of emergency. All incoming flights have been diverted to other airports."

"Mr. Ol, I'm glad to meet you. I'm Ray Darr, the air controller."

"What seems to be the trouble, Mr. Darr?" queried Cobb Ol.

"Well, Mr. Ol, the computer which controls the air traffic at this airport may have been sabotaged; it simply stopped functioning," he said in a most articulate manner.

"Has any change been made in the program recently?"

"Well, yes. There was a small section of new instructions added," explained Mr. Darr.

"I'd like to see a program listing," said Cobb.

"Mr. Ol, it will take hours to get a complete listing!" explained Darr.

"No, no, sir, I only need a listing of the latest additions to the program." Darr soon returned with the pages.

"Here you are, Mr. Ol."

"Thank you," answered the detective as he sat down to look over the instructions. After a few minutes, Cobb looked up.

"Isn't it strange that planes could be redirected because of an error in grammar?" said Cobb.

"An error in grammar?" asked Darr with a puzzled look on his face.

"COBOL grammar. This statement

```
PERFORM STEP1 THROUGH STEP2.
```

may seem correct in English, but it's not acceptable in certain COBOL compilers. Some insist it should be written

```
PERFORM STEP1 THRU STEP2."
```

"But, Mr. Ol, THRU is an English slang spelling of the word THROUGH," objected Darr.

"Even so."

"So, you mean to tell me that the entire system failed because of one word!" exclaimed Darr in disbelief.

"As every pilot knows," said Ol, "precision is essential."

10.3 THE PAYROLL PROBLEM

You know, of course, that in every business establishment the processing of the payroll data is of primary importance. In fact, it is often given priority over every other computational chore. For the purposes of the program at hand, let us assume that for each employee the payroll data are punched in the form shown in Figure 13.

What the program is designed to do is to read each data card and print out a listing showing, among other pertinent data, the gross pay based on the number of hours worked and the rate of pay. Since this is our first payroll program, we shall make a point of keeping it straightforward. Toward this end, we shall *not* take into consideration

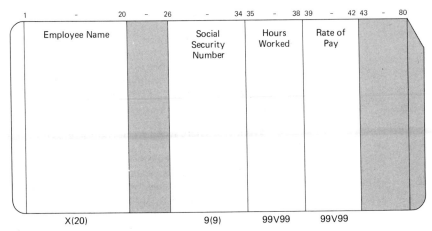

FIGURE 13

any overtime hours worked. Instead, all of the time worked will be paid at a uniform rate of pay. The output to Program 16 commences with a series of suitable headings. These are the card number, employee name, Social Security number, hours worked, rate of pay, and gross pay.

10.3.1 The WRITE . . . AFTER ADVANCING Option

In previous programs where the WRITE instruction was used, lines of output were printed in succession, no lines being skipped. For printing successive lines, the ordinary WRITE instruction is perfectly satisfactory. However, in order to enhance the appearance of output, it is often, if not always, desirable to skip lines at various points in the program. Although this can be done by using the ordinary WRITE instruction and arranging for blank lines to be printed, a much more elegant method is to use the WRITE statement with the AFTER ADVANCING option. A typical example is

```
WRITE PRINT–LINE–RECORD AFTER ADVANCING 3 LINES.
```

This has the effect of first skipping three lines before printing out the contents of PRINT–LINE–RECORD. Even if it is necessary to advance just *one* line before printing, the instruction must still be

```
WRITE PRINT–LINE–RECORD AFTER ADVANCING 1 LINES.
```

to avoid getting a diagnostic message.

There are two points to bear in mind when using this option. The first is that if it is used at all it must be used for *every* WRITE statement in the program for the output file. In other words, whichever WRITE statement appears first, all subsequent WRITE statements must be of the same type. Second, the print line is considered to have 133 positions rather than the 132 of the ordinary WRITE statement. Care must be taken, however, that the very first position is always a blank to allow for what is known as "carriage control" purposes. In effect, we still have 132 as the maximum number of characters which may appear on any one line.

Associated with this option is another which prints the output line *before* advancing. A typical example is

    WRITE PRINT–LINE–RECORD BEFORE ADVANCING 5 LINES.

Both forms of the ADVANCING option may be used with the FROM option, as explained earlier.

The generalized format for the WRITE statement is

$$\text{WRITE record-name-1 [\underline{FROM} record-name-2]} \left[\left\{ \begin{matrix} \underline{\text{BEFORE}} \\ \text{AFTER} \end{matrix} \right\} \underline{\text{ADVANCING}} \left\{ \begin{matrix} \text{integer LINES} \\ \text{data-name LINES} \\ \text{mnemonic-name} \end{matrix} \right\} \right]$$

In Program 16, notice that although the Social Security number is read in as a nine-digit number (thereby conserving space and effort), it is edited for the print-out with blanks separating the three parts of the number.

INPUT TO PROGRAM 16

```
GEORGE THOMAS      32564472842000625
EARL DENTOM        99966655534000455
BEATRICE TIER      42419552120250500
SAMUEL JONES       65478852235000525
WILLIAM TELLE      12354235409502000
CHESTER JAFFEE     78956123410000225
SUSAN PERLES       71155210035500080
STEVEN LEVY        08648282140000325
MARY HARTMAN       68742153635000350
```

PROGRAM 16
Payroll Program

```
00001        IDENTIFICATION DIVISION.
00002        PROGRAM-ID. PAYROLL.
00003        ENVIRONMENT DIVISION.
00004        CONFIGURATION SECTION.
00005        SOURCE-COMPUTER. IBM-370-145.
00006        OBJECT-COMPUTER. IBM-370-145.
00007        INPUT-OUTPUT SECTION.
00008        FILE-CONTROL.
00009            SELECT IN-FILE ASSIGN TO UT-S-READER.
00010            SELECT OUT-FILE ASSIGN TO UT-S-PRINTER.
00011        DATA DIVISION.
00012        FILE SECTION.
00013        FD  IN-FILE
00014            LABEL RECORDS ARE OMITTED.
00015        01  PAYROLL-IN.
00016            05  EMPLOYEE-NAME          PICTURE X(20).
```

```
00017                05  FILLER                PICTURE X(5).
00018                05  SOC-SEC-NO             PICTURE 9(9).
00019                05  HOURS-WORKED           PICTURE 99V99.
CC020                05  RATE-CF-PAY            PICTURE 99V99.
00021                05  FILLER                 PICTURE X(38).
00022         FD  OUT-FILE
00023         LABEL RECORDS ARE OMITTED.
00024         01  PRINT-LINE-RECORD.
00025                05  CARRIAGE-CONTROL       PICTURE X.
00026                05  PRINT-LINE             PICTURE X(132).
00027         WORKING-STORAGE SECTION.
00028         77  CARD-NUMBER                    PICTURE 999 VALUE ZERO.
00029         01  HEADER-1.
00030                05  FILLER           PICTURE X VALUE SPACE.
00031                05  FILLER           PICTURE X(11) VALUE 'CARD NUMBER'.
00032                05  FILLER           PICTURE X(02) VALUE SPACES.
00033                05  FILLER           PICTURE X(13) VALUE 'EMPLOYEE NAME'.
00034                05  FILLER           PICTURE X(07) VALUE SPACES.
00035                05  FILLER           PICTURE X(22) VALUE
00036         'SOCIAL SECURITY NUMBER'.
00037                05  FILLER           PICTURE X(4) VALUE SPACES.
00038                05  FILLER           PICTURE X(12) VALUE 'HOURS WORKED'.
00039                05  FILLER           PICTURE X(02) VALUE SPACES.
00040                05  FILLER           PICTURE X(11) VALUE 'RATE OF PAY'.
00041                05  FILLER           PICTURE X(02) VALUE SPACES.
00042                05  FILLER           PICTURE X(09) VALUE 'GROSS PAY'.
00043                05  FILLER           PICTURE X(37) VALUE SPACES.
00044         01  DETAIL-LINE.
00045                05  FILLER           PICTURE X(05) VALUE SPACES.
00046                05  CARD-NUMBER-OUT  PICTURE ZZ9.
00047                05  FILLER           PICTURE X(06) VALUE SPACES.
00048                05  EMPLOYEE-NAME-OUT PICTURE X(20).
00049                05  FILLER           PICTURE X(06) VALUE SPACES.
00050                05  SOC-SEC-NO-OUT   PICTURE 999B99B9999.
00051                05  FILLER           PICTURE X(11) VALUE SPACES.
00052                05  HOURS-WORKED-OUT PICTURE ZZ9.99.
00053                05  FILLER           PICTURE X(08) VALUE SPACES.
00054                05  RATE-OF-PAY-OUT  PICTURE Z9.99.
00055                05  FILLER           PICTURE X(05) VALUE SPACES.
00056                05  GROSS-PAY        PICTURE $$,$$$.99.
00057                05  FILLER           PICTURE X(38) VALUE SPACES.
00058         PROCEDURE DIVISION.
00059         START-HERE.
C0060              OPEN INPUT IN-FILE
00061                  OUTPUT OUT-FILE.
00062              WRITE PRINT-LINE-RECORD FROM HEADER-1 AFTER
00063                  ADVANCING 1 LINES.
00064         READ-DATA-CARD.
00065              READ IN-FILE AT END CLOSE IN-FILE, CLOSE OUT-FILE, STOP RUN.
C0066              ADD 1 TO CARD-NUMBER.
00067              MULTIPLY RATE-OF-PAY BY HOURS-WORKED GIVING GROSS-PAY.
00068              MOVE CARD-NUMBER TO CARD-NUMBER-OUT.
00069              MOVE EMPLOYEE-NAME TO EMPLOYEE-NAME-OUT.
00070              MOVE SOC-SEC-NO TO SOC-SEC-NO-OUT.
00071              MOVE HOURS-WORKED TO HOURS-WORKED-OUT.
00072              MOVE RATE-OF-PAY TO RATE-OF-PAY-OUT.
00073              WRITE PRINT-LINE-RECORD FROM DETAIL-LINE AFTER
00074                  ADVANCING 2 LINES.
00075              GO TO READ-DATA-CARD.
```

OUTPUT TO PROGRAM 16

CARD NUMBER	EMPLOYEE NAME	SOCIAL SECURITY NUMBER	HOURS WORKED	RATE OF PAY	GROSS PAY
1	GEORGE THOMAS	325 64 4728	42.00	6.25	$262.50
2	EARL DENTOM	999 66 6555	34.00	4.55	$154.70
3	BEATRICE TIER	424 19 5521	20.25	5.00	$101.25
4	SAMUEL JONES	654 78 8522	35.00	5.25	$183.75
5	WILLIAM TELLE	123 54 2354	9.50	20.00	$190.00
6	CHESTER JAFFEE	789 56 1234	10.00	2.25	$22.50
7	SUSAN PERLES	711 55 2100	35.50	8.00	$284.00
8	STEVEN LEVY	086 48 2821	40.00	3.25	$130.00
9	MARY HARTMAN	687 42 1536	35.00	3.50	$122.50

10.4 AN AMENDED PAYROLL PROBLEM

Now that we have become acquainted with the WRITE . . . AFTER ADVANCING instruction, we are ready to modify Program 16 so that we can take into account overtime pay. Let us assume that all time worked in excess of 35 hours is considered overtime which is paid at one and a half times the regular rate. In the Procedure Division, therefore, the number of hours worked is tested to see whether it is greater than 35. If it is, OVERTIME–HOURS is calculated and the associated OVERTIME–PAY computed. At this point, the numeric literal 35 is moved to REGULAR–HOURS. Otherwise, (read ELSE) ZERO is moved to OVERTIME–HOURS and to OVERTIME–PAY, and HOURS–WORKED in PAYROLL–IN is moved to REGULAR–HOURS. REGULAR–PAY is then calculated by multiplying REGULAR–HOURS by RATE–OF–PAY of PAYROLL–IN.

Notice this time that the nine-digit Social Security number has been edited to include hyphens as separators for the three parts of the number. Also notice the effect of the BLANK WHEN ZERO clauses when the field does, in fact, contain the value zero.

INPUT TO PROGRAM 17

```
GEORGE THOMAS      325644728420C0625
EARL DENTOM        999666555340C0455
BEATRICE TIER      4241955212C2505CC
SAMUEL JONES       65478852235000525
WILLIAM TELLE      1235423540950200C
CHESTER JAFFEE     78956123410C0C225
SUSAN PERLES       7115521C0355CC8CC
STEVEN LEVY        086482821400C0325
MARY HARTMAN       68742153635UCC35C
```

PROGRAM 17
An Amended Payroll Program

```
00001          IDENTIFICATION DIVISION.
00002          PROGRAM-ID. PAYROLL-2.
00003
00004          ENVIRONMENT DIVISION.
00005          CONFIGURATION SECTION.
00006          SOURCE-COMPUTER. IBM-370-145.
00007          OBJECT-COMPUTER. IBM-370-145.
00008          INPUT-OUTPUT SECTION.
00009          FILE-CONTROL.
00010              SELECT IN-FILE ASSIGN TO UT-S-READER.
00011              SELECT OUT-FILE ASSIGN TO UT-S-PRINTER.
00012
00013          DATA DIVISION.
00014          FILE SECTION.
00015          FD  IN-FILE
00016              LABEL RECORDS ARE OMITTED.
00017          01  PAYROLL-IN.
00018              05  EMPLOYEE-NAME          PICTURE X(15).
00019              05  FILLER                 PICTURE X(5).
00020              05  SOC-SEC-NO.
00021                  10  SOC-SEC-NO-1 PICTURE 999.
00022                  10  SOC-SEC-NO-2 PICTURE 99.
00023                  10  SOC-SEC-NO-3 PICTURE 9999.
00024              05  HOURS-WORKED           PICTURE 99V99.
00025              05  RATE-OF-PAY            PICTURE 99V99.
00026              05  FILLER                 PICTURE X(43).
00027
00028          FD  OUT-FILE
00029              LABEL RECORDS ARE OMITTED.
00030          01  PRINT-LINE-RECORD.
00031              05  CARRIAGE-CONTROL   PICTURE X.
```

```
00032              05  PRINT-LINE     PICTURE X(132).
00033
00034          WORKING-STORAGE SECTION.
00035          77  CARD-NUMBER         PICTURE 999 VALUE ZERO.
00036          77  OVERTIME-PAY        PICTURE 9999V99.
00037          77  OVERTIME-HOURS      PICTURE 99V99.
00038          77  REGULAR-HOURS       PICTURE 99V99.
00039          77  REGULAR-PAY         PICTURE 9999V99.
00040
00041          01  HEADER-1.
00042              05  FILLER          PICTURE X(38) VALUE SPACES.
00043              05  FILLER          PICTURE X(28) VALUE
00044              'W E E K L Y    P A Y R O L L'.
00045              05  FILLER          PICTURE X(67) VALUE SPACES.
00046
00047          01  HEADER-2.
00048              05  FILLER          PICTURE X(38) VALUE SPACES.
00049              05  FILLER          PICTURE X(28) VALUE ALL '*'.
00050              05  FILLER          PICTURE X(67) VALUE SPACES.
00051
00052          01  HEADER-3.
00053              05  FILLER          PICTURE X(47) VALUE SPACES.
00054              05  TODAYS-DATE     PICTURE X(8) VALUE SPACES.
00055              05  FILLER          PICTURE X(88) VALUE SPACES.
00056
00057          01  HEADER-4.
00058              05  FILLER          PICTURE X(33) VALUE SPACES.
00059              05  FILLER          PICTURE X(41) VALUE
00060              'INTERNATIONAL WIDGET COMPANY INCORPORATED'.
00061              05  FILLER          PICTURE X(59) VALUE SPACES.
00062
00063          01  HEADER-5.
00064              05  FILLER          PICTURE X(33) VALUE SPACES.
00065              05  FILLER          PICTURE X(41) VALUE ALL '='.
00066              05  FILLER          PICTURE X(59) VALUE SPACES.
00067
00068          01  HEADER-6.
00069              05  FILLER          PICTURE X VALUE SPACES.
00070              05  FILLER          PICTURE X(04) VALUE 'CARD'.
00071              05  FILLER          PICTURE X(02) VALUE SPACES.
00072              05  FILLER          PICTURE X(08) VALUE 'EMPLOYEE'.
00073              05  FILLER          PICTURE X(10) VALUE SPACES.
00074              05  FILLER          PICTURE X(08) VALUE 'SOC.SEC.'.
00075              05  FILLER          PICTURE X(04) VALUE SPACES.
00076              05  FILLER          PICTURE X(07) VALUE 'RATE OF'.
00077              05  FILLER          PICTURE X     VALUE SPACES.
00078              05  FILLER          PICTURE X(09) VALUE 'TOTAL HRS'.
00079              05  FILLER          PICTURE X(2)  VALUE SPACES.
00080              05  FILLER          PICTURE X(07) VALUE 'REGULAR'.
00081              05  FILLER          PICTURE X(05) VALUE SPACES.
00082              05  FILLER          PICTURE X(2)  VALUE SPACES.
00083              05  FILLER          PICTURE X(07) VALUE 'REGULAR'.
00084              05  FILLER          PICTURE X(3)  VALUE SPACES.
00085              05  FILLER          PICTURE X(08) VALUE 'OVERTIME'.
00086              05  FILLER          PICTURE X(2)  VALUE SPACES.
00087              05  FILLER          PICTURE X(08) VALUE 'OVERTIME'.
00088              05  FILLER          PICTURE X(3)  VALUE SPACES.
00089              05  FILLER          PICTURE X(05) VALUE 'TOTAL'.
00090              05  FILLER          PICTURE X(29) VALUE SPACES.
00091
00092          01  HEADER-7.
00093              05  FILLER          PICTURE X     VALUE SPACES.
00094              05  FILLER          PICTURE X(3)  VALUE 'NO.'.
00095              05  FILLER          PICTURE X(05) VALUE SPACES.
00096              05  FILLER          PICTURE X(4)  VALUE 'NAME'.
00097              05  FILLER          PICTURE X(13) VALUE SPACES.
00098              05  FILLER          PICTURE X(6)  VALUE 'NUMBER'.
00099              05  FILLER          PICTURE X(07) VALUE SPACES.
00100              05  FILLER          PICTURE X(3)  VALUE 'PAY'.
00101              05  FILLER          PICTURE X(05) VALUE SPACES.
00102              05  FILLER          PICTURE X(6)  VALUE 'WORKED'.
00103              05  FILLER          PICTURE X(04) VALUE SPACES.
00104              05  FILLER          PICTURE X(5)  VALUE 'HOURS'.
00105              05  FILLER          PICTURE X(10) VALUE SPACES.
00106              05  FILLER          PICTURE X(3)  VALUE 'PAY'.
00107              05  FILLER          PICTURE X(06) VALUE SPACES.
00108              05  FILLER          PICTURE X(5)  VALUE 'HOURS'.
00109              05  FILLER          PICTURE X(06) VALUE SPACES.
00110              05  FILLER          PICTURE X(3)  VALUE 'PAY'.
00111              05  FILLER          PICTURE X(07) VALUE SPACES.
00112              05  FILLER          PICTURE X(3)  VALUE 'PAY'.
00113              05  FILLER          PICTURE X(28) VALUE SPACES.
00114
```

```
00115           01  HEADER-8.
00116               05  FILLER          PICTURE X     VALUE SPACES.
00117               05  FILLER          PICTURE X(4)   VALUE ALL '*'.
00118               05  FILLER          PICTURE X(02)  VALUE SPACES.
00119               05  FILLER          PICTURE X(08)  VALUE ALL '*'.
C0120               05  FILLER          PICTURE X(10)  VALUE SPACES.
00121               05  FILLER          PICTURE X(08)  VALUE ALL '*'.
00122               05  FILLER          PICTURE X(04)  VALUE SPACES.
00123               05  FILLER          PICTURE X(07)  VALUE ALL '*'.
00124               05  FILLER          PICTURE X      VALUE SPACES.
00125               05  FILLER          PICTURE X(09)  VALUE ALL '*'.
00126               05  FILLER          PICTURE X(02)  VALUE SPACES.
00127               05  FILLER          PICTURE X(07)  VALUE ALL '*'.
0C128               05  FILLER          PICTURE X(07)  VALUE SPACES.
00129               05  FILLER          PICTURE X(07)  VALUE ALL '*'.
G0130               05  FILLER          PICTURE X(03)  VALUE SPACES.
00131               05  FILLER          PICTURE X(08)  VALUE ALL '*'.
00132               05  FILLER          PICTURE X(02)  VALUE SPACES.
00133               05  FILLER          PICTURE X(08)  VALUE ALL '*'.
00134               05  FILLER          PICTURE X(03)  VALUE SPACES.
00135               05  FILLER          PICTURE X(05)  VALUE ALL '*'.
00136               05  FILLER          PICTURE X(22)  VALUE SPACES.
00137
00138           01  DETAIL-LINE.
00139               05  FILLER          PICTURE X     VALUE SPACES.
00140               05  CARD-NUMBER-OUT    PICTURE ZZ9.
00141               05  FILLER          PICTURE X(3)   VALUE SPACES.
00142               05  EMPLOYEE-NAME PICTURE X(15).
00143               05  FILLER          PICTURE X(3)   VALUE SPACES.
00144               05  SOC-SEC-NO.
00145                   10  SOC-SEC-NO-1 PICTURE 999.
00146                   10  FILLER PICTURE X VALUE '-'.
0C147                   10  SOC-SEC-NC-2 PICTURE 99.
00148                   10  FILLER PICTURE X VALUE '-'.
00149                   10  SOC-SEC-NC-3 PICTURE 9999.
00150               05  FILLER          PICTURE X(2)   VALUE SPACES.
00151               05  RATE-OF-PAY        PICTURE Z9.99.
00152               05  FILLER          PICTURE X(5)   VALUE SPACES.
00153               05  HOURS-WORKED       PICTURE Z9.99.
00154               05  FILLER          PICTURE X(5)   VALUE SPACES.
00155               05  REGULAR-HOURS-OUT  PICTURE Z9.99.
00156               05  FILLER          PICTURE X(5)   VALUE SPACES.
00157               05  REGULAR-PAY-OUT    PICTURE $$,$$9.99.
C0158               05  FILLER          PICTURE X(5)   VALUE SPACES.
00159               05  OVERTIME-HOURS-OUT PICTURE Z9.99 BLANK WHEN ZERO.
00160               05  FILLER          PICTURE X(2)   VALUE SPACES.
00161               05  OVERTIME-PAY-OUT   PICTURE $$,$$9.99 BLANK WHEN ZERO.
00162               05  FILLER          PICTURE X      VALUE SPACES.
00163               05  GROSS-PAY-OUT      PICTURE $$$,$$9.99.
00164               05  FILLER          PICTURE X(23)  VALUE SPACES.
0C165
00166           PROCEDURE DIVISION.
0C167           START-HERE.
0C168               OPEN INPUT IN-FILE.
00169               OPEN OUTPUT OUT-FILE.
0C170               WRITE PRINT-LINE-RECORD FROM HEADER-1 AFTER
00171               ADVANCING 2 LINES.
00172               WRITE PRINT-LINE-RECORD FROM HEADER-2 AFTER
00173               ADVANCING 1 LINES.
00174               MOVE CURRENT-DATE TO TODAYS-DATE.
00175               WRITE PRINT-LINE-RECORD FROM HEADER-3 AFTER
00176               ADVANCING 2 LINES.
00177               WRITE PRINT-LINE-RECORD FRCM HEADER-4 AFTER
C0178               ADVANCING 2 LINES.
00179               WRITE PRINT-LINE-RECORD FRCM HEADER-5 AFTER
00180               ADVANCING 1 LINES.
00181               WRITE PRINT-LINE-RECORD FROM HEADER-6 AFTER
0C182               ADVANCING 5 LINES.
00183               WRITE PRINT-LINE-RECORD FROM HEADER-7 AFTER
00184               ADVANCING 1 LINES.
00185               WRITE PRINT-LINE-RECORD FROM HEADER-8 AFTER
00186               ADVANCING 1 LINES.
00187               MOVE SPACES TO PRINT-LINE-RECORD.
00188               WRITE PRINT-LINE-RECORD AFTER ADVANCING 1 LINES.
0C189
C0190           READ-DATA-CARD.
00191               READ IN-FILE AT END CLOSE IN-FILE, OUT-FILE, STOP RUN.
00192               ADD 1 TC CARD-NUMBER.
00193               IF HOURS-WORKED OF PAYROLL-IN > 35 THEN
00194                  SUBTRACT 35 FROM HOURS-WORKED IN PAYROLL-IN GIVING
00195                        OVERTIME-HOURS
00196                  COMPUTE OVERTIME-PAY = OVERTIME-HOURS * 1.5 * RATE-OF-PAY
00197                        IN PAYROLL-IN
```

```
00198          MOVE 35 TO REGULAR-HOURS
00199      ELSE
C0200          MOVE ZERO TO OVERTIME-HOURS, OVERTIME-PAY
00201          MOVE HOURS-WORKED IN PAYROLL-IN TO REGULAR-HOURS.
00202      MULTIPLY REGULAR-HOURS BY RATE-OF-PAY OF PAYROLL-IN
00203      GIVING REGULAR-PAY.
00204      MOVE CARD-NUMBER TO CARD-NUMBER-OUT.
00205      MOVE CORRESPONDING PAYROLL-IN TO DETAIL-LINE.
00206      MOVE REGULAR-HOURS TO REGULAR-HOURS-OUT.
00207      MOVE REGULAR-PAY TO REGULAR-PAY-OUT.
00208      MOVE OVERTIME-HOURS TO OVERTIME-HOURS-OUT.
00209      MOVE OVERTIME-PAY TO OVERTIME-PAY-OUT.
00210      ADD REGULAR-PAY, OVERTIME-PAY GIVING GROSS-PAY-OUT.
00211      WRITE PRINT-LINE-RECORD FROM DETAIL-LINE
00212      AFTER ADVANCING 2 LINES.
00213      GO TO READ-DATA-CARD.
```

OUTPUT TO PROGRAM 17

```
                   W E E K L Y   P A Y R O L L
                   *****************************

                         06/20/77

              INTERNATIONAL WIDGET COMPANY INCORPORATED
              ==========================================
```

CARD NO. ****	EMPLOYEE NAME ********	SOC.SEC. NUMBER ********	RATE OF PAY *******	TOTAL HRS WORKED *********	REGULAR HOURS *******	REGULAR PAY *******	OVERTIME HOURS ********	OVERTIME PAY ********	TOTAL PAY *****
1	GEORGE THOMAS	325-64-4728	6.25	42.00	35.00	$218.75	7.00	$65.62	$284.37
2	EARL DENTOM	999-66-6555	4.55	34.00	34.00	$154.70			$154.70
3	BEATRICE TIER	424-19-5521	5.00	20.25	20.25	$101.25			$101.25
4	SAMUEL JONES	654-78-8522	5.25	35.00	35.00	$183.75			$183.75
5	WILLIAM TELLE	123-54-2354	20.00	9.50	9.50	$190.00			$190.00
6	CHESTER JAFFEE	789-56-1234	2.25	10.00	10.00	$22.50			$22.50
7	SUSAN PERLES	711-55-2100	8.00	35.50	35.00	$280.00	0.50	$6.00	$286.00
8	STEVEN LEVY	086-48-2821	3.25	40.00	35.00	$113.75	5.00	$24.37	$138.12
9	MARY HARTMAN	687-42-1536	3.50	35.00	35.00	$122.50			$122.50

10.5 THE JULIAN DATE CONVERSION
PROBLEM

Most of us are accustomed to the conventional Gregorian method of describing a particular date. A typical example is October 15, 1976, which is generally written as

10/15/76

This is precisely the form in which the CURRENT-DATE prints the current date using the IBM 360–370 COBOL compiler.

For certain purposes, however, it is more convenient to express a date in terms of the last two digits of the year followed by three digits specifying that particular day of the year. For example, January 10, 1977, is the tenth day of the year 1977. The date may therefore be expressed as a *Julian date* in the form

77010

By the same token, December 31, 1978, is represented in Julian form as

78365

However, December 31, 1980, would have as its Julian date

80366

because 1980 is a leap year, making December 31 day 366 of that year. Expressing a date in the Julian style can be advantageous for those businesses in which the number of days elapsed between two periods becomes an integral part of a calculation. Banks, for example, sometimes charge interest by the day. In such cases it would be most helpful to have the date expressed as a Julian date rather than the conventional Gregorian date. In Program 18 a series of data cards is punched with dates expressed in the conventional Gregorian format. The first two columns are reserved for the month the, second two for the day, and columns five and six for the year. The purpose of the program is to convert the date punched on each input data card to its equivalent date on the Julian calendar. The period covered is 1965 through 1995. The leap years which occur during this period are 1968, 1972, 1976, 1980, 1984, 1988, and 1992. These years are defined as values for the condition-name LEAP–YEAR, which is an 88 level item associated with the 05 level data name YEAR–IN.

Several precautions have been taken in ensuring the validity of the input data. For example, each of the three fields of the input data is tested to be sure that they are numeric in class. Furthermore, since no month can have a numeric value less than 1 or greater than 12, MONTH–IN is tested to ensure that it does not exceed these limits. The same applies to the data name DAY–IN, which cannot have a value less than 1 or greater than 31. Provision has also been made to ensure that YEAR–IN does not fall out of the range prescribed by the program specifications. If any of these conditions are violated, the card number and the Gregorian date, with slashes separating the three fields, is printed out with the words ERROR FOUND in the Julian date field. For each input data card which passes these tests, the number of days accumulated during that year through the date specified is calculated with the help of a form of the GO TO statement which we have not as yet encountered in this text. It is called the GO TO . . . DEPENDING ON statement.

10.5.1 The GO TO . . . DEPENDING ON
Statement

A typical example of the GO TO . . . DEPENDING ON statement is:

```
GO TO PARA-1, PARA-2, PARA-3 DEPENDING ON J.
```

If J is equal to 1, control is sent directly to the *first*-named paragraph, which in this case is PARA-1. If J happens to have the value 2, it is the *second* paragraph, PARA-2, which will assume control. Similarly, if J takes on the value 3, control is sent to the *third*-named paragraph, PARA-3. Should J have a value other than 1, 2 or 3, the statement is ignored and control "falls through" to the next statement in line. In Program 18 the twelve months JAN through DEC are listed as elements of the GO TO . . . DEPENDING ON and MONTH-IN becomes the index, controlling the paragraph to which execution is transferred. If MONTH-IN has the value 1, for example, control is sent to the first paragraph named, which is JAN, skipping over each of the other paragraph names. The value of DAY-IN is then added to ACCUMULATED-DAYS, which is defined as a 77 level item in working storage and has an initial value of zero. It is in this paragraph that the condition-named LEAP-YEAR is tested. If the year happens to be a leap year and MONTH-IN is greater than 2, it is necessary to add 1 to ACCUMULATED-DAYS.

If, on the other hand, the value of MONTH-IN is 6, representing the month of June, control is sent to the paragraph labelled JUN. At this point, the number of days from the first of the year through the end of MAY are totalled in ACCUMULATED-DAYS by executing paragraphs MAY, APR, MAR, FEB and JAN successively. Finally, the value of DAY-IN is also added to ACCUMULATED-DAYS and the test for a leap year follows as before.

INPUT TO PROGRAM 18.

```
010175
010176
010376
123075
060559
121278
022875
130199
022876
022976
030175
 11376
170860
030176
```

PROGRAM 18
Julian Conversion Program

```
00001      IDENTIFICATION DIVISION.
00002      PROGRAM-ID. JULIAN.
00003      ENVIRONMENT DIVISION.
00004      CONFIGURATION SECTION.
00005      SOURCE-COMPUTER. IBM-370-145.
00006      OBJECT-COMPUTER. IBM-370-145.
```

```
00007            INPUT-OUTPUT SECTION.
00008            FILE-CONTROL.
00009                SELECT DATE-CARD-FILE ASSIGN TO UT-S-READER.
00010                SELECT OUTPUT-FILE ASSIGN TO UT-S-PRINTER.
00011            DATA DIVISION.
00012            FILE SECTION.
00013            FD  DATE-CARD-FILE
00014                LABEL RECORDS ARE OMITTED.
00015            01  DATE-CARD.
00016                05 MONTH-IN PICTURE 99.
00017                05 DAY-IN PICTURE 99.
00018                05 YEAR-IN PICTURE 99.
00019                   88 LEAP-YEAR  VALUE 68 72 76 80 84 88 92.
00020                05 FILLER PICTURE X(74).
00021            FD  OUTPUT-FILE
00022                LABEL RECORDS ARE OMITTED.
00023            01  OUT-LINE PICTURE X(132).
00024            WORKING-STORAGE SECTION.
00025            77  KOUNT PICTURE 999 VALUE ZERO.
00026            77  ACCUMULATED-DAYS PICTURE 999 VALUE ZERO.
00027            01  HEADER-1.
00028                05 FILLER       PICTURE X(3) VALUE SPACES.
00029                05 FILLER       PICTURE X(4) VALUE 'CARD'.
00030                05 FILLER       PICTURE X(3) VALUE SPACES.
00031                05 FILLER       PICTURE X(9) VALUE 'GREGORIAN'.
00032                05 FILLER       PICTURE X(2) VALUE SPACES.
00033                05 FILLER       PICTURE X(6) VALUE 'JULIAN'.
00034                05 FILLER       PICTURE X(105) VALUE SPACES.
00035            01  HEADER-2.
00036                05 FILLER       PICTURE X(3) VALUE SPACES.
00037                05 FILLER       PICTURE X(3) VALUE 'NO.'.
00038                05 FILLER       PICTURE X(6) VALUE SPACES.
00039                05 FILLER       PICTURE X(4) VALUE 'DATE'.
00040                05 FILLER       PICTURE X(6) VALUE SPACES.
00041                05 FILLER       PICTURE X(4) VALUE 'DATE'.
00042                05 FILLER       PICTURE X(106) VALUE SPACES.
00043            01  HEADER-3.
00044                05 FILLER       PICTURE X(3) VALUE SPACES.
00045                05 FILLER       PICTURE X(4) VALUE ALL '*'.
00046                05 FILLER       PICTURE X(3) VALUE SPACES.
00047                05 FILLER       PICTURE X(9) VALUE ALL '*'.
00048                05 FILLER       PICTURE X(2) VALUE SPACES.
00049                05 FILLER       PICTURE X(6) VALUE ALL '*'.
00050                05 FILLER       PICTURE X(105) VALUE SPACES.
00051            01  DETAIL-LINE-1.
00052                05  FILLER      PICTURE X(2) VALUE SPACES.
00053                05  NUM-OUT     PICTURE ZZ9.
00054                05  FILLER      PICTURE X VALUE '.'.
00055                05  FILLER      PICTURE X(4) VALUE SPACES.
00056                05  MONTH-OUT   PICTURE 99.
00057                05  FILLER      PICTURE X VALUE '/'.
00058                05  DAY-OUT     PICTURE 99.
00059                05  FILLER      PICTURE X VALUE '/'.
00060                05  YEAR-OUT    PICTURE 99.
00061                05  FILLER      PICTURE X(3) VALUE SPACES.
00062                05  JULIAN-YEAR PICTURE 99.
00063                05  JULIAN-DAY  PICTURE 999.
00064                05  FILLER      PICTURE X(106) VALUE SPACES.
00065            01  DETAIL-LINE-2.
00066                05  FILLER         PICTURE X(2) VALUE SPACES.
00067                05  NUM-OUT-ERROR  PICTURE ZZ9.
00068                05  FILLER         PICTURE X  VALUE '.'.
00069                05  FILLER         PICTURE X(4) VALUE SPACES.
00070                05  MONTH-OUT-ERROR PICTURE 99.
00071                05  FILLER         PICTURE X VALUE '/'.
00072                05  DAY-OUT-ERROR  PICTURE 99.
00073                05  FILLER         PICTURE X VALUE '/'.
00074                05  YEAR-OUT-ERROR PICTURE 99.
00075                05  FILLER         PICTURE X(3) VALUE SPACES.
00076                05  FILLER         PICTURE X(11) VALUE 'ERROR FOUND'.
00077                05  FILLER         PICTURE X(100) VALUE SPACES.
00078            PROCEDURE DIVISION.
00079            START-HERE.
00080                OPEN INPUT DATE-CARD-FILE
00081                     OUTPUT  OUTPUT-FILE.
00082                WRITE OUT-LINE FROM HEADER-1.
00083                WRITE OUT-LINE FROM HEADER-2.
00084                WRITE OUT-LINE FROM HEADER-3.
00085                MOVE SPACES TO OUT-LINE.
00086                WRITE OUT-LINE.
00087            MORE.
00088                READ DATE-CARD-FILE AT END CLOSE DATE-CARD-FILE,
00089                OUTPUT-FILE, STOP RUN.
```

```
C0090                     ADD 1 TO KOUNT.
00091                     IF MONTH-IN NOT NUMERIC
C0092                        OR DAY-IN NOT NUMERIC
00093                        OR YEAR-IN NOT NUMERIC
00094                        OR MONTH-IN < 1 OR > 12
00095                        OR DAY-IN < 1 OR > 31
00096                        OR YEAR-IN < 65 OR > 95
00097                           MOVE KOUNT TO NUM-OUT-ERROR
00098                           MOVE MONTH-IN TO MONTH-OUT-ERROR
00099                           MOVE DAY-IN TO DAY-OUT-ERROR
C0100                           MOVE YEAR-IN TO YEAR-OUT-ERROR
00101                           WRITE OUT-LINE FROM DETAIL-LINE-2
00102                           GO TO MORE
00103                     ELSE
00104                        GO TO JAN, FEB, MAR, APR, MAY, JUN, JLY, AUG, SEP,
00105                        OCT, NOV, DEC DEPENDING ON MONTH-IN.
00106    DEC.  ADD 30 TO ACCUMULATED-DAYS.
C0107    NOV.  ADD 31 TO ACCUMULATED-DAYS.
00108    OCT.  ADD 30 TO ACCUMULATED-DAYS.
00109    SEP.  ADD 31 TO ACCUMULATED-DAYS.
00110    AUG.  ADD 31 TO ACCUMULATED-DAYS.
00111    JLY.  ADD 30 TO ACCUMULATED-DAYS.
00112    JUN.  ADD 31 TO ACCUMULATED-DAYS.
00113    MAY.  ADD 30 TO ACCUMULATED-DAYS.
00114    APR.  ADD 31 TO ACCUMULATED-DAYS.
00115    MAR.  ADD 28 TO ACCUMULATED-DAYS.
00116    FEB.  ADD 31 TO ACCUMULATED-DAYS.
00117    JAN.  ADD DAY-IN TO ACCUMULATED-DAYS.
00118          IF LEAP-YEAR AND MONTH-IN > 2 ADD 1 TO ACCUMULATED-DAYS.
00119          MOVE KOUNT TO NUM-OUT.
00120          MOVE MONTH-IN TO MONTH-OUT.
00121          MOVE DAY-IN TO DAY-OUT.
00122          MOVE YEAR-IN TO YEAR-OUT.
00123          MOVE YEAR-IN TO JULIAN-YEAR.
00124          MOVE ACCUMULATED-DAYS TO JULIAN-DAY.
00125          WRITE OUT-LINE FROM DETAIL-LINE-1.
00126          MOVE ZERO TO ACCUMULATED-DAYS.
00127          GO TO MORE.
```

OUTPUT TO PROGRAM 18

CARD NO.	GREGORIAN DATE	JULIAN DATE
1.	01/01/75	75001
2.	01/01/76	76001
3.	01/03/76	76003
4.	12/30/75	75364
5.	06/05/59	ERROR FOUND
6.	12/12/78	78346
7.	02/28/75	75059
8.	13/01/99	ERROR FOUND
9.	02/28/76	76059
10.	02/29/76	76060
11.	03/01/75	75060
12.	1/13/76	ERROR FOUND
13.	17/08/60	ERROR FOUND
14.	03/01/76	76061

The output for input card number 12 is interesting. It is flagged as an error even though January 13, 1976 is a perfectly good date, falling well within the prescribed range of dates. The reason why the date has been rejected is that it is punched as 1/13/76 rather than 01/13/76. The leading blank is not a valid numeric and this is detected by the statement

IF MONTH-IN NOT NUMERIC.

10.6 THE COMMISSIONS PROBLEM

There are several purposes for presenting the commissions problem next in sequence. Not only is the calculation of commissions an essential part

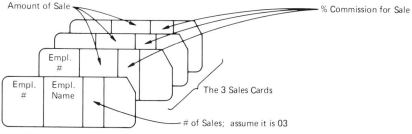

Amount of Sale

% Commission for Sale

Empl. #

Empl. # | Empl. Name

The 3 Sales Cards

# of Sales; assume it is 03

FIGURE 14

of much of data processing (as any salesman will eagerly confirm) but it introduces us to several additional features of the COBOL language.

The problem is basically simple in content. The input file is composed of a card itemizing an employee's number, name and number of sales, all punched on a single card, called in the program the *master–card*. If the number of separate sales, for example, is 3, three sales cards follow the master card. On each sales card is punched the employee number, the amount of the sale, and the percentage commission payable to that salesman for that particular sale. The input deck consists of many sets of such cards, the number of sales cards varying with each master card. A typical input set is shown in Figure 14.

The aim of the program is to read in as many sets of data as are present and to calculate from the sales cards the amount of commission payable to each salesman for each separate sale. After printing out all the relevant information for each particular salesman, the total commission payable to the salesman together with his sales volume are also printed. At the same time, a running account is kept of the grand total number of sales the grand total of commissions to be paid, and the grand total amount of sales made by all salesmen. In the event that any particular sale results in a commission which is greater than $100, a string of asterisks is printed alongside that amount to draw attention to this fact. This technique is used sometimes to alert the accounting department to the possibility of an error having been made in the data. On the other hand, it could just as easily be used as an indicator for awarding a bonus to the particular salesman.

The major point which should be emphasized in this program is that for the first time in the text we have an input file consisting of cards *not* identical in format. The format of the master card in each set is considerably different from that of the associated sales cards. When reading a data card into the input area of the computer, we have a space of eighty characters at our disposal; when reading each master or associated sales card into the memory of the computer, the single file IN–FILE permits us the use of this single 80-character area for storing the information. It is for this reason that under the FD for IN–FILE are *two*

126 SOME ILLUSTRATIVE COMPUTATIONAL PROBLEMS

separate 01 levels, namely MASTER–CARD and SALES–CARD respectively. It is the responsibility of the programmer to know which format he is dealing with at any given time. The first time the READ instruction is executed, the assumption made is that it is the master card of a set that is being read; to assume otherwise would make no sense. The READ instruction has to be executed subsequently so that the information on each of the sales cards can be read. In order to compare the employee number punched on the master card with the employee number punched on each of the associated sales cards, to ensure that the cards are in their correct order, it is essential to store the information from the first card in Working Storage. Otherwise, when the sales card is read the information on the master card will be erased in memory and no comparison can be made. Copying information to Working Storage applies equally to the field named NUMBER–OF–SALES in the master card. If it were not moved to NUMBER–OF–SALES–HOLD before subsequent cards are read in, its value would also no longer be available. Incidentally, it is for this reason that whenever we READ, we read a *file* and not a *record*. Each of the separate records has its own 01 level entry even though the file has only one FD entry.

At the beginning of the Working Storage Section are four 77 level items. Although these serve a very useful purpose, there are a few COBOL installations that not only frown upon the use of 77 level items but forbid their use outright. Such installations prefer that when the need for 77 level items arises, they be included in an 01 level description such as has been done in the record descriptions named TOTALS and GRAND–TOTALS, which immediately follow the 77 level items in Working Storage. The arguments underlying this philosophy seem to be that the absence of 77 level items precludes the possibility of their not preceding any 01 level entries. Also, it is felt that grouping them together under meaningful 01 level entry descriptions makes for easier debugging and greater program clarity.

All of the elementary items listed in the 01 level description can be cleared with a single instruction in the Procedure Division with an instruction such as

```
MOVE ZEROES TO TOTALS.
```

The WRITE . . . AFTER ADVANCING option has been used throughout the program which follows, but the careful reader will notice that in line 00160, for example, the instruction has been abbreviated to

```
WRITE PRINT–LINE–RECORD FROM HEADER–2 AFTER 1 LINES.
```

in which the word ADVANCING has been omitted. On most systems this abbreviation is perfectly acceptable. In the next statement, card 00161, the instruction

```
WRITE PRINT-LINE-RECORD FROM HEADER-3 AFTER 4.
```

the two words ADVANCING and LINES have both been omitted. Again, this is another acceptable abbreviation on most systems.

10.6.1 The PERFORM . . . VARYING . . . UNTIL . . . Statement

The final feature that requires special attention is the new form of the PERFORM statement which is used in lines 179 and 180. It says

```
PERFORM GET-SALES-CARD VARYING SALES-NUMBER FROM 1 BY 1
UNTIL SALES-NUMBER > NUMBER-OF-SALES-HOLD.
```

This is an alternative to the instruction

```
PERFORM GET-SALES-CARD NUMBER-OF-SALES-HOLD TIMES.
```

which, in principle, would appear to be the more obvious choice. However, using this more sophisticated form of PERFORM permits us to keep an automatic counter in increments of 1 of the sales number which is printed alongside each sales card in the report. It is advisable to become familiar with this version of PERFORM since its flexibility can be exploited in many different situations. Its general form is

```
PERFORM para-name VARYING data-item FROM constant-1
BY constant-2 UNTIL condition.
```

The paragraph is repeatedly executed (or PERFORMed) until the specified condition is met. Each time the paragraph is executed, the value of the data-item is automatically updated by adding constant-2 to its initial value of constant-1.

When this format is used, the specified paragraph name is performed until the specified condition is true. When this occurs, control is transferred to the statement following the PERFORM statement. However, the programmer is cautioned that if the condition is true at the time that the PERFORM statement is encountered, the specified procedure or procedures are not executed.

For this reason the PERFORM statement in Program 19 contains the UNTIL clause SALES-NUMBER > NUMBER-OF-SALES-HOLD rather than SALES-NUMBER = NUMBER-OF-SALES-HOLD. Use of the > operator becomes essential in order to read and execute the instructions relative to the last data card of the set.

It will be noticed once again that blank cards have been used to separate major sections of the program from each other in order to facilitate greater clarity in reading the program.

INPUT TO PROGRAM 19

```
666666JEFFREY KARP    04
666666800000100
666666770000600
666666002000300
666666500000300
123123WALTER GEISLER 02
123123650000200
123123440000500
552211MARGIE BRAND   03
552211453250020
552211250000500
552211030000500
654456ANDREA ROSS    05
6544563000U0100
654456025000100
654456600000400
654456745000200
654456650000300
232323ALINA CHU      05
232323640000200
232323520000325
232323552000350
232323250000700
232323600000210
252525GUY LAUWERS    03
252525784001600
252525098000400
252525572002200
```

PROGRAM 19
Commissions Report

```
00001          IDENTIFICATION DIVISION.
00002          PROGRAM-ID. COMMISSIONS.
00003
00004          ENVIRONMENT DIVISION.
00005          CONFIGURATION SECTION.
00006          SOURCE-COMPUTER. IBM-370-145.
00007          OBJECT-COMPUTER. IBM-370-145.
00008          INPUT-OUTPUT SECTION.
00009          FILE-CONTROL.
00010              SELECT IN-FILE ASSIGN TO UT-S-READER.
00011              SELECT OUT-FILE ASSIGN TO UT-S-PRINTER.
00012
00013          DATA DIVISION.
00014
00015          FILE SECTION.
00016          FD IN-FILE
00017              LABEL RECORDS ARE OMITTED.
00018
00019          01  MASTER-CARD.
00020              05 EMPLOYEE-NUMBER     PICTURE 9(6).
00021              05 EMPLOYEE-NAME       PICTURE X(15).
00022              05 NUMBER-OF-SALES     PICTURE 99.
00023              05 FILLER              PICTURE X(57).
00024
00025          01  SALES-CARD.
00026              05 EMPLOYEE-NUMBER-CHECK    PICTURE 9(6).
00027              05 AMOUNT-OF-SALE           PICTURE 999V99.
00028              05 PERCENTAGE-COMMISSION    PICTURE 99V99.
00029              05 FILLER           PICTURE X(65).
00030
00031          FD OUT-FILE
00032              LABEL RECORDS ARE OMITTED.
00033
00034          01  PRINT-LINE-RECORD.
00035              05 CARRIAGE-CONTROL PICTURE X(1).
00036              05 PRINT-LINE PICTURE X(132).
00037
00038          WORKING-STORAGE SECTION.
00039
00040          77  EMPLOYEE-NUMBER-HOLD PICTURE 9(6).
00041          77  NUMBER-OF-SALES-HOLD        PICTURE 99.
00042          77  SALES-NUMBER PICTURE 99.
00043          77  AMOUNT-OF-COMMISSION PICTURE 999V99.
00044
00045          01  TOTALS.
00046              05  TOTAL-COMMISSIONS  PICTURE 9(6)V99.
00047              05  TOTAL-AMOUNT-OF-SALES   PICTURE 9(6)V99.
00048
00049          01  GRAND-TOTALS.
00050              05 GRAND-TOTAL-NUMBER-OF-SALES PICTURE 9(4) VALUE ZERO.
00051              05 GRAND-TOTAL-AMOUNT-OF-SALES PICTURE 9(8)V99 VALUE ZERO.
00052              05  GRAND-TOTAL-COMMISSIONS PICTURE 9(8)V99 VALUE ZERO.
00053
00054          01  HEADER-1.
00055              05  FILLER          PICTURE X(32) VALUE SPACES.
00056              05  FILLER          PICTURE X(33) VALUE 'C O M M I S S I O N
00057       -                                          'R E P O R T'.
00058              05  FILLER          PICTURE X(68) VALUE SPACES.
00059
00060          01  HEADER-2.
00061              05  FILLER          PICTURE X(32) VALUE SPACES.
00062              05  FILLER          PICTURE X(33) VALUE ALL '*'.
00063              05  FILLER          PICTURE X(68) VALUE SPACES.
00064
00065          01  HEADER-3.
00066              05  FILLER          PICTURE X(4) VALUE SPACES.
00067              05  FILLER          PICTURE X(8) VALUE 'EMPLOYEE'.
00068              05  FILLER          PICTURE X(6) VALUE SPACES.
```

```
00069             05  FILLER        PICTURE X(8) VALUE 'NAME OF'.
00070             05  FILLER        PICTURE X(15) VALUE SPACES.
00071             05  FILLER        PICTURE X(4) VALUE 'SALE'.
00072             05  FILLER        PICTURE X(7) VALUE SPACES.
00073             05  FILLER        PICTURE X(9) VALUE 'AMOUNT OF'.
00074             05  FILLER        PICTURE X(4) VALUE SPACES.
00075             05  FILLER        PICTURE X(10) VALUE 'PERCENTAGE'.
00076             05  FILLER        PICTURE X(3) VALUE SPACES.
00077             05  FILLER        PICTURE X(10) VALUE 'AMOUNT  OF'.
00078             05  FILLER        PICTURE X(45) VALUE SPACES.
00079
00080         01  HEADER-4.
00081             05  FILLER        PICTURE X(05) VALUE SPACES.
00082             05  FILLER PICTURE X(06) VALUE 'NUMBER'.
00083             05  FILLER PICTURE X(07) VALUE SPACES.
00084             05  FILLER PICTURE X(08) VALUE 'SALESMAN'.
00085             05  FILLER PICTURE X(14) VALUE SPACES.
00086             05  FILLER PICTURE X(06) VALUE 'NUMBER'.
00087             05  FILLER PICTURE X(08) VALUE SPACES.
00088             05  FILLER PICTURE X(05) VALUE 'SALES'.
00089             05  FILLER PICTURE X(06) VALUE SPACES.
00090             05  FILLER PICTURE X(10) VALUE 'COMMISSION'.
00091             05  FILLER PICTURE X(03) VALUE SPACES.
00092             05  FILLER PICTURE X(10) VALUE 'COMMISSION'.
00093             05  FILLER        PICTURE X(45) VALUE SPACES.
00094
00095         01  HEADER-5.
00096             05  FILLER PICTURE X(04) VALUE SPACES.
00097             05  FILLER        PICTURE X(84) VALUE ALL '*'.
00098             05  FILLER        PICTURE X(45) VALUE SPACES.
00099
00100         01  DETAIL-LINE-1.
00101             05  FILLER PICTURE X(6) VALUE SPACES.
00102             05  EMPLOYEE-NUMBER-OUT PICTURE 9(6).
00103             05  FILLER PICTURE X(5) VALUE SPACES.
00104             05  EMPLOYEE-NAME-OUT PICTURE X(15).
00105             05  FILLER PICTURE X(101) VALUE SPACES.
00106
00107         01  DETAIL-LINE-2.
00108             05  FILLER PICTURE X(44) VALUE SPACES.
00109             05  SALES-NUMBER-OUT PICTURE Z9.
00110             05  FILLER PICTURE X(6) VALUE SPACES.
00111             05  AMOUNT-OF-SALE-OUT PICTURE $$$$.99.
00112             05  FILLER PICTURE X(10) VALUE SPACES.
00113             05  PERCENTAGE-COMMISSION-OUT PICTURE ZZ.99.
00114             05  FILLER PICTURE X(1) VALUE '%'.
00115             05  FILLER PICTURE X(6) VALUE SPACES.
00116             05  AMOUNT-OF-COMMISSION-OUT PICTURE $$$9.99.
00117             05  FILLER PICTURE X(6) VALUE SPACES.
00118             05  FLAG PICTURE X(14) VALUE SPACES.
00119
00120         01  DETAIL-LINE-3.
00121             05  FILLER PICTURE X(30) VALUE SPACES.
00122             05  FILLER PICTURE X(06) VALUE 'TOTALS'.
00123             05  FILLER PICTURE X(14) VALUE ALL '.'.
00124             05  TOTAL-AMOUNT-OF-SALES-OUT  PICTURE $$$$,$$$.
00125             05  FILLER PICTURE X(18)  VALUE SPACES.
00126             05  TOTAL-COMMISSIONS-OUT PICTURE $$$$,$$$.99.
00127             05  FILLER PICTURE X(46) VALUE SPACES.
00128
00129         01  DETAIL-LINE-4.
00130             05  FILLER PICTURE X(22) VALUE SPACES.
00131             05  FILLER PICTURE X(21) VALUE 'TOTAL NUMBER OF SALES'.
00132             05  FILLER PICTURE X(11) VALUE SPACES.
00133             05  GRAND-TOTAL-NUMBER-OF-SALES-OUT PICTURE ZZZ9.
00134             05  FILLER PICTURE X(75) VALUE SPACES.
00135
00136         01  DETAIL-LINE-5.
00137             05  FILLER PICTURE X(22) VALUE SPACES.
00138             05  FILLER PICTURE X(21) VALUE 'TOTAL AMOUNT OF SALES'.
00139             05  FILLER PICTURE X(04) VALUE SPACES.
00140             05  GRAND-TOTAL-AMOUNT-OF-SALES-OUT PICTURE $$$,$$$,$$$.
00141             05  FILLER PICTURE X(75) VALUE SPACES.
00142
00143         01  DETAIL-LINE-6.
00144             05  FILLER PICTURE X(22) VALUE SPACES.
00145             05  FILLER PICTURE X(17) VALUE 'TOTAL COMMISSIONS'.
00146             05  FILLER PICTURE X(08) VALUE SPACES.
00147             05  GRAND-TOTAL-COMMISSIONS-OUT PICTURE $$$,$$$,$$$.
00148             05  FILLER PICTURE X(75) VALUE SPACES.
00149
00150     PROCEDURE DIVISION.
00151
00152     LETS-GO.
00153         OPEN INPUT IN-FILE.
00154         OPEN OUTPUT OUT-FILE.
00155
00156     * PRINT HEADINGS
00157
00158         WRITE PRINT-LINE-RECORD FROM HEADER-1 AFTER ADVANCING
00159             2 LINES.
00160         WRITE PRINT-LINE-RECORD FROM HEADER-2 AFTER 1 LINES.
00161         WRITE PRINT-LINE-RECORD FROM HEADER-3 AFTER 4.
00162         WRITE PRINT-LINE-RECORD FROM HEADER-4 AFTER 1.
00163         WRITE PRINT-LINE-RECORD FROM HEADER-5 AFTER 1.
00164
00165     GET-MASTER-CARD.
00166         READ IN-FILE AT END GO TO PRINT-GRAND-TOTALS.
00167         MOVE ZEROES TO TOTALS.
00168
00169     * SET UP DETAIL-LINE-1
00170
00171         MOVE EMPLOYEE-NUMBER TO EMPLOYEE-NUMBER-HOLD,
00172             EMPLOYEE-NUMBER-OUT.
00173         MOVE EMPLOYEE-NAME TO EMPLOYEE-NAME-OUT.
00174         MOVE NUMBER-OF-SALES TO NUMBER-OF-SALES-HOLD.
00175         WRITE PRINT-LINE-RECORD FROM DETAIL-LINE-1 AFTER 3.
00176
00177     * READ IN EMPLOYEE SALES CARDS.
00178
00179         PERFORM GET-SALES-CARD VARYING SALES-NUMBER FROM 1 BY 1
00180             UNTIL SALES-NUMBER > NUMBER-OF-SALES-HOLD.
00181
00182         ADD NUMBER-OF-SALES-HOLD TO GRAND-TOTAL-NUMBER-OF-SALES.
00183         MOVE TOTAL-AMOUNT-OF-SALES TO TOTAL-AMOUNT-OF-SALES-OUT.
```

```
00184          MOVE TOTAL-COMMISSIONS TO TOTAL-COMMISSIONS-OUT.
00185          WRITE PRINT-LINE-RECORD FROM DETAIL-LINE-3 AFTER 2.
00186          GO TO GET-MASTER-CARD.
00187
00188     GET-SALES-CARD.
00189          READ IN-FILE AT END GO TO ERROR-ROUTINE-1.
00190          IF EMPLOYEE-NUMBER-CHECK NOT EQUAL EMPLOYEE-NUMBER-HOLD
00191               THEN GO TO ERROR-ROUTINE-2.
00192          ADD AMOUNT-OF-SALE TO  TOTAL-AMOUNT-OF-SALES,
00193                              GRAND-TOTAL-AMOUNT-OF-SALES.
00194          COMPUTE AMOUNT-OF-COMMISSION ROUNDED =
00195               AMOUNT-OF-SALE / 100 * PERCENTAGE-COMMISSION.
00196          ADD AMOUNT-OF-COMMISSION TO TOTAL-COMMISSIONS,
00197                              GRAND-TOTAL-COMMISSIONS.
00198
00199     * SET UP DETAIL-LINE-2
00200
00201          MOVE SALES-NUMBER TO SALES-NUMBER-OUT.
00202          MOVE AMOUNT-OF-SALE TO AMOUNT-OF-SALE-OUT.
00203          MOVE PERCENTAGE-COMMISSION TO PERCENTAGE-COMMISSION-OUT.
00204          MOVE AMOUNT-OF-COMMISSION TO AMOUNT-OF-COMMISSION-OUT.
00205          IF AMOUNT-OF-COMMISSION IS GREATER THAN 100 THEN
00206               MOVE '************' TO FLAG
00207          ELSE  MOVE SPACES TO FLAG.
00208          WRITE PRINT-LINE-RECORD FROM DETAIL-LINE-2 AFTER 1.
00209
00210     ERROR-ROUTINE-1.
00211          DISPLAY '*** ERROR - NOT ENOUGH SALES CARDS FOR LAST EMPLOYEE
00212     -          ', PROGRAM EXECUTION TERMINATED.'.
00213          CLOSE IN-FILE.
00214          CLOSE OUT-FILE.
00215          STOP RUN.
00216
00217     ERROR-ROUTINE-2.
00218          DISPLAY EMPLOYEE-NUMBER-CHECK, AMOUNT-OF-SALE,
00219               PERCENTAGE-COMMISSION, ' *** CARD OUT OF SEQUENCE OR
00220     -          'MISPUNCHED, EXECUTION TERMINATED.'.
00221          CLOSE IN-FILE, OUT-FILE.
00222          STOP RUN.
00223
00224     PRINT-GRAND-TOTALS.
00225          MOVE GRAND-TOTAL-NUMBER-OF-SALES TO
00226               GRAND-TOTAL-NUMBER-OF-SALES-OUT.
00227          MOVE GRAND-TOTAL-AMOUNT-OF-SALES TO
00228               GRAND-TOTAL-AMOUNT-OF-SALES-OUT.
```

6

```
00229          MOVE GRAND-TOTAL-COMMISSIONS TO GRAND-TOTAL-COMMISSIONS-OUT.
00230          WRITE PRINT-LINE-RECORD FROM DETAIL-LINE-4 AFTER 5.
00231          WRITE PRINT-LINE-RECORD FROM DETAIL-LINE-5 AFTER 2.
00232          WRITE PRINT-LINE-RECORD FROM DETAIL-LINE-6 AFTER 2.
00233          CLOSE IN-FILE, OUT-FILE.
00234          STOP RUN.
```

OUTPUT TO PROGRAM 19

```
                    C O M M I S S I O N   R E P O R T
                    **********************************
```

EMPLOYEE NUMBER	NAME OF SALESMAN	SALE NUMBER	AMOUNT OF SALES	PERCENTAGE COMMISSION	AMOUNT OF COMMISSION
666666	JEFFREY KARP				
		1	$800.00	1.00%	$8.00
		2	$770.00	6.00%	$46.20
		3	$2.00	3.00%	$0.06
		4	$500.00	3.00%	$15.00
	TOTALS...............		$2,072		$69.26
123123	WALTER GEISLER				
		1	$650.00	2.00%	$13.00
		2	$440.00	5.00%	$22.00
	TOTALS...............		$1,090		$35.00
552211	MARGIE BRAND				
		1	$453.25	.20%	$0.91
		2	$250.00	5.00%	$12.50
		3	$30.00	5.00%	$1.50
	TOTALS...............		$733		$14.91

654456	ANDREA ROSS					
		1	$300.00	1.00%	$3.00	
		2	$25.00	1.00%	$0.25	
		3	$600.00	4.00%	$24.00	
		4	$745.00	2.00%	$14.90	
		5	$650.00	3.00%	$19.50	
	TOTALS.............		$2,320		$61.65	
232323	ALINA CHU					
		1	$640.00	2.00%	$12.80	
		2	$520.00	3.25%	$16.90	
		3	$552.00	3.50%	$19.32	
		4	$250.00	7.00%	$17.50	
		5	$600.00	2.10%	$12.60	
	TOTALS.............		$2,562		$79.12	
252525	GUY LAUWERS					
		1	$784.00	16.00%	$125.44	************
		2	$98.00	4.00%	$3.92	
		3	$572.00	22.00%	$125.84	************
	TOTALS.............		$1,454		$255.20	

TOTAL NUMBER OF SALES	22
TOTAL AMOUNT OF SALES	$10,231
TOTAL COMMISSIONS	$515

Before leaving the PERFORM statement, we will look at yet another version which permits even greater flexibility even though it admittedly looks somewhat forbidding. We will include it here for the sake of completeness but will not use it until the last program in the book. It has the following structure:

PERFORM procedure-name-1   [THRU procedure-name-2]

$$\underline{\text{VARYING}} \begin{Bmatrix} \text{index-1} \\ \text{data-name-1} \end{Bmatrix} \underline{\text{FROM}} \begin{Bmatrix} \text{index-2} \\ \text{constant-2} \\ \text{data-name-2} \end{Bmatrix}$$

$$\underline{\text{BY}} \begin{Bmatrix} \text{constant-3} \\ \text{data-name-3} \end{Bmatrix} \qquad \underline{\text{UNTIL}} \quad \text{condition-1}$$

$$[\underline{\text{AFTER}} \begin{Bmatrix} \text{index-4} \\ \text{data-name-4} \end{Bmatrix} \quad \underline{\text{FROM}} \begin{Bmatrix} \text{index-5} \\ \text{constant-5} \\ \text{data-name-5} \end{Bmatrix}$$

$$\underline{\text{BY}} \begin{Bmatrix} \text{constant-6} \\ \text{data-name-6} \end{Bmatrix} \qquad \underline{\text{UNTIL}} \text{ condition-2}$$

$$[AFTER \begin{Bmatrix} \text{index-7} \\ \text{data-name-7} \end{Bmatrix} \underline{FROM} \begin{Bmatrix} \text{index-8} \\ \text{constant-8} \\ \text{data-name-8} \end{Bmatrix}$$

$$\underline{BY} \begin{Bmatrix} \text{constant-9} \\ \text{data-name-9} \end{Bmatrix} \qquad \underline{UNTIL} \text{ condition-3]]}$$

When the PERFORM statement is entered, each of the index names or data names is initialized to its corresponding FROM value.

```
PEFORM PARA
    VARYING A FROM 1 BY 1 UNTIL A > 10
        AFTER B FROM 1 BY 1 UNTIL B > 10
            AFTER C FROM 1 BY 1 UNTIL C > 10
```

It will be advantageous to conceptualize this PERFORM instruction as a "nest." For example:

```
PERFORM PARA
    VARYING A FROM 1 BY 1
        AFTER B FROM 1 BY 1
            AFTER C FROM 1 BY 1


            UNTIL C > 10
        UNTIL B > 10
    UNTIL A > 10
```

It is clear from the above schematic representation that there is an outer loop where A is varied, a middle loop with B being varied, and an inner loop where C is varied. After A, B, and C are individually initialized to 1 the *inner* loop is executed until the condition (C > 10) is satisfied. Once this is achieved B is incremented by 1 and the inner loop executed afresh, until once again C > 10. This sequence is repeated until B > 10 at which point the middle loop is satisfied. The outer loop is now activated. Its value of A is incremented by 1 and the two inner loops executed anew as shown above. This sequence is repeated for each value of A until A > 10.

10.6.2. Comment Cards

In this program, for the first time, we have improved the internal documentation of the program by resorting to *comment cards.* A comment card is characterized by an asterisk punched in column 7. Anything else punched on this card is completely ignored by the compiler but appears in the listing of the program. Some explanation or other may be punched on a comment card describing the logic of a particularly difficult section

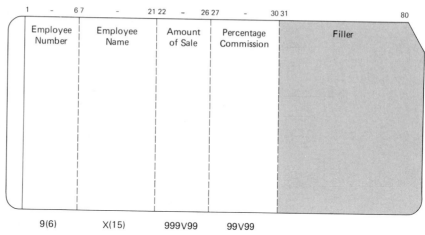

FIGURE 15

of a program, thereby making it easier for the programmer (or his successor) to follow the program at some later date.

Incidentally, if, as has been done several times in Program 19, a data name exceeds the permissible 30 characters, the compiler prints out a message to the effect that it has truncated the name to 30 characters. The exact diagnostic printed by the system is

WORD OR PICTURE EXCEEDS 30 CHARACTERS TRUNCATED TO 30 CHARACTERS

Since no other data name in the program has the same first 30 characters, no harm results from this minor violation. The advantages gained in retaining completely explicit and unabbreviated names like

```
        GRAND-TOTAL-NUMBER-OF-SALES-OUT
and     GRAND-TOTAL-AMOUNT-OF-SALES-OUT
```

far outweighs the disadvantages.

10.7 A MODIFIED COMMISSIONS REPORT

In the previous program we dealt with a COBOL program in which a file is composed of records with different formats. For the purpose of presenting further new features of the COBOL repertoire, we shall now modify Program 19. The input data to the modified program contains similar information punched in the format shown in Figure 15.

We have often made the point that a great deal of COBOL programming effort is devoted to the printing of a report for a given business situation.

It has also been pointed out that when printing a report it is always a good idea to take pains to make the output look elegant so that it is esthetically pleasing to read. With these aims in mind, our commissions report will now be modified to accomplish the following additional tasks:

1. To instruct the printer attached to the computer to go to the top of a new page at an appropriate point in the program.
2. To paginate each page in a report, that is, to number each page consecutively beginning at 1.
3. To print an attractive report heading on the first page of the report.
4. To print an identical caption known as a page heading at the top of each page of the report.
5. Whenever there is a change in employee number in the data cards, indicating the conclusion of a particular data set and the start of a new one, the total sales and total commissions for the particular salesman is printed underneath the regular detail lines and preparation made for the printing and summing of these sales for the next employee number. This information is spoken of in COBOL jargon as *control footings* and *control headings*. Since this action is triggered by a change in employee number, the employee number is known as a *control switch*.
6. At the end of the report we shall print the grand total number of sales, the grand totals for sales volume and the grand total commissions to be paid.

10.7.1 The SPECIAL–NAMES Option

The COBOL programmer is able to control the movement of paper through the printer by means of a paragraph name called SPECIAL–NAMES, which appears in the Environment Division after SOURCE–COMPUTER. Inside the printer is a carriage tape which is divided into various channels. When channel 01 is activated, the printer automatically brings the next new page into the print area so that any printing that is executed appears on the top line of the new page. In order to invoke channel 01 the abbreviation C01 (C-zero-1, not C-Oh-1) is associated with a data name indicating the top of a page. For example, TOP–OF–PAGE would be an ideal selection as would NEW–PAGE, FRESH–PAGE, NEXT–PAGE, and so on. Whatever mnemonic name is selected is associated with C01 in the SPECIAL–NAMES Paragraph according to the following generalized formats.

```
SPECIAL-NAMES. C01 IS data-name-for-new-page
```

The following are therefore valid:

```
SPECIAL-NAMES. C01 IS TOP-OF-PAGE.
SPECIAL-NAMES. C01 IS NEW-PAGE.
SPECIAL-NAMES. C01 IS NEXT-PAGE.
```

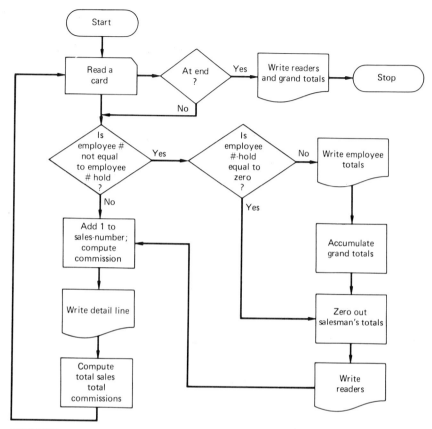

FIGURE 16

The name selected is then used in a WRITE statement using the ADVANCING option. For example,

```
WRITE RECORD-1 AFTER ADVANCING TOP-OF-PAGE.
```

This advances the output sheets to the top of a new page, then writes the appropriate record.

Now that we know how to signal the printer to go to the top of a new page, we have the ability to keep a running counter for the number of pages being printed. All this means is that we initialize some suitable data name to an appropriate value. In the program we have given the name PAGE-KOUNTER to the page counter. The reason why it is spelled this way is that PAGE-COUNTER is a reserved word. Each time a new page is activated, 1 is added to the page counter. The printing of the report heading on the first page of the report and the printing of the identical headings on each subsequent page are under the control of the logic of the program.

To assist the reader to follow the logic of this program, which admittedly requires considerable concentration, the flowchart in Figure 16 illustrates in schematic form the control of flow through the program.

INPUT TO PROGRAM 20

```
666666JEFFREY KARP      800000100
666666JEFFREY KARP      770000600
666666JEFFREY KARP      002000300
666666JEFFREY KARP      500000300
123123WALTER GEISLER    650000200
123123WALTER GEISLER    440000500
552211MARGIE BRAND      453250020
552211MARGIE BRAND      250000500
552211MARGIE BRAND      030000500
654456ANDREA ROSS       300000100
654456ANDREA ROSS       025000100
654456ANDREA ROSS       660000400
654456ANDREA ROSS       745000200
654456ANDREA ROSS       650000300
232323ALINA CHU         640000200
232323ALINA CHU         520000325
232323ALINA CHU         552000350
232323ALINA CHU         250000700
232323ALINA CHU         600000210
252525GUY LAUWERS       784001600
252525GUY LAUWERS       098000400
252525GUY LAUWERS       572002200
252525GUY LAUWERS       001000100
```

PROGRAM 20
Modified Commissions Report

```
00001          IDENTIFICATION DIVISION.
00002          PROGRAM-ID.  MODIFIED COMMISSIONS.
00003
00004          ENVIRONMENT DIVISION.
00005          CONFIGURATION SECTION.
00006          SOURCE-COMPUTER. IBM-370-145.
00007          OBJECT-COMPUTER. IBM-370-145.
00008          SPECIAL-NAMES.
00009               C01 IS NEW-PAGE.
00010          INPUT-OUTPUT SECTION.
00011          FILE-CONTROL.
00012               SELECT IN-FILE ASSIGN TO UT-S-READER.
00013               SELECT OUT-FILE ASSIGN TO UT-S-PRINTER.
00014
00015          DATA DIVISION.
00016
00017          FILE SECTION.
00018          FD  IN-FILE
00019               LABEL RECORDS ARE OMITTED.
00020
00021          01  SALES-CARD.
00022               05  EMPLOYEE-NUMBER PICTURE 9(6).
00023               05  EMPLOYEE-NAME PICTURE X(15).
00024               05  AMOUNT-OF-SALE PICTURE 999V99.
00025               05  PERCENTAGE-COMMISSION PICTURE 99V99.
00026               05  FILLER PICTURE X(50).
00027
00028          FD  OUT-FILE
00029               LABEL RECORDS ARE OMITTED.
00030
00031          01  PRINT-LINE-RECORD.
00032               05  CARRIAGE-CONTROL PICTURE X(1).
00033               05  PRINT-LINE PICTURE X(132).
00034
00035          WORKING-STORAGE SECTION.
00036
00037          77  PAGE-KOUNTER PICTURE 9999 VALUE 1.
00038          77  EMPLOYEE-NUMBER-HOLD PICTURE 9(6).
00039          77  SALES-NUMBER PICTURE 99.
00040          77  AMOUNT-OF-COMMISSION PICTURE 999V99.
00041
00042          01  TOTALS.
00043               05  TOTAL-COMMISSIONS PICTURE 9(6)V99.
00044               05  TOTAL-AMOUNT-OF-SALES PICTURE 9(6)V99.
```

```
00045
00046          01  GRAND-TOTALS.
00047              05 GRAND-TOTAL-NUMBER-OF-SALES PICTURE 9(4) VALUE ZERO.
00048              05 GRAND-TOTAL-AMOUNT-OF-SALES PICTURE 9(8)V99 VALUE ZERO.
00049              05  GRAND-TOTAL-COMMISSIONS PICTURE 9(8)V99 VALUE ZERO.
00050
00051          01  HEADER-1.
00052              05  FILLER          PICTURE X(32) VALUE SPACES.
00053              05  FILLER PICTURE X(33) VALUE
00054                  'COMMISSION      REPORT'.
00055              05  FILLER PICTURE X(25) VALUE SPACES.
00056              05   FILLER PICTURE X(6) VALUE 'PAGE  '.
00057              05  PAGE-KOUNTER-OUT PICTURE Z9.
00058              05  FILLER PICTURE X(35) VALUE SPACES.
00059
00060          01  HEADER-2.
00061              05  FILLER          PICTURE X(32) VALUE SPACES.
00062              05  FILLER          PICTURE X(33) VALUE ALL '*'.
00063              05  FILLER          PICTURE X(68) VALUE SPACES.
00064
00065          01  HEADER-3.
00066              05  FILLER          PICTURE X(4) VALUE SPACES.
00067              05  FILLER          PICTURE X(8) VALUE 'EMPLOYEE'.
00068              05  FILLER          PICTURE X(6) VALUE SPACES.
00069              05  FILLER          PICTURE X(8) VALUE 'NAME  OF'.
00070              05  FILLER          PICTURE X(15) VALUE SPACES.
00071              05  FILLER          PICTURE X(4) VALUE 'SALE'.
00072              05  FILLER          PICTURE X(7) VALUE SPACES.
00073              05  FILLER          PICTURE X(9) VALUE 'AMOUNT OF'.
00074              05  FILLER          PICTURE X(4) VALUE SPACES.
00075              05  FILLER          PICTURE X(10) VALUE 'PERCENTAGE'.
00076              05  FILLER          PICTURE X(3) VALUE SPACES.
00077              05  FILLER          PICTURE X(10) VALUE 'AMOUNT  OF'.
00078              05  FILLER          PICTURE X(45) VALUE SPACES.
00079
00080          01  HEADER-4.
00081              05  FILLER          PICTURE X(05) VALUE SPACES.
00082              05  FILLER PICTURE X(06) VALUE 'NUMBER'.
00083              05  FILLER PICTURE X(07) VALUE SPACES.
00084              05  FILLER PICTURE X(08) VALUE 'SALESMAN'.
00085              05  FILLER PICTURE X(14) VALUE SPACES.
00086              05  FILLER PICTURE X(06) VALUE 'NUMBER'.
00087              05  FILLER PICTURE X(08) VALUE SPACES.
00088              05  FILLER PICTURE X(05) VALUE 'SALES'.
00089              05  FILLER PICTURE X(06) VALUE SPACES.
00090              05  FILLER PICTURE X(10) VALUE 'COMMISSION'.
00091              05  FILLER PICTURE X(03) VALUE SPACES.
00092              05  FILLER PICTURE X(10) VALUE 'COMMISSION'.
00093              05  FILLER          PICTURE X(45) VALUE SPACES.
00094
00095          01  HEADER-5.
00096              05  FILLER PICTURE X(04) VALUE SPACES.
00097              05  FILLER          PICTURE X(84) VALUE ALL '*'.
00098              05  FILLER          PICTURE X(45) VALUE SPACES.
00099
00100          01  DETAIL-LINE-1.
00101              05  FILLER PICTURE X(6) VALUE SPACES.
00102              05  EMPLOYEE-NUMBER-OUT PICTURE 9(6) BLANK WHEN ZERO.
00103              05  FILLER PICTURE X(5) VALUE SPACES.
00104              05  EMPLOYEE-NAME-OUT PICTURE X(15).
00105              05  FILLER PICTURE X(12) VALUE SPACES.
00106              05  SALES-NUMBER-OUT PICTURE Z9.
00107              05  FILLER PICTURE X(6) VALUE SPACES.
00108              05  AMOUNT-OF-SALE-OUT      PICTURE $$$$.99.
00109              05  FILLER PICTURE X(10) VALUE SPACES.
00110              05  PERCENTAGE-COMMISSION-OUT PICTURE ZZ.99.
00111              05  FILLER PICTURE X(1) VALUE '%'.
00112              05  FILLER PICTURE X(6) VALUE SPACES.
00113              05  AMOUNT-OF-COMMISSION-OUT PICTURE $$$.99.
00114              05  FILLER PICTURE X(20) VALUE SPACES.
00115
00116          01  DETAIL-LINE-2.
00117              05  FILLER PICTURE X(30) VALUE SPACES.
00118              05  FILLER PICTURE X(06) VALUE 'TOTALS'.
00119              05  FILLER PICTURE X(14) VALUE ALL '.'.
00120              05  TOTAL-AMOUNT-OF-SALES-OUT  PICTURE $$$$,$$$.
00121              05  FILLER PICTURE X(18) VALUE SPACES.
00122              05  TOTAL-COMMISSIONS-OUT PICTURE $$$$,$$$.99.
00123              05  FILLER PICTURE X(46) VALUE SPACES.
00124          01  DETAIL-LINE-3.
00125              05 FILLER PICTURE X(22) VALUE SPACES.
00126              05 FILLER PICTURE X(27) VALUE 'GRAND TOTAL NUMBER OF SALES'.
00127              05 FILLER PICTURE X(11) VALUE SPACES.
```

```
00128           05  GRAND-TOTAL-NUMBER-OF-SALES-OUT PICTURE ZZZ9.
00129           05  FILLER PICTURE X(69) VALUE SPACES.
C0130
00131       01  DETAIL-LINE-4.
00132           05  FILLER PICTURE X(22) VALUE SPACES.
00133           05  FILLER PICTURE X(27) VALUE 'GRAND TOTAL AMOUNT OF SALES'.
00134           05  FILLER PICTURE X(04) VALUE SPACES.
00135           05  GRAND-TOTAL-AMOUNT-OF-SALES-OUT PICTURE $$$,$$$,$$$.
C0136           05  FILLER PICTURE X(69) VALUE SPACES.
00137
00138       01  DETAIL-LINE-5.
00139           05  FILLER PICTURE X(22) VALUE SPACES.
00140           05  FILLER PICTURE X(23) VALUE 'GRAND TOTAL COMMISSIONS'.
00141           05  FILLER PICTURE X(08) VALUE SPACES.
00142           05  GRAND-TOTAL-COMMISSIONS-OUT PICTURE $$$,$$$,$$$.
00143           05  FILLER PICTURE X(69) VALUE SPACES.
00144
00145       01  REPORT-HEADING-1.
00146           05  FILLER PICTURE X(75) VALUE SPACES.
00147           05  FILLER PICTURE X(5) VALUE 'PAGE'.
00148           05  FILLER PICTURE 99     VALUE 1.
00149           05  FILLER PICTURE X(51) VALUE SPACES.
CC150
00151       01  REPORT-HEADING-2.
00152           05  FILLER PICTURE X(30) VALUE SPACES.
00153           05  FILLER PICTURE X(30) VALUE
00154               'MULLGHAN MANUFACTURING COMPANY'.
00155           05  FILLER PICTURE X(73) VALUE SPACES.
C0156
00157       01  REPORT-HEADING-3.
C0158           05  FILLER PICTURE X(32) VALUE SPACES.
00159           05  FILLER PICTURE X(25) VALUE
00160               'MONTHLY COMMISSION REPORT'.
00161           05  FILLER PICTURE X(76) VALUE SPACES.
00162
00163       01  REPORT-HEADING-4.
00164           05  FILLER PICTURE X(38) VALUE SPACES.
00165           05  FILLER PICTURE X(07) VALUE 'AS OF
00166           05  CURRENT-DATE-OUT  PICTURE X(8).
C0166           05  FILLER PICTURE X(80) VALUE SPACES.
00167
00168
00169       01  REPORT-HEADING-5.
00170           05  FILLER PICTURE X(42) VALUE SPACES.
00171           05  FILLER PICTURE X(09) VALUE ALL '*'.
00172           05  FILLER PICTURE X(82) VALUE SPACES.
C0173
CC174       01  REPORT-HEADING-6.
00175           05  FILLER PICTURE X(43) VALUE SPACES.
00176           05  FILLER PICTURE X(07) VALUE ALL '*'.
00177           05  FILLER PICTURE X(83) VALUE SPACES.
CC178
00179       01  REPORT-HEADING-7.
C0180           05  FILLER PICTURE X(44) VALUE SPACES.
00181           05  FILLER PICTURE X(05) VALUE ALL '*'.
00182           05  FILLER PICTURE X(84) VALUE SPACES.
C0183
00184       01  REPORT-HEADING-8.
00185           05  FILLER PICTURE X(45) VALUE SPACES.
00186           05  FILLER PICTURE X(03) VALUE ALL '*'.
00187           05  FILLER PICTURE X(85) VALUE SPACES.
0C188
00189       01  REPORT-HEADING-9.
C0190           05  FILLER PICTURE X(46) VALUE SPACES.
00191           05  FILLER PICTURE X(01) VALUE ALL '*'.
00192           05  FILLER PICTURE X(86) VALUE SPACES.
00193
00194       PROCEDURE DIVISION.
CC195       OPEN-FILES.
00196           OPEN INPUT IN-FILE, OUTPUT OUT-FILE.
00197           MOVE ZERO TO EMPLOYEE-NUMBER-HOLD.
C0198
00199       PRINT-REPORT-HEADINGS.
C0200           MOVE CURRENT-DATE TO CURRENT-DATE-OUT.
00201           WRITE PRINT-LINE-RECORD FROM REPORT-HEADING-1 AFTER ADVANCING
00202               NEW-PAGE.
0U203           WRITE PRINT-LINE-RECORD FROM REPORT-HEADING-2 AFTER ADVANCING
00204               20 LINES.
00205           WRITE PRINT-LINE-RECORD FROM REPORT-HEADING-3 AFTER ADVANCING
00206               03 LINES.
00207           WRITE PRINT-LINE-RECORD FROM REPORT-HEADING-4 AFTER ADVANCING
C0208               03 LINES.
00209           WRITE PRINT-LINE-RECORD FROM REPORT-HEADING-5 AFTER ADVANCING
CC210               03 LINES.
00211           WRITE PRINT-LINE-RECORD FROM REPORT-HEADING-6 AFTER ADVANCING
00212               01 LINES.
```

```
00213              WRITE PRINT-LINE-RECORD FROM REPORT-HEADING-7 AFTER ADVANCING
00214                   01 LINES.
00215              WRITE PRINT-LINE-RECORD FROM REPORT-HEADING-8 AFTER ADVANCING
00216                   01 LINES.
00217              WRITE PRINT-LINE-RECORD FROM REPORT-HEADING-9 AFTER ADVANCING
00218                   01 LINES.
00219
00220          READ-SALES-CARD.
00221              READ IN-FILE AT END
00222                   PERFORM WRITE-TOTALS THRU ACCUMULATE-GRAND-TOTALS,
00223                   GO TO PRINT-GRAND-TOTALS.
00224              IF EMPLOYEE-NUMBER NOT EQUAL EMPLOYEE-NUMBER-HOLD THEN
00225                   PERFORM WRITE-TOTALS THRU WRITE-HEADINGS
00226                   MOVE EMPLOYEE-NAME TO EMPLOYEE-NAME-OUT
00227                   MOVE EMPLOYEE-NUMBER TO EMPLOYEE-NUMBER-OUT,
00228                        EMPLOYEE-NUMBER-HOLD.
00229              ADD 1 TO SALES-NUMBER.
00230              MOVE SALES-NUMBER TO SALES-NUMBER-OUT.
00231              MOVE AMOUNT-OF-SALE TO AMOUNT-OF-SALE-OUT.
00232              MOVE PERCENTAGE-COMMISSION TO PERCENTAGE-COMMISSION-OUT.
00233              COMPUTE AMOUNT-OF-COMMISSION ROUNDED = AMOUNT-OF-SALE / 100
00234                   * PERCENTAGE-COMMISSION.
00235              MOVE AMOUNT-OF-COMMISSION TO AMOUNT-OF-COMMISSION-OUT.
00236              WRITE PRINT-LINE-RECORD FROM DETAIL-LINE-1 AFTER ADVANCING
00237                   3 LINES.
00238              MOVE SPACES TO EMPLOYEE-NAME-OUT.
00239              MOVE ZEROES TO EMPLOYEE-NUMBER-OUT.
00240
00241          ACCUMULATE-TOTALS.
00242              ADD AMOUNT-OF-SALE TO TOTAL-AMOUNT-OF-SALES.
00243              ADD AMOUNT-OF-COMMISSION TO TOTAL-COMMISSIONS.
00244              GO TO READ-SALES-CARD.
00245
00246          WRITE-TOTALS.
00247              IF EMPLOYEE-NUMBER-HOLD EQUAL ZERO THEN
00248                   GO TO INITIALIZE-TOTALS.
00249              MOVE TOTAL-AMOUNT-OF-SALES TO TOTAL-AMOUNT-OF-SALES-OUT.
00250              MOVE TOTAL-COMMISSIONS TO TOTAL-COMMISSIONS-OUT.
00251              WRITE PRINT-LINE-RECORD FROM DETAIL-LINE-2 AFTER ADVANCING
00252                   5 LINES.
00253
00254          ACCUMULATE-GRAND-TOTALS.
00255              ADD TOTAL-AMOUNT-OF-SALES TO GRAND-TOTAL-AMOUNT-OF-SALES.
00256              ADD TOTAL-COMMISSIONS TO GRAND-TOTAL-COMMISSIONS.
00257              ADD SALES-NUMBER TO GRAND-TOTAL-NUMBER-OF-SALES.
00258
00259          INITIALIZE-TOTALS.
00260              MOVE ZEROES TO TOTALS, SALES-NUMBER.
00261
00262          WRITE-HEADINGS.
00263              ADD 1 TO PAGE-KOUNTER.
00264              MOVE PAGE-KOUNTER TO PAGE-KOUNTER-OUT.
00265              WRITE PRINT-LINE-RECORD FROM HEADER-1 AFTER ADVANCING
00266                   NEW-PAGE.
00267              WRITE PRINT-LINE-RECORD FROM HEADER-2 AFTER ADVANCING
00268                   1 LINES.
00269              WRITE PRINT-LINE-RECORD FROM HEADER-3 AFTER ADVANCING
00270                   3 LINES.
00271              WRITE PRINT-LINE-RECORD FROM HEADER-4 AFTER ADVANCING
00272                   1 LINES.
00273              WRITE PRINT-LINE-RECORD FROM HEADER-5 AFTER ADVANCING
00274                   1 LINES.
00275
00276          PRINT-GRAND-TOTALS.
00277              ADD 1 TO PAGE-KOUNTER.
00278              MOVE PAGE-KOUNTER TO PAGE-KOUNTER-OUT.
00279              WRITE PRINT-LINE-RECORD FROM HEADER-1 AFTER ADVANCING
00280                   NEW-PAGE.
00281              WRITE PRINT-LINE-RECORD FROM HEADER-2 AFTER ADVANCING
00282                   1 LINES.
00283              MOVE GRAND-TOTAL-NUMBER-OF-SALES TO
00284                   GRAND-TOTAL-NUMBER-OF-SALES-OUT.
00285              MOVE GRAND-TOTAL-AMOUNT-OF-SALES TO
00286                   GRAND-TOTAL-AMOUNT-OF-SALES-OUT.
00287              MOVE GRAND-TOTAL-COMMISSIONS TO GRAND-TOTAL-COMMISSIONS-OUT.
00288              WRITE PRINT-LINE-RECORD FROM DETAIL-LINE-3 AFTER ADVANCING
00289                   25 LINES.
00290              WRITE PRINT-LINE-RECORD FROM DETAIL-LINE-4 AFTER ADVANCING
00291                   3 LINES.
00292              WRITE PRINT-LINE-RECORD FROM DETAIL-LINE-5 AFTER ADVANCING
00293                   3 LINES.
00294
00295          END-OF-JOB.
00296              CLOSE IN-FILE, OUT-FILE.
00297              STOP RUN.
```

OUTPUT TO PROGRAM 20

MULLCHAN MANUFACTURING COMPANY   PAGE 01

MONTHLY COMMISSION REPORT

AS OF   06/20/77

COMMISSION   REPORT   PAGE   2
****

EMPLOYEE NUMBER	NAME OF SALESMAN	SALE NUMBER	AMOUNT OF SALES	PERCENTAGE COMMISSION	AMOUNT OF COMMISSION
666666	JEFFREY KARP	1	$800.00	1.00%	$8.00
		2	$770.00	6.00%	$46.20
		3	$2.00	3.00%	$0.06
		4	$500.00	3.00%	$15.00
		TOTALS.............	$2,072		$69.26

COMMISSION   REPORT   PAGE   3
****

EMPLOYEE NUMBER	NAME OF SALESMAN	SALE NUMBER	AMOUNT OF SALES	PERCENTAGE COMMISSION	AMOUNT OF COMMISSION
123123	WALTER GEISLER	1	$650.00	2.00%	$13.00
		2	$440.00	5.00%	$22.00
		TOTALS.............	$1,090		$35.00

COMMISSION   REPORT   PAGE   4
****

EMPLOYEE NUMBER	NAME OF SALESMAN	SALE NUMBER	AMOUNT OF SALES	PERCENTAGE COMMISSION	AMOUNT OF COMMISSION
552211	MARGIE BRAND	1	$453.25	.20%	$0.91
		2	$250.00	5.00%	$12.50
		3	$30.00	5.00%	$1.50
		TOTALS.............	$733		$14.91

EMPLOYEE NUMBER	NAME OF SALESMAN	SALE NUMBER	AMOUNT OF SALES	PERCENTAGE COMMISSION	AMOUNT OF COMMISSION
654456	ANDREA ROSS	1	$300.00	1.00%	$3.00
		2	$25.00	1.00%	$0.25
		3	$600.00	4.00%	$24.00
		4	$745.00	2.00%	$14.90
		5	$650.00	3.00%	$19.50
	TOTALS...............		$2,320		$61.65

EMPLOYEE NUMBER	NAME OF SALESMAN	SALE NUMBER	AMOUNT OF SALES	PERCENTAGE COMMISSION	AMOUNT OF COMMISSION
232323	ALINA CHU	1	$640.00	2.00%	$12.80
		2	$520.00	3.25%	$16.90
		3	$552.00	3.50%	$19.32
		4	$250.00	7.00%	$17.50
		5	$600.00	2.10%	$12.60
	TOTALS...............		$2,562		$79.12

EMPLOYEE NUMBER	NAME OF SALESMAN	SALE NUMBER	AMOUNT OF SALES	PERCENTAGE COMMISSION	AMOUNT OF COMMISSION
252525	GUY LAUWERS	1	$784.00	16.00%	$125.44
		2	$98.00	4.00%	$3.92
		3	$572.00	22.00%	$125.84
		4	$1.00	1.00%	$0.01
	TOTALS...............		$1,455		$255.21

```
              C O M M I S S I O N   R E P O R T                    PAGE   8
              *******************************

GRAND TOTAL NUMBER OF SALES           23

GRAND TOTAL AMOUNT OF SALES       $10,232

GRAND TOTAL COMMISSIONS             $515
```

COBB OL MYSTERY #8

The world-famous detective was just about to start the main course at the testimonial dinner when the waiter informed him of an important phone call. Cobb went to the phone.

"Hello, this is Ol," said the detective.

"This is Mr. Chip," said the voice on the other end of the line. "I'm from the Calco Electronic Calculator Company. We need your help, Mr. Ol. The computer which controls all our assembly line operations refuses to function. This breakdown is holding up all production. If you can't help us, we will soon be way behind on meeting the orders for our new calculator model."

"I'll be there shortly," answered Cobb.

"It's late, so why don't you meet me in the machine room," said Chip.

"That's perfectly satisfactory."

The detective asked the waiter to have his Bentley brought to the front.

The machine room at the Calco factory was extremely quiet.

"Good evening, Mr. Ol. I'm glad to meet you. I'm Mr. Chip."

"How do you do, Mr. Chip," politely replied Ol. "I'd like to see a listing of the program, if you please."

"Oh, certainly," mumbled Mr. Chip as he hurried away.

"Here is the listing, sir. I can't figure out what is wrong. This new program cost the company $25,000 to write."

"The error will probably be easily detected," replied Cobb quietly as he perused the pages. "Mr. Chip, do you know COBOL?"

"No, sir, I don't."

"I'm glad of that because any elementary COBOL student could have detected this error. This PERFORM statement is incorrect:

```
PERFORM STEP1 THRU STEP4 UNTIL FINISHED."
```

"That looks innocent enough to me," said Chip.

"Ah, but when the UNTIL clause is included in a PERFORM statement, it *must* be followed by a conditional clause such as A = B," explained the detective.

"Oh, I see; even though the word FINISHED looks correct, it really is meaningless to the computer. Right?" asked Chip.

"Very good," said the detective.

"That's exactly right. Of course, if the word FINISHED had been defined as an 88 level condition name, the statement might indeed have been valid.

"Thanks very much" said Chip," I don't know what I would have done without you. I'll have one of the new calculators sent to you, compliments of our company."

"You're most welcome, Mr. Chip, I'll have my bill sent to you, compliments of my office," said Cobb. "Now if you'll excuse me, I would like to return to my dessert."

As the world-famous detective left the factory, he brushed some dust off the sleeve of his tuxedo.

10.8 REVIEW QUESTIONS AND EXERCISES

1. Referring to the murder problem (Program 14) assume that the first two letters of the car manufacturer's name are punched in columns 7 and 8 of the data cards. For example, CH could stand for Chevrolet, FO for Ford, PO for Pontiac, and so on. Assume also that another witness has been found who remembers the make of the escape vehicle. Rewrite the program to take advantage of this additional information, again printing out all the relevant information including the percentage of suspects.

2. Assume a deck of 80-column student registration cards is punched with the student name, ID number, address, and the number of credits to be taken in the forthcoming semester. Select any columns you desire for the individual fields. Write a program that will print, for the benefit of the college bursar, the tuition costs for each student and the total tuition for all students.

   If the student registers for less than 12 credits, he or she is charged $100 per credit. If the student takes between 12 and 18 credits, the charge is a flat fee of $1500. For more than 18 credits, the student is charged the flat fee of $1500 plus $100 for every credit over 18.

3. A salesman employed by the McKay T-Shirt Company sells three types of T-shirts only:
   (a) plain white at $2.95 a shirt
   (b) imprinted with the name in black at $3.95 a shirt.
   (c) imprinted with the name in color at $5.95 a shirt.
   Assume that a card for each sale is punched as follows:

   columns 1–20: salesman's name

   column 25: type of shirt sold (1, 2, or 3 as detailed above)

   columns 30–33: number of shirts sold

   The salesman earns 5% commission on every shirt of type 1, 9% on every shirt of type 2, and 15% on every shirt of type 3. Write a program that prints and calculates:
   (a) a report of all the transactions
   (b) the commission for each sale
   (c) the gross amount for each sale
   (d) the total commission for each salesman
   (e) The grand total of sales
   (f) the grand total commission.
   It may be assumed that all the data cards are sorted by salesman's name.

4. Write a COBOL program to process a monthly payroll. There is an input file and an output file. The cards in the input file are punched as follows:

col 1–25	employee name
26–29	blank
30–33	hours worked 999V9
34–35	blank
36–39	rate of pay per hour 99V99
40–80	bank

   The program should print out
   (a) a count of the cards
   (b) employee name
   (c) gross pay (hours worked times rate)

(d) Social Security tax (0.0585 times gross pay)

(e) net pay (gross pay less tax).

   If a net pay exceeds $1000.00, print out 10 asterisks alongside the line so that it can be checked for accuracy. Each output field must be edited as necessary. Use all the options you know, but do not concern yourself with elaborate cosmetics.

5. Assume the following two records that contain identical names.

```
01   CLUB–MEMBER.
        NAME–OF–MEMBER          PICTURE X(25).
        ADDRESS–OF–MEMBER       PICTURE X(50).
        MEMBERSHIP–NUMBER       PICTURE 9(5).

01   GALA–INVITATION.
        NAME–OF–MEMBER          PICTURE X(20).
        ADDRESS–OF–MEMBER       PICTURE X(55).
        MEMBERSHIP–NUMBER       PICTURE 9(5).
```

   Which of the following MOVE instructions is invalid? State your reason in each case.

(a) MOVE NAME–OF–MEMBER OF CLUB–MEMBER TO NAME–OF–MEMBER OF GALA–INVITATION.

(b) MOVE NAME–OF–MEMBER IN CLUB–MEMBER TO NAME–OF–MEMBER OF GALA–INVITATION.

(c) MOVE SPACES TO ADDRESS–OF–MEMBER.

(d) MOVE MEMBERSHIP–NUMBER TO MEMBERSHIP–NUMBER OF GALA-INVI-TATION.

(e) MOVE ZERO TO MEMBERSHIP–NUMBER OF CLUB–MEMBER.

6. For a series of special courses given by a leading university, attendance is recorded by punching a card for each student for every meeting of the class. The card is punched by columns as follows:

```
1–20    name
  25    attendance code (A = Absent
                         P = Present
                         E = excused)
28–31   course number
  80    section number
```

   List all the cards, printing the course number and section number once only each time there is a change either in the course number or the class number. Be sure that only attendance codes A, P, and E are used. At the end of the job, beginning on a new page, print the grand total absent, grand total present, the grand total excused, followed by the grand total listed, and the grand total of errors punched in column 25.

7. The input deck for a factory's payroll is punched as follows:

```
1–5     department number
10–18   Social Security number
20–24   rate per hour 99V999
31–34   hours worked (straight time) 99V99
41–44   hours worked (at time and a half) 99V99
```

Write a program which prints the department number, Social Security number, rate per hour, straight hours worked, straight pay, overtime hours worked, overtime pay, and gross pay. Appropriate headings including the current date should be provided.

There should be a totals line showing the totals for straight time, straight pay, overtime, overtime pay, and gross pay.

To impress your teacher with your proficiency, you may wish to print subtotals for each department.

8. Sloppy Sam wanted to amuse himself by writing a short COBOL program that appears below to sum all the integers from 1 to 10. He made sure that all his data names were correctly defined. From his knowledge of mathematics he was convinced that the sum of the integers from 1 to 10 was 55. For some unexplained reason, however, he could not get the computer to confirm this result. Like most novices, he suspected at first that the computer had made an error. What, in fact, is the reason for the incorrect result?

```
MOVE ZERO TO TOTAL.
PERFORM PARA-1 VARYING POINTER
    FROM 1 BY 1 UNTIL
    POINTER > 10.


PARA-1.     ADD POINTER TO TOTAL.
```

9. Suppose that the Procedure Division of a program consists of three paragraphs named PARA–A, PARA–B and PARA–C respectively. Write the correct PERFORM instructions to process:
   (a) PARA–A once only
   (b) PARA–A six times
   (c) PARA–A, PARA–B and PARA–C once only in sequence
   (d) PARA–A twice and PARA–C four times.

10. Write a COBOL program using the PERFORM . . . VARYING . . . UNTIL version of PERFORM to print the following output:

```
6 BOTTLES OF BEER ON THE WALL,
6 BOTTLES OF BEER,
  IF ONE OF THE BOTTLES SHOULD HAPPEN TO FALL,
5 BOTTLES OF BEER ON THE WALL.

5 BOTTLES OF BEER ON THE WALL,
5 BOTTLES OF BEER,
  IF ONE OF THE BOTTLES SHOULD HAPPEN TO FALL,
4 BOTTLES OF BEER ON THE WALL.

4 BOTTLES OF BEER ON THE WALL,
4 BOTTLES OF BEER,
  IF ONE OF THE BOTTLES SHOULD HAPPEN TO FALL,
3 BOTTLES OF BEER ON THE WALL.

3 BOTTLES OF BEER ON THE WALL,
3 BOTTLES OF BEER,
  IF ONE OF THE BOTTLES SHOULD HAPPEN TO FALL,
2 BOTTLES OF BEER ON THE WALL.

2 BOTTLES OF BEER ON THE WALL,
2 BOTTLES OF BEER,
  IF ONE OF THE BOTTLES SHOULD HAPPEN TO FALL,
1 BOTTLES OF BEER ON THE WALL.

1 BOTTLES OF BEER ON THE WALL,
1 BOTTLES OF BEER,
  IF ONE OF THE BOTTLES SHOULD HAPPEN TO FALL,
0 BOTTLES OF BEER ON THE WALL.
```

REPORT WRITER FEATURE

In Chapter 10 we saw how writing a report can make for a somewhat lengthy Procedure Division. Depending upon the depth of detail required, the logic can become quite complicated. Since the writing of reports plays such a major role in business data processing, ANSI COBOL provides us with a special module known as the Report Writer Feature. This gives us the ability to print a heading to a report, a page heading at the top of each page, detail lines of various kinds—the major substance of the report, page footings at the bottom of each page of the report, footings for subtotals and totals, and, finally, a report footing for the conclusion of the report.

Some COBOL programmers are repeatedly asked to program a report for a great number of purposes. For those programmers the Report Writer feature will be of particular interest since it relieves the programmer of a great deal of housekeeping chores. In Report Writer the programmer is given the opportunity to describe the physical appearance of a report rather than having to specify the precise, detailed procedures which otherwise would be necessary to produce that report. As a result the amount of coding in the Procedure Division is radically reduced and the task made that much easier.

As is usual in life, one doesn't get something for nothing. If advantage is to be taken of the Report Writer Feature, a certain amount of effort must be expended in learning the rules regarding it. It is true that when seen for the first time, the amount of detail that has to be absorbed and correctly implemented looks complicated and possibly overwhelming. The way it is often presented gives the impression that however effective a tool the Report Writer might be, it certainly isn't worth the learning. This is simply not so. It does require a certain amount of strict attention

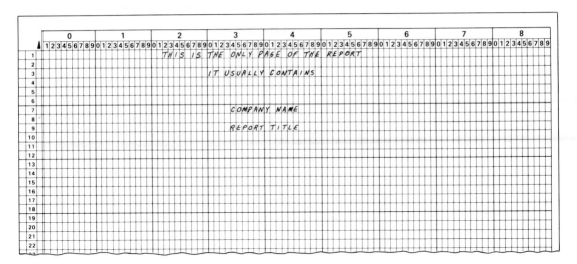

FIGURE 17 **The Format of the Report**

to detail but, for that matter, what worthwhile doesn't? Once the Report Writer has been mastered, it can then be applied in all manner of reports, thereby easing the burden on the programmer to a considerable extent.

11.1 A ONE-PAGE REPORT

Rather than get involved in a complicated program, or at least a complicated *looking* program as our first illustration, we shall take an atypical example first, one which requires no computation and no input data. All Program 20 will do is to print in a predetermined manner a heading to a report. The design of the heading—the report heading—is first sketched out on a special format sheet called a *print layout form,* which is usually supplied by the manufacturer. A completed print layout form is presented here to show what we want to accomplish. One could easily write suitable Data and Procedure Division instructions to produce this output without resorting to the Report Writer feature, but the point is how do we do it by *using* the Report Writer.

When the Report Writer is used all reports are automatically started at the top of a new page. Our task at the moment is to print a single page with a particular format. It is nothing more than a title page which begins on the top line of the new page. Specifically, we note that the first line which reads

    THIS IS THE ONLY PAGE OF THE REPORT

begins in column 22 and is composed of 35 alphabet characters. The next line of output which is

IT USUALLY CONTAINS

is a 19-alphabetic character literal which begins two lines after the previous printed line and commences in column 30. Then we come to the third line

COMPANY NAME

which is printed four lines after the previous one. The phrase begins in column 34 and consists of 12 alphabetic characters. Finally, two lines below the last line (which was written on line 7 of the chart), we print the 12-character alphabetic literal

REPORT TITLE

beginning in column 34, thus lining up directly with the printed line above it. This represents the conclusion of the output.

What we have outlined is the crux of the so-called Report Section, which must be included in any COBOL program utilizing the Report Writer feature. We shall now state some of the rules which apply to the Report Writer feature, and show how the detailed description fits into the general pattern.

1. A name must be selected for the report file. We have named it, expectedly, REPORT-FILE. Since this file is our output file, it is assigned to the printer in the SELECT clause and a file description—the usual FD—must be specified.

This file description differs from all those others we have encountered thus far in that on all previous occasions it was not necessary to include a REPORT IS clause. When using the Report Writer feature, however, this clause is mandatory. It is encumbent upon us now to give a name to the report. What better name could we choose than ONLY-PAGE? So the FD must include the clause

REPORT IS ONLY-PAGE

2. A new section must now be introduced. It is called the Report Section. It is a detailed description of the report. In the same way that a file description is specified by an FD level entry, so the report file description is specified by an RD level entry. Under this entry we can stipulate the maximum number of lines to be printed per page. It has arbitrarily been decided to limit the number of lines per page to 30. Furthermore, we may specify under the RD level entry the line number on which the heading is to appear. According to the print layout form, the heading is to begin on the top line of the page. All this information is stated in a most succinct form by the following:

```
REPORT SECTION.
RD   ONLY-PAGE
     PAGE LIMIT IS 30 LINES
     HEADING 1.
```

Analogous to the 01 level of an FD level entry is an 01 level for an RD level entry. A name is selected for the 01 level—in our case we choose COVER-PAGE. This is followed by a so-called TYPE clause. There are a variety of TYPE clauses, but the one we are interested in right now is the one called report heading, which may be specified by its abbreviation RH.

Subordinate to the 01 level we specify in terms of line number, column number, and line content the precise information we wish to print in the report. Referring to the print layout form and the description which immediately follows it, we describe the successive lines of the report in almost identical language. The first line, for example, is specified within the 01 level entry:

```
01 COVER-PAGE
   TYPE IS REPORT HEADING
   05 LINE NUMBER IS 1
      COLUMN NUMBER IS 22 PICTURE A (35)
      VALUE 'THIS IS THE ONLY PAGE OF THE REPORT'.
```

The second line is specified by the 05 level entry

```
05 LINE PLUS 2
   COLUMN 30 PICTURE A (19)
   VALUE 'IT USUALLY CONTAINS'.
```

This has the effect of printing the phrase 'IT USUALLY CONTAINS' on line 3, (plus two lines from the previous printed line). This is a *relative* way of specifying a line position, as opposed to the *direct* method.

The only portion of the program left to describe is the Procedure Division.

3. The output file is opened in the ordinary way. (This particular program does not have an input file).

4. The report specified in the FD and the RD entries must be activated by the INITIATE verb. It has the effect of initializing certain important counters provided by the Report Writer feature.

5. The report is generated internally by the GENERATE verb.

6. At the end of the job the processing of the report is completed by the TERMINATE verb. Although the TERMINATE instruction completes the processing of the report, it does not close the file. This must be done in the ordinary way.

Here is the complete program producing a single-page report (albeit an elementary one) generated by the Report Writer feature of COBOL.

PROGRAM 21
Report A

```
00001
00002          IDENTIFICATION DIVISION.
00003          PROGRAM-ID. REPORT-A.
00004          REMARKS. THIS THE FIRST ATTEMPT AT THE REPORT WRITER FEATURE.
00005          AUTHOR. ELI J.OPAS.
00006
00007          ENVIRONMENT DIVISION.
00008          CONFIGURATION SECTION.
00009          SOURCE-COMPUTER. IBM-370-145.
00010          OBJECT-COMPUTER. IBM-370-145.
00011          INPUT-OUTPUT SECTION.
00012          FILE-CONTROL.
00013              SELECT REPORT-FILE ASSIGN TO UT-S-PRINTER.
00014
00015          DATA DIVISION.
00016          FILE SECTION.
00017          FD  REPORT-FILE
00018              LABEL RECORDS ARE OMITTED
00019              REPORT IS ONLY-PAGE.
00020
00021          REPORT SECTION.
00022          RD  ONLY-PAGE
00023              PAGE LIMIT IS 30 LINES
00024              HEADING 1.
00025
00026          01  COVER-PAGE
00027              TYPE IS REPORT HEADING.
00028              05  LINE NUMBER IS 1
00029                  COLUMN NUMBER IS 22 PICTURE A(35)
00030                  VALUE 'THIS IS THE ONLY PAGE OF THE REPORT'.
00031              05  LINE PLUS 2
00032                  COLUMN 30 PICTURE A(15)
00033                  VALUE 'IT USUALLY CONTAINS'.
00034              05  LINE PLUS 4
00035                  COLUMN 34 PICTURE A(12)
00036                  VALUE 'COMPANY NAME'.
00037              05  LINE PLUS 2
00038                  COLUMN 34 PICTURE A(12)
00039                  VALUE 'REPORT TITLE'.
00040
00041          PROCEDURE DIVISION.
00042          HERE-WE-GO.
00043              OPEN OUTPUT REPORT-FILE.
00044              INITIATE ONLY-PAGE.
00045          WRITE-COVER-PAGE.
00046              GENERATE ONLY-PAGE.
00047          EOJ.
00048              TERMINATE ONLY-PAGE.
00049              CLOSE REPORT-FILE.
00050              STOP RUN.
```

OUTPUT TO PROGRAM 21

```
THIS IS THE ONLY PAGE OF THE REPORT

    IT USUALLY CONTAINS



    COMPANY NAME

    REPORT TITLE
```

11.2 DIRECT LINE REFERENCING

Another way of specifying the position of the line being printed is to refer directly to the line number. In other words, we may specify a line position "absolutely" rather than by referring to a previous program line. A rule which must be observed, however, is that once a relative reference has been used in any group, it cannot be followed by a direct reference.

What follows is a program similar to the previous one except that all the line references are direct or absolute. The output is identical to the previous one.

PROGRAM 22
Report B

```
00001
00002        IDENTIFICATION DIVISION.
00003        PROGRAM-ID. REPORT-B.
00004        REMARKS. THIS IS THE SECOND ATTEMPT AT THE REPORT WRITER FEATURE.
C0005        AUTHOR. ELI J.OPAS.
00006
00007        ENVIRONMENT DIVISION.
00008        CONFIGURATION SECTION.
00009        SOURCE-COMPUTER. IBM-370-145.
00010        OBJECT-COMPUTER. IBM-370-145.
00011        INPUT-OUTPUT SECTION.
00012        FILE-CONTROL.
00013            SELECT REPORT-FILE ASSIGN TO UT-S-PRINTER.
00014
00015        DATA DIVISION.
00016        FILE SECTION.
00017        FD  REPORT-FILE
00018            LABEL RECORDS ARE OMITTED
00019            REPORT IS ONLY-PAGE.
00020
00021        REPORT SECTION.
00022        RD  ONLY-PAGE
00023            PAGE LIMIT IS 30 LINES
00024            HEADING 1.
00025        01  COVER-PAGE
00026            TYPE IS REPORT HEADING.
00027            05  LINE NUMBER IS 1
00028                COLUMN NUMBER IS 22 PICTURE A(35)
00029                VALUE 'THIS IS THE ONLY PAGE OF THE REPORT'.
00030            05  LINE NUMBER IS 3
00031                COLUMN 30 PICTURE A(19)
00032                VALUE 'IT USUALLY CONTAINS'.
00033            05 LINE NUMBER IS 7
00034                COLUMN 34 PICTURE A(12)
00035                VALUE 'COMPANY NAME'.
00036            05  LINE NUMBER IS 9
00037                COLUMN 34 PICTURE A(12)
00038                VALUE 'REPORT TITLE'.
00039
00040        PROCEDURE DIVISION.
00041        HERE-WE-GO.
00042            OPEN OUTPUT REPORT-FILE.
C0043            INITIATE ONLY-PAGE.
00044        WRITE-COVER-PAGE.
00045            GENERATE ONLY-PAGE.
0C046        EOJ.
00047            TERMINATE ONLY-PAGE.
00048            CLOSE REPORT-FILE.
00049            STOP RUN.
```

OUTPUT TO PROGRAM 22

THIS IS THE ONLY PAGE OF THE REPORT

IT USUALLY CONTAINS

COMPANY NAME

REPORT TITLE

11.3 A PROGRAM WITH
A CONTROL BREAK

Programs 21 and 22 were presented merely to familiarize the reader with some of the basic considerations when writing a report by means of

1 — 21	22 — 26	27 - 29 30	80
Name	Item-No.	Qty. Sold	Filler
X(21)	9(5)	9(3)	

FIGURE 18

the Report Writer feature. It is most unlikely that any COBOL programmer would resort to Report Writer merely to prepare a one-page report. A more realistic situation presents itself in the next program, where the input deck is composed of a series of cards, each of which is punched with a salesman's name, a product item number and the quantity of items sold. The data is punched in the format shown in Figure 18.

The data cards are arranged such that all cards bearing the same salesman's name are grouped together. The purpose of the program is merely to produce a report using the Report Writer feature that lists the salesman's name, item number, and quantity sold, all preceded by a suitable title page. However, each time there is a change of salesman's

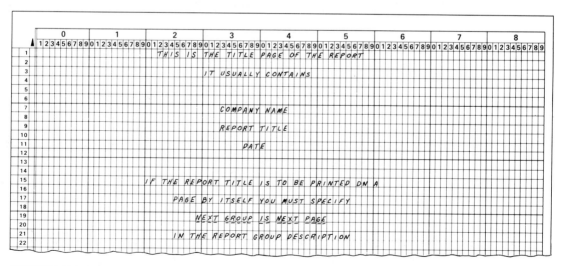

FIGURE 19

name, we wish to total the quantity sold by that salesman and print it out with an appropriate control footing. We have selected as a control footing the phrase SALESMAN TOTAL >>---->, followed by a line of asterisks. For each salesman the name is printed once only.

The most important point to understand in the program which follows is that it is the change of salesman's name which triggers the printing of the control footing, the total quantity sold by that salesman, and so on. For this reason the salesman's name is considered to be a *control break*.

Here is the outline of the title page described by the first 01 level entry of the Report Section. It is similar in most respects to what we have already encountered in the two previous programs, but we have introduced two new features, which will be described shortly.

DESCRIPTION OF REPORT SECTION
IN PROGRAM 23

Once again the Report Description is prefaced by the section header REPORT SECTION and is followed by the RD level entry in which it is stated in succinct form that the data name NAME is the control break. All we need write is

    CONTROL IS NAME

The page limit is again set to 30 lines and this limit applies to every page generated by the report. All headings will begin on line 1 since we have specified

    HEADING 1

Since we wish to start the first detail line on line 3 and the last on line 25, we include the clauses

    FIRST DETAIL 3
    LAST DETAIL 25.

The phrase NEXT GROUP IS NEXT PAGE causes the printing described in the next 01 level entry to be printed on a new page. It is an option which, if used, is incorporated into the TYPE clause. If it is omitted and the page limit is not exceeded, the next group described will be printed on the same page as the title page.

The underlining of the phrase

    NEXT GROUP IS NEXT PAGE

is accomplished by printing a succession of underbar symbols on the *same* line as the phrase to be underlined. By writing

LINE PLUS 0

(in line 0006) we suppress the line feed of the printer. Consequently, the printer overprints the same line, thus underlining the line already printed.

Another TYPE clause is PAGE HEADING, which identifies the group entry called PAGE–HEAD as the group containing all the information to be printed at the top of each successive page. The abbreviation PH may be used instead of PAGE HEADING.

Yet another clause is DETAIL, which may be abbreviated to DE. It appears in the 01 level entry DETAIL–LINE. As its name implies, it contains the information required for the printing out of each detail line in the report. In the RD level entry described above, the FIRST DETAIL line of each page is specified to be printed on line 3. In the same group entry is another clause we have not yet encountered, the GROUP INDICATE clause. It provides the means to suppress the printing of any elementary level item in the DETAIL group except for its first appearance after a control break or when a new page is triggered, even though a control break has not occurred. Since this is an output item, it must be accompanied by a suitable PICTURE clause. The specific data name to be "group indicated" is included in the SOURCE IS clause. It is obvious, then, that the SOURCE IS clause is nothing other than the familiar MOVE verb where the item to be moved is specified by the SOURCE IS clause. In our case it is NAME, a field specified in the input field called INPUT–CARD. Although both ITEM–NO and QTY–SOLD are included in the DETAIL–LINE group, they are not affected by the GROUP INDICATE clause and therefore are not suppressed at all. If the intention had been to GROUP INDICATE *each* of these items, a separate GROUP INDICATE clause would have had to appear.

Finally we come to the last of the 01 level entries, that whose type is CONTROL FOOTING. CONTROL FOOTING applies to the data name we called NAME in the program. Whenever a control break on NAME occurs, the relevant information from this group entry is printed out according to the manner specified within the group. This footing will be automatically printed *before* the detail line for the new name which triggers the control break.

However, we have yet another special word, namely SUM. The role of SUM is to maintain an accumulative total for the designated data name. Since we have the value QTY–SOLD qualified by the SUM clause, the Report Writer feature sets up a counter whose value is printed out at each control break. Not only that, but after printed out it is being reset to zero for the next accumulation.

In the Procedure Division it is once again SALES–REPORT which is INITIATEd. The major difference is with respect to the GENERATE statement. Since the bulk of the report is concerned with the printing of the detail line, it is DETAIL–LINE which must now be GENERATEd. This has the effect of performing all the automatic operations within the Report Writer program and, in addition, produces the printed detail line.

All the above is included in Program 23, which follows immediately after the print layout form which was used to establish the format of the layout.

PRINT LAYOUT FORM FOR PROGRAM 23

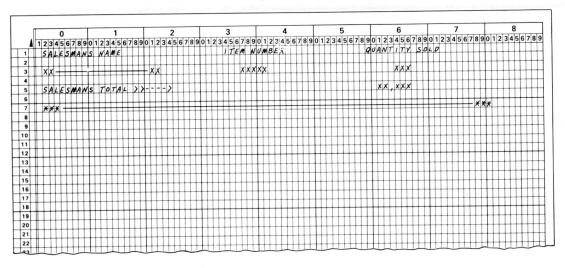

INPUT TO PROGRAM 23

SUPER SAM	45214536
SUPER SAM	63255421
SUPER SAM	12254336
SUPER SAM	63589742
SUPER SAM	25542361
SUPER SAM	99986532
SUPER SAM	66652148
SUPER SAM	6665321C
SUPER SAM	12345678
SUPER SAM	87654321
SUPER SAM	98886C02
SUPER SAM	99986001
SUPER SAM	66532012
SUPER SAM	99965842
SUPER SAM	9885321C
SUPER SAM	96653214
SUPER SAM	98853CC2
SUPER SAM	96655423
JCE SHMC	11111111
JCE SHMC	96632C2C
JOE SHMO	96653210
JCE SHMO	96655632
JCE SHMO	98852012
JCE SHMO	66653214
JCE SHMO	66632554
JCE SHMO	96653214
JCE SHMC	99965213
JCE SHMC	33300001
JCE SHMC	C0G01001
JOE SHMO	88865321
JCE SHMC	96632562
JOE SHMC	96653215
JCE SHMO	86562120

```
JOE  SHMO              98653212
JOE  SHMO              96653254
Y  PEERIM              63352102
Y  PEERIM              65532102
Y  PEERIM              96653254
Y  PEERIM              96653254
Y  PEERIM              96653254
Y  PEERIM              96653210
Y  PEERIM              96658723
Y  PEERIM              85563214
DAVIS  JONES           32235642
DAVIS  JONES           65532102
DAVIS  JONES           858956312
DAVIS  JONES           12365498
DAVIS  JONES           96653254
DAVIS  JONES           96653245
BILLY  BOY             32231456
BILLY  BOY             63256421
BILLY  BOY             96653215
BILLY  BOY             89965321
ROBERT  SMITH          56632541
ROBERT  SMITH          96653245
ROBERT  SMITH          63356421
BO  DIDLY              36653214
BO  DIDLY              36652145
ALAN  ROBERTS          36652458
H  NACHTOP             03323125
H  NACHTOP             36652145
H  NACHTOP             96655321
H  NACHTOP             96653254
H  NACHTOP             32256425
H  NACHTOP             65524531
H  NACHTOP             66355216
H  NACHTOP             36652153
H  NACHTOP             96655896
H  NACHTOP             63356452
H  NACHTOP             52245214
H  NACHTOP             98896532
H  NACHTOP             00005001
H  NACHTOP             33325642
JOHN  JOHNS            33325647
JOHN  JOHNS            63356854
JOHN  JOHNS            66653254
JOHN  JOHNS            98856324
JOHN  JOHNS            66635521
JOHN  JOHNS            96656320
```

PROGRAM 23
Report C

```
00001          IDENTIFICATION DIVISION.
00002          PROGRAM-ID. REPORT-C.
00003          REMARKS. THIS PROGRAM HAS A CONTROL BREAK.
00004          AUTHOR. ELI J.OPAS.
00005
00006          ENVIRONMENT DIVISION.
00007          CONFIGURATION SECTION.
00008          SOURCE-COMPUTER. IBM-370-145.
00009          OBJECT-COMPUTER. IBM-370-145.
00010          INPUT-OUTPUT SECTION.
00011          FILE-CONTROL.
00012              SELECT CARD-FILE ASSIGN TO UT-S-READER.
00013              SELECT REPORT-FILE ASSIGN TO UT-S-PRINTER.
00014
00015          DATA DIVISION.
00016          FILE SECTION.
00017          FD  CARD-FILE
00018              LABEL RECORDS ARE OMITTED.
00019
00020          01  INPUT-CARD.
00021              05 NAME        PICTURE X(21).
00022              05 ITEM-NO     PICTURE 9(5).
00023              05 QTY-SOLD    PICTURE 9(3).
00024              05 FILLER      PICTURE X(51).
00025          FD  REPORT-FILE
00026              LABEL RECORDS ARE OMITTED
00027              REPORT IS SALES-REPORT.
00028          REPORT SECTION.
00029          RD  SALES-REPORT
00030              CONTROL IS NAME
00031              PAGE LIMIT IS 30 LINES
```

```
00032                    HEADING 1
00033                    FIRST DETAIL 3
00034                    LAST DETAIL 25.
00035
00036            01  FIRST-PAGE
00037                    TYPE IS REPORT HEADING NEXT GROUP IS NEXT PAGE.
00038                    05  LINE NUMBER IS 1
00039                    COLUMN 22 PICTURE A(36)
00040                       VALUE 'THIS IS THE TITLE PAGE OF THE REPORT'.
00041                    05  LINE PLUS 2
00042                       COLUMN 30 PICTURE A(19)
00043                       VALUE 'IT USUALLY CONTAINS'.
00044                    05  LINE PLUS 4
00045                       COLUMN 34 PICTURE A(12)
00046                       VALUE 'COMPANY NAME'.
00047                    05  LINE PLUS 2
00048                       COLUMN 34 PICTURE A(12)
00049                       VALUE 'REPORT TITLE'.
00050                    05  LINE PLUS 2
00051                       COLUMN 38 PICTURE A(4)
00052                       VALUE 'DATE'.
00053                    05  LINE PLUS 4
00054                       COLUMN 20 PICTURE A(41)
00055                       VALUE 'IF THE REPORT TITLE IS TO BE PRINTED ON A'.
00056                    05  LINE PLUS 2
00057                       COLUMN 25 PICTURE A(31)
00058                       VALUE 'PAGE BY ITSELF YOU MUST SPECIFY'.
00059                    05  LINE PLUS 2
00060                       COLUMN 29 PICTURE A(23)
00061                       VALUE 'NEXT GROUP IS NEXT PAGE'.
00062                    05  LINE PLUS 0
00063                       COLUMN 29 PICTURE A(23)
00064                       VALUE '____ _____ __ ____ ____'.
00065                    05  LINE PLUS 2
00066                       COLUMN 25 PICTURE A(31)
00067                       VALUE 'IN THE REPORT GROUP DESCRIPTION'.
00068
00069            01  PAGE-HEAD
00070                    TYPE IS PAGE HEADING
00071                    LINE NUMBER IS 1.
00072                    05  COLUMN IS 2
00073                       PICTURE IS A(14)
00074                       VALUE IS 'SALESMANS NAME'.
00075                    05  COLUMN IS 34
00076                       PICTURE IS A(11)
00077                       VALUE IS 'ITEM NUMBER'.
00078                    05  COLUMN IS 59
00079                       PICTURE IS A(13)
00080                       VALUE IS 'QUANTITY SOLD'.
00081
00082            01  DETAIL-LINE
00083                    TYPE IS DETAIL
00084                    LINE NUMBER IS PLUS 1.
00085                    05  COLUMN IS 2
00086                       GROUP INDICATE
00087                       PICTURE IS A(21)
00088                       SOURCE IS NAME.
00089                    05  COLUMN IS 37
00090                       PICTURE IS X(5)
00091                       SOURCE IS ITEM-NO.
00092                    05  COLUMN IS 64
00093                       PICTURE IS ZZ9
00094                       SOURCE IS QTY-SOLD.
00095
00096            01  TYPE IS CONTROL FOOTING NAME
00097                    LINE NUMBER IS PLUS 2.
00098                    05 COLUMN IS 2
00099                       PICTURE IS X(24)
00100                       VALUE 'SALESMANS TOTAL >>---->'.
00101                    05 COLUMN 61
00102                       PICTURE ZZ,9(3)
00103                       SUM QTY-SOLD.
00104                    05 LINE PLUS 1
00105                       COLUMN 2
00106                       PICTURE X(78)
00107                       VALUE ALL '*'.
00108
00109            PROCEDURE DIVISION.
00110            LETS-GO.
00111                OPEN INPUT CARD-FILE, OUTPUT REPORT-FILE.
00112                INITIATE SALES-REPORT.
00113
00114            READ-A-CARD.
00115                READ CARD-FILE AT END GO TO E-O-J.
00116                GENERATE DETAIL-LINE.
```

```
00117                GO TO READ-A-CARD.
00118
00119        E-O-J.
00120            TERMINATE SALES-REPORT.
00121            CLOSE CARD-FILE, REPORT-FILE.
00122            STOP RUN.
```

OUTPUT TO PROGRAM 23

```
THIS IS THE TITLE PAGE OF THE REPORT

    IT USUALLY CONTAINS


        COMPANY NAME

        REPORT TITLE

          DATE



IF THE REPORT TITLE IS TO BE PRINTED ON A

    PAGE BY ITSELF YOU MUST SPECIFY

        NEXT GROUP IS NEXT PAGE

    IN THE REPORT GROUP DESCRIPTION
```

SALESMANS NAME	ITEM NUMBER	QUANTITY SOLD
SUPER SAM	45214	536
	63255	421
	12254	336
	63585	742
	25542	361
	99986	532
	66652	148
	66653	210
	12345	678
	87654	321
	98886	2
	99986	1
	66532	12
	99965	842
	98853	210
	96653	214
	98853	2
	96655	423

```
SALESMANS TOTAL >>---->                        5,991
***************************************************************************
```

JOE SHMO	11111	111
	96632	20

SALESMANS NAME	ITEM NUMBER	QUANTITY SOLD
JOE SHMO	96653	210
	96655	632
	98852	12
	66653	214
	66632	554
	96653	214
	99965	213
	33300	1
	00001	1
	88865	321
	96632	562
	96653	215
	86562	120
	98653	212
	96653	254

```
SALESMANS TOTAL >>---->                        3,866
***************************************************************************
```

Y PEERIM	63352	102
	65532	102
	96653	254
	96653	254
	96653	254

SALESMANS NAME	ITEM NUMBER	QUANTITY SOLD
Y PEERIM	96653	210
	96658	723
	85563	214
SALESMANS TOTAL >>---->		2,113

****

DAVIS JONES	32235	642
	65532	102
	89895	631
	12365	498
	96653	254
	96653	245
SALESMANS TOTAL >>---->		2,372

****

BILLY BOY	32231	456
	63256	421
	96653	215
	89965	321
SALESMANS TOTAL >>---->		1,413

****

ROBERT SMITH	56632	541

SALESMANS NAME	ITEM NUMBER	QUANTITY SOLD
ROBERT SMITH	96653	245
	63356	421
SALESMANS TOTAL >>---->		1,207

****

BO DIDLY	36653	214
	36652	145
SALESMANS TOTAL >>---->		359

****

ALAN ROBERTS	36652	458
SALESMANS TOTAL >>---->		458

****

H NACHTOP	03323	125
	36652	145
	96655	321
	96653	254
	32256	425
	65524	531
	66355	216
	36652	153
	96655	896

SALESMANS NAME	ITEM NUMBER	QUANTITY SOLD
H NACHTOP	63356	452
	52245	214
	98896	532
	00005	1
	33325	642
SALESMANS TOTAL >>---->		4,907

****

JOHN JOHNS	33325	647
	63356	854
	66653	254
	98856	324
	66635	521
	96656	320
SALESMANS TOTAL >>---->		2,920

****

11.4 A PROGRAM WITH TWO CONTROL BREAKS

The input to the next illustration of the Report Writer is identical to that of Program 23. It is a set of cards punched with a salesman's name in columns 1–21, product item number in columns 22–26, and the quantity of products sold in columns 27–29. The report, however, differs in several respects:

1. There is no title page (this is always the programmer's prerogative).
2. A report title is printed once, and once only, at the top of the first page (again, this is at the programmer's discretion).
3. There are two control breaks.
4. Advantage is taken of the COBOL reserved word PAGE–COUNTER.
5. We encounter two new TYPE clauses.

Here is the print layout form designed for Program 24, which follows immediately. We shall discuss the program itself in detail in the text following the output.

PRINT LAYOUT FORM FOR PROGRAM 24

```
                                    HENRY AND ELI SALES COMPANY

                                           SALES REPORT


     SALESMANS NAME                   ITEM NUMBER              QUANTITY SOLD

     XX                    XX         XXXXX                    XXX

     SALESMANS TOTAL >>----->                                 XX,XXX

     XXX                                                                    XXX

     TOTAL QUANTITY SOLD >>----->                             XXX,XXX




                                                              PAGE NUMBER  XX

                                           END OF REPORT
```

INPUT TO PROGRAM 24

```
SUPER SAM        63255421
SUPER SAM        12254336
SUPER SAM        63585742
SUPER SAM        25542361
SUPER SAM        99986532
SUPER SAM        66652148
SUPER SAM        66653210
SUPER SAM        12345678
SUPER SAM        87654321
SUPER SAM        98886002
SUPER SAM        99986001
SUPER SAM        66532012
SUPER SAM        99965842
SUPER SAM        98853210
SUPER SAM        96653214
SUPER SAM        98853002
SUPER SAM        96655423
SUPER SAM        45214536
```

```
JOE   SHMO              11111111
JOE   SHMO              96632020
JOE   SHMO              9665321C
JOE   SHMO              96655632
JOE   SHMO              98852012
JOE   SHMO              66653214
JOE   SHMO              66632554
JOE   SHMO              96653214
JOE   SHMO              99965213
JOE   SHMO              33300001
JOE   SHMO              00001001
JOE   SHMO              88865321
JOE   SHMO              96632562
JOE   SHMO              96653215
JOE   SHMO              86562120
JOE   SHMO              98653212
JOE   SHMO              96653254
Y PEERIM                63352102
Y PEERIM                65532102
Y PEERIM                96653254
Y PEERIM                96653254
Y PEERIM                96653254
Y PEERIM                9665321C
Y PEERIM                96658723
Y PEERIM                85563214
DAVIS JONES             32235642
DAVIS JONES             65532102
CAVIS JCNES             898956312
DAVIS JONES             12365498
CAVIS JONES             96653254
DAVIS JONES             96653245
BILLY BOY               32231456
BILLY BOY               63256421
BILLY BOY               96653215
BILLY BOY               89965321
ROBERT SMITH            56632541
ROBERT SMITH            96653245
ROBERT SMITH            63356421
BC DIDLY                36653214
BO DIDLY                36652145
ALAN ROBERTS            36652458
H NACHTOP               03323125
H NACHTOP               36652145
H NACHTOP               96655321
H NACHTOP               96653254
H NACHTOP               32256425
H NACHTOP               65524531
H NACHTOP               66355216
H NACHTOP               36652153
H NACHTOP               96655896
H NACHTOP               63356452
H NACHTOP               52245214
H NACHTOP               98896532
H NACHTOP               00005001
H NACHTOP               33325642
JOHN JOHNS              33325647
JOHN JOHNS              63356854
JOHN JOHNS              66653254
JOHN JOHNS              98856324
JOHN JOHNS              66635521
JOHN JOHNS              96656320
```

PROGRAM 24
Report D

```
00001        IDENTIFICATION DIVISION.
00002        PROGRAM-ID. REPORT-D.
00003        REMARKS. THIS PROGRAM HAS TWO CONTROL BREAKS.
00004        AUTHOR. ELI J. OPAS.
00005
00006        ENVIRONMENT DIVISION.
00007        CONFIGURATION SECTION.
00008        SOURCE-COMPUTER. IBM-370-145.
00009        OBJECT-COMPUTER. IBM-370-145.
00010        INPUT-OUTPUT SECTION.
00011        FILE-CONTROL.
00012            SELECT CARD-FILE ASSIGN TO UT-S-READER.
00013            SELECT REPORT-FILE ASSIGN TO UT-S-PRINTER.
00014
00015        DATA DIVISION.
00016        FILE SECTION.
```

```
00017          FD   CARD-FILE
00018               LABEL RECORDS ARE OMITTED.
00019
00020          01   INPUT-CARD.
00021               05 NAME          PICTURE X(21).
00022               05 ITEM-NO       PICTURE 9(5).
00023               05 QTY-SOLD      PICTURE 9(3).
00024               05 FILLER        PICTURE X(51).
00025          FD   REPORT-FILE
00026               LABEL RECORDS ARE OMITTED
00027               REPORT IS SALES-REPORT.
00028          REPORT SECTION.
00029          RD   SALES-REPORT
00030               CONTROLS ARE FINAL, NAME
00031               PAGE LIMIT IS 32 LINES
00032               HEADING 1
00033               FIRST DETAIL 8
00034               LAST DETAIL 23
00035               FOOTING 28.
00036
00037          01   TYPE IS REPORT HEADING.
00038               05 LINE NUMBER IS 1
00039                  COLUMN NUMBER IS 27
00040                  PICTURE IS A(27)
00041                  VALUE IS 'HENRY AND ELI SALES COMPANY'.
00042               05 LINE NUMBER IS 3
00043                  COLUMN NUMBER IS 34
00044                  PICTURE IS A(12)
00045                  VALUE IS 'SALES REPORT'.
00046
00047          01   PAGE-HEAD
00048               TYPE IS PAGE HEADING.
00049               05 LINE NUMBER IS 6.
00050                  10 COLUMN IS 2
00051                     PICTURE IS A(14)
00052                     VALUE IS 'SALESMANS NAME'.
00053                  10 COLUMN IS 34
00054                     PICTURE IS A(11)
00055                     VALUE IS 'ITEM NUMBER'.
00056                  10 COLUMN IS 59
00057                     PICTURE IS A(13)
00058                     VALUE IS 'QUANTITY SOLD'.
00059
00060          01   DETAIL-LINE
00061               TYPE IS DETAIL LINE NUMBER IS PLUS 1.
00062               05 COLUMN IS 2
00063                  GROUP INDICATE
00064                     PICTURE IS A(21)
00065                     SOURCE IS NAME.
00066               05 COLUMN IS 37
00067                  PICTURE IS X(5)
00068                  SOURCE IS ITEM-NO.
00069               05 COLUMN IS 64
00070                  PICTURE IS ZZ9
00071                  SOURCE IS QTY-SOLD.
00072
00073          01   TYPE IS CONTROL FOOTING NAME.
00074               05 LINE NUMBER IS PLUS 2.
00075                  10 COLUMN IS 2
00076                     PICTURE IS X(24)
00077                     VALUE 'SALESMANS TOTAL >>---->'.
00078                  10 SUB
00079                     COLUMN 61
00080                     PICTURE   ZZ,9(3)
00081                     SUM QTY-SOLD.
00082               05 LINE PLUS 1.
00083                  10 COLUMN 2
00084                     PICTURE X(78)
00085                     VALUE ALL '*'.
00086
00087          01   TYPE IS CONTROL FOOTING FINAL LINE NEXT PAGE.
00088               05 COLUMN 2
00089                  PICTURE X(27)
00090                  VALUE 'TOTAL QUANTITY SOLD >>---->'.
00091               05 COLUMN 60
00092                  PICTURE ZZ9,9(3)
00093                  SUM SUB.
00094
00095          01   TYPE PAGE FOOTING LINE 30.
00096               05 COLUMN 62  PICTURE X(11) VALUE 'PAGE NUMBER'.
00097               05 COLUMN 76  PICTURE Z9    SOURCE PAGE-COUNTER.
00098
00099          01   TYPE REPORT FOOTING
00100               LINE PLUS 2
```

```
00101                    COLUMN 33
00102                    PICTURE X(13)
00103                    VALUE 'END OF REPORT'.
00104
00105           PROCEDURE DIVISION.
00106           STARTUP.
00107               OPEN INPUT CARD-FILE, OUTPUT REPORT-FILE.
00108               INITIATE SALES-REPORT.
00109
00110           READ-CARD.
00111               READ CARD-FILE AT END GO TO EOJ.
00112               GENERATE DETAIL-LINE.
00113               GO TO READ-CARD.
00114
00115           EOJ.
00116               TERMINATE SALES-REPORT.
00117               CLOSE CARD-FILE, REPORT-FILE.
00118               STOP RUN.
```

OUTPUT TO PROGRAM 24

```
                         HENRY AND ELI SALES COMPANY

                              SALES REPORT


     SALESMANS NAME                  ITEM NUMBER          QUANTITY SOLD

     SUPER SAM                          63255                  421
                                        12254                  336
                                        63589                  742
                                        25542                  361
                                        99986                  532
                                        66652                  148
                                        66653                  210
                                        12345                  678
                                        87654                  321
                                        98886                    2
                                        99986                    1
                                        66532                   12
                                        59965                  842
                                        98853                  210
                                        96653                  214
                                        98853                    2




                                                      PAGE NUMBER    1


     SALESMANS NAME                  ITEM NUMBER          QUANTITY SOLD

     SUPER SAM                          96655                  423
                                        45214                  536

     SALESMANS TOTAL >>---->                               5,991
     ***********************************************************************
     JOE SHMO                           11111                  111
                                        96632                   20
                                        96653                  210
                                        96655                  632
                                        98852                   12
                                        66653                  214
                                        66632                  554
                                        96653                  214
                                        99965                  213
                                        33300                    1
                                        00001                    1




                                                      PAGE NUMBER    2
```

SALESMANS NAME	ITEM NUMBER	QUANTITY SOLD
JOE SHMO	88865	321
	96632	562
	96653	215
	86562	120
	98653	212
	96653	254
SALESMANS TOTAL >>---->		3,866

****

Y PEERIM	63352	102
	65532	102
	96653	254
	96653	254
	96653	254
	96653	210
	96658	723

PAGE NUMBER   3

SALESMANS NAME	ITEM NUMBER	QUANTITY SOLD
Y PEERIM	85563	214
SALESMANS TOTAL >>---->		2,113

****

DAVIS JONES	32235	642
	65532	102
	89895	631
	12365	498
	96653	254
	96653	245
SALESMANS TOTAL >>---->		2,372

****

BILLY BOY	32231	456
	63256	421
	96653	215

PAGE NUMBER   4

SALESMANS NAME	ITEM NUMBER	QUANTITY SOLD
BILLY BOY	89965	321
SALESMANS TOTAL >>---->		1,413

****

ROBERT SMITH	56632	541
	96653	245
	63356	421
SALESMANS TOTAL >>---->		1,207

****

BO DIDLY	36653	214
	36652	145
SALESMANS TOTAL >>---->		359

****

ALAN ROBERTS	36652	458
SALESMANS TOTAL >>---->		458

****

PAGE NUMBER   5

```
SALESMANS NAME              ITEM NUMBER              QUANTITY SOLD

H NACHTOP                       03323                     125
                                36652                     145
                                96655                     321
                                96653                     254
                                32256                     425
                                65524                     531
                                66355                     216
                                36652                     153
                                96655                     896
                                63356                     452
                                52245                     214
                                98896                     532
                                00005                       1
                                33325                     642

SALESMANS TOTAL >>---->                                 4,907
*************************************************************************
```

```
                                                        PAGE NUMBER    6


SALESMANS NAME              ITEM NUMBER              QUANTITY SOLD

JOHN JOHNS                      33325                     647
                                63356                     854
                                66653                     254
                                98856                     324
                                66635                     521
                                96656                     320

SALESMANS TOTAL >>---->                                 2,920
*************************************************************************
```

```
                                                        PAGE NUMBER    7


SALESMANS NAME              ITEM NUMBER              QUANTITY SOLD

TOTAL QUANTITY SOLD >>---->                             25,606
```

```
                                                        PAGE NUMBER    8
                        END OF REPORT
```

DISCUSSION OF PROGRAM 24

The CONTROL IS or the CONTROLS ARE clause in the RD level entry is the means by which the Report Writer feature is advised of the control breaks. This time there are two such control breaks: FINAL and NAME.

FINAL is a COBOL reserved word. It is a control break condition activated by the end of the data. Following the word FINAL in the CONTROLS ARE clause is NAME, which also acts as a control break whenever there is a change in the NAME field of the input data. Of course, one may have a long list of other control breaks, but the order in which these appear in the list is significant. The control break which appears first is the *most* inclusive of the control breaks; that which appears last is the *least* inclusive. When controls are tested, the most inclusive (highest) control is tested first, then the second, and so on.

These terms might seem somewhat strange at first. All that is implied is a system of hierarchy of levels. For example, at New York University there is a renowned College of the Arts and Sciences; within the College is a School of Mathematics, which includes the Computer Science department, which in turn offers an excellent course in COBOL programming. In this system, the most inclusive level is New York University and the least inclusive is the course in COBOL. New York University would therefore be the first to be mentioned and COBOL the last. Another example might be country, region, state, and city.

In order to print certain information at the foot of each page of the report, a special TYPE clause is used. It is the PAGE FOOTING clause, which may be abbreviated to PF. The PAGE FOOTING in the program specifies that information is to be printed on line 30. In particular, the literal PAGE NUMBER is to appear starting in column 62. Following this phrase the actual page number is to be printed. This role, however, is taken care of automatically by the Report Writer feature. A page counter called PAGE–COUNTER is incremented each time a new page is printed. Therefore, by specifying SOURCE IS PAGE–COUNTER this information is accessed directly.

Finally, at the foot of the report, that is, at its conclusion, we want to print the phrase END OF REPORT. This is accomplished by resorting to the special TYPE called REPORT FOOTING, which may be abbreviated to RF.

11.5 REVIEW EXERCISES

1. Select any program you have written and rewrite it using the Report Writer Feature.
2. Write a program using Report Writer which will read in as input a set of accounts receivable cards sorted by month and punched in the following format:

col	1–15	name of month
	21–46	customer name
	61–65	amount due (999V99)
	76–80	invoice number

Generate a report which lists and totals all the accounts receivable for each of the months. Each month's transactions should appear on a separate page with a suitable heading including a page number.

At the end of the report, the total accounts receivable for the year should be printed.

3. Write a report using Report Writer to process salesmen's commissions. The commission a salesman is paid is based on his number of years of service with the company, in accordance with the following table:

YEARS OF SERVICE	RATE OF COMMISSION
1	5.0%
2	6.8%
3	7.5%
4	8.0%
5	10.0%
6	11.0%
7	13.0%
8	15.0%
9	17.5%
10 or more	20.0%

The input cards are punched as follows:

col	1–20	salesman's name
	30–35	number of items sold
	40–45	price per item (9999V99)
	50–51	number of years of service

TABLE HANDLING

In business transactions one frequently comes upon situations in which a discount varies according to the volume purchased, a salesman's percentage commission depends upon his seniority in the firm, a citizen's income tax is dependent upon the number of allowable exemptions, the cost of mailing a package varies with its weight, and so on. The range of such situations is extremely wide. Each of these different relationships can be expressed most conveniently by *tables,* that is, in tabular form. These tables have proved so useful it is inevitable a way would be found in COBOL to implement them. Here are some examples of tables:

(1)

VOLUME IN DOZENS	PERCENTAGE DISCOUNT
1	0.50
2	0.75
3	1.10
4	1.23
5	1.57
6	1.83
7	1.97
8	2.03
9	2.34
10	2.50

(2)

YEARS OF SERVICE	PERCENTAGE COMMISSION
1	0.25
2	0.41
3	0.50
4	0.62
5	0.70
6	0.75

(2) YEARS OF SERVICE	PERCENTAGE COMMISSION
7	0.85
8	1.00
9	1.25
10 or more	2.00

(3) WEIGHT IN POUNDS	MAILING COST IN DOLLARS
0.25	1.00
0.50	1.46
0.75	1.74
1.00	1.88
1.25	2.04
1.50	2.26
1.75	2.52
2.00	2.65

(4)   ONE-WAY AIRFARE FROM N.Y.

City 1 Columbus	City 2 Chicago	City 3 Denver	City 4 Los Angeles	City 5 Las Vegas
$61.00	$80.00	$143.00	$162.00	$185.00

Looking at table 4, for example, we can easily determine at a glance the cost of a one-way flight from New York to any of the five cities mentioned in the table. This procedure is often called "table look-up". In order to simulate such a table in a COBOL program, it is necessary to store the required information in Working-Storage using a series of FILLER statements and appropriate VALUE clauses. The *first* entry refers to City 1 (Columbus), the *second* to City 2 (Chicago), the *third* to City 3 (Denver), the *fourth* to City 4 (Los Angeles) and the *fifth* to City 5 (Las Vegas).

12.1 THE OCCURS CLAUSE

The OCCURS clause eliminates the need for the repeated entry of similar data. In our case, although the actual values of RATE–TABLE–VALUES are different in themselves, their format, that is, their PICTURE specifications, are identical. In fact, the PICTURE 999V99 occurs 5 times. In defining tables the OCCURS clause plays a prominent role. Once the table is defined, it may be retained in memory for the complete run of the program and accessed as often as is necessary.

12.1.1 The REDEFINES Clause

In order to set up the table, we have to redefine the entries for RATE– TABLE–VALUES by using the REDEFINES clause. The REDEFINES clause merely permits us to refer to the table entries by a different name. Let this different name be RATE–TABLE. Now we combine the entries for RATE–TABLE–VALUES with the REDEFINES and the OCCURS clauses in the following way:

```
WORKING-STORAGE SECTION.
01 RATE-TABLE-VALUES.
   05 FILLER PICTURE 999V99 VALUE 061.00.
   05 FILLER PICTURE 999V99 VALUE 080.00.
   05 FILLER PICTURE 999V99 VALUE 143.00.
   05 FILLER PICTURE 999V99 VALUE 162.00.
   05 FILLER PICTURE 999V99 VALUE 185.00.
01 RATE-TABLE REDEFINES RATE-TABLE-VALUES.
   05 AIRFARE PICTURE 999V99 OCCURS 5 TIMES.
```

Once the values have been redefined by RATE-TABLE and its subordinate OCCURS clause, we can refer to each value of AIRFARE by its order of occurrence. This is done by what is known as *subscripting*.

12.1.2 Subscripting

To refer to the *first* AIRFARE of RATE-TABLE, we use a subscript of 1 in the following way:

```
AIRFARE (1)
```

Which contains the value 061.00 in the table. Similarly, to refer to the second element or item, we write:

```
AIRFARE (2)
```

which has the value of 080.00. The subscript can be expressly defined in an input card or may be created by a PERFORM statement, in which case the subscript must be a data name. Note that there must be at least one space between the subscripted item and its subscript.

12.2 ACCESSING A SINGLE LEVEL TABLE USING SUBSCRIPTS

For our first illustrative program using tables, the subscript of 1 through 5 is punched in column 80 of the data cards. In other words, if the destination for a particular transaction is Columbus, Ohio, which is coded 1 for our purposes, the 1 appears in column 80 of that card. In Program 25 this field is referred to as DESTINATION-KOD. It will always assume the value 1, 2, 3, 4, or 5 to correspond to the first, second, third, fourth or fifth occurrence, respectively, of AIRFARE as defined in the RATE-TABLE.

The input deck is made up of a series of data cards punched according to the format shown in Figure 20.

The purpose of the program is to read in each data card. The contents of column 80, DESTINATION-KOD, is then used as a subscript for AIRFARE and, depending upon the value of the subscript, the appropriate cost for the trip is accessed. The output is a simple invoice containing the

| 1 | - | 21 22 | - | 42 43 | - | 63 64 | - | 79 80 |

Name.	Street Address	City State Zip	Filler
X(21)	X(21)	X(21)	

Destination Code
PICTURE 9.

FIGURE 20

customer's name and address, a statement of the amount to be paid, and where the remittance should be sent.

The table in this program is rather short compared to those customarily used in the real world of data processing. But in essence this program shows what is entailed in constructing and looking up a table in COBOL, regardless of its length.

INPUT TO PROGRAM 25

```
ARTHUR FIELDS        1155 BLEECKER STREET  NEW YORK, N.Y. 10005    4
HENRY MULLISH        100 BLEECKER STREET   NEW YORK, N.Y. 10012    2
JANE MORROW          45 WEST 37 STREET     NEW YORK, N.Y. 10014    3
ELI OPAS             1514 EAST 56 STREET   BROOKLYN, N.Y. 11236    5
MARY JANE            23 MAIN STREET        ITHACA, N.Y. 52100      1
ANN ASTER            14 ELM LANE           BROOKLYN, N.Y. 54211    5
SAMUEL R SMITH       6 ANSI COURT          SPRING GELEN,N.Y.       4
JOHN ADAMS           3321 ASTER PLACE      QUEENS, N.Y. 12230      3
HARRY JONES          2 HOLIDAY WAY         ALBANY, N.Y. 14452      2
HARVEY RENMAN        1 LONGACER ROAD       KINGS POINT, N.Y.       5
```

PROGRAM 25
Lookup 1

```
00001     IDENTIFICATION DIVISION.
00002     PROGRAM-ID. LOOKUP-1.
00003     REMARKS. THIS IS A TABLE LOOK-UP USING SUBSCRIPTING.
00004     AUTHOR. ELI J. OPAS.
00005
00006     ENVIRONMENT DIVISION.
00007     CONFIGURATION SECTION.
00008     SOURCE-COMPUTER. IBM-370-145.
00009     OBJECT-COMPUTER. IBM-370-145.
00010     SPECIAL-NAMES.
00011         C01 IS TO-TOP-OF-PAGE.
00012     INPUT-OUTPUT SECTION.
00013     FILE-CONTROL.
00014         SELECT IN-FILE  ASSIGN TO UT-S-READER.
00015         SELECT OUT-FILE ASSIGN TO UT-S-PRINTER.
00016
00017     DATA DIVISION.
00018
00019     FILE SECTION.
00020
00021     FD  IN-FILE
00022         LABEL RECORDS ARE OMITTED.
```

```
00023
00024            01  FARE-CARD.
00025                05 NAME            PICTURE X(21).
00026                05 STREET-ADDRESS  PICTURE X(21).
00027                05 CITY-STATE-ZIP  PICTURE X(21).
00028                05 FILLER          PICTURE X(16).
00029                05 DESTINATION-KOD PICTURE 9.
00030
00031        FD  OUT-FILE
00032            LABEL RECORDS ARE OMITTED.
00033
00034            01  AIRFARE-BILL.
00035                05 FILLER          PICTURE X(133).
00036
00037        WORKING-STORAGE SECTION.
00038        77  LINE-KOUNTER        PICTURE 99 VALUE ZERO.
00039
00040            01  LINE-1.
00041                05 FILLER          PICTURE X VALUE SPACES.
00042                05 NAME            PICTURE X(21) VALUE SPACES.
00043                05 FILLER          PICTURE X(111) VALUE SPACES.
00044
00045            01  LINE-2.
00046                05 FILLER          PICTURE X VALUE SPACES.
00047                05 STREET-ADDRESS  PICTURE X(21) VALUE SPACES.
00048                05 FILLER          PICTURE X(111) VALUE SPACES.
00049
00050            01  LINE-3.
00051                05 FILLER          PICTURE X VALUE SPACES.
00052                05 CITY-STATE-ZIP  PICTURE X(21) VALUE SPACES.
00053                05 FILLER          PICTURE X(111) VALUE SPACES.
00054
00055            01  LINE-4.
00056                05 FILLER          PICTURE X VALUE SPACES.
00057                05 FILLER          PICTURE X(13) VALUE 'PLEASE REMIT '.
00058                05 FARE            PICTURE $Z99.99.
00059                05 FILLER          PICTURE X(32) VALUE
00060                ' FOR AIRFARE ON COBOL AIP LINES'.
00061                05 FILLER          PICTURE X(80) VALUE SPACES.
00062
00063            01  LINE-5.
00064                05 FILLER          PICTURE X VALUE SPACES.
00065                05 FILLER          PICTURE X(49) VALUE
00066                'MAIL CHECKS TO P.O. BOX 913, NEW YORK, N.Y. 10019'.
00067                05 FILLER          PICTURE X(83) VALUE SPACES.
00068
00069            01  LINE-6.
00070                05 FILLER          PICTURE X VALUE SPACES.
00071                05 FILLER          PICTURE X(79) VALUE ALL '*'.
00072                05 FILLER          PICTURE X(53) VALUE SPACES.
00073
00074            01  RATE-TABLE-VALUES.
00075                05 FILLER          PICTURE 999V99 VALUE 061.00.
00076                05 FILLER          PICTURE 999V99 VALUE 080.00.
00077                05 FILLER          PICTURE 999V99 VALUE 143.00.
00078                05 FILLER          PICTURE 999V99 VALUE 162.00.
00079                05 FILLER          PICTURE 999V99 VALUE 185.00.
00080
00081            01  RATE-TABLE REDEFINES RATE-TABLE-VALUES.
00082                05  AIRFARE        PICTURE 999V99 OCCURS 5 TIMES.
00083
00084        PROCEDURE DIVISION.
00085
00086        START-UP.
00087            OPEN INPUT IN-FILE, OUTPUT OUT-FILE.
00088            MOVE SPACES TO AIRFARE-BILL.
00089
00090        HERE-WE-GO.
00091            READ IN-FILE AT END GO TO E-O-J.
00092            MOVE NAME IN FARE-CARD TO NAME IN LINE-1.
00093            MOVE STREET-ADDRESS IN FARE-CARD TO STREET-ADDRESS IN LINE-2.
00094            MOVE CITY-STATE-ZIP IN FARE-CARD TO CITY-STATE-ZIP IN LINE-3.
00095            MOVE AIRFARE (DESTINATION-KOD) TO FARE IN LINE-4.
00096
00097        WRITE-BILL.
00098            IF LINE-KOUNTER > 59 MOVE ZERO TO LINE-KOUNTER,
00099            WRITE AIRFARE-BILL FROM LINE-1 AFTER ADVANCING TO-TOP-OF-PAGE
00100                ELSE WRITE AIRFARE-BILL FROM LINE-1 AFTER ADVANCING 2.
00101            WRITE AIRFARE-BILL FROM LINE-2 AFTER ADVANCING 1.
00102            WRITE AIRFARE-BILL FROM LINE-3 AFTER ADVANCING 1.
00103            WRITE AIRFARE-BILL FROM LINE-4 AFTER ADVANCING 3.
00104            WRITE AIRFARE-BILL FROM LINE-5 AFTER ADVANCING 2.
00105            WRITE AIRFARE-BILL FROM LINE-6 AFTER ADVANCING 5.
```

```
00106              ADD 15 TO LINE-KOUNTER.
00107              GO TO HERE-WE-GO.
00108
00109        E-O-J.
00110              CLOSE IN-FILE, OUT-FILE.
00111              STOP RUN.
```

OUTPUT TO PROGRAM 25

```
ARTHUR FIELDS
1155 BLEECKER STREET
NEW YORK, N.Y. 10005

PLEASE REMIT $162.00  FOR AIRFARE ON COBOL AIR LINES

MAIL CHECKS TO P.O. BOX 913, NEW YORK, N.Y. 10019




********************************************************************************

HENRY MULLISH
100 BLEECKER STREET
NEW YORK, N.Y. 10012

PLEASE REMIT $ 80.00  FOR AIRFARE ON COBOL AIR LINES

MAIL CHECKS TO P.O. BOX 913, NEW YORK, N.Y. 10019




********************************************************************************

JANE MORROW
45 WEST 37 STREET
NEW YORK, N.Y. 10014

PLEASE REMIT $143.00  FOR AIRFARE ON COBOL AIR LINES

MAIL CHECKS TO P.O. BOX 913, NEW YORK, N.Y. 10019




********************************************************************************

ELI OPAS
1514 EAST 96 STREET
BROOKLYN, N.Y. 11236

PLEASE REMIT $185.00  FOR AIRFARE ON COBOL AIR LINES

MAIL CHECKS TO P.O. BOX 913, NEW YORK, N.Y. 10019




********************************************************************************

MARY JANE
23 MAIN STREET
ITHACA, N.Y. 52100

PLEASE REMIT $ 61.00  FOR AIRFARE ON COBOL AIR LINES

MAIL CHECKS TO P.O. BOX 913, NEW YORK, N.Y. 10019




********************************************************************************
```

```
            ANN ASTER
            14 ELM LANE
            BROOKLYN, N.Y. 54211


            PLEASE REMIT $185.00  FOR AIRFARE ON COBOL AIR LINES

            MAIL CHECKS TO P.O. BOX 913, NEW YORK, N.Y. 10019



            ******************************************************************************
            SAMUEL R SMITH
            6 ANSI COURT
            SPRING GELEN,N.Y.


            PLEASE REMIT $162.00  FOR AIRFARE ON COBOL AIR LINES

            MAIL CHECKS TO P.O. BOX 913, NEW YORK, N.Y. 10019



            ******************************************************************************
            JOHN ADAMS
            3321 ASTER PLACE
            QUEENS, N.Y. 12230


            PLEASE REMIT $143.00  FOR AIRFARE ON COBOL AIR LINES

            MAIL CHECKS TO P.O. BOX 913, NEW YORK, N.Y. 10019



            ******************************************************************************
            HARRY JONES
            2 HOLIDAY WAY
            ALBANY, N.Y. 14452


            PLEASE REMIT $ 80.00  FOR AIRFARE ON COBOL AIR LINES

            MAIL CHECKS TO P.O. BOX 913, NEW YORK, N.Y. 10019



            ******************************************************************************
            HARVEY RENMAN
            1 LONGACER ROAD
            KINGS POINT, N.Y.


            PLEASE REMIT $185.00  FOR AIRFARE ON COBOL AIR LINES

            MAIL CHECKS TO P.O. BOX 913, NEW YORK, N.Y. 10019



            ******************************************************************************
```

12.3 ANOTHER METHOD OF ACCESSING A TABLE

In Program 25 the information punched in column 80 was used as the subscript. It was given the name DESTINATION–KOD and its value was always between 1 and 5 inclusive. Whatever value it had acted as the subscript to AIRFARE. For example, when DESTINATION–KOD was equal to 4, as was the case on the first data card, AIRFARE (DESTINATION–KOD) was accessed. In other words, AIRFARE (4) was referenced, and since the *fourth* item in RATE–TABLE–VALUES (later redefined to RATE–TABLE with the data name AIRFARE specified by an OCCURS clause to occur 5 times) had the value 162.00, the invoice was printed for the value $162.00. No more than four invoices were printed per page and the string of asterisks which separates each invoice from the next might well symbolize a perforation in the paper enabling each invoice to be separated easily.

In the modification to Program 25 which follows (as Program 26), a different approach is taken. This time the destination code is no longer confined to a single digit punched in column 80 but rather to a double-digit number punched in columns 79 and 80. Furthermore, the 12 codes permitted representing various cities are 1, 2, 5, 6, 7, 10, 11, 12, 15, 16, 18, and 19. The fact that the codes are not consecutive could easily reflect the fact that certain destinations have been dropped by the airline company.

Furthermore, the city codes are included in the table alongside the corresponding airfare. For example, City 1 with an airfare of $142.00 is specified by the entry

01142.00

and City 19 with an airfare of $195.00 by the entry

19195.00

The manner in which the entry is broken up into its constituent parts is by an appropriate redefinition of the table. RATE–TABLE redefines RATE–TABLE–VALUES on the 01 level, exactly as was done in the previous example. But a data name TABLE–DETAIL is specified on the 05 level as occurring 12 times. This is further broken down into two 10 level entries:

```
05 TABLE-DETAIL OCCURS 12 TIMES.
   10 CITY-KODE PICTURE 99.
   10 AIRFARE PICTURE 999V99.
```

In other words, for each TABLE–DETAIL (there are 12 of them) the city code is specified by the first two digits and its corresponding airfare by the remaining part of the value designated by the picture 999V99. Also, since these two elementary items are subordinate to a group item which in turn is part of an OCCURS clause, these elementary items must be subscripted when used.

Now in order to access any particular item in the table, a subscript is created by means of a 77 level item called SUBSCRIPT, which is set initially to 00. SUBSCRIPT can never be greater than 12 in our example because there are only 12 destinations. If it is greater than 12, an error is indicated and an error routine is activated, causing an appropriate printout to be made. Suppose, for example, as is the case with the first two data cards, the destination code as punched in columns 79 and 80 is 02. In the paragraph LOOK–UP–FARE, 1 is first added to SUBSCRIPT, giving it the value 1. After the subscript value passes the test against 12, the destination code is tested against CITY–KODE (01). In other words, the city code of 01 is matched against the destination code on the data card, which is 02. Since the test fails, the ELSE clause is executed and control is sent to the paragraph LOOK–UP–FARE again. This time the value of SUBSCRIPT is incremented to 02. The code 02 is not greater than 12; the test is again made to determine whether DESTINATION–KOD is equal to CITY–KODE (SUBSCRIPT). On this time around, 02 is indeed equal to the 02 located in the second entry of the table and a successful match is made. As a result, an invoice is printed and the value of SUBSCRIPT is reinitialized to zero before the next data card is read.

The destination code of the third data card is 09. The value of SUBSCRIPT increments to 01 and again a match is attempted between 09 and each of the city codes in the table. But 09 is not a legitimate city code and SUBSCRIPT is repeatedly incremented by 1. When it reaches the value 13, control is sent to the error routine where the pertinent information is printed out and SUBSCRIPT once again reinitialized to zero before processing resumes.

Here is Program 26 together with its output. It deserves very careful study.

INPUT TO PROGRAM 26

```
ARTHUR FIELDS      1155 BLEECKER STREET  NEW YORK, N.Y. 10005      02
HENRY MULLISH      100 BLEECKER STREET   NEW YORK, N.Y. 10012      02
HARVEY RENMAN      1 LONGACER ROAD       KINGS PCINT, N.Y.         09
JANE MORROW        45 WEST 37 STREET     NEW YORK, N.Y. 10014      15
ELI OPAS           1514 EAST 96 STREET   BROOKLYN, N.Y. 11236      19
ALFRED NEWMAN      14 WARREN STREET      SENECA ,N.Y. 22103        12
MARY JANE          23 MAIN STREET        ITHACA N.Y. 12345         05
ANN ASTER          14 ELM LANE           BROOKLYN, N.Y. 54211      18
JOHN ADAMS         3321 ASTER PLACE      QUEENS, N.Y. 12230        16
HARRY JONES        2 HOLIDAY WAY         ALBANY, N.Y. 14452        01
SAMUEL R SMITH     6 ANSI COURT          SPRING GELEN,N.Y.         07
```

PROGRAM 26
Lookup 2

```
00001          IDENTIFICATION DIVISION.
C0002          PROGRAM-ID. LCCKUP-2.
00003          REMARKS. ANOTHER METHOD OF TABLE LOOK-UP.
C0004          AUTHOR. ELI J. OPAS.
00005
00006          ENVIRONMENT DIVISION.
C0C07          CONFIGURATION SECTION.
C0008          SOURCE-COMPUTER. IBM-370-145.
00009          OBJECT-COMPUTER. IBM-370-145.
00010          SPECIAL-NAMES.
C0011              C01 IS TO-TOP-OF-PAGE.
C0012          INPUT-OUTPUT SECTION.
G0013          FILE-CONTROL.
00014              SELECT IN-FILE  ASSIGN TO UT-S-READER.
C0015              SELECT OUT-FILE ASSIGN TO UT-S-PRINTER.
```

```
00016
00017            DATA DIVISION.
00018
00019            FILE SECTION.
00020
00021            FD  IN-FILE
00022                LABEL RECORDS ARE OMITTED.
00023
00024            01  FARE-CARD.
00025                05 NAME              PICTURE X(21).
00026                05 STREET-ADDRESS    PICTURE X(21).
00027                05 CITY-STATE-ZIP    PICTURE X(21).
00028                05 FILLER            PICTURE X(15).
00029                05 DESTINATION-KOD   PICTURE 99.
00030
00031            FD  OUT-FILE
00032                LABEL RECORDS ARE OMITTED.
00033
00034            01  AIRFARE-BILL.
00035                05 FILLER            PICTURE X.
00036                05 OUTPUT-LINE       PICTURE X(132).
00037
00038            WORKING-STORAGE SECTION.
00039            77  LINE-KOUNTER         PICTURE 99 VALUE ZERO.
00040            77  SUBSCRIPT            PICTURE 99 VALUE ZERO.
00041
00042            01  LINE-1.
00043                05 FILLER            PICTURE X VALUE SPACES.
00044                05 NAME              PICTURE X(21) VALUE SPACES.
00045                05 FILLER            PICTURE X(111) VALUE SPACES.
00046
00047            01  LINE-2.
00048                05 FILLER            PICTURE X VALUE SPACES.
00049                05 STREET-ADDRESS    PICTURE X(21) VALUE SPACES.
00050                05 FILLER            PICTURE X(111) VALUE SPACES.
00051
00052            01  LINE-3.
00053                05 FILLER            PICTURE X VALUE SPACES.
00054                05 CITY-STATE-ZIP    PICTURE X(21) VALUE SPACES.
00055                05 FILLER            PICTURE X(111) VALUE SPACES.
00056
00057            01  LINE-4.
00058                05 FILLER            PICTURE X VALUE SPACES.
00059                05 FILLER            PICTURE X(13) VALUE 'PLEASE REMIT '.
00060                05 FARE              PICTURE $Z99.99.
00061                05 FILLER            PICTURE X(32) VALUE
00062              ' FOR AIRFARE ON COBOL AIR LINES'.
00063                05 FILLER            PICTURE X(80) VALUE SPACES.
00064
00065            01  LINE-5.
00066                05 FILLER            PICTURE X VALUE SPACES.
00067                05 FILLER            PICTURE X(49) VALUE
00068              'MAIL CHECKS TO P.O. BOX 913, NEW YORK, N.Y. 10019'.
00069                05 FILLER            PICTURE X(83) VALUE SPACES.
00070
00071            01  LINE-6.
00072                05 FILLER            PICTURE X VALUE SPACES.
00073                05 FILLER            PICTURE X(79) VALUE ALL '*'.
00074                05 FILLER            PICTURE X(53) VALUE SPACES.
00075
00076            01  RATE-TABLE-VALUES.
00077                05 FILLER            PICTURE 9(5)V99 VALUE 01142.00.
00078                05 FILLER            PICTURE 9(5)V99 VALUE 02221.00.
00079                05 FILLER            PICTURE 9(5)V99 VALUE 05109.50.
00080                05 FILLER            PICTURE 9(5)V99 VALUE 06078.50.
00081                05 FILLER            PICTURE 9(5)V99 VALUE 07100.00.
00082                05 FILLER            PICTURE 9(5)V99 VALUE 10210.50.
00083                05 FILLER            PICTURE 9(5)V99 VALUE 11335.75.
00084                05 FILLER            PICTURE 9(5)V99 VALUE 12250.50.
00085                05 FILLER            PICTURE 9(5)V99 VALUE 15110.00.
00086                05 FILLER            PICTURE 9(5)V99 VALUE 16210.00.
00087                05 FILLER            PICTURE 9(5)V99 VALUE 18485.00.
00088                05 FILLER            PICTURE 9(5)V99 VALUE 19195.00.
00089
00090            01  RATE-TABLE REDEFINES RATE-TABLE-VALUES.
00091                05 TABLE-DETAIL OCCURS 12 TIMES.
00092                   10 CITY-KODE       PICTURE 99.
00093                   10 AIRFARE         PICTURE 999V99.
00094
00095            PROCEDURE DIVISION.
00096
00097            START-UP.
00098                OPEN INPUT IN-FILE, OUTPUT OUT-FILE.
```

```
00099                    MOVE SPACES TC AIRFARE-BILL.
00100
00101          READ-DATA.
00102              READ IN-FILE AT END GC TC E-O-J.
00103
00104          LCCK-UP-FARE.
00105              ADD 1 TO SUBSCRIPT.
00106              IF SUBSCRIPT > 12 GO TC ERRCR-RTN.
00107              IF DESTINATICN-KCD = CITY-KCDE (SUBSCRIPT)
00108                  MOVE AIRFARE (SUBSCRIPT) TC FARE IN LINE-4
00109                  GO TO WRITE-INVOICE
00110              ELSE
00111                  GO TC LCCK-UP-FARE.
00112
00113          WRITE-INVOICE.
00114              MOVE NAME IN FARE-CARD TO NAME IN LINE-1.
00115              MOVE STREET-ADDRESS IN FARE-CARD TO STREET-ADDRESS IN LINE-2.
00116              MOVE CITY-STATE-ZIP IN FARE-CARD TO CITY-STATE-ZIP IN LINE-3.
00117              IF LINE-KCUNTER > 59 MCVE ZERO TO LINE-KOUNTER,
00118              WRITE AIRFARE-BILL FRCM LINE-1 AFTER ADVANCING TO-TOP-OF-PAGE
00119                  ELSE WRITE AIRFARE-BILL FROM LINE-1 AFTER ACVANCING 2.
00120              WRITE AIRFARE-BILL FRCM LINE-2 AFTER ADVANCING 1.
00121              WRITE AIRFARE-BILL FRCM LINE-3 AFTER ADVANCING 1.
00122              WRITE AIRFARE-BILL FRCM LINE-4 AFTER ADVANCING 4.
00123              WRITE AIRFARE-BILL FRCM LINE-5 AFTER ADVANCING 2.
00124              WRITE AIRFARE-BILL FRCM LINE-6 AFTER ADVANCING 5.
00125              ADD 15 TO LINE-KCUNTER.
00126              MOVE ZERC TC SUBSCRIPT.
00127              GO TO READ-DATA.
00128
00129          ERROR-RTN.
00130              MOVE SPACES TC AIRFARE-BILL.
00131              MOVE FARE-CARC TO OUTPLT-LINE.
00132              WRITE AIRFARE-BILL AFTER ADVANCING 5.
00133              MOVE
00134              '                    ***ERKOR***ERROR***ERKOR***ERROR***'
00135              TO AIRFARE-BILL.
00136              WRITE AIRFARE-BILL AFTER ADVANCING 2.
00137              MOVE
00138              '                        DESTINATICN CODE INVALID'
00139              TO AIRFARE-BILL.
00140              WRITE AIRFARE-BILL AFTER ACVANCING 1.
00141              WRITE AIRFARE-BILL FRCM LINE-6 AFTER ADVANCING 5.
00142              ADD 15 TO LINE-KCUNTER.
00143              MOVE ZERC TC SUBSCRIPT.
00144              GO TO READ-DATA.
00145
00146          E-O-J.
00147              CLOSE IN-FILE, OUT-FILE.
00148              STOP RUN.
```

OUTPUT TO PROGRAM 26

```
ARTHUR FIELDS
1155 BLEECKER STREET
NEW YORK, N.Y. 10005



PLEASE REMIT $221.00  FOR AIRFARE ON CDBGL AIR LINES

MAIL CHECKS TO P.C. BCX 913, NEW YCRK, N.Y. 1C019




*****************************************************************************************
HENRY MULLISH
100 BLEECKER STREET
NEW YORK, N.Y. 10012



PLEASE REMIT $221.00  FOR AIRFARE ON CDBCL AIR LINES

MAIL CHECKS TO P.C. BCX 913, NEW YCRK, N.Y. 1C019




*****************************************************************************************
```

```
HARVEY RENMAN         1 LONGACER ROAD      KINGS POINT, N.Y.                    09
                    ***ERROR***ERROR***ERROR***ERROR***
                      DESTINATION CODE INVALID



*************************************************************************************

JANE MORROW
45 WEST 37 STREET
NEW YORK, N.Y. 10014


PLEASE REMIT $110.00  FOR AIRFARE ON COBOL AIR LINES

MAIL CHECKS TO P.O. BOX 913, NEW YORK, N.Y. 10019



*************************************************************************************

ELI OPAS
1514 EAST 96 STREET
BROOKLYN, N.Y. 11236


PLEASE REMIT $195.00  FOR AIRFARE ON COBOL AIR LINES

MAIL CHECKS TO P.O. BOX 913, NEW YORK, N.Y. 10019



*************************************************************************************

ALFRED NEWMAN
14 WARREN STREET
SENECA ,N.Y. 22103


PLEASE REMIT $250.50  FOR AIRFARE ON COBOL AIR LINES

MAIL CHECKS TO P.O. BOX 913, NEW YORK, N.Y. 10019



*************************************************************************************

MARY JANE
23 MAIN STREET
ITHACA N.Y. 12345


PLEASE REMIT $109.50  FOR AIRFARE ON COBOL AIR LINES

MAIL CHECKS TO P.O. BOX 913, NEW YORK, N.Y. 10019



*************************************************************************************

ANN ASTER
14 ELM LANE
BROOKLYN, N.Y. 54211


PLEASE REMIT $485.00  FOR AIRFARE ON COBOL AIR LINES

MAIL CHECKS TO P.O. BOX 913, NEW YORK, N.Y. 10019



*************************************************************************************
```

```
JOHN ADAMS
3321 ASTER PLACE
QUEENS, N.Y. 12230


PLEASE REMIT $210.00  FOR AIRFARE ON COBOL AIR LINES

MAIL CHECKS TO P.O. BOX 913, NEW YORK, N.Y. 10019



**********************************************************************************
HARRY JONES
2 HOLIDAY WAY
ALBANY, N.Y. 14452


PLEASE REMIT $142.00  FOR AIRFARE ON COBOL AIR LINES

MAIL CHECKS TO P.O. BOX 913, NEW YORK, N.Y. 10019



**********************************************************************************
SAMUEL R SMITH
6 ANSI COURT
SPRING GELEN,N.Y.


PLEASE REMIT $100.00  FOR AIRFARE ON COBOL AIR LINES

MAIL CHECKS TO P.O. BOX 913, NEW YORK, N.Y. 10019



**********************************************************************************
```

12.4 YET ANOTHER APPROACH TO TABLE LOOKUP

The data to the next problem is identical to that used in Program 26 and, in fact, so is the output. The purpose of presenting it is to illustrate the use of the somewhat sophisticated version of the PERFORM statement. It is written in Program 27 as

```
PERFORM TABLE-LOOKUP THRU EXIT-ROUTINE
    VARYING SUBSCRIPT FROM 1 BY 1 UNTIL SUBSCRIPT > 12.
```

This statement enables us to initialize the value of SUBSCRIPT to 1, from which value it is incremented by 1 until it is greater than 12. As soon as its value is greater than 12, PERFORM is no longer executed. It is the range of PERFORM that we would like to concentrate upon now.

The paragraph names executed by PERFORM are:

```
TABLE-LOOKUP
WRITE-INVOICE
EXIT-ROUTINE
```

The sole entry in the paragraph EXIT-ROUTINE is the word EXIT. This is a COBOL reserved word which performs a very valuable function. If during a paragraph which is being PERFORMed, a test is made, and if as a result, nothing other than a continuation of the PERFORM is required, control can be sent to the paragraph name containing the EXIT instruction (in margin B, of course). In a sense it's a do-nothing verb, merely permitting PERFORM to continue its role without leaving its range. Once control is sent out of the range, it is not ordinarily possible to enter it again.

In paragraph TABLE-LOOKUP a test is made to determine whether DESTI-NATION-KOD is unequal to CITY-KODE (SUBSCRIPT). If it is, control is sent to EXIT-ROUTINE, the terminal paragraph of the range of PERFORM, and SUBSCRIPT is automatically incremented. Each time a successful match is made, the appropriate invoice is printed. If a data card is present which does not have a destination code coinciding with those in the table, the value of SUBSCRIPT will eventually exceed 12, in which case control "falls through" to the ERROR-RTN paragraph, which prints out the relevant error information as before.

PROGRAM 27
Lookup 3

```
00001          IDENTIFICATION DIVISION.
00002          PROGRAM-ID. LOOKUP3.
00003          AUTHOR. ELI J. OPAS.
00004          REMARKS. THIS IS YET ANOTHER APPROACH TO TABLE LOOK-UP.
00005
00006          ENVIRONMENT DIVISION.
00007          CONFIGURATION SECTION.
00008          SOURCE-COMPUTER. IBM-370-145.
00009          OBJECT-COMPUTER. IBM-370-145.
00010          SPECIAL-NAMES.
00011               C01 IS TO-TOP-OF-PAGE.
00012          INPUT-OUTPUT SECTION.
00013          FILE-CONTROL.
00014               SELECT  IN-FILE  ASSIGN TO UR-S-READER.
00015               SELECT  OUT-FILE ASSIGN TO UR-S-PRINTER.
00016
00017          DATA DIVISION.
00018
00019          FILE SECTION.
00020
00021          FD  IN-FILE
00022               LABEL RECORDS ARE OMITTED.
00023
00024          01  FARE-CARD.
00025               05 NAME           PICTURE X(21).
00026               05 STREET-ADDRESS PICTURE X(21).
00027               05 CITY-STATE-ZIP PICTURE X(21).
00028               05 FILLER         PICTURE X(15).
00029               05 DESTINATION-KOD PICTURE 99.
00030
00031          FD  OUT-FILE
00032               LABEL RECORDS ARE OMITTED.
00033
00034          01  AIRFARE-BILL.
00035               05 FILLER         PICTURE X.
00036               05 OUTPUT-LINE    PICTURE X(132).
00037
00038          WORKING-STORAGE SECTION.
00039          77  LINE-KOUNTER       PICTURE 99    VALUE ZERO.
00040          77  SUBSCRIPT          PICTURE 99    VALUE ZERO.
00041
00042          01  LINE-1.
00043               05  FILLER        PICTURE X     VALUE SPACES.
00044               05  NAME          PICTURE X(21) VALUE SPACES.
00045               05  FILLER        PICTURE X(111) VALUE SPACES.
```

```
00046
00047      01  LINE-2.
00048          05  FILLER                   PICTURE X VALUE SPACES.
00049          05  STREET-ADDRESS           PICTURE X(21)  VALUE SPACES.
00050          05  FILLER                   PICTURE X(111) VALUE SPACES.
00051
00052      01  LINE-3.
00053          05  FILLER                   PICTURE X     VALUE SPACES.
00054          05  CITY-STATE-ZIP           PICTURE X(21)  VALUE SPACES.
00055          05  FILLER                   PICTURE X(111) VALUE SPACES.
00056
00057      01  LINE-4.
00058          05  FILLER                   PICTURE X      VALUE SPACES.
00059          05  FILLER                   PICTURE X(13)  VALUE 'PLEASE REMIT
00060          05  FARE                     PICTURE $Z99.99.
00061          05  FILLER                   PICTURE X(32)  VALUE
00062      '  FOR AIRFARE ON CCBOL AIR LINES'.
00063          05  FILLER                   PICTURE X(80)  VALUE SPACES.
00064
00065      01  LINE-5.
00066          05  FILLER                   PICTURE X      VALUE SPACES.
00067          05  FILLER                   PICTURE X(49)  VALUE
00068      'MAIL CHECKS TO P.O. BCX 913, NEW YORK, N.Y. 10019'.
00069          05  FILLER                   PICTURE X(83)  VALUE SPACES.
00070
00071      01  LINE-6.
00072          05  FILLER                   PICTURE X      VALUE SPACES.
00073          05  FILLER                   PICTURE X(79)  VALUE ALL '*'.
00074          05  FILLER                   PICTURE X(53)  VALUE SPACES.
00075
00076      01  RATE-TABLE-VALUES.
00077          05  FILLER          PICTURE 9(5)V99 VALUE 01142.00.
00078          05  FILLER          PICTURE 9(5)V99 VALUE 02221.00.
00079          05  FILLER          PICTURE 9(5)V99 VALUE 05109.50.
00080          05  FILLER          PICTURE 9(5)V99 VALUE 06078.50.
00081          05  FILLER          PICTURE 9(5)V99 VALUE 07100.00.
00082          05  FILLER          PICTURE 9(5)V99 VALUE 10210.50.
00083          05  FILLER          PICTURE 9(5)V99 VALUE 11335.75.
00084          05  FILLER          PICTURE 9(5)V99 VALUE 12250.50.
00085          05  FILLER          PICTURE 9(5)V99 VALUE 15110.00.
00086          05  FILLER          PICTURE 9(5)V99 VALUE 16210.00.
00087          05  FILLER          PICTURE 9(5)V99 VALUE 18485.00.
00088          05  FILLER          PICTURE 9(5)V99 VALUE 19195.00.
00089
00090      01  RATE-TABLE REDEFINES RATE-TABLE-VALUES.
00091          05  TABLE-DETAIL OCCURS 12 TIMES.
00092              10  CITY-KODE   PICTURE 99.
00093              10  AIRFARE     PICTURE 999V99.
00094
00095      PROCEDURE DIVISION.
00096
00097      START-UP.
00098          OPEN INPUT IN-FILE, OUTPUT OUT-FILE.
00099          MOVE SPACES TO AIRFARE-BILL.
00100
00101      READ-DATA.
00102          READ IN-FILE AT END GO TO E-O-J.
00103
00104      LOOK-UP-FARE.
00105          PERFORM TABLE-LOOKUP THRU EXIT-ROUTINE
00106              VARYING SUBSCRIPT FROM 1 BY 1 UNTIL SUBSCRIPT > 12.
00107
00108
00109      ERROR-RTN.
00110          MOVE SPACES TO AIRFARE-BILL.
00111          MOVE FARE-CARD TO OUTPUT-LINE.
00112          WRITE AIRFARE-BILL AFTER ADVANCING 5.
00113          MOVE
00114      '                     ***ERROR***ERROR***ERROR***ERROR***'
00115          TO AIRFARE-BILL.
00116          WRITE AIRFARE-BILL AFTER ADVANCING 2.
00117          MOVE
00118      '                              DESTINATION CODE INVALID'
00119          TO AIRFARE-BILL.
00120          WRITE AIRFARE-BILL AFTER ADVANCING 1.
00121          WRITE AIRFARE-BILL FROM LINE-6 AFTER ADVANCING 5.
00122          ADD 15 TO LINE-KOUNTER.
00123          GO TO READ-DATA.
00124
00125      TABLE-LOOKUP.
00126          IF DESTINATION-KOD NOT EQUAL CITY-KODE (SUBSCRIPT) THEN
00127              GO TO EXIT-ROUTINE.
00128
00129      WRITE-INVOICE.
```

```
C0130           MOVE NAME IN FARE-CARD TO NAME IN LINE-1.
00131           MOVE STREET-ADDRESS IN FARE-CARD TO STREET-ADDRESS IN LINE-2.
00132           MOVE CITY-STATE-ZIP IN FARE-CARD TO CITY-STATE-ZIP IN LINE-3.
00133           IF LINE-KOUNTER > 59 MOVE ZERO TO LINE-KOUNTER,
00134           WRITE AIRFARE-BILL FROM LINE-1 AFTER ADVANCING TO-TOP-OF-PAGE
00135           ELSE WRITE AIRFARE-BILL FROM LINE-1 AFTER ADVANCING 2.
00136           WRITE AIRFARE-BILL FROM LINE-2 AFTER ADVANCING 1.
00137           WRITE AIRFARE-BILL FROM LINE-3 AFTER ADVANCING 1.
00138           MOVE AIRFARE (SUBSCRIPT) TO FARE IN LINE-4.
00139           WRITE AIRFARE-BILL FROM LINE-4 AFTER ADVANCING 4.
C0140           WRITE AIRFARE-BILL FROM LINE-5 AFTER ADVANCING 2.
00141           WRITE AIRFARE-BILL FROM LINE-6 AFTER ADVANCING 5.
00142           ADD 15 TO LINE-KOUNTER.
00143           GO TO READ-DATA.
0C144
00145       EXIT-ROUTINE.
C0146           EXIT.
00147
00148       E-O-J.
C0149           CLOSE IN-FILE, OUT-FILE.
00150           STOP RUN.
```

12.4.1. A Closer Look at Program 27

Program 27 was run again, on another compiler, the WATBOL version for the IBM 370, and it unexpectedly terminated abnormally. In computer science jargon, it "bombed." Here is the total output produced by the WATBOL run:

```
ARTHUR FIELDS
1155 BLEECKER STREET
NEW YORK, N.Y. 10005


PLEASE REMIT $221.00  FOR AIRFARE ON COBOL AIR LINES

MAIL CHECKS TO P.O. BOX 913, NEW YORK, N.Y. 10019


***********************************************************************************
***** ERROR 66 ILLEGAL ATTEMPT TO REENTER PERFORM.
PROGRAM WAS EXECUTING LINE   38 IN ROUTINE LOOKUP03 WHEN TERMINATION OCCURRED.
```

How is it possible for a program to run correctly on one compiler and not on another? Because not all compilers for a given computer language are alike. Some do a more thorough job of optimizing the generated machine level code while others, such as the WATBOL compiler, have better diagnostic capabilities. It is clear that the program contains an error which was not picked up by the regular IBM compiler but was detected by the WATBOL compiler.

What then is the source of the error?

A close look at the paragraph LOOK–UP–FARE, which contains the PERFORM statement, will help us to pinpoint the error. Each time the PERFORM instruction is encountered, the paragraphs TABLE–LOOKUP through EXIT–ROUTINE are executed a maximum of 12 times. The paragraphs are performed until either of the following two conditions are met:

1. The value of SUBSCRIPT is greater than 12.
2. DESTINATION–KOD is equal to CITY–CODE (SUBSCRIPT).

Terminating when the first condition holds is perfectly valid because when SUBSCRIPT is greater than 12, PERFORM will have relinquished its control.

Terminating when the second condition holds will inevitably lead to problems. The reason for this is that an attempt will have been made to re-execute PERFORM while it is still active. In the case in question, the value of DESTINATION–KOD (punched in columns 79–80) of the first data card is 02. Once this data card is read, PERFORM is activated and SUBSCRIPT is set to 1. At TABLE–LOOKUP a test is made to determine if the value of DESTINATION–KOD is equal to CITY–KODE (1). Since the value of CITY–KODE (1) is 01 (the first element of the table), control is sent to EXIT–ROUTINE. The value of SUBSCRIPT is then automatically incremented to 2 and the DESTINATION–KOD of 02 is tested against CITY–KODE (2). As will be seen from the table, CITY–KODE (2) is in fact equal to 02, so a match is made. As a result, the instructions in paragraph WRITE–INVOICE are executed, including the GO TO READ–DATA instruction. The next data card is read and control drops through to the next instruction, which happens to be the still active PERFORM. Remember that this is so because SUBSCRIPT is not yet greater than 12. An attempt to execute a still active PERFORM violates the rules of COBOL. One is left to ponder how a full COBOL compiler can permit such an error to go through undetected.

How can we rectify the problem?

Since the trouble arises because the PERFORM statement is still active after a match had been effected, an obvious solution is to deactivate the PERFORM by artificially satisfying the UNTIL condition before reading the next data card. Moving 13 to SUBSCRIPT will exhaust the PERFORM. This will satisfy the UNTIL condition so that by the time the EXIT statement is executed PERFORM will have completed its cycle.

In order to prevent ERROR–RTN from being executed erroneously, a flag device can be set up by means of a simple 77 level item called, say, FOUND. Moving 'YES' to FOUND signifies that a match has been made. Control can then be sent directly to the read paragraph, thereby preventing the error routine from being incorrectly executed.

These amendments have been included in the Program 27A. The output which is not shown is identical to that of Program 27.

PROGRAM 27A
Lookup 3A

```
00001        IDENTIFICATION DIVISION.
00002        PROGRAM-ID. LOOKUP3A.
00003        AUTHOR. ELI J. OPAS.
00004        REMARKS. THIS IS ANOTHER APPROACH TO TABLE LOOK-UP.
00005
00006        ENVIRONMENT DIVISION.
00007        CONFIGURATION SECTION.
00008        SOURCE-COMPUTER. IBM-370-145.
00009        OBJECT-COMPUTER. IBM-370-145.
00010        SPECIAL-NAMES.
00011            C01 IS TO-TOP-OF-PAGE.
```

```
00012               INPUT-OUTPUT SECTICN.
00013               FILE-CONTROL.
00014                   SELECT  IN-FILE  ASSIGN TC UR-S-READER.
00015                   SELECT  OUT-FILE ASSIGN TC UR-S-PRINTER.
00016
00017               DATA DIVISION.
00018
00019               FILE SECTION.
00020
00021               FD  IN-FILE
00022                   LABEL RECORDS ARE OMITTED.
00023
00024               01  FARE-CARD.
00025                   05 NAME            PICTURE X(21).
00026                   05 STREET-ADDRESS  PICTURE X(21).
00027                   05 CITY-STATE-ZIP  PICTURE X(21).
00028                   05 FILLER          PICTURE X(15).
00029                   05 DESTINATION-KOD PICTURE 99.
00030
00031               FD  OUT-FILE
00032                   LABEL RECORDS ARE OMITTED.
00033
00034               01  AIRFARE-BILL.
00035                   05 FILLER          PICTURE X.
00036                   05 OUTPUT-LINE     PICTURE X(132).
00037
00038               WORKING-STORAGE SECTION.
00039               77  FOUND              PICTURE X(3).
00040               77  LINE-KOUNTER       PICTURE 99 VALUE ZERO.
00041               77  SUBSCRIPT          PICTURE 99.
00042
00043               01  LINE-1.
00044                   05 FILLER          PICTURE X VALUE SPACES.
00045                   05 NAME            PICTURE X(21) VALUE SPACES.
00046                   05 FILLER          PICTURE X(111) VALUE SPACES.
00047
00048               01  LINE-2.
00049                   05 FILLER          PICTURE X VALUE SPACES.
00050                   05 STREET-ADDRESS  PICTURE X(21) VALUE SPACES.
00051                   05 FILLER          PICTURE X(111) VALUE SPACES.
00052
00053               01  LINE-3.
00054                   05 FILLER          PICTURE X VALUE SPACES.
00055                   05 CITY-STATE-ZIP  PICTURE X(21) VALUE SPACES.
00056                   05 FILLER          PICTURE X(111) VALUE SPACES.
00057
00058               01  LINE-4.
00059                   05 FILLER          PICTURE X VALUE SPACES.
00060                   05 FILLER          PICTURE X(13) VALUE 'PLEASE REMIT '.
00061                   05 FARE            PICTURE $Z99.99.
00062                   05 FILLER          PICTURE X(32) VALUE
00063                   ' FOR AIRFARE ON COBOL AIR LINES'.
00064                   05 FILLER          PICTURE X(80) VALUE SPACES.
00065
00066               01  LINE-5.
00067                   05 FILLER          PICTURE X VALUE SPACES.
00068                   05 FILLER          PICTURE X(49) VALUE
00069                   'MAIL CHECKS TO P.O. BCX 913, NEW YORK, N.Y. 10019'.
00070                   05 FILLER          PICTURE X(83) VALUE SPACES.
00071
00072               01  LINE-6.
00073                   05 FILLER          PICTURE X VALUE SPACES.
00074                   05 FILLER          PICTURE X(79) VALUE ALL '*'.
00075                   05 FILLER          PICTURE X(53) VALUE SPACES.
00076
00077               01  RATE-TABLE-VALUES.
00078                   05 FILLER          PICTURE 9(5)V99 VALUE 01142.00.
00079                   05 FILLER          PICTURE 9(5)V99 VALUE 02221.00.
00080                   05 FILLER          PICTURE 9(5)V99 VALUE 05109.50.
00081                   05 FILLER          PICTURE 9(5)V99 VALUE 06078.50.
00082                   05 FILLER          PICTURE 9(5)V99 VALUE 07100.00.
00083                   05 FILLER          PICTURE 9(5)V99 VALUE 10210.50.
00084                   05 FILLER          PICTURE 9(5)V99 VALUE 11335.75.
00085                   05 FILLER          PICTURE 9(5)V99 VALUE 12250.50.
00086                   05 FILLER          PICTURE 9(5)V99 VALUE 15110.00.
00087                   05 FILLER          PICTURE 9(5)V99 VALUE 16210.00.
00088                   05 FILLER          PICTURE 9(5)V99 VALUE 18485.00.
00089                   05 FILLER          PICTURE 9(5)V99 VALUE 19195.00.
00090
00091               01  RATE-TABLE REDEFINES RATE-TABLE-VALUES.
00092                   05 TABLE-DETAIL OCCURS 12 TIMES.
00093                      10 CITY-KODE    PICTURE 99.
00094                      10 AIRFARE      PICTURE 999V99.
```

```
00095
00096              PROCEDURE DIVISION.
00097
00098              START-UP.
00099                  OPEN INPUT IN-FILE, OUTPUT OUT-FILE.
00100                  MOVE SPACES TO AIRFARE-BILL.
00101
00102              READ-DATA.
00103                  READ IN-FILE AT END GO TO E-O-J.
00104                  MOVE 'NO' TO FOUND.
00105
00106              LOOK-UP-FARE.
00107                  PERFORM TABLE-LOOKUP THRU EXIT-ROUTINE
00108                      VARYING SUBSCRIPT FROM 1 BY 1 UNTIL SUBSCRIPT > 12.
00109
00110                  IF FOUND = 'YES' THEN GO TO READ-DATA.
00111
00112              ERROR-RTN.
00113                  MOVE SPACES TO AIRFARE-BILL.
00114                  MOVE FARE-CARD TO OUTPUT-LINE.
00115                  WRITE AIRFARE-BILL AFTER ADVANCING 5.
00116                  MOVE
00117                  '                    ***ERROR***ERROR***ERROR***ERROR***'
00118                  TO AIRFARE-BILL.
00119                  WRITE AIRFARE-BILL AFTER ADVANCING 2.
00120                  MOVE
00121                  '                         DESTINATION CODE INVALID'
00122                  TO AIRFARE-BILL.
00123                  WRITE AIRFARE-BILL AFTER ADVANCING 1.
00124                  WRITE AIRFARE-BILL FROM LINE-6 AFTER ADVANCING 5.
00125                  ADD 15 TO LINE-KOUNTER.
00126                  GO TO READ-DATA.
00127
00128              TABLE-LOOKUP.
00129                  IF DESTINATION-KOD NOT EQUAL CITY-KODE (SUBSCRIPT) THEN
00130                      GO TO EXIT-ROUTINE.
00131
00132              WRITE-INVOICE.
00133                  MOVE NAME IN FARE-CARD TO NAME IN LINE-1.
00134                  MOVE STREET-ADDRESS IN FARE-CARD TO STREET-ADDRESS IN LINE-2.
00135                  MOVE CITY-STATE-ZIP IN FARE-CARD TO CITY-STATE-ZIP IN LINE-3.
00136                  IF LINE-KOUNTER > 59 MOVE ZERO TO LINE-KOUNTER.
00137                  WRITE AIRFARE-BILL FROM LINE-1 AFTER ADVANCING TO-TOP-OF-PAGE
00138                      ELSE WRITE AIRFARE-BILL FROM LINE-1 AFTER ADVANCING 2.
00139                  WRITE AIRFARE-BILL FROM LINE-2 AFTER ADVANCING 1.
00140                  WRITE AIRFARE-BILL FROM LINE-3 AFTER ADVANCING 1.
00141                  MOVE AIRFARE (SUBSCRIPT) TO FARE IN LINE-4.
00142                  WRITE AIRFARE-BILL FROM LINE-4 AFTER ADVANCING 4.
00143                  WRITE AIRFARE-BILL FROM LINE-5 AFTER ADVANCING 2.
00144                  WRITE AIRFARE-BILL FROM LINE-6 AFTER ADVANCING 5.
00145                  ADD 15 TO LINE-KOUNTER.
00146                  MOVE 13 TO SUBSCRIPT.
00147                  MOVE 'YES' TO FOUND.
00148
00149              EXIT-ROUTINE.
00150                  EXIT.
00151
00152              E-O-J.
00153                  CLOSE IN-FILE, OUT-FILE.
00154                  STOP RUN.
```

12.5 AND YET ANOTHER APPROACH TO TABLES

In the definition of RATE–TABLE–VALUES in Program 28, each of the 12 codes is contained as an alphanumeric value with a PICTURE of X. Each of the four 21 character strings is enclosed by a beginning quote and is terminated by a quote sign, even though each item is numeric. However, when RATE–TABLE–VALUES is redefined by RATE–TABLE, the elementary items CITY–KODE and AIRFARE are specified with numeric pictures, thereby making possible arithmetic comparisons. The output to Program 28 is identical to that produced by Program 27.

PROGRAM 28
Lookup 4

```
00001          IDENTIFICATION DIVISION.
00002          PROGRAM-ID. LOOKUP-4.
00003          REMARKS. AND YET ANOTHER APPROACH TO TABLES.
C0004          AUTHOR. ELI J. OPAS.
C0005
C0006          ENVIRONMENT DIVISION.
0C007          CONFIGURATION SECTION.
C0008          SOURCE-COMPUTER. IBM-370-145.
00009          OBJECT-COMPUTER. IBM-370-145.
00010          SPECIAL-NAMES.
C0011              C01 IS TO-TOP-OF-PAGE.
00012          INPUT-OUTPUT SECTION.
00013          FILE-CONTROL.
00014              SELECT IN-FILE  ASSIGN TO UT-S-READER.
C0015              SELECT OUT-FILE ASSIGN TO UT-S-PRINTER.
C0016
00017          DATA DIVISION.
C0018
00019          FILE SECTION.
C0020
C0021          FD  IN-FILE
00022              LABEL RECORDS ARE OMITTED.
00023
00024          01  FARE-CARD.
C0025              05 NAME            PICTURE X(21).
00026              05 STREET-ADDRESS  PICTURE X(21).
00027              05 CITY-STATE-ZIP  PICTURE X(21).
00028              05 FILLER          PICTURE X(15).
00029              05 DESTINATION-KOD PICTURE 99.
C0030
00031          FD  OUT-FILE
00032              LABEL RECORDS ARE OMITTED.
00033
00034          01  AIRFARE-BILL.
00035              05 FILLER          PICTURE X.
C0036              05 OUTPUT-LINE     PICTURE X(132).
00037
00C38          WORKING-STORAGE SECTION.
00039          77  LINE-KOUNTER       PICTURE 99 VALUE ZERO.
C0040          77  SUBSCRIPT          PICTURE 99.
00041          77  FOUND              PICTURE X(3).
00042
00043          01  LINE-1.
00044              05 FILLER          PICTURE X VALUE SPACES.
00045              05 NAME            PICTURE X(21) VALUE SPACES.
00046              05 FILLER          PICTURE X(111) VALUE SPACES.
00047
00048          01  LINE-2.
00049              05 FILLER          PICTURE X VALUE SPACES.
00050              05 STREET-ADDRESS  PICTURE X(21) VALUE SPACES.
00051              05 FILLER          PICTURE X(111) VALUE SPACES.
C0052
00053          01  LINE-3.
00054              05 FILLER          PICTURE X VALUE SPACES.
C0055              05 CITY-STATE-ZIP  PICTURE X(21) VALUE SPACES.
00056              05 FILLER          PICTURE X(111) VALUE SPACES.
00057
C0058          01  LINE-4.
00059              05 FILLER          PICTURE X VALUE SPACES.
C0060              05 FILLER          PICTURE X(13) VALUE 'PLEASE REMIT '.
C0061              05 FARE            PICTURE $299.99.
00062              05 FILLER          PICTURE X(32) VALUE
C0063          ' FOR AIRFARE ON COBOL AIR LINES'.
C0064              05 FILLER          PICTURE X(80) VALUE SPACES.
CC065
0C066          01  LINE-5.
C0067              05 FILLER          PICTURE X VALUE SPACES.
CC068              05 FILLER          PICTURE X(45) VALUE
CC069          'MAIL CHECKS TO P.C. BOX 513, NEW YORK, N.Y. 10019'.
CC070              05 FILLER          PICTURE X(83) VALUE SPACES.
CC071
CCC72          01  LINE-6.
00073              05 FILLER          PICTURE X VALUE SPACES.
00074              05 FILLER          PICTURE X(79) VALUE ALL '*'.
CC075              05 FILLER          PICTURE X(53) VALUE SPACES.
CC076
00077          01  RATE-TABLE-VALUES.
C0078              05 FILLER          PICTURE X(21) VALUE
```

```
00079                                      '01142000222100051055C'.
00080              05 FILLER                PICTURE X(21) VALUE
00081                                      '06078500071C00010210500'.
00082              05 FILLER                PICTURE X(21) VALUE
00083                                      '1133575122505C1511000'.
00084              05 FILLER                PICTURE X(21) VALUE
00085                                      '1621000184850C1519500'.
00086
00087       01  RATE-TABLE REDEFINES RATE-TABLE-VALUES.
00088            05 TABLE-DETAIL OCCURS 12 TIMES.
00089               10 CITY-KODE    PICTURE 99.
00090               10 AIRFARE      PICTURE 999V99.
00091
00092       PROCEDURE DIVISION.
00093
00094       START-UP.
00095            OPEN INPUT IN-FILE, OUTPUT OUT-FILE.
00096            MOVE SPACES TO AIRFARE-BILL.
00097
00098       READ-DATA.
00099            READ IN-FILE AT END GO TO E-O-J.
00100
00101       LOOK-UP-FARE.
00102            MOVE 'NO' TO FOUND.
00103            PERFORM TABLE-LOOKUP THRU EXIT-ROUTINE
00104                 VARYING SUBSCRIPT FROM 1 BY 1 UNTIL SUBSCRIPT > 12.
00105            IF FOUND = 'YES' GO TO READ-DATA.
00106
00107       ERROR-RTN.
00108            MOVE SPACES TO AIRFARE-BILL.
00109            MOVE FARE-CARD TO OUTPUT-LINE.
00110            WRITE AIRFARE-BILL AFTER ADVANCING 5.
00111            MOVE
00112            '                    ***ERROR***ERROR***ERROR***ERROR***'
00113            TO AIRFARE-BILL.
00114            WRITE AIRFARE-BILL AFTER ADVANCING 2.
00115            MOVE
00116            '                    DESTINATION CODE INVALID'
00117            TO AIRFARE-BILL.
00118            WRITE AIRFARE-BILL AFTER ADVANCING 1.
00119            WRITE AIRFARE-BILL FROM LINE-6 AFTER ADVANCING 5.
00120            ADD 15 TO LINE-KOUNTER.
00121            GO TO READ-DATA.
00122
00123       TABLE-LOOKUP.
00124            IF DESTINATION-KOD NOT EQUAL CITY-KODE (SUBSCRIPT) THEN
00125                 GO TO EXIT-ROUTINE.
00126
00127       WRITE-INVOICE.
00128            MOVE NAME IN FARE-CARD TO NAME IN LINE-1.
00129            MOVE STREET-ADDRESS IN FARE-CARD TO STREET-ADDRESS IN LINE-2.
00130            MOVE CITY-STATE-ZIP IN FARE-CARD TO CITY-STATE-ZIP IN LINE-3.
00131            IF LINE-KOUNTER > 59 MOVE ZERO TO LINE-KOUNTER,
00132            WRITE AIRFARE-BILL FROM LINE-1 AFTER ADVANCING TO-TOP-OF-PAGE
00133                 ELSE WRITE AIRFARE-BILL FROM LINE-1 AFTER ADVANCING 2.
00134            WRITE AIRFARE-BILL FROM LINE-2 AFTER ADVANCING 1.
00135            WRITE AIRFARE-BILL FROM LINE-3 AFTER ADVANCING 1.
00136            MOVE AIRFARE (SUBSCRIPT) TO FARE IN LINE-4.
00137            WRITE AIRFARE-BILL FROM LINE-4 AFTER ADVANCING 4.
00138            WRITE AIRFARE-BILL FROM LINE-5 AFTER ADVANCING 2.
00139            WRITE AIRFARE-BILL FROM LINE-6 AFTER ADVANCING 5.
00140            ADD 15 TO LINE-KOUNTER.
00141            MOVE 13 TO SUBSCRIPT.
00142            MOVE 'YES' TO FOUND.
00143
00144       EXIT-ROUTINE.
00145            EXIT.
00146
00147       E-O-J.
00148            CLOSE IN-FILE, OUT-FILE.
00149            STOP RUN.
```

12.6 A TABLE SEARCH USING INDEXING

Even though many programmers might jump to the conclusion that indexing and subscripting are identical operations, the fact is that in COBOL they are quite distinct, even though there are definite similarities between the two and their purposes are analogous.

| 1 | - | 21 22 | - | 32 33 | - | 76 77 | 78 79 | 80 |

Name of Employee X(21)	Employee # (soc-sec-no) X(11)	Filler X(44)	Hours Wkd. 99	Pay Class 99

FIGURE 21

When subscripting is used, as was the case in each of the four previous programs, it is the responsibility of the programmer not only to initialize the value of the subscript but also to arrange for a method of increasing or, as one says in computing circles, incrementing the value of the subscript. In *indexing* the initial value of the index is set by the SET verb while the index is incremented automatically. The program which will shortly follow introduces us to several interesting features which will be discussed further on.

The input to Program 29 is a series of weekly time cards, each of which is punched in the format shown in Figure 21.

This is the actual data that was used in running the program:

COLUMN 1	COLUMN 22	COLUMN 77	COLUMN 79
BERT STURZA	451–02–1411	3209	
HAIM TOPOL	888–25–4758	3603	
ANITA BORG	117–44–9161	3201	
ALAN LEVINE	444–55–3625	4508	
MOISHA OYSHER	456–78–1238	3007	
ROSEMARY CORTELYOU	586–36–1425	2001	
ALFRED FREEMAN	356–23–3658	4012	
GEORGE WASHINGTON	120–35–1234	3605	
ROSE HAN	789–25–4758	3510	
JAY BLAIRE	365–25–1346	4002	
SUE MAILMAN	578–45–0102	3005	
MINDY WACHTEL	214–23–3214	3605	

Each employee's hourly rate of pay falls into a pay class which ranges from 01 to 10. The weekly salary is computed by multiplying the number of hours worked during the week by the rate specified by the pay class. The object of the program is to print the check for the weekly salary, without taking into account any of the usual deductions since this will unnecessarily complicate the discussion of the underlying principles.

12.6.1. The INDEXED BY and SET Clauses

The 10 pay classes and their corresponding hourly rates are incorporated into the table called TABLE–VALUES. This table is then redefined by HOURLY–WAGE on the 01 level. On the 05 level we indicate that the TABLE–PAIR (composed of HW–PAY–CLASS and HW–HOURLY–WAGE) occurs 10 times and each is indexed by HW–INDEX. The INDEXED BY clause defines the name of the index, thereby relieving the programmer of the responsibility of making provisions for the index in Working-Storage, as has to be done when subscripting is used. The programmer does not have to be concerned at all with assigning a PICTURE to the index, since it does not take one.

The INDEXED BY clause in Program 29 specifies that the index to be used is HW-INDEX. The initial value of HW–INDEX is set to 1 by the instruction

```
SET HW–INDEX TO 1
```

in the Procedure Division.

From a conceptual point of view, both subscript and index refer to that occurrence of the data name included by the OCCURS clause as specified by the value of the subscript or the index. In other words, if the subscript or the index have the value of, say, 4, it is the *fourth* occurrence in the table that is being referenced in both cases. What then is the advantage of one approach over the other? The index is stored internally as a binary value without having to undergo any sort of conversion and as a result is faster so far as execution of the program is concerned. Actually, the value of an index points to an element in the table relative to the beginning of the table, but this is of no direct concern to the programmer.

Let us return to the Procedure Division; the input file PAYROLL–FILE is opened and so is the output file PAY–CHECK. The first data card of the input file is then read; it has a pay class of 09 and the hours worked are 32. The paragraph SEARCH–TABLE is then encountered and it is here that HW–INDEX is set to 1. Now we will search the table for a pay class of 09. If one is found (and notice that the ninth element of the table has the value 09501, meaning class 09, hourly wage $5.01) we want to "extract" the value $5.01 and multiply it by the number of hours worked as punched on the input card in order to calculate the amount of the pay check.

12.6.2. The SEARCH and WHEN Clauses

The group item TABLE–PAIR is searched by the COBOL phrase

```
SEARCH TABLE-PAIR
```

However, this verb acts in a manner reminiscent of the READ instruction. The SEARCH verb too has an AT END clause. Now, with HW–INDEX set to the value 1, HW–PAY–CLASS (1) is compared to the value of PAY–CLASS punched on the data card. If they match, the associated HW–HOURLY–WAGE (1) is moved to Working-Storage for subsequent computation. If they don't match, the value of HW–INDEX is automatically incremented so that it points to the second occurrence of the table. All this is accomplished in COBOL by the SEARCH verb and its associated WHEN clause, which acts as an IF statement.

Each time a match is made the weekly wage is computed and a payroll check printed out. If, however, the entire table is searched and a pay class punched on the data card is not matched successfully with any pay class in the table, it is assumed that the data card in question is incorrectly punched. The AT END clause is then invoked and the entire card-contents printed out accompanied by a suitable message.

12.6.3. The JUSTIFIED RIGHT Clause

Another feature mentioned but not yet discussed has been introduced into this program. It concerns the printing out of a non-numeric literal. Normally, if a non-numeric literal is moved to an X field, it is left-adjusted, with any remaining space being filled with blanks. On occasions it is convenient to deliberately right-adjust the information. This is done in LINE-1 and LINE-5, where the COBOL phrase JUSTIFIED RIGHT has been abbreviated to its equally acceptable JUST RIGHT, or even JUST. Oddly enough one cannot achieve this result using the regular MOVE instruction.

PROGRAM 29
Index 1

```
00001        IDENTIFICATION DIVISION.
00002
00003        PROGRAM-ID. INDEX-1.
00004        AUTHOR. ELI J. OPAS.
00005        REMARKS. THIS IS A FIRST ATTEMPT AT INDEXING.
00006
00007        ENVIRONMENT DIVISION.
00008
00009        CONFIGURATION SECTION.
00010        SOURCE-COMPUTER. IBM-370-145.
00011        OBJECT-COMPUTER. IBM-370-145.
00012
00013        SPECIAL-NAMES.
00014            C01 IS TO-TOP-OF-PAGE.
00015
00016        INPUT-OUTPUT SECTION.
00017
00018        FILE-CONTROL.
00019
00020            SELECT PAYROLL-FILE ASSIGN TO UT-S-READER.
00021            SELECT PAY-CHECK ASSIGN TO UT-S-PRINTER.
00022
00023        DATA DIVISION.
00024
00025        FILE SECTION.
00026
00027        FD  PAYROLL-FILE
00028            LABEL RECORDS ARE OMITTED.
00029
00030        01  EMPLOYEE-CARD.
```

```
00031                05   NAME              PICTURE X(21).
00032                05   EMPLOYEE-NO       PICTURE X(11).
00033                05   FILLER            PICTURE X(44).
00034                05   HOURS-WORKED      PICTURE 99.
00035                05   PAY-CLASS         PICTURE 99.
00036
00037        FD   PAY-CHECK
00038             LABEL RECORDS ARE OMITTED.
00039
00040        01   PAYROLL-CHECK.
00041             05 CC                     PICTURE X.
00042             05 OUTPUT-LINE            PICTURE X(132).
00043
00044        WORKING-STORAGE SECTION.
00045
00046        77   W-S-HOURLY-WAGE      PICTURE 9V99.
00047        77   LINE-KOUNTER         PICTURE 99 VALUE ZERO.
00048
00049        01   TABLE-VALUES.
00050             05 FILLER            PICTURE X(25) VALUE
00051                                  '0118502193032040422305268'.
00052             05 FILLER            PICTURE X(25) VALUE
00053                                  '0632507347084720950110624'.
00054
00055        01   HOURLY-WAGE REDEFINES TABLE-VALUES.
00056             05 TABLE-PAIR OCCURS 10 TIMES INDEXED BY HW-INDEX.
00057                10 HW-PAY-CLASS PICTURE 99.
00058                10 HW-HOURLY-WAGE PICTURE 9V99.
00059
00060        01   LINE-1.
00061             05 FILLER            PICTURE X(52) VALUE
00062                                  'ANSI CORP. PAYROLL ACCOUNT' JUST RIGHT.
00063
00064        01   LINE-2.
00065             05 FILLER            PICTURE X(72) VALUE SPACES.
00066             05   DAYTE           PICTURE X(8) VALUE SPACES.
00067
00068        01   LINE-3.
00069             05 FILLER            PICTURE X(21) VALUE
00070                                  ' PAY TO THE ORDER CF '.
00071             05 NAME              PICTURE X(21) VALUE SPACES.
00072             05 FILLER            PICTURE X(31) VALUE SPACES.
00073             05 WEEKLY-PAY        PICTURE $Z99.99.
00074
00075        01   LINE-4.
00076             05 FILLER            PICTURE X(17) VALUE
00077                                  ' EMPLOYEE NUMBER '.
00078             05 EMPLOYEE-NO       PICTURE X(11) VALUE SPACES.
00079             05 FILLER            PICTURE X(52) VALUE SPACES.
00080
00081        01   LINE-5.
00082             05 FILLER            PICTURE X(80) VALUE
00083                                  'PETER PRESIDENT' JUST RIGHT.
00084
00085        01   LINE-6.
00086             05 FILLER            PICTURE X VALUE SPACES.
00087             05 FILLER            PICTURE X(79) VALUE ALL '*'.
00088
00089        PROCEDURE DIVISION.
00090
00091        LETS-GO.
00092             OPEN INPUT PAYROLL-FILE, OUTPUT PAY-CHECK.
00093
00094        READ-A-CARD.
00095             READ PAYROLL-FILE AT END GO TO E-C-J.
00096
00097        SEARCH-TABLE.
00098             SET HW-INDEX TO 1.
00099             SEARCH TABLE-PAIR AT END GO TO ERROR-RTN,
00100             WHEN HW-PAY-CLASS (HW-INDEX) = PAY-CLASS
00101             MOVE HW-HOURLY-WAGE (HW-INDEX) TO W-S-HOURLY-WAGE.
00102
00103        SET-UP-CHECK.
00104             COMPUTE WEEKLY-PAY ROUNDED = HOURS-WORKED * W-S-HOURLY-WAGE.
00105             MOVE NAME IN EMPLOYEE-CARD TO NAME IN LINE-3.
00106             MOVE CURRENT-DATE TO DAYTE.
00107             MOVE EMPLOYEE-NO IN EMPLOYEE-CARD TO EMPLOYEE-NO IN LINE-4.
00108
00109        WRITE-PAY-CHECK.
00110             IF LINE-KOUNTER > 59 WRITE PAYROLL-CHECK FROM LINE-1
00111                AFTER ADVANCING TO-TOP-OF-PAGE,
00112                MOVE ZERO TO LINE-KOUNTER
00113             ELSE
```

```
C0114            WRITE PAYROLL-CHECK FROM LINE-1 AFTER ADVANCING 2.
00115            WRITE PAYROLL-CHECK FROM LINE-2 AFTER ADVANCING 3.
00116            WRITE PAYROLL-CHECK FROM LINE-3 AFTER ADVANCING 3.
C0117            WRITE PAYROLL-CHECK FROM LINE-4 AFTER ADVANCING 2.
00118            WRITE PAYROLL-CHECK FROM LINE-5 AFTER ADVANCING 3.
00119            WRITE PAYROLL-CHECK FROM LINE-6 AFTER ADVANCING 2.
C0120            ADD 15 TO LINE-KOUNTER.
00121            GO TC READ-A-CARD.
00122
00123        ERROR-RTN.
00124            MOVE EMPLOYEE-CARD TO CUTPUT-LINE.
00125            WRITE PAYROLL-CHECK AFTER ADVANCING 3.
C0126            MOVE
00127               '                         ***ERROR***ERROR***ERROR***'
00128            TO CUTPUT-LINE.
C0129            WRITE PAYROLL-CHECK AFTER ADVANCING 3.
00130            MOVE
00131               '                         PAY-CLASS NOT FOUND'
00132            TO CUTPUT-LINE.
00133            WRITE PAYROLL-CHECK AFTER ADVANCING 3.
00134            WRITE PAYROLL-CHECK FROM LINE-6 AFTER ADVANCING 6.
C0135            ADD 15 TO LINE-KOUNTER.
C0136            GO TO READ-A-CARD.
0C137
00138        E-O-J.
00139            CLOSE PAYROLL-FILE, PAY-CHECK.
C0140            STOP RUN.
```

OUTPUT TO PROGRAM 29

```
                        ANSI CORP. PAYROLL ACCOUNT


                                                              06/20/77


PAY TO THE ORDER OF BERT STURZA                              $160.32

EMPLOYEE NUMBER 451-02-1411


                                                    PETER PRESIDENT

********************************************************************************
                        ANSI CORP. PAYROLL ACCOUNT


                                                              06/20/77


PAY TO THE ORDER CF HAIM TOPOL                               $ 73.44

EMPLOYEE NUMBER 888-25-4758


                                                    PETER PRESIDENT

********************************************************************************
                        ANSI CORP. PAYROLL ACCOUNT


                                                              06/20/77


PAY TO THE ORDER OF ANITA BORG                               $ 59.20

EMPLOYEE NUMBER 117-44-9161


                                                    PETER PRESIDENT

********************************************************************************
```

```
                      ANSI CORP. PAYROLL ACCOUNT


                                                          06/20/77

PAY TO THE ORDER OF ALAN LEVINE                          $212.40
EMPLOYEE NUMBER 444-55-3625


                                                    PETER PRESIDENT
*****************************************************************************

                      ANSI CORP. PAYROLL ACCOUNT


                                                          06/20/77

PAY TO THE ORDER OF MOISHA OYSHER                        $104.10
EMPLOYEE NUMBER 456-78-1238


                                                    PETER PRESIDENT
*****************************************************************************

                      ANSI CORP. PAYROLL ACCOUNT


                                                          06/20/77

PAY TO THE ORDER OF ROSEMARY CORTELYOU                   $ 37.00
EMPLOYEE NUMBER 586-36-1425


                                                    PETER PRESIDENT
*****************************************************************************

ALFRED FREEMAN          356-23-3658                           4012

                    ***ERROR***ERROR***ERROR***

                        PAY-CLASS NOT FOUND



*****************************************************************************

                      ANSI CORP. PAYROLL ACCOUNT


                                                          06/20/77

PAY TO THE ORDER OF GEORGE WASHINGTON                    $ 96.48
EMPLOYEE NUMBER 120-35-1234


                                                    PETER PRESIDENT
*****************************************************************************
```

```
                          ANSI CORP. PAYROLL ACCOUNT


                                                                     06/20/77


         PAY TO THE ORDER OF ROSE HAN                                $218.40

         EMPLOYEE NUMBER 789-25-4758


                                                                 PETER PRESIDENT
         ****************************************************************************
                          ANSI CORP. PAYROLL ACCOUNT


                                                                     06/20/77


         PAY TO THE ORDER OF JAY BLAIRE                             $  77.20

         EMPLOYEE NUMBER 365-25-1346


                                                                 PETER PRESIDENT
         ****************************************************************************
                          ANSI CORP. PAYROLL ACCOUNT


                                                                     06/20/77


         PAY TO THE ORDER OF SUE MAILMAN                            $  96.48

         EMPLOYEE NUMBER 578-45-0102


                                                                 PETER PRESIDENT
         ****************************************************************************
                          ANSI CORP. PAYROLL ACCOUNT


                                                                     06/20/77


         PAY TO THE ORDER OF MINDY WACHTEL                          $  96.48

         EMPLOYEE NUMBER 214-23-3214


                                                                 PETER PRESIDENT
         ****************************************************************************
```

12.7 A TABLE LOOKUP WITH BOTH INDEXING AND SUBSCRIPTING

We have seen how both indexing and subscripting may be used to reference a table in a COBOL program. In each of the programs thus far, only one table has been included. But a program can contain more than one table. In the program which follows two tables are specified. For the sake of illustration the first table uses subscripting while the second uses indexing.

The input deck to the program consists of a series of daily time cards, each of which is punched as shown in Figure 22.

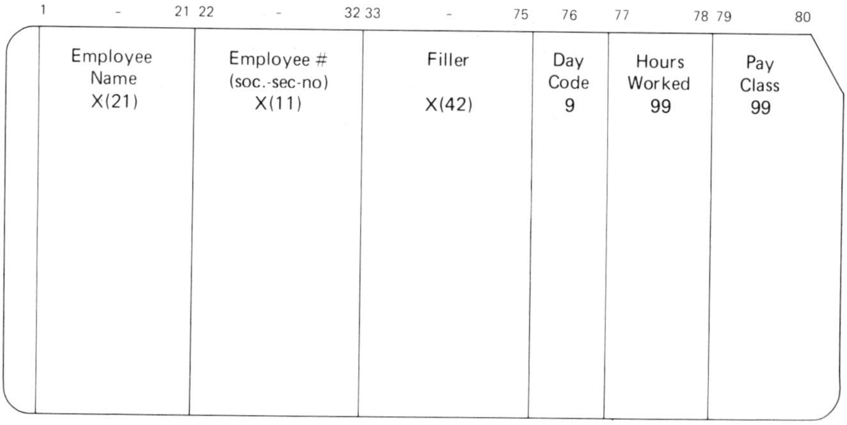

1	-	21 22	-	32 33	-	75	76	77	78 79	80

Employee Name X(21)	Employee # (soc.-sec-no) X(11)	Filler X(42)	Day Code 9	Hours Worked 99	Pay Class 99

FIGURE 22

DAY–CODE is a single digit field in which the digits 1 through 7 represent a particular day of the week, according to the following scheme:

1 = Monday
2 = Tuesday
3 = Wednesday
4 = Thursday
5 = Friday
6 = Saturday
7 = Sunday

Whatever day of the week a particular time card represents, the appropriate code number is punched in column 76.

Each employee is assigned a pay class which determines the amount to be paid per hour. The rates are as follows:

PAY CLASS	RATE PER HOUR
1	$1.25
2	1.57
3	1.84
4	1.98
5	2.03
6	2.18
7	2.23
8	2.38
9	2.87
10	3.09

The purpose of the program is to compute a summary of each employee's daily earnings. The summary is to print out the employee's name, the actual day of the week spelled out in full, and the wages earned for each day. Then the week's total wages is to be calculated together with the average daily earnings.

In the event that an error has been punched for the day, such as a value of less than 1 or greater than 7, an appropriate message is printed out on a separate page in the report detailing the nature of the error; the employee's daily time card is printed out as a reminder to correct the invalid data card. A flag of '***' prints out to identify a day code error. If, on the other hand, an error in the pay class has been made, for example, a code less than 01 or greater than 10, has been detected, the same action is taken but it is flagged with '**' and is included on the separate page summarizing the errors detected.

Attention is drawn to the use of the DISPLAY statements, two of which are included in Program 30. As mentioned earlier on in the text, the DISPLAY statement, if used at all, should be restricted to low volume output. It is used in Program 30 to flag input errors which are not really expected. Of course, in order to be sure that the test works correctly, we have included some invalid data. This is always a good practice; it might be termed "defensive programming."

The displayed comments appear on a fresh page rather than in the expected logical sequence because this arrangement has been determined by an appropriate job control statement. This statement will be discussed in detail when we deal with the concepts underlying JCL (job control language).

INPUT TO PROGRAM 30

```
FERN FRIEDMAN      123-25-4789              10805
FERN FRIEDMAN      123-25-4789              21405
FERN FRIEDMAN      123-25-4789              30205
FERN FRIEDMAN      123-25-4789              41105
FERN FRIEDMAN      123-25-4789              50505
BARBARA HODGES     645-23-6632              22009
BARBARA HODGES     645-23-6632              30709
BARBARA HODGES     645-23-6632              51209
BARBARA HODGES     645-23-6632              61121
BARBARA HODGES     645-23-6632              95120
SALLY DEMBERG      554-61-3214              20306
SALLY DEMBERG      554-61-3214              30706
SALLY DEMBERG      554-61-3214              61506
SALLY DEMBERG      554-61-3214              70206
JACKIE MURDOCK     225-32-1122              20301
JACKIE MURDOCK     225-32-1122              30501
JACKIE MURDOCK     225-32-1122              40501
JACKIE MURDOCK     225-32-1122              50601
MARY LAGOUMIS      521-23-9876              11001
MARY LAGOUMIS      521-23-9876              21201
MARY LAGOUMIS      521-23-9876              30501
```

PROGRAM 30
Index 2

```
00001          IDENTIFICATION DIVISION.
00002          PROGRAM-ID. INDEX-2.
00003          AUTHOR. ELI J. OPAS.
00004          REMARKS. A TABLE LOOK-UP WITH BOTH INDEXING AND SUBSCRIPTING.
00005
00006          ENVIRONMENT DIVISION.
00007
00008          CONFIGURATION SECTION.
```

```
00009          SOURCE-COMPUTER. IBM-370-145.
00010          OBJECT-COMPUTER. IBM-370-145.
00011
00012          SPECIAL-NAMES.
00013
00014              C01 IS TO-TOP-OF-PAGE.
00015          INPUT-OUTPUT SECTION.
00016
00017          FILE-CONTROL.
00018
00019              SELECT IN-FILE ASSIGN TO UT-S-READER.
00020              SELECT OUT-FILE ASSIGN TO UT-S-PRINTER.
00021
00022          DATA DIVISION.
00023
00024          FILE SECTION.
00025          FD  IN-FILE
00026              LABEL RECORDS ARE OMITTED.
00027
00028          01  EMPLOYEE-CARD.
00029              05 NAME          PICTURE X(21).
00030              05 EMPLOYEE-NO    PICTURE X(11).
00031              05 FILLER        PICTURE X(43).
00032              05 DAY-CODE      PICTURE 9.
00033              05 HOURS-WORKED  PICTURE 99.
00034              05 PAY-CLASS     PICTURE 99.
00035
00036          FD  OUT-FILE
00037              LABEL RECORDS ARE OMITTED.
00038
00039          01  REPORT-LINE.
00040              05 CARRIAGECONTROL PICTURE X.
00041              05 OUTPUT-LINE    PICTURE X(132).
00042
00043          WORKING-STORAGE SECTION.
00044
00045          77  FIRST-TIME-FLAG   PICTURE X(3) VALUE 'YES'.
00046          77  ANY-ERRORS-FOUND  PICTURE X(03)     VALUE 'NO'.
00047          77  DAY-KOUNTER       PICTURE 99 VALUE ZERO.
00048          77  WAGE-KOUNTER      PICTURE 9(3)V99 VALUE ZERO.
00049          77  W-S-WAGES         PICTURE 9(3)V99 VALUE ZERO.
00050          77  W-S-HOURLY-RATE   PICTURE 9V99.
00051          77  W-S-NAME          PICTURE X(21) VALUE SPACES.
00052
00053          01  HEADER-1.
00054              05 FILLER           PICTURE X(53) VALUE
00055                                  'SUMMARY OF DAILY EARNINGS' JUST RIGHT.
00056              05 FILLER           PICTURE X(27) VALUE SPACES.
00057
00058          01  HEADER-2.
00059              05 FILLER           PICTURE X(42) VALUE
00060                                  'WEEK ENDING ' JUST RIGHT.
00061              05 DAYTE            PICTURE X(8).
00062              05 FILLER           PICTURE X(30) VALUE SPACES.
00063
00064          01  HEADER-3.
00065              05 FILLER           PICTURE X(10) VALUE ' EMPLOYEES'.
00066              05 FILLER           PICTURE X(55) VALUE 'WEEKLY' JUST RIGHT.
00067              05 FILLER           PICTURE X(15) VALUE 'AVERAGE' JUST RIGHT.
00068
00069          01  HEADER-4.
00070              05 FILLER           PICTURE X(5) VALUE ' NAME'.
00071              05 FILLER           PICTURE X(27) VALUE 'DAY' JUST RIGHT.
00072              05 FILLER           PICTURE X(18) VALUE 'WAGES' JUST RIGHT.
00073              05 FILLER           PICTURE X(14) VALUE 'TOTAL' JUST RIGHT.
00074              05 FILLER           PICTURE X(16) VALUE 'EARNINGS' JUST RIGHT.
00075
00076          01  DETAIL-LINE.
00077              05 FILLER           PICTURE X VALUE SPACES.
00078              05 NAME             PICTURE X(21) VALUE SPACES.
00079              05 FILLER           PICTURE X(7) VALUE SPACES.
00080              05 DAY-OF-THE-WEEK PICTURE X(9) VALUE SPACES.
00081              05 FILLER           PICTURE X(7) VALUE SPACES.
00082              05 WAGES            PICTURE $299.99.
00083              05 FILLER           PICTURE X(28) VALUE SPACES.
00084
00085          01  TOTAL-LINE.
00086              05 FILLER           PICTURE X(59) VALUE SPACES.
00087              05 WK-TOTAL         PICTURE $299.99.
00088              05 FILLER           PICTURE X(6) VALUE SPACES.
00089              05 AVERAGE          PICTURE $299.99 VALUE ZERO.
00090              05 FILLER           PICTURE X VALUE SPACES.
00091
```

```
00092          01  DAY-TABLE-VALUES.
00093              05 FILLER           PICTURE X(9) VALUE 'MONDAY   '.
00094              05 FILLER           PICTURE X(9) VALUE 'TUESDAY  '.
00095              05 FILLER           PICTURE X(9) VALUE 'WEDNESDAY'.
00096              05 FILLER           PICTURE X(9) VALUE 'THURSDAY '.
00097              05 FILLER           PICTURE X(9) VALUE 'FRIDAY   '.
00098              05 FILLER           PICTURE X(9) VALUE 'SATURDAY '.
00099              05 FILLER           PICTURE X(9) VALUE 'SUNDAY   '.
00100
00101          01  DAYS REDEFINES DAY-TABLE-VALUES.
00102              05 DAY-NAME          PICTURE X(9) OCCURS 7 TIMES.
00103
00104          01  RATE-TABLE-VALUES.
00105              05 FILLER            PICTURE X(25) VALUE
00106                                   '0112502157031840419805203'.
00107              05 FILLER            PICTURE X(25) VALUE
00108                                   '0621807223082380928710309'.
00109
00110          01  RATE-TABLE REDEFINES RATE-TABLE-VALUES.
00111              05  TABLE-PAIR OCCURS 10 TIMES INDEXED BY RATE-INDEX.
00112                  10 CLASS         PICTURE 99.
00113                  10 RATE          PICTURE 9V99.
00114
00115          PROCEDURE DIVISION.
00116
00117          LETS-GET-GOING.
00118              OPEN INPUT IN-FILE, OUTPUT OUT-FILE.
00119              MOVE CURRENT-DATE TO DAYTE.
00120              PERFORM HEADING-RTN.
00121
00122          WE-READ-A-FILE.
00123              READ IN-FILE AT END GO TO WE-ARE-DONE.
00124              IF FIRST-TIME-FLAG = 'YES' MOVE 'NO' TO FIRST-TIME-FLAG,
00125                  MOVE NAME IN EMPLOYEE-CARD TO W-S-NAME.
00126                  GO TO WE-FIND-THE-DAY.
00127              IF NAME IN EMPLOYEE-CARD NOT = W-S-NAME
00128                  PERFORM WE-COMPUTE-THE-AVERAGE THRU TOTAL-EXIT,
00129                  PERFORM HEADING-RTN.
00130              MOVE NAME IN EMPLOYEE-CARD TO W-S-NAME.
00131
00132          WE-FIND-THE-DAY.
00133              IF DAY-CODE > 0 AND < 8 NEXT SENTENCE,
00134                  ELSE GO TO DAY-CODE-ERROR-RTN.
00135              MOVE DAY-NAME (DAY-CODE) TO DAY-OF-THE-WEEK.
00136              ADD 1 TO DAY-KOUNTER.
00137
00138          WE-FIND-THE-RATE.
00139              SET RATE-INDEX TO 1.
00140              SEARCH TABLE-PAIR AT END GO TO PAY-CLASS-ERROR-RTN,
00141              WHEN CLASS (RATE-INDEX) = PAY-CLASS
00142              MOVE RATE (RATE-INDEX) TO W-S-HOURLY-RATE.
00143
00144          WE-COMPUTE-THE-WAGES.
00145              COMPUTE W-S-WAGES = W-S-HOURLY-RATE * HOURS-WORKED.
00146              MOVE W-S-WAGES TO WAGES.
00147              ADD W-S-WAGES TO WAGE-KOUNTER.
00148
00149          WE-WRITE-A-RECORD.
00150              MOVE CORRESPONDING EMPLOYEE-CARD TO DETAIL-LINE.
00151              WRITE REPORT-LINE FROM DETAIL-LINE AFTER ADVANCING 3.
00152              GO TO WE-READ-A-FILE.
00153
00154          WE-COMPUTE-THE-AVERAGE.
00155              COMPUTE AVERAGE = WAGE-KOUNTER / DAY-KOUNTER.
00156              MOVE WAGE-KOUNTER TO WK-TOTAL.
00157              MOVE ZERO TO WAGE-KOUNTER, DAY-KOUNTER.
00158
00159          WE-WRITE-THE-AVERAGE-AND-TOTAL.
00160              WRITE REPORT-LINE FROM TOTAL-LINE AFTER ADVANCING 4.
00161
00162          TOTAL-EXIT.
00163              EXIT.
00164
00165          DAY-CODE-ERROR-RTN.
00166              MOVE
00167              '**WARNING**DAY-CODE NOT FOUND-DISREGARD TOTAL AND AVERAGE'
00168              TO OUTPUT-LINE.
00169              WRITE REPORT-LINE AFTER ADVANCING 3.
00170              DISPLAY EMPLOYEE-CARD ' ***'.
00171              MOVE 'YES' TO ANY-ERRORS-FOUND.
00172              GO TO WE-READ-A-FILE.
00173
00174          PAY-CLASS-ERROR-RTN.
00175              MOVE
```

```
00176                    '**WARNING**PAY-CLASS NOT FOUND-DISREGARD TOTAL AND AVERAGE'
00177                    TO OUTPUT-LINE.
00178                    WRITE REPORT-LINE AFTER ADVANCING 3.
00179                    DISPLAY EMPLOYEE-CARD ' **'.
00180                    MOVE 'YES' TO ANY-ERRORS-FOUND.
00181                    GO TO WE-READ-A-FILE.
00182
00183         HEADING-RTN.
00184                    WRITE REPORT-LINE FROM HEADER-1
00185                    AFTER ADVANCING TO-TOP-OF-PAGE.
00186                    WRITE REPORT-LINE FROM HEADER-2 AFTER ADVANCING 1.
00187                    WRITE REPORT-LINE FROM HEADER-3 AFTER ADVANCING 3.
00188                    WRITE REPORT-LINE FROM HEADER-4 AFTER ADVANCING 1.
00189         WE-ARE-DONE.
00190                    PERFORM WE-COMPUTE-THE-AVERAGE THRU TOTAL-EXIT.
00191                    IF ANY-ERRORS-FOUND = 'YES'
00192                       MOVE
00193                       ' (PLEASE CORRECT CARDS DISPLAYED ON FOLLOWING PAGE)'
00194                       TO OUTPUT-LINE
00195                       WRITE REPORT-LINE AFTER ADVANCING 3
00196                       MOVE
00197                       ' (*** = ERROR IN DAY-CODE  ** = ERROR IN PAY-CLASS)'
00198                       TO OUTPUT-LINE
00199                       WRITE REPORT-LINE AFTER ADVANCING 1.
00200                    CLOSE IN-FILE, OUT-FILE.
00201                    STOP RUN.
```

OUTPUT TO PROGRAM 30

SUMMARY OF DAILY EARNINGS
WEEK ENDING 07/20/77

EMPLOYEES NAME	DAY	WAGES	WEEKLY TOTAL	AVERAGE EARNINGS
FERN FRIEDMAN	MONDAY	$ 16.24		
FERN FRIEDMAN	TUESDAY	$ 28.42		
FERN FRIEDMAN	WEDNESDAY	$ 04.06		
FERN FRIEDMAN	THURSDAY	$ 22.33		
FERN FRIEDMAN	FRIDAY	$ 10.15		
			$ 81.20	$ 16.24

SUMMARY OF DAILY EARNINGS
WEEK ENDING 07/20/77

EMPLOYEES NAME	DAY	WAGES	WEEKLY TOTAL	AVERAGE EARNINGS
BARBARA HODGES	TUESDAY	$ 57.40		
BARBARA HODGES	WEDNESDAY	$ 20.09		
BARBARA HODGES	FRIDAY	$ 34.44		

WARNINGPAY-CLASS NOT FOUND-DISREGARD TOTAL AND AVERAGE

WARNINGDAY-CODE NOT FOUND-DISREGARD TOTAL AND AVERAGE

			$111.93	$ 27.98

```
                        SUMMARY OF DAILY EARNINGS
                          WEEK ENDING 07/20/77

     EMPLOYEES                                         WEEKLY        AVERAGE
     NAME                     DAY          WAGES        TOTAL         EARNINGS

     SALLY DEMBERG            TUESDAY      $ 06.54

     SALLY DEMBERG            WEDNESDAY    $ 15.26

     SALLY DEMBERG            SATURDAY     $ 32.70

     SALLY DEMBERG            SUNDAY       $ 04.36


                                                       $ 58.86      $ 14.71

                        SUMMARY OF DAILY EARNINGS
                          WEEK ENDING 07/20/77

     EMPLOYEES                                         WEEKLY        AVERAGE
     NAME                     DAY          WAGES        TOTAL         EARNINGS

     JACKIE MURDOCK           TUESDAY      $ 03.75

     JACKIE MURDOCK           WEDNESDAY    $ 06.25

     JACKIE MURDOCK           THURSDAY     $ 06.25

     JACKIE MURDOCK           FRIDAY       $ 07.50


                                                       $ 23.75      $ 05.93

                        SUMMARY OF DAILY EARNINGS
                          WEEK ENDING 07/20/77

     EMPLOYEES                                         WEEKLY        AVERAGE
     NAME                     DAY          WAGES        TOTAL         EARNINGS

     MARY LAGOUMIS            MONDAY       $ 12.50

     MARY LAGOUMIS            TUESDAY      $ 15.00

     MARY LAGOUMIS            WEDNESDAY    $ 06.25


                                                       $ 33.75      $ 11.25


     (PLEASE CORRECT CARDS DISPLAYED ON FOLLOWING PAGE)
     (*** = ERROR IN DAY-CODE   ** = ERROR IN PAY-CLASS)

     BARBARA HODGES       645-23-6632                           61121 **
     BARBARA HODGES       645-23-6632                           95120 ***
```

Notice that the program has detected two data cards which are in error. The first is in error because it is punched with a PAY-CLASS of 21 whereas the maximum permitted is 10. This error is detected when the table is searched. Since there is no PAY-CLASS of 21 in the table, the AT

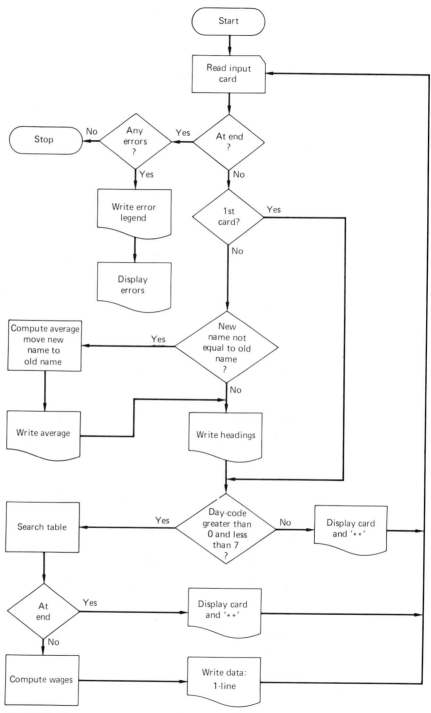

FIGURE 23

END condition is triggered, control is sent to PAY–CLASS–ERROR–RTN, and an appropriate error displayed.

The second error is caused by the data card having a PAY–CODE of 09 whereas, only codes 01 through 07 are permitted. This error was detected in the paragraph named WE–FIND–THE–DAY, in which control is sent to DAY–CODE–ERROR–RTN, which prints out an appropriate message and three asterisks. Note, however, that columns 79 and 80 are punched with 20 rather than the correct DAY–CODE of 09.

All three errors are corrected and the program resubmitted for execution. The program is identical to that already shown; here is the correct output.

OUTPUT TO PROGRAM 30 (RERUN)

SUMMARY OF DAILY EARNINGS
WEEK ENDING 07/20/77

EMPLOYEES NAME	DAY	WAGES	WEEKLY TOTAL	AVERAGE EARNINGS
FERN FRIEDMAN	MONDAY	$ 16.24		
FERN FRIEDMAN	TUESDAY	$ 28.42		
FERN FRIEDMAN	WEDNESDAY	$ 04.06		
FERN FRIEDMAN	THURSDAY	$ 22.33		
FERN FRIEDMAN	FRIDAY	$ 10.15		
			$ 81.20	$ 16.24

SUMMARY OF DAILY EARNINGS
WEEK ENDING 07/20/77

EMPLOYEES NAME	DAY	WAGES	WEEKLY TOTAL	AVERAGE EARNINGS
BARBARA HODGES	TUESDAY	$ 57.40		
BARBARA HODGES	WEDNESDAY	$ 20.09		
BARBARA HODGES	FRIDAY	$ 34.44		
BARBARA HODGES	SATURDAY	$ 31.57		
BARBARA HODGES	SUNDAY	$146.37		
			$289.87	$ 57.97

SUMMARY OF DAILY EARNINGS
WEEK ENDING 07/20/77

EMPLOYEES NAME	DAY	WAGES	WEEKLY TOTAL	AVERAGE EARNINGS
SALLY DEMBERG	TUESDAY	$ 06.54		
SALLY DEMBERG	WEDNESDAY	$ 15.26		
SALLY DEMBERG	SATURDAY	$ 32.70		
SALLY DEMBERG	SUNDAY	$ 04.36		
			$ 58.86	$ 14.71

SUMMARY OF DAILY EARNINGS
WEEK ENDING 07/20/77

EMPLOYEES NAME	DAY	WAGES	WEEKLY TOTAL	AVERAGE EARNINGS
JACKIE MURDOCK	TUESDAY	$ 03.75		
JACKIE MURDOCK	WEDNESDAY	$ 06.25		
JACKIE MURDOCK	THURSDAY	$ 06.25		
JACKIE MURDOCK	FRIDAY	$ 07.50		
			$ 23.75	$ 05.93

SUMMARY OF DAILY EARNINGS
WEEK ENDING 07/20/77

EMPLOYEES NAME	DAY	WAGES	WEEKLY TOTAL	AVERAGE EARNINGS
MARY LAGOUMIS	MONDAY	$ 12.50		
MARY LAGOUMIS	TUESDAY	$ 15.00		
MARY LAGOUMIS	WEDNESDAY	$ 06.25		
			$ 33.75	$ 11.25

12.8 A TWO-DIMENSIONAL TABLE LOOKUP

In each of the previous programs where tables were used, we stored the data in memory in what is known as a "single level" table. What this implies is that in each case there is only a *single* item which appears in the OCCURS clause and, as a result, only a *single* subscript or index is necessary to access any particular item. But one is not confined to single levels in COBOL. Suppose, for example, that we are considering automobile insurance, where the rate one pays depends upon both age and sex. This may be represented diagrammatically as

AGE	RATE	
	Men	Women
18–21	XXX.XX	YYY.YY
22–35	XXX.XX	YYY.YY
35–65	XXX.XX	YYY.YY
65–over	XXX.XX	YYY.YY

From the above chart it will be noticed that the age group occurs four times. But within each age category the rate occurs two times, where the first occurrence relates to the rate for men and the second to the rate for women. This may be expressed in COBOL with an entry in which the OCCURS clause appears twice. Here are the symbolic COBOL entries to represent the two-dimensioned table which will appear in the Working-Storage Section of the DATA DIVISION.

```
01   RATE-TABLE-VALUES.
     05   FILLER PICTURE X(11) VALUE '1XXXXXYYYYY'.
     05   FILLER PICTURE X(11) VALUE '2XXXXXYYYYY'.
     05   FILLER PICTURE X(11) VALUE '3XXXXXYYYYY'.
     05   FILLER PICTURE X(11) VALUE '4XXXXXYYYYY'.
01   RATE–TABLE REDEFINES RATE–TABLE–VALUES.
     05   AGE OCCURS 4 TIMES.
     10 AGE-CODE PICTURE 9.
     10 RATE     PICTURE 9(3)V99   OCCURS 2 TIMES.
```

where codes 1, 2, 3 and 4 represent the four age groups 18–21, 22–35, 35–65 and 65 and over respectively. It will be noticed—and you must be sure to notice it—that AGE OCCURS 4 times and *within each occurrence* of AGE, the item RATE OCCURS 2 times.

Another example of a two level table is the train fare chart which follows:

		ONE-WAY	ROUND-TRIP	UNLIMITED
1–4 yr	(1)	AAA.AA	BBB.BB	CCC.CC
5–12	(2)	DDD.DD	EEE.EE	FFF.FF
Adult	(3)	GGG.GG	HHH.HH	III.II
Senior Citizen	(4)	JJJ.JJ	KKK.KK	LLL.LL

Such a table may be stored in the memory of the computer by the following symbolic COBOL code:

```
01  RATE-TABLE-VALUES.
    05  FILLER PICTURE X(16) VALUE '1AAAAABBBBBCCCCC'.
    05  FILLER PICTURE X(16) VALUE '2DDDDDEEEEEFFFFF'.
    05  FILLER PICTURE X(16) VALUE '3GGGGGHHHHHIIIII'.
    05  FILLER PICTURE X (16) VALUE '4JJJJJKKKKKLLLLL'.
01  RATE–TABLE REDEFINES RATE-TABLE-VALUES.
    05  AGE–GROUP OCCURS 4 TIMES.
        10 AGE–CATEGORY PICTURE 9.
        10 FARE PICTURE 9(3)V99 OCCURS 3 TIMES.
```

Here an AGE–CATEGORY of 1, 2, 3, or 4 corresponds to the appropriate age category.

The AGE–GROUP OCCURS 4 times, and within each occurrence of AGE–GROUP the item FARE OCCURS 3 times. This is therefore a two level table.

The final illustration of a two level table will actually be programmed. It is designed to calculate the room charges for hotel room rental. The individual charges are shown in the following chart:

	DAY	WEEK	MONTH	YEAR
Single	$14.00	$89.00	$349.00	$1384.00
Double	$27.00	$152.00	$658.00	$2486.00

This table may be written in COBOL:

```
01  CHARGE-TABLE-VALUES.
    05 FILLER PICTURE X(25) VALUE '1001400008900034900138400'.
    05 FILLER PICTURE X(25) VALUE '2002700015200065800248600'.
01  CHARGE-TABLE REDEFINES CHARGE–TABLE–VALUES.
    05 RM–TYPE OCCURS 2 TIMES.
        10 TYPE-CODE PICTURE 9.
        10 CHARGE OCCURS 4 TIMES PICTURE 9(4)V99.
```

The input to Program 31 is punched as shown in Figure 24:

CODING OF CARD.

1. Room type: 1 for single room
                2 for double room
2. Period of stay: 1 for payment by the day
                     2 for payment by the week
                     3 for payment by the month
                     4 for payment by the year

| 1 | - | 21 | 22 | 23 | . | 24 | 25 26 | - | 80 |

Name	Room Type	Period of Stay	Unit of Stay	Filler
X(21)	9	9	99	X(55)

FIGURE 24

3. Unit of stay: For day-rate values of 01–13 only are valid.

For week-rate values of 01–52 only are valid.

For monthly-rate values of 01–12 only are valid.

For yearly-rate only a 01 is valid.

The purpose of the program is to read in all of the data cards and validate the data punched on them. If no errors are detected, then the program is to calculate the total room charge for each guest and print out in a report the guest's name, period of stay in units of days, weeks, months, or year (spelled out), the room size (single or double, again spelled out), the rate and the total charge for each customer. At the end of the report, an accumulated total of the charges is to be printed out.

If, on the other hand, any errors at all are detected, the room charge for each valid guest card is still calculated, but the accumulated total is neither maintained nor printed. Instead, each invalid guest card is displayed on a separate page together with an appropriate message at the end of the report.

The program makes abundant use of 88 level items which were discussed in detail earlier in the text. Without further ado here is the program, which is run with the following input data. Two of the input cards are in error.

INPUT TO PROGRAM 31

```
FRANZ LISTZ           1101
WINSTON CHURCHILL     2202
JACKIE ROBINSON       1209
DIANE CORAN           2244
PETER MCKAY           1310
LETITIA YZARRIE       2311
ERWIN CHUA            1401
LEN VANEK             2199
PAT HOULIHAN          2312
ROXANNE HOFFMAN       1212
```

```
DAVID BLAUSTEIN      1204
KIMBERLEY CLARK      2213
HARRIET TUBMAN       2312
JOHN BEETHOVEN       2111
EDITH DEAK           2105
GREGORY SMITH        2401
RICHARD SAKOWSKI     8311
```

PROGRAM 31
Two Levels

```
C0001          IDENTIFICATION DIVISION.
00002          PROGRAM-ID. TWO-LEVEL.
00003          AUTHOR. ELI J. CPAS.
00004          REMARKS. A TWO DIMENSIONAL TABLE LOOK-UP.
00005
00006          ENVIRONMENT DIVISION.
00007
00008          CONFIGURATION SECTION.
00009
00010          SOURCE-COMPUTER. IBM-370-145.
00011          OBJECT-COMPUTER. IBM-370-145.
00012
00013          SPECIAL-NAMES.
00014
00015              C01 IS TO-TOP-OF-PAGE.
00016
00017          INPUT-OUTPUT SECTION.
00018
00019          FILE-CONTROL.
00020
00021              SELECT IN-FILE ASSIGN TO UT-S-READER.
00022              SELECT OUT-FILE ASSIGN TO UT-S-PRINTER.
00023
00024          DATA DIVISION.
00025
00026          FILE SECTION.
00027
00028          FD  IN-FILE
00029              LABEL RECORDS ARE OMITTED.
00030
00031          01  GUEST-CARD.
00032              05  NAME            PICTURE X(21).
00033              05  ROOM-TYPE       PICTURE 9.
00034                  88  SINGLE          VALUE 1.
00035                  88  DOUBLE          VALUE 2.
00036              05  PERIOD-OF-STAY  PICTURE 9.
00037                  88  DAYS            VALUE 1.
00038                  88  WEEK            VALUE 2.
00039                  88  MONTH           VALUE 3.
00040                  88  YEAR            VALUE 4.
00041              05  UNIT-OF-STAY    PICTURE 99.
00042              05  FILLER          PICTURE X(55).
00043
00044          FD  OUT-FILE
00045              LABEL RECORDS ARE OMITTED.
00046
00047          01  REPORT-LINE.
00048              05  CARRIAGECONTROL PICTURE X.
00049              05  OUTPUT-LINE     PICTURE X(132).
00050
00051          WORKING-STORAGE SECTION.
00052
00053          77  W-S-CHARGE          PICTURE 9(4)V99.
00054          77  CHARGE-KOUNTER      PICTURE 9(5)V99 VALUE ZERO.
00055          77  LINE-KOUNTER        PICTURE 99 VALUE ZERO.
00056          77  ERROR-FLAG          PICTURE X(3) VALUE 'NO'.
00057
00058          01  HEADER-1.
00059              05  FILLER          PICTURE X(48) VALUE
00060                                  'HEARTBREAK HOTEL' JUST RIGHT.
00061              05  FILLER          PICTURE X(32) VALUE SPACES.
00062
00063          01  HEADER-2.
00064              05  FILLER          PICTURE X(56) VALUE
00065                  'ANNUAL ROOM RENTAL REVENUE REPORT' JUST RIGHT.
00066              05  FILLER          PICTURE X(24) VALUE SPACES.
00067
00068          01  HEADER-3.
00069              05  FILLER          PICTURE X(48) VALUE
00070                                  'FOR THE YEAR 1977' JUST RIGHT.
```

```
00071                05 FILLER          PICTURE X(32) VALUE SPACES.
C0072
C0073           01  HEADER-4.
00074                05 FILLER          PICTURE X(12) VALUE
00075                                   'GUESTS NAME' JUST RIGHT.
00076                05 FILLER          PICTURE X(29) VALUE
00077                                   'PERIOD OF STAY' JUST RIGHT.
C0078                05 FILLER          PICTURE X(15) VALUE
00079                                   'ROOM SIZE' JUST RIGHT.
C0080                05 FILLER          PICTURE X(8) VALUE
00081                                   'RATE' JUST RIGHT.
C0082                05 FILLER          PICTURE X(15) VALUE
C0083                                   'CHARGE' JUST RIGHT.
00084                05 FILLER          PICTURE X(3) VALUE SPACES.
00085
C0086           01  DETAIL-LINE.
CC087                05 FILLER          PICTURE X VALUE SPACES.
00088                C5 NAME            PICTURE X(21).
00089                05 FILLER          PICTURE X(5) VALUE SPACES.
C0090                05 UNIT-OF-STAY    PICTURE Z9.
00091                05 FILLER          PICTURE X VALUE SPACES.
0C092                05 KIND            PICTURE X(8).
00093                05 FILLER          PICTURE X(9) VALUE SPACES.
00094                05 TYPE-OF-ROOM    PICTURE X(6).
00095                05 FILLER          PICTURE X(7) VALUE SPACES.
00096                05 RATE            PICTURE $Z,Z99.99.
00097                05 FILLER          PICTURE X(4) VALUE SPACES.
00098                05 ROOM-CHARGE     PICTURE $ZZ,Z99.99.
00099
C0100           01  CHARGE-TABLE-VALUES.
00101                05 FILLER          PICTURE X(25) VALUE
C0102                                   '10014000089000349000138400'.
CC103                05 FILLER          PICTURE X(25) VALUE
CC104                                   '20027000015200065800248600'.
CC105
00106           01  CHARGE-TABLE REDEFINES CHARGE-TABLE-VALUES.
C0107                05 RM-TYPE         OCCURS 2 TIMES.
00108                     10 TYPE-CODE  PICTURE 9.
00109                     10 CHARGE     OCCURS 4 TIMES,
CC110                                   PICTURE 9(4)V99.
00111
00112           PROCEDURE DIVISION.
00113           WE-BEGIN.
00114                OPEN INPUT IN-FILE, OUTPUT OUT-FILE.
00115                PERFORM HEADING-RTN.
CC116
00117           READ-THE-GUEST-CARD.
00118                READ IN-FILE AT END GO TO END-OF-JOB.
0C119
00120           VALIDATE-THE-GUEST-CARD.
00121                IF NOT SINGLE AND NOT DOUBLE GO TO ERROR-RTN.
00122                IF DAYS AND UNIT-OF-STAY OF GUEST-CARD > 13 GO TO ERROR-RTN.
00123                IF WEEK AND UNIT-OF-STAY OF GUEST-CARD > 52 GO TO ERROR-RTN.
00124                IF MONTH AND UNIT-OF-STAY OF GUEST-CARD > 12 GO TO ERROR-RTN.
00125                IF YEAR AND UNIT-OF-STAY OF GUEST-CARD > 1 GO TO ERROR-RTN.
00126                IF PERIOD-OF-STAY < 0 OR > 4 GO TO ERROR-RTN.
0C127
00128           COMPUTE-THE-CHARGE.
00129                COMPUTE W-S-CHARGE =
00130                     CHARGE (ROOM-TYPE, PERIOD-OF-STAY) * UNIT-OF-STAY OF
00131                                           GUEST-CARD.
00132
00133           WRITE-DETAIL-LINE.
00134                MOVE CHARGE (ROOM-TYPE, PERIOD-OF-STAY) TO RATE.
00135                MOVE CORRESPONDING GUEST-CARD TO DETAIL-LINE.
00136                IF DAYS MOVE 'DAYS' TO KIND.
0C137                IF WEEK MOVE 'WEEKS' TO KIND.
00138                IF MONTH MOVE 'MONTHS' TO KIND.
00139                IF YEAR MOVE 'YEAR' TO KIND.
00140                IF SINGLE MOVE 'SINGLE' TO TYPE-OF-ROOM.
00141                IF DOUBLE MOVE 'DOUBLE' TO TYPE-OF-ROOM.
00142                MOVE W-S-CHARGE TO ROOM-CHARGE.
00143                IF ERROR-FLAG = 'NO' ADD W-S-CHARGE TO CHARGE-KOUNTER.
00144                IF LINE-KOUNTER > 14 MOVE ZERO TO LINE-KOUNTER,
00145                PERFORM HEADING-RTN.
00146                WRITE REPORT-LINE FROM DETAIL-LINE AFTER ADVANCING 2.
00147                ADD 2 TO LINE-KOUNTER.
C0148                GO TO READ-THE-GUEST-CARD.
0C149
CC150           ERROR-RTN.
00151                MOVE 'YES' TO ERROR-FLAG.
00152                DISPLAY GUEST-CARD.
00153                GO TO READ-THE-GUEST-CARD.
00154
00155           HEADING-RTN.
```

```
00156                    WRITE REPORT-LINE FROM HEADER-1
00157                        AFTER ADVANCING TO-TOP-OF-PAGE.
00158                    WRITE REPORT-LINE FROM HEADER-2 AFTER ADVANCING 1.
00159                    WRITE REPORT-LINE FROM HEADER-3 AFTER ADVANCING 1.
00160                    WRITE REPORT-LINE FROM HEADER-4 AFTER ADVANCING 3.
00161
00162           END-OF-JOB.
00163                    IF ERROR-FLAG = 'YES' MOVE
00164                    'ERRORS HAVE BEEN DETECTED ON GUEST-CARD DISPLAYED'
00165                        TO OUTPUT-LINE
00166                      WRITE REPORT-LINE AFTER ADVANCING 3
00167                        MOVE
00168                       'ON FOLLOWING PAGE-PLEASE CORRECT AND RESUBMIT'
00169                          TO OUTPUT-LINE
00170                           WRITE REPORT-LINE AFTER ADVANCING 1
00171                             MOVE
00172                             'TOTAL NOT COMPUTED'
00173                                TO OUTPUT-LINE
00174                                 WRITE REPORT-LINE AFTER ADVANCING 1
00175                    ELSE
00176                      MOVE
00177                      'TOTAL FOR 1977  >>------>    ' TO OUTPUT-LINE
00178                       WRITE REPORT-LINE AFTER ADVANCING 3
00179                        MOVE SPACES TO DETAIL-LINE
00180                         MOVE CHARGE-KOUNTER TO ROOM-CHARGE
00181                          MOVE DETAIL-LINE TO REPORT-LINE
00182                           WRITE REPORT-LINE AFTER ADVANCING 1.
00183                    CLOSE IN-FILE, OUT-FILE.
00184                    STOP RUN.
```

OUTPUT TO PROGRAM 31

HEARTBREAK HOTEL
ANNUAL ROOM RENTAL REVENUE REPORT
FOR THE YEAR 1977

GUESTS NAME	PERIOD OF STAY	ROOM SIZE	RATE	CHARGE
FRANZ LISTZ	1 DAYS	SINGLE	$ 14.00	$ 14.00
WINSTON CHURCHILL	2 WEEKS	DOUBLE	$ 152.00	$ 304.00
JACKIE ROBINSON	9 WEEKS	SINGLE	$ 89.00	$ 801.00
DIANE CORAN	44 WEEKS	DOUBLE	$ 152.00	$ 6,688.00
PETER MCKAY	10 MONTHS	SINGLE	$ 349.00	$ 3,490.00
LETITIA YZARRIE	11 MONTHS	DOUBLE	$ 658.00	$ 7,238.00
ERWIN CHUA	1 YEAR	SINGLE	$1,384.00	$ 1,384.00
PAT HOULIHAN	12 MONTHS	DOUBLE	$ 658.00	$ 7,896.00

HEARTBREAK HOTEL
ANNUAL ROOM RENTAL REVENUE REPORT
FOR THE YEAR 1977

GUESTS NAME	PERIOD OF STAY	ROOM SIZE	RATE	CHARGE
ROXANNE HOFFMAN	12 WEEKS	SINGLE	$ 89.00	$ 1,068.00
DAVID BLAUSTEIN	4 WEEKS	SINGLE	$ 89.00	$ 356.00
KIMBERLEY CLARK	13 WEEKS	DOUBLE	$ 152.00	$ 1,976.00
HARRIET TUBMAN	12 MONTHS	DOUBLE	$ 658.00	$ 7,896.00
JOHN BEETHOVEN	11 DAYS	DOUBLE	$ 27.00	$ 297.00
EDITH DEAK	5 DAYS	DOUBLE	$ 27.00	$ 135.00
GREGORY SMITH	1 YEAR	DOUBLE	$2,486.00	$ 2,486.00

ERRORS HAVE BEEN DETECTED ON GUEST-CARD DISPLAYED
ON FOLLOWING PAGE-PLEASE CORRECT AND RESUBMIT
TOTAL NOT COMPUTED

```
LEN VANEK          2199
RICHARD SAKOWSKI   8311
```

As will be noticed from the output, errors have been detected on two of the input data cards. Specifically, in the first card in error, the code of 2199 specifies that the client is registered for a double room on a daily basis for 99 days. But for such a period of time, a daily rate is not appropriate. For the second card in error, with a code of 8311, there is no room type with a classification of 8; this is also flagged as an error. According to the advice printed at the end of the report, the errors were corrected (the cards were changed to 2101 and 1311, respectively) and the program resubmitted. Here then is the output using the corrected input data.

OUTPUT PROGRAM 31 (RERUN)

HEARTBREAK HOTEL
ANNUAL ROOM RENTAL REVENUE REPORT
FOR THE YEAR 1977

GUESTS NAME	PERIOD OF STAY	ROOM SIZE	RATE	CHARGE
FRANZ LISTZ	1 DAYS	SINGLE	$ 14.00	$ 14.00
ROXANNE HOFFMAN	12 WEEKS	SINGLE	$ 89.00	$ 1,068.00
DAVID BLAUSTEIN	4 WEEKS	SINGLE	$ 89.00	$ 356.00
KIMBERLEY CLARK	13 WEEKS	DOUBLE	$ 152.00	$ 1,976.00
HARRIET TUBMAN	12 MONTHS	DOUBLE	$ 658.00	$ 7,896.00
JOHN BEETHOVEN	11 DAYS	DOUBLE	$ 27.00	$ 297.00
EDITH DEAK	5 DAYS	DOUBLE	$ 27.00	$ 135.00
GREGORY SMITH	1 YEAR	DOUBLE	$2,486.00	$ 2,486.00

HEARTBREAK HOTEL
ANNUAL ROOM RENTAL REVENUE REPORT
FOR THE YEAR 1977

GUESTS NAME	PERIOD OF STAY	ROOM SIZE	RATE	CHARGE
WINSTON CHURCHILL	2 WEEKS	DOUBLE	$ 152.00	$ 304.00
JACKIE ROBINSON	9 WEEKS	SINGLE	$ 89.00	$ 801.00
DIANE CORAN	44 WEEKS	DOUBLE	$ 152.00	$ 6,688.00
PETER MCKAY	10 MONTHS	SINGLE	$ 349.00	$ 3,490.00
LETITIA YZARRIE	11 MONTHS	DOUBLE	$ 658.00	$ 7,238.00
ERWIN CHUA	1 YEAR	SINGLE	$1,384.00	$ 1,384.00
LEN VANEK	1 DAYS	DOUBLE	$ 27.00	$ 27.00
PAT HOULIHAN	12 MONTHS	DOUBLE	$ 658.00	$ 7,896.00

HEARTBREAK HOTEL
ANNUAL ROOM RENTAL REVENUE REPORT
FOR THE YEAR 1977

GUESTS NAME	PERIOD OF STAY	ROOM SIZE	RATE	CHARGE
RICHARD SAKOWSKI	11 MONTHS	SINGLE	$ 349.00	$ 3,839.00

TOTAL FOR 1977   >>------>

$45,895.00

12.9. A THREE-DIMENSIONAL
TABLE USING SUBSCRIPTING

We have now seen how a table may be composed of two levels or, as it is commonly known, of two dimensions. In point of fact it is possible in COBOL to have a maximum of three levels for any particular table. It is perfectly conceivable for a professional COBOL program to consist of a long series of three-dimensional tables.

In Program 32 we have devised a three-dimensional table to calculate excursion package tours from New York to London using subscripts. The fictitious package tours table is shown:

EXCURSION-RATE TABLE (NEW YORK–LONDON)

OCCUPANCY (PER PERSON)	One-Way (1)		Round-Trip (2)	
	Map (1)	European (2)	Map (1)	European (2)
Single (1)	285.00	254.00	594.00	578.00
Double (2)	276.00	243.00	542.00	518.00

A preliminary examination of the table will reveal that the occupancy falls into 2 categories, single or double. Occupancy therefore occurs twice. For each kind of occupancy two kinds of trip-types are available, one-way or round-trip. For each of these trip-types there are therefore two different fare-rates. One is called Modified American Plan (MAP) and the other is European Plan. Thus the rate to be charged occurs twice.

The complete statement of the table is therefore written

```
01  EXCURSION–RATE–TABLE.
    05   FILLER PICTURE X(21) VALUE '128500254005940057800'.
    05   FILLER PICTURE X(21) VALUE '227600243005420051800'.
01  EXCURSION–RATES REDEFINES EXCURSION–RATE–TABLE.
    05   ER–OCCUPANCY OCCURS 2 TIMES.
        10  OCCUPANCY PICTURE 9.
        10  TRIP–TYPE OCCURS 2 TIMES.
            15  ER–RATE OCCURS 2 TIMES PICTURE 9(3)V99.
```

The reader's attention is drawn to the PICTURE of 9 for OCCUPANCY. This refers to the *first* digit in the value clause in each of the 05 levels of the EXCURSION-RATE TABLE. It specifies whether ER–OCCUPANCY is single (code 1) or double (code 2).

The purpose of Program 32 is to print out a confirmation letter detailing the cost of the proposed trip and the kind of options requested. The input data to the program is punched according to the format shown in Figure 25.

The actual data used for the first run of the program follows. It will be noticed that the first data card contains an error in column 77.

COLUMN 1	COLUMN 12	COLUMN 22	COLUMN 77
FREGA	MICHAEL	40 WEST 4TH STREET NEW YORK 10012	3118
GREENSTONE	TEDDY	123 MAIN STREET NEW YORK 10023	2215
MAILMAN	SUSAN	25 ELDORADO ST. ENGLEWOOD N.J. 07070	1126
OPAS	ELI	1514 EAST 96TH STREET BROOKLYN N.Y. 11236	2122
MULLISH	HENRY	100 BLEEKER STREET NEW YORK 10012	2121

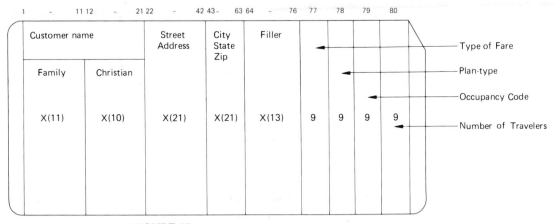

FIGURE 25

The data punched in columns 77, 78 and 79 are separate values and are used as the three subscripts to the data-name ER–RATE.

PROGRAM 32
Three Levels

```
00001        IDENTIFICATION DIVISION.
00002        PROGRAM-ID. THREE-LEVEL.
00003        AUTHOR. ELI J. OPAS.
00004        REMARKS. A THREE DIMENSIONAL TABLE LOOK-UP USING SUBSCRIPTS.
00005
00006        ENVIRONMENT DIVISION.
00007
00008        CONFIGURATION SECTION.
00009
00010        SOURCE-COMPUTER. IBM-370-145.
00011        OBJECT-COMPUTER. IBM-370-145.
00012
00013        SPECIAL-NAMES.
00014
00015            C01 IS TO-TOP-OF-PAGE.
00016
00017        INPUT-OUTPUT SECTION.
00018
00019        FILE-CONTROL.
00020
00021            SELECT IN-FILE ASSIGN TO UT-S-READER.
00022            SELECT OUT-FILE ASSIGN TO UT-S-PRINTER.
00023
00024        DATA DIVISION.
00025
00026        FILE SECTION.
00027
00028        FD  IN-FILE
```

```
00029               LABEL RECORDS ARE OMITTED.
00030
00031          01  RESERVATION-CARD.
00032              05  NAME.
00033                  10  FAMILY      PICTURE X(11).
00034                  10  CHRISTIAN   PICTURE X(10).
00035              05  STREET-ADDRESS  PICTURE X(21).
00036              05  CITY-STATE-ZIP  PICTURE X(21).
00037              05  FILLER          PICTURE X(13).
00038              05  TYPE-OF-FARE    PICTURE 9.
00039                  88  ONE-WAY     VALUE 1.
00040                  88  ROUND-TRIP  VALUE 2.
00041              05  PLAN-TYPE       PICTURE 9.
00042                  88  MAP         VALUE 1.
00043                  88  EUROPEAN    VALUE 2.
00044              05  OCCUPANCY-CODE  PICTURE 9.
00045                  88  SINGLE      VALUE 1.
00046                  88  DOUBLE      VALUE 2.
00047              05  NO-OF-TRAVELERS PICTURE 9.
00048
00049          FD  OUT-FILE
00050              LABEL RECORDS ARE OMITTED.
00051          01  OUTPUT-LINE.
00052              05  CC          PICTURE X.
00053              05  PRINT-LINE  PICTURE X(79).
00054          WORKING-STORAGE SECTION.
00055          77  ERROR-FLAG      PICTURE X(3) VALUE 'NO'.
00056          01  EXCURSION-RATE-TABLE.
00057              05  FILLER          PICTURE X(21) VALUE
00058                  '12950025400594005780O'.
00059              05  FILLER          PICTURE X(21) VALUE
00060                  '22760024300542005180O'.
00061
00062          01  EXCURSION-RATES REDEFINES EXCURSION-RATE-TABLE.
00063              05  ER-OCCUPANCY    OCCURS 2 TIMES.
00064                  10  OCCUPANCY   PICTURE 9.
00065                  10  TRIP-TYPE   OCCURS 2 TIMES.
00066                      15  ER-RATE OCCURS 2 TIMES
00067                          PICTURE 9(3)V99.
00068          01  LINE-1.
00069              05  FILLER      PICTURE X VALUE SPACES.
00070              05  NAME        PICTURE X(21).
00071              05  FILLER      PICTURE X(58) VALUE SPACES.
00072
00073          01  LINE-2.
00074              05  FILLER          PICTURE X VALUE SPACES.
00075              05  STREET-ADDRESS  PICTURE X(21).
00076              05  FILLER          PICTURE X(58) VALUE SPACES.
00077
00078          01  LINE-3.
00079              05  FILLER          PICTURE X VALUE SPACES.
00080              05  CITY-STATE-ZIP  PICTURE X(21).
00081              05  FILLER          PICTURE X(58) VALUE SPACES.
00082
00083          01  LINE-4.
00084              05  FILLER      PICTURE X VALUE SPACES.
00085              05  FILLER      PICTURE X(15) VALUE
00086                  'DEAR PASSENGER '.
00087              05  FAMILY      PICTURE X(11).
00088              05  FILLER      PICTURE X(53) VALUE SPACES.
00089
00090          01  LINE-5.
00091              05  FILLER      PICTURE X VALUE SPACES.
00092              05  FILLER      PICTURE X(53) VALUE
00093                  'WORLD-WIDE TRAVEL IS PLEASED TO INFORM YOU THAT YOUR'.
00094              05  FILLER      PICTURE X(26) VALUE SPACES.
00095
00096          01  LINE-6.
00097              05  FILLER          PICTURE X VALUE SPACES.
00098              05  FILLER          PICTURE X(27) VALUE
00099                  'RESERVATION FOR A PARTY OF '.
00100              05  NO-OF-TRAVELERS PICTURE 9.
00101              05  FILLER          PICTURE X(19) VALUE
00102                  ' TO LONDON HAS BEEN'.
00103              05  FILLER          PICTURE X(32) VALUE SPACES.
00104
00105          01  LINE-7.
00106              05  FILLER          PICTURE X VALUE SPACES.
00107              05  FILLER          PICTURE X(32) VALUE
00108                  'RECEIVED. YOUR ARRANGEMENTS FOR '.
00109              05  TYPE-OF-FARE    PICTURE X(10).
00110              05  FILLER          PICTURE X(9) VALUE
00111                  ' AIR-FARE'.
```

```
00112              05 FILLER          PICTURE X(28) VALUE SPACES.
00113
00114         01  LINE-8.
00115              05 FILLER          PICTURE X(01) VALUE SPACES.
00116              05 FILLER          PICTURE X(04) VALUE 'AND '.
00117              05 OCCUPANCY       PICTURE X(16).
00118              05 FILLER          PICTURE X(01) VALUE SPACES.
00119              05 PLAN-TYPE       PICTURE X(13).
00120              05 FILLER          PICTURE X(08) VALUE ' WILL BE'.
00121              05 FILLER          PICTURE X(37) VALUE SPACES.
00122
00123         01  LINE-9.
00124              05 FILLER          PICTURE X(01) VALUE SPACES.
00125              05 FILLER          PICTURE X(51) VALUE
00126              'CONFIRMED UPON RECEIPT OF YOUR CHECK OR MONEY ORDER'.
00127              05 FILLER          PICTURE X(28) VALUE SPACES.
00128
00129         01  LINE-10.
00130              05 FILLER          PICTURE X(01) VALUE SPACES.
00131              05 FILLER          PICTURE X(15) VALUE
00132              'FOR THE SUM OF '.
00133              05 RATE            PICTURE $$$,999.99.
00134              05 FILLER          PICTURE X(01) VALUE '.'.
00135              05 FILLER          PICTURE X(53) VALUE SPACES.
00136
00137         01  LINE-11.
00138              05 FILLER          PICTURE X(53) VALUE 'WORLD-WIDE TRAVEL'
00139              JUSTIFIED RIGHT.
00140              05 FILLER          PICTURE X(27) VALUE SPACES.
00141
00142          PROCEDURE DIVISION.
00143      GO-TO-IT.
00144          OPEN INPUT IN-FILE, OUTPUT OUT-FILE.
00145      GO-GET-EM.
00146          READ IN-FILE AT END GO TO GO-HOME.
00147      VALIDATE.
00148          IF TYPE-OF-FARE IN RESERVATION-CARD < 0 OR > 2
00149              GO TO LET-EM-HAVE-IT.
00150          IF PLAN-TYPE IN RESERVATION-CARD < 0 OR > 2
00151              GO TO LET-EM-HAVE-IT.
00152          IF OCCUPANCY-CODE < 0 OR > 2 GO TO LET-EM-HAVE-IT.
00153          IF NO-OF-TRAVELERS OF RESERVATION-CARD < 0 OR > 9
00154              GO TO LET-EM-HAVE-IT.
00155      PREPARE-TO-WRITE.
00156          MOVE NAME IN RESERVATION-CARD TO NAME IN LINE-1.
00157          MOVE STREET-ADDRESS IN RESERVATION-CARD
00158              TO STREET-ADDRESS IN LINE-2.
00159          MOVE CITY-STATE-ZIP IN RESERVATION-CARD TO
00160              CITY-STATE-ZIP IN LINE-3.
00161          MOVE FAMILY IN RESERVATION-CARD TO FAMILY IN LINE-4.
00162          MOVE NO-OF-TRAVELERS IN RESERVATION-CARD TO
00163              NO-OF-TRAVELERS IN LINE-6.
00164          IF ONE-WAY MOVE 'ONE-WAY' TO TYPE-OF-FARE IN LINE-7,
00165              ELSE MOVE 'ROUND-TRIP' TO TYPE-OF-FARE IN LINE-7.
00166          IF SINGLE MOVE 'SINGLE OCCUPANCY' TO OCCUPANCY IN LINE-8
00167              ELSE MOVE 'DOUBLE OCCUPANCY' TO OCCUPANCY IN LINE-8.
00168          IF MAP MOVE 'MAP' TO PLAN-TYPE IN LINE-8,
00169              ELSE MOVE 'EUROPEAN PLAN' TO PLAN-TYPE IN LINE-8.
00170          COMPUTE RATE =
00171              ER-RATE (OCCUPANCY-CODE, TYPE-OF-FARE IN RESERVATION-CARD,
00172              PLAN-TYPE IN RESERVATION-CARD) * NO-OF-TRAVELERS OF
00173              RESERVATION-CARD.
00174      WRITE-THE-LETTER.
00175          WRITE OUTPUT-LINE FROM LINE-1 AFTER ADVANCING
00176              TO-TOP-OF-PAGE.
00177          WRITE OUTPUT-LINE FROM LINE-2 AFTER ADVANCING 1 LINES.
00178          WRITE OUTPUT-LINE FROM LINE-3 AFTER ADVANCING 1 LINES.
00179          WRITE OUTPUT-LINE FROM LINE-4 AFTER ADVANCING 3 LINES.
00180          WRITE OUTPUT-LINE FROM LINE-5 AFTER ADVANCING 3 LINES.
00181          WRITE OUTPUT-LINE FROM LINE-6 AFTER ADVANCING 2 LINES.
00182          WRITE OUTPUT-LINE FROM LINE-7 AFTER ADVANCING 2 LINES.
00183          WRITE OUTPUT-LINE FROM LINE-8 AFTER ADVANCING 2 LINES.
00184          WRITE OUTPUT-LINE FROM LINE-9 AFTER ADVANCING 2 LINES.
00185          WRITE OUTPUT-LINE FROM LINE-10 AFTER ADVANCING 2 LINES.
00186          WRITE OUTPUT-LINE FROM LINE-11 AFTER ADVANCING 3 LINES.
00187          GO TO GO-GET-EM.
00188      LET-EM-HAVE-IT.
00189          MOVE 'YES' TO ERROR-FLAG.
00190          DISPLAY RESERVATION-CARD.
00191          GO TO GO-GET-EM.
00192      GO-HOME.
00193          IF ERROR-FLAG = 'YES' DISPLAY
00194          'INVALID DATA-CARDS -- CORRECT AND RESUBMIT'.
00195          CLOSE IN-FILE, OUT-FILE.
00196          STOP RUN.
```

OUTPUT TO PROGRAM 32

```
GREENSTONE  TEDDY
123 MAIN STREET
N.Y.  10023

DEAR PASSENGER GREENSTONE

WORLD-WIDE TRAVEL IS PLEASED TO INFORM YOU THAT YOUR

RESERVATION FOR A PARTY OF 5 TO LONDON HAS BEEN

RECEIVED. YOUR ARRANGEMENTS FOR ROUND-TRIP AIR-FARE

AND SINGLE OCCUPANCY EUROPEAN PLAN WILL BE

CONFIRMED UPON RECEIPT OF YOUR CHECK OR MONEY ORDER

FOR THE SUM OF  $2,890.00.

                              WORLD-WIDE TRAVEL


MAILMAN    SUSAN
25 ELDORADO ST
ENGLEWOOD, N.J. 07070

DEAR PASSENGER MAILMAN

WORLD-WIDE TRAVEL IS PLEASED TO INFORM YOU THAT YOUR

RESERVATION FOR A PARTY OF 6 TO LONDON HAS BEEN

RECEIVED. YOUR ARRANGEMENTS FOR ONE-WAY    AIR-FARE

AND DOUBLE OCCUPANCY MAP           WILL BE

CONFIRMED UPON RECEIPT OF YOUR CHECK OR MONEY ORDER

FOR THE SUM OF  $1,656.00.

                              WORLD-WIDE TRAVEL


MULLISH    HENRY
100 BLEEKER STREET
NEW YORK CITY 10012

DEAR PASSENGER MULLISH

WORLD-WIDE TRAVEL IS PLEASED TO INFORM YOU THAT YOUR

RESERVATION FOR A PARTY OF 1 TO LONDON HAS BEEN

RECEIVED. YOUR ARRANGEMENTS FOR ROUND-TRIP AIR-FARE

AND DOUBLE OCCUPANCY MAP           WILL BE

CONFIRMED UPON RECEIPT OF YOUR CHECK OR MONEY ORDER

FOR THE SUM OF    $542.00.

                              WORLD-WIDE TRAVEL


OPAS       ELI
1514 EAST 96TH STREET
BROOKLYN, N.Y. 11236

DEAR PASSENGER OPAS

WORLD-WIDE TRAVEL IS PLEASED TO INFORM YOU THAT YOUR

RESERVATION FOR A PARTY OF 2 TO LONDON HAS BEEN
```

```
RECEIVED. YOUR ARRANGEMENTS FOR ROUND-TRIP AIR-FARE
AND DOUBLE OCCUPANCY MAP          WILL BE
CONFIRMED UPON RECEIPT OF YOUR CHECK OR MONEY ORDER
FOR THE SUM OF  $1,084.00.

                         WORLD-WIDE TRAVEL

FREGA     MICHAEL    40 WEST 4TH STREET    NEW YORK 10012        3118
INVALID DATA-CARDS -- CORRECT AND RESUBMIT
```

Column 77 (type of fare) of the invalid data card is corrected to a 1 (one-way fare) and the program rerun. Here is the printed output for the second run.

OUTPUT TO PROGRAM 32 (RERUN)

```
FREGA     MICHAEL
40 WEST 4TH STREET
NEW YORK 10012

DEAR PASSENGER FREGA

WORLD-WIDE TRAVEL IS PLEASED TO INFORM YOU THAT YOUR
RESERVATION FOR A PARTY OF 8 TO LONDON HAS BEEN
RECEIVED. YOUR ARRANGEMENTS FOR ONE-WAY    AIR-FARE
AND SINGLE OCCUPANCY MAP          WILL BE
CONFIRMED UPON RECEIPT OF YOUR CHECK OR MONEY ORDER
FOR THE SUM OF  $2,280.00.

                         WORLD-WIDE TRAVEL

GREENSTONE TEDDY
123 MAIN STREET
N.Y.  10023

DEAR PASSENGER GREENSTONE

WORLD-WIDE TRAVEL IS PLEASED TO INFORM YOU THAT YOUR
RESERVATION FOR A PARTY OF 5 TO LONDON HAS BEEN
RECEIVED. YOUR ARRANGEMENTS FOR ROUND-TRIP AIR-FARE
AND SINGLE OCCUPANCY EUROPEAN PLAN WILL BE
CONFIRMED UPON RECEIPT OF YOUR CHECK OR MONEY ORDER
FOR THE SUM OF  $2,890.00.

                         WORLD-WIDE TRAVEL

MAILMAN    SUSAN
25 ELDORADO ST
ENGLEWOOD, N.J. 07070

DEAR PASSENGER MAILMAN

WORLD-WIDE TRAVEL IS PLEASED TO INFORM YOU THAT YOUR
RESERVATION FOR A PARTY OF 6 TO LONDON HAS BEEN
```

```
RECEIVED. YOUR ARRANGEMENTS FOR ONE-WAY     AIR-FARE

AND DOUBLF OCCUPANCY MAP           WILL BE

CONFIRMED UPON RECEIPT OF YOUR CHECK OR MONEY ORDER

FOR THE SUM OF  $1,656.00.


                             WORLD-WIDE TRAVEL


OPAS       ELI
1514 EAST 96TH STREET
BROOKLYN, N.Y. 11236


DEAR PASSENGER OPAS


WORLD-WIDE TRAVEL IS PLEASED TO INFORM YOU THAT YOUR

RESERVATION FOR A PARTY OF 2 TO LONDON HAS BEEN

RECEIVED. YOUR ARRANGEMENTS FOR ROUND-TRIP AIR-FARE

AND DOUBLE OCCUPANCY MAP           WILL BE

CONFIRMED UPON RECEIPT OF YOUR CHECK OR MONEY ORDER

FOR THE SUM OF  $1,084.00.


                             WORLD-WIDE TRAVEL


MULLISH     HENRY
100 BLEEKER STREET
NEW YORK CITY 10012


DEAR PASSENGER MULLISH


WORLD-WIDE TRAVEL IS PLEASED TO INFORM YOU THAT YOUR

RESERVATION FOR A PARTY OF 1 TO LONDON HAS BEEN

RECEIVED. YOUR ARRANGEMENTS FOR ROUND-TRIP AIR-FARE

AND DOUBLF OCCUPANCY MAP           WILL BE

CONFIRMED UPON RECEIPT OF YOUR CHECK OR MONEY ORDER

FOR THE SUM OF    $542.00.


                             WORLD-WIDE TRAVEL
```

12.10 A THREE LEVEL TABLE
USING INDEXING

In order to re-emphasize the fact that when operating upon tables in COBOL it is always possible to work with the indexing feature rather than with subscripts, the identical data is run with a modified version of the previous program. In Program 33 the data stored in the three-dimensional table is accessed by means of indexing. The invalid data card left in for the first run is corrected for the second run of the program.

PROGRAM 33
Three Level Index

```
00001        IDENTIFICATION DIVISION.
00002        PROGRAM-ID. THREE-LEVEL-INDEX.
00003        AUTHOR. ELI J. OPAS.
00004        REMARKS. A THREE DIMENSIONAL TABLE LOOK-UP USING INDEXING.
```

```
00005
00006              ENVIRONMENT DIVISION.
00007
00008              CONFIGURATION SECTION.
00009
00010              SOURCE-COMPUTER. IBM-370-145.
00011              OBJECT-COMPUTER. IBM-370-145.
00012
00013              SPECIAL-NAMES.
00014
00015                  C01 IS TO-TOP-OF-PAGE.
00016
00017              INPUT-OUTPUT SECTION.
00018
00019              FILE-CONTROL.
00020
00021                  SELECT IN-FILE ASSIGN TO UT-S-READER.
00022                  SELECT OUT-FILE ASSIGN TO UT-S-PRINTER.
00023
00024              DATA DIVISION.
00025
00026              FILE SECTION.
00027
00028              FD  IN-FILE
00029                  LABEL RECORDS ARE OMITTED.
00030
00031              01  RESERVATION-CARD.
00032                  05 NAME.
00033                      10 FAMILY       PICTURE X(11).
00034                      10 CHRISTIAN    PICTURE X(10).
00035                  05 STREET-ADDRESS   PICTURE X(21).
00036                  05 CITY-STATE-ZIP   PICTURE X(21).
00037                  05 FILLER           PICTURE X(13).
00038                  05 TYPE-OF-FARE     PICTURE 9.
00039                      88 ONE-WAY      VALUE 1.
00040                      88 ROUND-TRIP   VALUE 2.
00041                  05 PLAN-TYPE        PICTURE 9.
00042                      88 MAP          VALUE 1.
00043                      88 EUROPEAN     VALUE 2.
00044                  05 OCCUPANCY-CODE   PICTURE 9.
00045                      88 SINGLE       VALUE 1.
00046                      88 DOUBLE       VALUE 2.
00047                  05 NO-OF-TRAVELERS PICTURE 9.
00048
00049              FD  OUT-FILE
00050                  LABEL RECORDS ARE OMITTED.
00051              01  OUTPUT-LINE.
00052                  05 CC               PICTURE X.
00053                  05 PRINT-LINE       PICTURE X(79).
00054              WORKING-STORAGE SECTION.
00055              77 ERROR-FLAG           PICTURE X(3) VALUE 'NO'.
00056              01 EXCURSION-RATE-TABLE.
00057                  05 FILLER           PICTURE X(21) VALUE
00058                                      '128500254005940057800'.
00059                  05 FILLER           PICTURE X(21) VALUE
00060                                      '227600243005420051800'.
00061
00062              01  EXCURSION-RATES REDEFINES EXCURSION-RATE-TABLE.
00063                  05 ER-OCCUPANCY     OCCURS 2 TIMES,
00064                                      INDEXED BY OCCUPANCY-INDEX.
00065                      10 OCCUPANCY    PICTURE 9.
00066                      10 TRIP-TYPE    OCCURS 2 TIMES,
00067                                      INDEXED BY TYPE-INDEX.
00068                          15 ER-RATE  OCCURS 2 TIMES,
00069                                      INDEXED BY RATE-INDEX,
00070                                      PICTURE 9(3)V99.
00071              01  LINE-1.
00072                  05 FILLER           PICTURE X VALUE SPACES.
00073                  05 NAME             PICTURE X(21).
00074                  05 FILLER           PICTURE X(58) VALUE SPACES.
00075
00076              01  LINE-2.
00077                  05 FILLER           PICTURE X VALUE SPACES.
00078                  05 STREET-ADDRESS   PICTURE X(21).
00079                  05 FILLER           PICTURE X(58) VALUE SPACES.
00080
00081              01  LINE-3.
00082                  05 FILLER           PICTURE X VALUE SPACES.
00083                  05 CITY-STATE-ZIP   PICTURE X(21).
00084                  05 FILLER           PICTURE X(58) VALUE SPACES.
00085
00086              01  LINE-4.
00087                  05 FILLER           PICTURE X VALUE SPACES.
```

```
00088            05 FILLER           PICTURE X(15) VALUE
00089                                'DEAR PASSENGER '.
00090            05 FAMILY           PICTURE X(11).
00091            05 FILLER           PICTURE X(53) VALUE SPACES.
00092
00093        01  LINE-5.
00094            05 FILLER           PICTURE X VALUE SPACES.
00095            05 FILLER           PICTURE X(53) VALUE
00096            'WORLD-WIDE TRAVEL IS PLEASED TO INFORM YOU THAT YOUR'.
00097            05 FILLER           PICTURE X(26) VALUE SPACES.
00098
00099        01  LINE-6.
00100            05 FILLER           PICTURE X VALUE SPACES.
00101            05 FILLER           PICTURE X(27) VALUE
00102            'RESERVATION FOR A PARTY OF '.
00103            05 NO-OF-TRAVELERS PICTURE 9.
00104            05 FILLER           PICTURE X(19) VALUE
00105            ' TO LONDON HAS BEEN'.
00106            05 FILLER           PICTURE X(32) VALUE SPACES.
00107
00108        01  LINE-7.
00109            05 FILLER           PICTURE X VALUE SPACES.
00110            05 FILLER           PICTURE X(32) VALUE
00111            'RECEIVED. YOUR ARRANGEMENTS FOR '.
00112            05 TYPE-OF-FARE      PICTURE X(10).
00113            05 FILLER           PICTURE X(9) VALUE
00114            ' AIR-FARE'.
00115            05 FILLER           PICTURE X(28) VALUE SPACES.
00116
00117        01  LINE-8.
00118            05 FILLER           PICTURE X(01) VALUE SPACES.
00119            05 FILLER           PICTURE X(04) VALUE 'AND '.
00120            05 OCCUPANCY         PICTURE X(16).
00121            05 FILLER           PICTURE X(01) VALUE SPACES.
00122            05 PLAN-TYPE         PICTURE X(13).
00123            05 FILLER           PICTURE X(08) VALUE ' WILL BE'.
00124            05 FILLER           PICTURE X(37) VALUE SPACES.
00125
00126        01  LINE-9.
00127            05 FILLER           PICTURE X(01) VALUE SPACES.
00128            05 FILLER           PICTURE X(51) VALUE
00129               'CONFIRMED UPON RECEIPT OF YOUR CHECK OR MONEY ORDER'.
00130            05 FILLER           PICTURE X(28) VALUE SPACES.
00131
00132        01  LINE-10.
00133            05 FILLER           PICTURE X(01) VALUE SPACES.
00134            05 FILLER                   PICTURE X(15) VALUE
00135               'FOR THE SUM OF '.
00136            05 RATE              PICTURE $$$,999.99.
00137            05 FILLER           PICTURE X(01) VALUE '.'.
00138            05 FILLER           PICTURE X(53) VALUE SPACES.
00139
00140        01  LINE-11.
00141            05 FILLER              PICTURE X(53) VALUE 'WORLD-WIDE TRAVEL'
00142               JUSTIFIED RIGHT.
00143            05 FILLER           PICTURE X(27) VALUE SPACES.
00144
00145        PROCEDURE DIVISION.
00146        GO-TO-IT.
00147            OPEN INPUT IN-FILE, OUTPUT OUT-FILE.
00148        GO-GET-EM.
00149            READ IN-FILE AT END GO TO GO-HOME.
00150        VALIDATE.
00151            IF TYPE-OF-FARE IN RESERVATION-CARD < 0 OR > 2
00152                GO TO LET-EM-HAVE-IT.
00153            IF PLAN-TYPE IN RESERVATION-CARD < 0 OR > 2
00154                GO TO LET-EM-HAVE-IT.
00155            IF OCCUPANCY-CODE < 0 OR > 2 GO TO LET-EM-HAVE-IT.
00156            IF NO-OF-TRAVELERS OF RESERVATION-CARD < 0 OR > 9
00157                    GO TO LET-EM-HAVE-IT.
00158
00159        PREPARE-TO-WRITE.
00160            MOVE NAME IN RESERVATION-CARD TO NAME IN LINE-1.
00161            MOVE STREET-ADDRESS IN RESERVATION-CARD
00162                TO STREET-ADDRESS IN LINE-2.
00163            MOVE CITY-STATE-ZIP IN RESERVATION-CARD TO
00164                CITY-STATE-ZIP IN LINE-3.
00165            MOVE FAMILY IN RESERVATION-CARD TO FAMILY IN LINE-4.
00166            MOVE NO-OF-TRAVELERS IN RESERVATION-CARD TO
00167                NO-OF-TRAVELERS IN LINE-6.
00168            IF ONE-WAY MOVE 'ONE-WAY' TO TYPE-OF-FARE IN LINE-7,
00169            ELSE MOVE 'ROUND-TRIP' TO TYPE-OF-FARE IN LINE-7.
00170            IF SINGLE MOVE 'SINGLE OCCUPANCY' TO OCCUPANCY IN LINE-8
```

```
00171                    ELSE MOVE 'DOUBLE OCCUPANCY' TO OCCUPANCY IN LINE-8.
00172                  IF MAP MOVE 'MAP' TO PLAN-TYPE IN LINE-8,
00173                    ELSE MOVE 'EUROPEAN PLAN' TO PLAN-TYPE IN LINE-8.
00174              COMPUTE-THE-RATE.
00175                  SET OCCUPANCY-INDEX TO OCCUPANCY-CODE.
00176                  SET TYPE-INDEX TO TYPE-OF-FARE IN RESERVATION-CARD.
00177                  SET RATE-INDEX TO PLAN-TYPE IN RESERVATION-CARD.
00178                  COMPUTE RATE =
00179                      ER-RATE (OCCUPANCY-INDEX, TYPE-INDEX, RATE-INDEX)
00180                      * NO-OF-TRAVELERS IN RESERVATION-CARD.
00181
00182              WRITE-THE-LETTER.
00183                  WRITE OUTPUT-LINE FROM LINE-1 AFTER ADVANCING
00184                      TO-TOP-OF-PAGE.
00185                  WRITE OUTPUT-LINE FROM LINE-2 AFTER ADVANCING 1 LINES.
00186                  WRITE OUTPUT-LINE FROM LINE-3 AFTER ADVANCING 1 LINES.
00187                  WRITE OUTPUT-LINE FROM LINE-4 AFTER ADVANCING 3 LINES.
00188                  WRITE OUTPUT-LINE FROM LINE-5 AFTER ADVANCING 3 LINES.
00189                  WRITE OUTPUT-LINE FROM LINE-6 AFTER ADVANCING 2 LINES.
00190                  WRITE OUTPUT-LINE FROM LINE-7 AFTER ADVANCING 2 LINES.
00191                  WRITE OUTPUT-LINE FROM LINE-8 AFTER ADVANCING 2 LINES.
00192                  WRITE OUTPUT-LINE FROM LINE-9 AFTER ADVANCING 2 LINES.
00193                  WRITE OUTPUT-LINE FROM LINE-10 AFTER ADVANCING 2 LINES.
00194                  WRITE OUTPUT-LINE FROM LINE-11 AFTER ADVANCING 3 LINES.
00195                  GO TO GO-GET-EM.
00196              LET-EM-HAVE-IT.
00197                  MOVE 'YES' TO ERROR-FLAG.
00198                  DISPLAY RESERVATION-CARD.
00199                  GO TO GO-GET-EM.
00200              GO-HOME.
00201                  IF ERROR-FLAG = 'YES' DISPLAY
00202                  'INVALID DATA-CARDS -- CORRECT AND RESUBMIT'.
00203                  CLOSE IN-FILE, OUT-FILE.
00204                  STOP RUN.
```

OUTPUT TO PROGRAM 33

```
GREENSTONE TEDDY
123 MAIN STREET
N.Y.  10023


DEAR PASSENGER GREENSTONE


WORLD-WIDE TRAVEL IS PLEASED TO INFORM YOU THAT YOUR

RESERVATION FOR A PARTY OF 5 TO LONDON HAS BEEN

RECEIVED. YOUR ARRANGEMENTS FOR ROUND-TRIP AIR-FARE

AND SINGLE OCCUPANCY EUROPEAN PLAN WILL BE

CONFIRMED UPON RECEIPT OF YOUR CHECK OR MONEY ORDER

FOR THE SUM OF  $2,890.00.


                                   WORLD-WIDE TRAVEL


MAILMAN    SUSAN
25 ELDORADO ST
ENGLEWOOD, N.J.  07070


DEAR PASSENGER MAILMAN


WORLD-WIDE TRAVEL IS PLEASED TO INFORM YOU THAT YOUR

RESERVATION FOR A PARTY OF 6 TO LONDON HAS BEEN

RECEIVED. YOUR ARRANGEMENTS FOR ONE-WAY    AIR-FARE

AND DOUBLE OCCUPANCY MAP          WILL BE

CONFIRMED UPON RECEIPT OF YOUR CHECK OR MONEY ORDER

FOR THE SUM OF  $1,656.00.


                                   WORLD-WIDE TRAVEL
```

```
OPAS      ELI
1514 EAST 96TH STREET
BROOKLYN, N.Y. 11236

DEAR PASSENGER OPAS

WORLD-WIDE TRAVEL IS PLEASED TO INFORM YOU THAT YOUR

RESERVATION FOR A PARTY OF 2 TO LONDON HAS BEEN

RECEIVED. YOUR ARRANGEMENTS FOR ROUND-TRIP AIR-FARE

AND DOUBLE OCCUPANCY MAP          WILL BE

CONFIRMED UPON RECEIPT OF YOUR CHECK OR MONEY ORDER

FOR THE SUM OF  $1,084.00.

                              WORLD-WIDE TRAVEL



MULLISH    HENRY
100 BLEEKER STREET
NEW YORK CITY 10012

DEAR PASSENGER MULLISH

WORLD-WIDE TRAVEL IS PLEASED TO INFORM YOU THAT YOUR

RESERVATION FOR A PARTY OF 1 TO LONDON HAS BEEN

RECEIVED. YOUR ARRANGEMENTS FOR ROUND-TRIP AIR-FARE

AND DOUBLE OCCUPANCY MAP          WILL BE

CONFIRMED UPON RECEIPT OF YOUR CHECK OR MONEY ORDER

FOR THE SUM OF     $542.00.

                              WORLD-WIDE TRAVEL



FREGA     MICHAEL    40 WEST 4TH STREET   NEW YORK 10012              3118
INVALID DATA-CARDS -- CORRECT AND RESUBMIT
```

OUTPUT TO PROGRAM 33 (RERUN)

```
FREGA      MICHAEL
40 WEST 4TH STREET
NEW YORK 10012

DEAR PASSENGER FREGA

WORLD-WIDE TRAVEL IS PLEASED TO INFORM YOU THAT YOUR

RESERVATION FOR A PARTY OF 8 TO LONDON HAS BEEN

RECEIVED. YOUR ARRANGEMENTS FOR ONE-WAY    AIR-FARE

AND SINGLE OCCUPANCY MAP          WILL BE

CONFIRMED UPON RECEIPT OF YOUR CHECK OR MONEY ORDER

FOR THE SUM OF  $2,280.00.

                              WORLD-WIDE TRAVEL
```

```
GREENSTONE TEDDY
123 MAIN STREET
N.Y.  10023
```

DEAR PASSENGER GREENSTONE

WORLD-WIDE TRAVEL IS PLEASED TO INFORM YOU THAT YOUR
RESERVATION FOR A PARTY OF 5 TO LONDON HAS BEEN
RECEIVED. YOUR ARRANGEMENTS FOR ROUND-TRIP AIR-FARE
AND SINGLE OCCUPANCY EUROPEAN PLAN WILL BE
CONFIRMED UPON RECEIPT OF YOUR CHECK OR MONEY ORDER
FOR THE SUM OF $2,890.00.

                               WORLD-WIDE TRAVEL


```
MAILMAN    SUSAN
25 ELDORADO ST
ENGLEWOOD, N.J. 07070
```

DEAR PASSENGER MAILMAN

WORLD-WIDE TRAVEL IS PLEASED TO INFORM YOU THAT YOUR
RESERVATION FOR A PARTY OF 6 TO LONDON HAS BEEN
RECEIVED. YOUR ARRANGEMENTS FOR ONE-WAY   AIR-FARE
AND DOUBLE OCCUPANCY MAP   WILL BE
CONFIRMED UPON RECEIPT OF YOUR CHECK OR MONEY ORDER
FOR THE SUM OF $1,656.00.

                               WORLD-WIDE TRAVEL


```
OPAS         FLT
1514 EAST 96TH STREET
BROOKLYN, N.Y. 11236
```

DEAR PASSENGER OPAS

WORLD-WIDE TRAVEL IS PLEASED TO INFORM YOU THAT YOUR
RESERVATION FOR A PARTY OF 2 TO LONDON HAS BEEN
RECEIVED. YOUR ARRANGEMENTS FOR ROUND-TRIP AIR-FARE
AND DOUBLE OCCUPANCY MAP   WILL BE
CONFIRMED UPON RECEIPT OF YOUR CHECK OR MONEY ORDER
FOR THE SUM OF $1,084.00.

                               WORLD-WIDE TRAVEL


```
MULLISH    HENRY
100 BLEEKER STREET
NEW YORK CITY 10012
```

DEAR PASSENGER MULLISH

WORLD-WIDE TRAVEL IS PLEASED TO INFORM YOU THAT YOUR
RESERVATION FOR A PARTY OF 1 TO LONDON HAS BEEN

RECEIVED. YOUR ARRANGEMENTS FOR ROUND-TRIP AIR-FARE

AND DOUBLE OCCUPANCY MAP   WILL BE

CONFIRMED UPON RECEIPT OF YOUR CHECK OR MONEY ORDER

FOR THE SUM OF $542.00.

                                   WORLD-WIDE TRAVEL

12.11 LOADING A FIXED-LENGTH TABLE INTO STORAGE

Throughout this chapter we have dealt with tables whose entries were defined in the Working-Storage section of the program where they were also redefined and converted to a table proper by means of the occurs clause.

It is not necessary, however, to define a table only in this manner. It is possible in COBOL to read in the values of a table from data cards as is illustrated in Program 34. If realistic considerations lead one to the conclusion that it will become necessary to change the contents of a table relatively frequently, it would be advantageous to resort to this method of loading a table. When using this method, it is not necessary to change repeatedly the program itself; all that is necessary is a change in the data cards.

The inventory table to be loaded for Program 34 is punched on data cards. Since the table is fixed at 20 entries, there are 20 data cards punched with the following information:

COLUMN 1	COLUMN 5	
0010	1234	
0020	4321	
0030	4521	Inventory as of
0040	0023	previous run,
0050	8752	called QUANTITY
0060	6044	in program
0070	4563	
0080	9632	
0090	5879	
0100	0032	
0110	6532	
0120	3524	
0130	2547	
0140	2563	
0150	2546	
0160	2356	
0170	2587	
0180	2546	
0190	0235	
0200	3654	

Product code, called PRODUCT-CODE in program

The first four columns of each data card is punched with a product code number; this is followed immediately with the quantity in stock (as of the last inventory) punched in columns 5 through 8. These 20 data cards represent the input to the input file IN–FILE described in the record entry named INVENTORY. The product codes are in ascending order starting with 0010 and going up to 0200.

After the files have been opened in the Procedure Division, an index called TABLE–INDEX is set to 1 before the data cards are read. If the value of this index becomes greater than 20, this indicates an error in loading the table and control is sent directly to a load-error routine. The phrase

'INVENTORY–CARDS EXCEED TABLE SIZE––PROGRAM TERMINATED'

is displayed. On the assumption that this does not occur, a check is made to determine whether the product code is in correct sequence. If it isn't, another error message is printed out specifying the nature of the error, and again the program is terminated.

Attention is now drawn to the record entry INVENTORY–TABLE in Working-Storage. It is stated as follows:

```
01  INVENTORY–TABLE.
    05 TABLE–VALUES OCCURS 20 TIMES
                    INDEXED BY TABLE–INDEX.
        10 TV–PRODUCT–CODE   PICTURE 9(4).
        10 TV–QUANTITY       PICTURE 9(4).
```

This is the entry which sets up the area in memory for the loading of the table. The 05 level entry TABLE–VALUES contains the OCCURS clause and the specification that the table is indexed by TABLE–INDEX. You will recall that this was initialized to 1 at the beginning of the Procedure Division.

In the Procedure Division, with TABLE–INDEX set to 1, the value of PRODUCT–CODE (from the first data card) is moved to TV–PRODUCT–CODE indexed by 1. Similarly, QUANTITY (also of the first data card) is moved to TV–QUANTITY (1) and the value of the product code is saved in Working Storage for subsequent comparison. At this point it is necessary to advance the value of the index TABLE–INDEX by 1 prior to reading the next data card. This is done by a form of the SET instruction we have not yet encountered.

12.11.1. The SET Index UP Instruction

It will be recalled that in a previous program when the SET instruction was used under the control of the SEARCH verb, the value of the index was *automatically* incremented. In the paragraph LOAD–TABLE, however, the SEARCH verb is absent. For this reason we must incorporate into the program a means of incrementing the index. We cannot MOVE a number to an index as we can an ordinary data name. In COBOL provision is made to decrement or increment an index. If we want to increment the index by 1, we write as in our case:

SET TABLE–INDEX UP BY 1.

By the same token, if we wanted to decrement the index by 1, we would have written:

SET TABLE–INDEX DOWN BY 1.

Once the index has been incremented, the next data card is read. This process is repeated until the whole table is loaded. At this point the paragraph WRITE–TABLE–VALUES is encountered. After going to the top of a new page, the index INDEX–TABLE is reinitialized to 1 and, under the control of the PERFORM the index is again incremented from 1 to 20, printing out the contents of the table on a separate line with each pass.

It should be noted that when a table is loaded from data it is not necessary to REDEFINE the area of the table.

PROGRAM 34
Fixed Load

```
00001          IDENTIFICATION DIVISION.
00002          PROGRAM-ID. FIXEDLOAD.
00003          AUTHOR. ELI J. OPAS.
00004          REMARKS. LOADING A FIXED LENGTH TABLE.
00005
00006          ENVIRONMENT DIVISION.
00007
00008          CONFIGURATION SECTION.
00009
00010          SOURCE-COMPUTER. IBM-370-145.
00011          OBJECT-COMPUTER. IBM-370-145.
00012
00013          SPECIAL-NAMES.
00014
00015              C01 IS TO-TOP-OF-PAGE.
00016
00017          INPUT-OUTPUT SECTION.
00018
00019          FILE-CONTROL.
00020
00021              SELECT IN-FILE ASSIGN TO UT-S-READER.
00022              SELECT OUT-FILE ASSIGN TO UT-S-PRINTER.
00023
00024          DATA DIVISION.
00025
00026          FILE SECTION.
00027
00028          FD  IN-FILE
00029              LABEL RECORDS ARE OMITTED.
00030
00031          01  INVENTORY-CARD.
00032              05 PRODUCT-CODE      PICTURE 9(4).
00033              05 QUANTITY          PICTURE 9(4).
00034              05 FILLER            PICTURE X(72).
00035
00036          FD  OUT-FILE
00037              LABEL RECORDS ARE OMITTED.
00038
00039          01  TABLE-LIST.
00040              05 FILLER            PICTURE X(80).
00041
00042          WORKING-STORAGE SECTION.
00043
00044          77  PRODUCT-CODE-SAVE  PICTURE 9(4) VALUE ZERO.
```

```
00045
00046          01  INVENTORY-TABLE.
00047              05  TABLE-VALUES      OCCURS 20 TIMES,
00048                                    INDEXED BY TABLE-INDEX.
00049                  10 IV-PRODUCT-CODE PICTURE 9(4).
00050                  10 IV-QUANTITY     PICTURE 9(4).
00051
00052          01  HEADER.
00053              05  FILLER            PICTURE X(13) VALUE ' PRODUCT CODE'.
00054              05  FILLER            PICTURE X(18) VALUE 'QUANTITY' JUST RIGHT.
00055              05  FILLER            PICTURE X(49) VALUE SPACES.
00056
00057          01  TABLE-LISTING.
00058              05  FILLER            PICTURE X VALUE SPACES.
00059              05  PRODUCT-CODE-OUT  PICTURE 9(4).
00060              05  FILLER            PICTURE X(18) VALUE SPACES.
00061              05  QUANTITY-OUT      PICTURE 9(4).
00062              05  FILLER            PICTURE X(53) VALUE SPACES.
00063
00064          PROCEDURE DIVISION.
00065
00066          START-UP.
00067              OPEN INPUT IN-FILE, OUTPUT OUT-FILE.
00068
00069          PREPARE-TO-LOAD.
00070              SET TABLE-INDEX TO 1.
00071
00072          READ-TABLE-VALUES.
00073              READ IN-FILE AT END GO TO WRITE-TABLE-VALUES.
00074
00075          LOAD-TABLE.
00076              IF TABLE-INDEX > 20 GO TO LOAD-ERROR.
00077              IF PRODUCT-CODE NOT > PRODUCT-CODE-SAVE
00078                  GO TO OUT-OF-SEQUENCE.
00079              MOVE PRODUCT-CODE TO IV-PRODUCT-CODE (TABLE-INDEX).
00080              MOVE QUANTITY TO IV-QUANTITY (TABLE-INDEX).
00081              MOVE PRODUCT-CODE TO PRODUCT-CODE-SAVE.
00082              SET TABLE-INDEX UP BY 1.
00083              GO TO READ-TABLE-VALUES.
00084
00085          WRITE-TABLE-VALUES.
00086              WRITE TABLE-LIST FROM HEADER AFTER ADVANCING TO-TOP-OF-PAGE.
00087              PERFORM TABLE-VALUES-LISTING
00088                  VARYING TABLE-INDEX FROM 1 BY 1
00089                      UNTIL TABLE-INDEX > 20.
00090              GO TO END-OF-JOB.
00091
00092          TABLE-VALUES-LISTING.
00093              MOVE IV-PRODUCT-CODE (TABLE-INDEX) TO PRODUCT-CODE-OUT.
00094              MOVE IV-QUANTITY (TABLE-INDEX) TO QUANTITY-OUT.
00095              WRITE TABLE-LIST FROM TABLE-LISTING AFTER ADVANCING 2.
00096
00097          LOAD-ERROR.
00098              DISPLAY
00099                  'INVENTORY-CARDS EXCEED TABLE SIZE-PROGRAM TERMINATED'.
00100              GO TO END-OF-JOB.
00101
00102          OUT-OF-SEQUENCE.
00103              DISPLAY INVENTORY-CARD
00104                  'INVENTORY-CARD OUT OF SEQUENCE-PROGRAM TERMINATED'.
00105
00106          END-OF-JOB.
00107              CLOSE IN-FILE, OUT-FILE.
00108              STOP RUN.
```

OUTPUT TO PROGRAM 34

PRODUCT CODE	QUANTITY
0010	1234
0020	4321
0030	4521
0040	0023
0050	8752
0060	6544
0070	4563

0080	9632
0090	5879
0100	0032
0110	6532
0120	3524
0130	2547
0140	2563
0150	2546
0160	2356
0170	2587
0180	2546
0190	0235
0200	3654

12.12 LOADING A VARIABLE-LENGTH TABLE

In Program 34 we loaded a table of exactly 20 entries. It often transpires, however, that the actual length a table will assume can vary from run to run, from one period to another. In such situations a method may be used in which a certain maximum length can be decided upon, one which will be large enough to accommodate any reasonable demand in the foreseeable future. Once this maximum length has been decided, any length table up to and including that maximum may be loaded. The method used is one commonly found in other programming languages and is called the *trailer card* technique.

12.12.1. The Trailer Card Technique

This very useful and simple technique rests on the fact that for a given list of items it is invariably possible to select a value which, for reasons of logic or reasonableness, can never be a legitimate member of that list. A telephone number composed of seven consecutive zeros is such a number, or a person's age over 200 years, and so on. This fictitious number is punched on a card which is placed all the way at the end of the data deck; since it "trails" at the end, it is called a trailer card. Now, as *each* data card is read, it is checked to determine whether it is the trailer card or not. As soon as the trailer card is encountered, it is a clear signal that the end of the table has been loaded, and no further action is taken with the trailer card. Nor is it read in as part of the table, of course.

In Program 35, which follows, the input cards are punched with a product code and a quantity on hand in columns 1 through 4 and 5 through 8 respectively. Behind these cards a trailer card is punched with the "phoney" product number of 9999. The program is designed to allow for a maximum table length of 999 entries. This is implemented by means of the table defined as

```
01  PRODUCT-TABLE.
    05 TABLE-VALUES   OCCURS 1 TO 999 TIMES,
                      DEPENDING ON VALUE-COUNTER,
                      INDEXED BY PT-INDEX.
        10 PT-PRODUCT-CODE   PICTURE 9(4).
        10 PT-QUANTITY       PICTURE 9(4).
```

12.12.2. The OCCURS . . . DEPENDING ON Clause

As will be noticed, a new form of the OCCURS clause has been introduced. It is the OCCURS . . . DEPENDING ON clause. It provides the programmer with the ability to specify a variable number of table entries. The exact number is specified for a particular run by the value of the data name which follows the phrase DEPENDING ON. In our case this data name is VALUE–COUNTER. This value is initially set to zero, and each time a bona fide data card is read (as opposed to the trailer card), it is incremented by 1 in the program. The final value that VALUE–COUNTER attains is the number of times that will be associated with the OCCURS clause.

In summary, the program loads a table, checking for a trailer card with 9999 punched in the first four columns. The product code is checked for sequence; if a card is detected to be out of sequence an appropriate comment is printed out and the program is terminated. If the end of data is reached before the trailer card is encountered—indicating that the trailer card has been omitted—again a statement to that effect is printed and the program terminated. Provided the table has been successfully loaded, it is searched sequentially and each product code together with its associated quantity are listed in a report.

INPUT TO PROGRAM 35

```
00011234
00023225
00033256
00046633
00053256
00062541
00075842
00085632
00094587
00103256
00111245
00124527
00135897
00149865
00158752
00163254
00175865
00185647
00195863
00203568
00213564
00222587
```

```
00235698
00245287
00251236
00263598
00275412
00285876
00296532
00301478
9999
```

PROGRAM 35
Varying Length

```
00001        IDENTIFICATION DIVISION.
00002        PROGRAM-ID. VARYLEN.
00003        AUTHOR. ELI J. OPAS.
00004        REMARKS. LOADING A VARIABLE LENGTH TABLE.
00005
00006        ENVIRONMENT DIVISION.
00007
00008        CONFIGURATION SECTION.
00009
00010        SOURCE-COMPUTER. IBM-370-145.
00011        OBJECT-COMPUTER. IBM-370-145.
00012
00013        SPECIAL-NAMES.
00014
00015            C01 IS TO-TOP-OF-PAGE.
00016
00017        INPUT-OUTPUT SECTION.
00018
00019        FILE-CONTROL.
00020
00021            SELECT IN-FILE ASSIGN TO UT-S-READER.
00022            SELECT OUT-FILE ASSIGN TO UT-S-PRINTER.
00023
00024        DATA DIVISION.
00025
00026        FILE SECTION.
00027
00028        FD  IN-FILE
00029            LABEL RECORDS ARE OMITTED.
00030
00031        01  VALUES-CARD.
00032            05 PRODUCT-CODE     PICTURE 9(4).
00033            05 QUANTITY         PICTURE 9(4).
00034            05 FILLER           PICTURE X(72).
00035
00036        FD  OUT-FILE
00037            LABEL RECORDS ARE OMITTED.
00038
00039        01  TABLE-VALUES-LIST.
00040            05 FILLER           PICTURE X(80).
00041
00042        WORKING-STORAGE SECTION.
00043
00044        77  VALUE-COUNTER       PICTURE 9(4)  VALUE ZERO.
00045        77  PRODUCT-CODE-SAVE   PICTURE 9(4) VALUE ZERO.
00046
00047        01  PRODUCT-TABLE.
00048            05 TABLE-VALUES         OCCURS 1 TO 999 TIMES,
00049                                    DEPENDING ON VALUE-COUNTER,
00050                                    INDEXED BY PT-INDEX.
00051            10 PT-PRODUCT-CODE PICTURE 9(4).
00052            10 PT-QUANTITY      PICTURE 9(4).
00053
00054        01  HEADER.
00055            05 FILLER           PICTURE X(13) VALUE
00056                                'PRODUCT CODE' JUST RIGHT.
00057            05 FILLER           PICTURE X(18) VALUE 'QUANTITY' JUST RIGHT.
00058            05 FILLER           PICTURE X(49) VALUE SPACES.
00059
00060        01  OUTPUT-LINE.
00061            05 FILLER           PICTURE X VALUE SPACES.
00062            05 PRODUCT-CODE-OUT PICTURE 9(4).
00063            05 FILLER           PICTURE X(18) VALUE SPACES.
00064            05 QUANTITY-OUT     PICTURE 9(4).
00065            05 FILLER           PICTURE X(53) VALUE SPACES.
00066
```

```
00067          PROCEDURE DIVISION.
00068
00069      HOUSEKEEPING.
00070          OPEN INPUT IN-FILE, OUTPUT OUT-FILE.
00071          WRITE TABLE-VALUES-LIST FROM HEADER
00072              AFTER ADVANCING TO-TOP-OF-PAGE.
00073          SET PT-INDEX TO 1.
00074
00075      TABLE-LOAD.
00076          READ IN-FILE AT END GO TO NO-TRAILER.
00077          IF PRODUCT-CODE NOT > PRODUCT-CODE-SAVE GO TO SEQUENCE-ERROR.
00078          IF PRODUCT-CODE = 9999 GO TO TABLE-SEARCH.
00079          MOVE PRODUCT-CODE TO PT-PRODUCT-CODE (PT-INDEX).
00080          MOVE QUANTITY TO PT-QUANTITY (PT-INDEX).
00081          ADD 1 TO VALUE-COUNTER.
00082          MOVE PRODUCT-CODE TO PRODUCT-CODE-SAVE.
00083          SET PT-INDEX UP BY 1.
00084          IF VALUE-COUNTER < 999 GO TO TABLE-LOAD,
00085              ELSE
00086          DISPLAY 'TABLE ENTRIES EXCEED 999' GO TO END-OF-JOB.
00087
00088      TABLE-SEARCH.
00089          PERFORM WRITE-VALUES-LIST
00090              VARYING PT-INDEX FROM 1 BY 1
00091                  UNTIL PT-INDEX > VALUE-COUNTER.
00092          GO TO END-OF-JOB.
00093
00094      WRITE-VALUES-LIST.
00095          MOVE PT-PRODUCT-CODE (PT-INDEX) TO PRODUCT-CODE-OUT.
00096          MOVE PT-QUANTITY (PT-INDEX) TO QUANTITY-OUT.
00097          WRITE TABLE-VALUES-LIST FROM OUTPUT-LINE AFTER ADVANCING 1.
00098
00099      SEQUENCE-ERROR.
00100          DISPLAY
00101              PRODUCT-CODE
00102              'VALUE CARD OUT OF SEQUENCE-PROGRAM TERMINATED'.
00103          GO TO END-OF-JOB.
00104
00105      NO-TRAILER.
00106          DISPLAY
00107          'END OF DATA REACHED BEFORE TRAILER. PROGRAM TERMINATED'.
00108          GO TO END-OF-JOB.
00109
00110      END-OF-JOB.
00111          CLOSE IN-FILE, OUT-FILE.
00112          STOP RUN.
```

OUTPUT TO PROGRAM 35

PRODUCT CODE	QUANTITY
0001	1234
0002	3225
0003	3256
0004	6633
0005	3256
0006	2541
0007	5842
0008	5632
0009	4587
0010	3256
0011	1245
0012	4527
0013	5897
0014	9865
0015	8752
0016	3254
0017	5865
0018	5647
0019	5863
0020	3568
0021	3564
0022	2587
0023	5698
0024	5287
0025	1236
0026	3598
0027	5412
0028	9876
0029	6532
0030	1478

12.13 SCANNING A TABLE WITH A BINARY SEARCH

For the purposes of the next program a correspondence is set up between 10 product numbers and their associated product description. This correspondence is quite arbitrary and forms the basis of a table which is defined in the program as shown under the name PRODUCT–TABLE– VALUES.

PRODUCT NUMBER	PRODUCT NAME
0100	peas
0200	carrots
0300	tomatoes
0400	beans
0500	potatoes
0600	peaches
0700	pears
0800	cherries
0900	sardines
1000	olives

In order to convert these entries into a table, PRODUCTS redefines PRODUCT–TABLE–VALUES with the subordinate 05 level TABLE–PAIR specified to OCCUR 10 times. Within this level entry are two separate clauses, one of which is familiar to us, namely the INDEXED BY clause whereas the second is quite strange. Perhaps we ought to discuss it now.

12.13.1. KEY Fields

The product number in the table is in ascending order. It begins with 0100 and the last entry is 1000. When a match is to be made with a field which is in either ascending or descending order, one may take advantage of a special option available in many COBOL compilers. It is the SEARCH ALL option, which searches a key field which must be in either ascending or descending order—it makes no difference which of the two it is. In our case PRODUCT–CODE is a key field, the field which is to be searched, and since it is in ascending order it is a suitable candidate for the SEARCH ALL option. This is why the clause

```
ASCENDING KEY IS PRODUCT-CODE
```

is included in the 05 level entry for the table PRODUCTS.

The search effected by the SEARCH ALL option is known as a *binary* search as opposed to the *sequential* search which results when the SEARCH verb is used without the ALL option. The reason this search is called binary is that a match is first attempted with an element near the middle of the table. Depending upon the result of this attempt, either the first half or the second half of the table is selected for subsequent attempts.

The table half selected is itself divided in half and the process is repeated until a match is effected or, if no match succeeds, the AT END option is executed. It is on account of the search area continually being divided into halves that the method is described as a binary search. The binary search was implemented because it could be 10, 20, or even more times faster than the sequential search, always an important consideration in business processing.

The input to Program 36 is

```
0100
0800
0200
0700
0500
0900
1700
1000
0400
0300
0600
```

The table in the program is searched for the product number punched on each data card and the corresponding product name is printed alongside the product number. It will be noticed that the product number 1700 falls out of the range of the table and consequently is printed by a DISPLAY statement.

PROGRAM 36
Search-all

```
00001          IDENTIFICATION DIVISION.
00002          PROGRAM-ID. SEARCH-ALL.
00003          AUTHOR. ELI J. CPAS.
00004          REMARKS. USING THE SEARCH ALL VERB.
00005
C0006          ENVIRONMENT DIVISION.
00007
C0008          CONFIGURATION SECTION.
00009
00010          SOURCE-COMPUTER. IBM-370-145.
00011          OBJECT-COMPUTER. IBM-370-145.
00012
00013          SPECIAL-NAMES.
00014
00015              C01 IS TO-TOP-CF-PAGE.
00016
00017          INPUT-OUTPUT SECTION.
00018
00019          FILE-CONTROL.
C0020
00021              SELECT IN-FILE ASSIGN TO UT-S-READER.
00022              SELECT OUT-FILE ASSIGN TO UT-S-PRINTER.
C0023
00024          DATA DIVISION.
00025
OCC26          FILE SECTION.
00027
C0028          FD  IN-FILE
00029              LABEL RECORDS ARE OMITTED.
00030
00031          01  PRODUCT-CARD.
```

```
00032                05 PRODUCT-NUMBER  PICTURE 9(4).
00033                05 FILLER          PICTURE X(76).
00034
00035        FD  OUT-FILE
00036            LABEL RECORDS ARE OMITTED.
00037
00038        01  PRODUCT-LIST.
00039                05 FILLER          PICTURE X(80).
00040
00041        WORKING-STORAGE SECTION.
00042        01  PRODUCT-TABLE-VALUES.
00043                05 FILLER          PICTURE X(12) VALUE '0100PEAS    '.
00044                05 FILLER          PICTURE X(12) VALUE '0200CARROTS '.
00045                05 FILLER          PICTURE X(12) VALUE '0300TOMATOES'.
00046                05 FILLER          PICTURE X(12) VALUE '0400BEANS   '.
00047                05 FILLER          PICTURE X(12) VALUE '0500POTATOES'.
00048                05 FILLER          PICTURE X(12) VALUE '0600PEACHES '.
00049                05 FILLER          PICTURE X(12) VALUE '0700PEARS   '.
00050                05 FILLER          PICTURE X(12) VALUE '0800CHERRIES'.
00051                05 FILLER          PICTURE X(12) VALUE '0900SARDINES'.
00052                05 FILLER          PICTURE X(12) VALUE '1000OLIVES  '.
00053        01  PRODUCTS REDEFINES PRODUCT-TABLE-VALUES.
00054                05 TABLE-PAIR      OCCURS 10 TIMES,
00055                                   ASCENDING KEY IS PRODUCT-CODE,
00056                                   INDEXED BY PRODUCT-INDEX.
00057                    10 PRODUCT-CODE PICTURE 9(4).
00058                    10 PRODUCT-NAME PICTURE X(8).
00059
00060        01  HEADER.
00061                05 FILLER          PICTURE X(15) VALUE ' PRODUCT NUMBER'.
00062                05 FILLER          PICTURE X(22) VALUE
00063                                   'PRODUCT NAME' JUST RIGHT.
00064                05 FILLER          PICTURE X(43) VALUE SPACES.
00065
00066        01  PRODUCT-LISTING.
00067                05 FILLER          PICTURE X VALUE SPACES.
00068                05 NUMBER-OUT      PICTURE 9(4).
00069                05 FILLER          PICTURE X(20) VALUE SPACES.
00070                05 NAME-OUT        PICTURE X(8).
00071                05 FILLER          PICTURE X(47) VALUE SPACES.
00072
00073        PROCEDURE DIVISION.
00074
00075        LETS-BEGIN.
00076            OPEN INPUT IN-FILE, OUTPUT OUT-FILE.
00077            WRITE PRODUCT-LIST FROM HEADER
00078                AFTER ADVANCING TO-TOP-OF-PAGE.
00079
00080        READ-A-RECORD.
00081            READ IN-FILE AT END GO TO E-O-J.
00082
00083        SEARCH-TABLE.
00084            SET PRODUCT-INDEX TO 1.
00085            SEARCH ALL TABLE-PAIR AT END GO TO INVALID-PRODUCT-NUMBER
00086                WHEN PRODUCT-NUMBER = PRODUCT-CODE (PRODUCT-INDEX)
00087                    GO TO WRITE-LISTING.
00088
00089        WRITE-LISTING.
00090            MOVE PRODUCT-NUMBER TO NUMBER-OUT.
00091            MOVE PRODUCT-NAME (PRODUCT-INDEX) TO NAME-OUT.
00092            WRITE PRODUCT-LIST FROM PRODUCT-LISTING AFTER ADVANCING 2.
00093            GO TO READ-A-RECORD.
00094
00095        INVALID-PRODUCT-NUMBER.
00096            DISPLAY PRODUCT-NUMBER '    INVALID PRODUCT NUMBER'.
00097            GO TO READ-A-RECORD.
00098
00099        E-O-J.
00100            CLOSE IN-FILE, OUT-FILE.
00101            STOP RUN.
```

OUTPUT TO PROGRAM 36

PRODUCT NUMBER	PRODUCT NAME
0100	PEAS
0800	CHERRIES
0200	CARROTS
0700	PEARS

0500	POTATCES
0900	SARDINES
1000	OLIVES
0400	BEANS
0300	TOMATOES
0600	PEACHES
1700	INVALID PRODUCT NUMBER

12.14 REVIEW QUESTIONS AND EXERCISES

1. The Lobbus Manufacturing Co., Inc. records on 80-column cards each sale in the following fashion:

1–5	salesman number
6–8	product number
13–18	quantity sold
19–26	total sale price 9(6)V99

   Stored in a table is the product number together with its associated manufacturer's cost per unit item.

   Write a program which prints a listing, one line per card, showing salesman number, product number, quantity sold, manufacturer's cost (quantity sold times cost per item), sales price, and net profit on loss per sale. For each salesman, a total line should be printed showing total quantity, total sales, and total profit or loss. Finally, a grand total line should be printed showing the total quantity sold, total or sales, and total profit or loss. Assume that the input deck is sorted in order of salesman number.

   ### TABLE OF UNIT COSTS

PRODUCT NUMBER	COST PER UNIT ITEM
001	00.019
005	00.912
011	01.622
019	04.915
077	00.125
078	00.115
084	08.652
100	10.115
125	02.225
350	05.350
412	05.500

2. A local philanthropist in a moment of extreme gratitude to his alma mater decided to contribute towards the tuition costs of each paying student in the current academic year according to the following scheme:

1. Freshmen	20%
2. Sophomores	18%
3. Juniors	12%
4. Seniors	10%
5. Graduate	15%
6. Doctoral candidate	40%

For each student a card is punched in the following way:

columns	1–25	student's name
	30–38	Social Security number
	40	academic category (1 = Freshmen . . .
		6 = doctoral candidate)
	46–55	student's address
	70–73	regular annual fees 9(4)

Write a COBOL program that uses a table to print a listing made up of

(1) edited card count (assume about 10,000 students are registered)
(2) student's name
(3) student's address
(4) academic category (Freshmen, . . . doctoral candidate)
(5) Social Security number with 2 blanks as separators
(6) percentage reduction
(7) regular annual fees (edited)
(8) amount of discount (edited)
(9) balance to be paid by student (edited)
(10) In the middle of the next new page, the edited total amount to be paid by the benefactor should be printed, together with some pertinent comments about how much his efforts are appreciated, how long he will be remembered with esteem in the halls of academia . . .

3. Write a COBOL program to process a payroll file composed of data cards punched according to the following format:

col	1–25	name of employee
	30–31	number of dependents
	50–54	gross pay (999V99)

A table should be set up in memory (details follow the statement of this problem). It shows the tax rates for all employees, depending upon the number of dependents. For each employee calculate the amount of witholding tax and the net pay after deducting the tax from the gross pay. The tax is computed by multiplying the gross pay by the tax rate. Keep a count of the cards and print out the following:

(1) card sequence number (edited)
(2) name of employee
(3) gross pay (edited)
(4) number of dependents (edited)
(5) the applicable tax rate (edited)
(6) the amount of tax (edited)
(7) the net pay (edited).

If the number of dependents is less than 1 or greater than 10, display an error message but continue processing.

As an additional exercise on a separate page print the total gross pay, total tax witheld, and total net pay for the whole file of cards.

TAX RATE BASED ON DEPENDENTS

NUMBER OF DEPENDENTS	TAX RATE (PERCENT)
1	10.00
2	7.00
3	5.90
4	5.00
5	4.30
6	3.85
7	3.30
8	2.90
9	2.60
10 or more	2.35

4. The Acme Tool Company receives a series of orders from their customers. The orders are transcribed to punch cards in the following format:

col   1–20   customer name
      25–27   item number
      30–34   quantity of items ordered

Assume a table of 10 item entries containing the following information:

PRODUCT NUMBER	PRICE	ITEM NAME
004	$ 1.23	screws
009	2.49	nails
012	1.58	nuts
013	2.95	bolts
015	5.00	hammers
017	2.48	screwdrivers
020	12.50	drills
022	6.50	pliers
026	3.25	wrenches
030	11.98	saws

Write a COBOL program to read in a maximum of 5000 data cards. Calculate the cost per order and add to each order an 8-percent sales tax. The output should contain:

(1)   a sequential card number counter
(2)   customer name
(3)   item number
(4)   item name
(5)   quantity purchased
(6)   cost before tax is added
(7)   net cost (cost + 8% tax).

On a separate page print the

(a)   the total tax charged
(b)   the total cost before taxes
(c)   the grand total cost including taxes.

13

UPDATING
FILES

It probably would not be an exaggeration to say that one of the most common—if not the most important—business data processing activities is that of maintaining files. A typical commercial company will maintain a file of its employees, for example. Now this file hardly ever remains static, especially in a large firm. Employees retire, quit, or are relocated. Their records would therefore have to be deleted from the file. New employees are hired on occasion and naturally their records have to be added to the file. An employee might change his or her name, address, or whatever, in which case the appropriate records would have to be changed. If any one of these three possibilities occurs, the employee file would have to be updated at the appropriate time in order that it correctly reflect the current status. The same applies to those massive files usually associated with insurance premiums, motor vehicle licenses, automobile registration, income tax reports, mailing lists, and so on. One large insurance company has a computer system which supports a file of more than four million policies, with as many as 3000 address changes daily.

What is common to each of these situations is that the current file, usually known as the *master* file, is updated by a series of new records constituting what is known as the *transaction* file. In addition to whatever other information is punched on the transaction file cards, these cards will also have to bear some kind of code indicating whether the information is to be *added* to the master file or *deleted* from the master file, or whether the corresponding records in the master file are to be *changed* or *corrected*. It would not be surprising, therefore, to find that the master file is invariably considerably longer than the transaction file. The process of updating the master file may be done on a daily, weekly, monthly, or even an annual basis, depending upon the nature of the business concerned. In any case, the result of the procedure is an updated, current master file, the previous master file being known as the *old* master file.

13.1 UPDATING A PARTY LIST

Before we become involved in the manner in which the updating process is implemented on a computer, it would be instructive to consider a common but analogous situation in which similar logical thinking is required. Suppose, for example, we are planning to throw a New Year's Eve party to which we would like to invite a number of our friends, many of whom were invited to the previous party. In fact, the list of names (in alphabetical order) used for the previous party could be used as the basis for the new list, with some minor corrections. Some of the guests might have since moved abroad; their names would have to be deleted. Some of them might have ceased being very friendly, so their names, too, might be deleted. Some of them might have had their last names changed for reasons of marriage (or divorce) and it would be courteous, if not mandatory, to correct those names. Also, we might want to add the names of the new neighbors who moved next door subsequent to the last party. Our task is to make up the new list, keeping it in alphabetical order.

One approach we may adopt is to place the listing of the previous invitees, alphabetized according to **first** name, on a table to our left and the alphabetized list (also according to first name) of the "transaction" names to our right. Directly in front we place a blank sheet of paper on which we are going to write the new, updated list of names. Let each of the "transaction" names have a suitable code letter attached to it to indicate the nature of the transaction. Perhaps "A" for "add to the list," "D" for "delete from the list," and "C" for "change or correct the name." Figure 26 is a diagram of the situation.

Alphabetizing the lists according to first names assumes, of course, that each name is unique. It would not work, for example, if two Alinas were present. But for the purpose of illustration the analogy holds, even if it is not feasible for commercial situations. By the same token more than one person can have the same last name. It is clear therefore that sorting by name is not the most advisable method of maintaining a file. In business it is common practice to assign unique numbers to employees or customers, which will be illustrated once this analogy has been completed.

PROCEDURE FOR CREATING THE
UPDATED LIST OF NAMES

1. Look at the first-listed name in the old list in preparation for a comparison with the first name listed on the transaction list. If the name on the transaction list is to be added, an "A" will appear beside the name. Compare this name with the name from

Old List Arranged Alphabetically by First Name	Blank sheet for Updated List	List of Amendments, Also Arranged in Alphabetical Order of First Name	
ALINA PRESTON		ALINA SMITH	C
GLADYS ZELLIG		BETTY FORD	A
JOAN BERGER		CATHY ROSE	A
JOHN MCKAY		JOHN MCKAY	D
MARION ANDERSON		SUE DEMBERG	C
NANCY KRUGER			
ROBERT CHADWICK			
ROBERTA ROSENTEL			
SUE DEMSBERG			
WAYNE NUTLEY			

FIGURE 26

the old list in order to determine which is to be written first on the new list. If the name on the old list comes before the name in the transaction list, it must be written on the new list and the next name read from the old list. If, on the other hand, the name from the old list comes alphabetically after the name on the transaction list, the latter is written down on the new list, and the next transaction name is read. A comparison of the current pair of names is now made, repeating the actions just described.

2. If the name on the transaction pile is marked as a deletion (indicated by a "D"), it must of necessity correspond with a name already on the old list. Until its matching name is found on the old list, each successive old-list name is added to the new list. Once the match is found, both names are ignored and a new name from each pile is read. The process is then repeated.

3. If the code on the transaction name indicates it is a change (that is, the name is marked with a "C") the successive names on the old list are written on the new list until a match is found. Now, instead of discarding both names as we did in the deletion process described in (2), the name on the transaction list is added to the new list. A new name from each pile is now read and the process repeated.

4. This entire process is repeated until either list is exhausted. If the old list is exhausted first, all the remaining names on the transaction list are added to the new list and our work is done. If the transaction list is the first to become exhausted, then the remaining names from the old list are added to the new list.

5. The process is now complete, leaving us with an updated new list (Figure 27).

Old List (with first name in alphabetical order)	New Updated List	Transaction List	
ALINA PRESTON GLADYS ZELLIG JOAN BERGER JOHN MCKAY MARION ANDERSON NANCY KRUGER ROBERT CHANDWICK ROBERTA ROSENTEL SUE DEMSBERG WAYNE NUTLEY	ALINA SMITH BETTY FORD CATHY ROSE GLADYS ZELLIG JOAN BERGER MARION ANDERSON NANCY KRUGER ROBERT CHADWICK ROBERTA ROSENTEL SUE DEMBERG WAYNE NUTLEY	ALINA SMITH BETTY FORD CATHY ROSE JOHN MCKAY SUE DEMBERG	C A A D C

FIGURE 27

It might appear that we have made a simple job seem fairly complicated. The fact of the matter is that we have merely formalized the steps that one would have to go through at least intuitively to accomplish the simple task of updating a list. The computer, unfortunately, is utterly devoid of intuition or original thought, or, indeed, of intelligence in general. It is encumbent upon us, the warm-blooded, thinking programmers, to carefully instruct the computer through the program how to carry out, step by step, the decision-making process and how to act on the basis of its various conclusions.

The following series of programs illustrates the manner in which these decisions may be made on a computer. In order to clarify the various aspects of the update, we have broken the process down into its three different, characteristic functions, namely those of adding (or inserting), deleting, and changing. Instead of updating a list of party names, the programs update a club membership list.

13.2 UPDATING A FILE WITH ADDITIONS ONLY

The master list of membership cards may be assumed to run into the hundred or maybe thousands, but for illustrating our updating techniques, the number of members is kept down to 20. The cards are already sorted in ascending order of membership number, which, having nine-digits, could easily be each member's Social Security number.

In order to expedite matters, the master file is stored neither on cards nor on magnetic tape but rather on a magnetic disk (how data are written on disk need not be of concern to the reader at this point). In COBOL (but not in WATBOL, the fast student COBOL compiler about which we shall have more to say in a later chapter) one can access data stored on disk very rapidly.

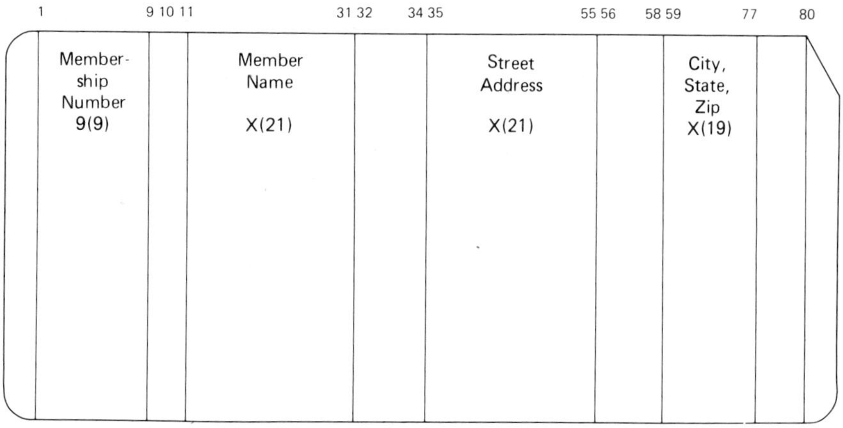

FIGURE 28

In the update programs which follow a club's membership is stored on disk in the format shown in Figure 28:

Here is a listing of the master list which is to be updated:

```
012341253  MARGIE BRAND          2650 E 12 STREET            BROOKLYN, N.Y. 11235
102035456  DAVID FIFE            5900 PALEYBRIDGE AVENUE      BROOKLYN, N.Y.10463
103065997  LILITA PUON           505 10 STREET               BROOKLYN, 11215
110225477  DENNIS SCHWARTZ       840 THERIOT AVENUE          BRONX N.Y. 10473
245799210  WENDY WONG            14 MONTH COURT              CLIFTON, N.J. 07013
302021475  MITCHEL RUBIN         2542 W 2 STREET             BROOKLYN, N.Y.11223
302145785  GOOK CHIN             78 PERSIAN DRIVE            NEW ROCHELLE 10801
410235478  ANDREA ROTH           66 GLORY STREET             IRVINGTON, N.J.07411
442030156  PETER GARCIA          5711 YORK AVENUE            N.Y.  10021
542003214  ALINA CHOOCHOO        71 APPLE STREET             N.Y. 10012
552021417  ROBERT BALCOMF        8312 35 STREET              J.HTS. N.Y. 11372
558553210  BARBARA HOUGIE        423 76 STREET               S.BERGEN N.J. 07047
664012354  ELSIE SCHMITT         74-25 84 STREET             GLENDALE N.Y. 11227
705010665  WENDY POITMAN         2469 HARBOR LANE            BELLEMORE 11710
732596315  KATIE SOMMER          61 SOMERSET STREET          GARDEN CITY 11530
774222541  DEBBIE FELDT          14 FLOREN PLACE             SCARSDALE  10583
885444602  ANDREW WEISSMAN       5 UNIVERSITY PLACE          N.Y.   10003
885446320  ANDY DAVIS            99 FLEECKER STREET          N.Y.   10012
903335478  BARRIE LOWENDORF      6000 TOENAIL ROAD           YONKERS 10710
999522140  CARMELLA CARNOVALT    11 CEDAR STREET             N.Y.  11570
```

13.2.1. Adding Cards

The first updating program UPDATE–ADD, which follows, has as its input a series of cards to be added to those already on disk. The input cards are punched in exactly the same format as those on disk except that column 80 is punched with the letter A. Here is a listing of the transaction file—those records which are to update the old list. Notice that the first card is in error since it is punched with a code of C rather than A. Also notice that the last card is not punched at all with a code. This card also should be flagged by the program as an error.

```
000356878  RONALD S. PHIFER      170-30 1130 AVE             ALANTOWN, PA           C
002606108  DEL T. A. PHI         146 W. 4TH                  N.Y. NY 10012          A
021879654  KOSEPH JAISER         747 CALLE CONTRAIGALIA      BALONA, ITALY          A
123458975  JOE MANDELSKY         1001 BINARY ROAD            BKLYN N.Y. 13421       A
127403158  PETER M C MCKAY       104 CALLE ANASCO            SANTURCE PUERTO RICO   A
789456123  STEWART S. KAPLAN     37 MAIN STREET              LINSCOTT L.I. 18976
```

In order that we may see the result of the updating process, the output is printed on paper rather than written on disk, which might ordinarily be the case. In other words, we shall not alter the card images on disk although this can easily be done as well.

For the first time in this text we have three SELECT clauses in the file section. The master list on disk is assigned to the disk file, the transaction cards to the input file, and a third SELECT clause to the printer for the writing of the updated report. It is for this reason that three FD's are described. The disk file FD has some additional information, namely:

```
LABEL RECORDS ARE STANDARD,
RECORDING MODE IS F,
RECORD CONTAINS 80 CHARACTERS,
BLOCK CONTAINS 80 CHARACTERS.
```

This is merely the COBOL method of advising the system that the label records are "standard" (instead of "omitted," as has always been the case when cards are the medium of input). This is required for identification purposes when either disks or tapes are used for input files. The recording mode is F, which means that each record is of *fixed* length, and each record and block contains 80 characters. This is another way of saying that each block contains one record. In both of the other FD's, the label records are omitted in the usual way.

In the Procedure Division the two input files and the single output file are opened and the two header lines are printed. A blank line is printed below the headers by moving spaces to the output record and printing the blank line. Similar headers are printed by the DISPLAY statement for invalid data cards to be listed on a separate page after the main output. So much for the cosmetics of the program; now for the updating itself.

The disk is read with the usual READ verb and, as always, it has an AT END clause. The card image from disk is sent to its input area and, as soon as the card file is read, a card record from the transaction file goes into the other input area. Since for the purposes of this program we are confining ourselves to transaction cards with an A punched in column 80, a test of this column is made. If it is not punched with an A, it is flagged and printed by the DISPLAY as an error and the card is ignored by simply reading the next transaction card.

The membership number of the card on disk is now compared with that of the transaction card. If they agree the transaction card is in error because when inserting an "add" transaction card its absence in the master file is implied. If a match is made, therefore, the complete contents of the offending card is printed out together with a suitable comment reminding the user to check the code on that card. This card is then ignored and the next card read. If, on the other hand, the disk number is not equal to the card number, the card to be added is in order, and what

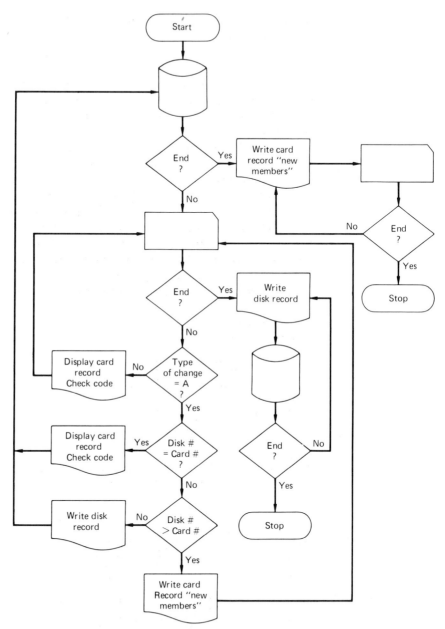

FIGURE 29 **Flowchart for Program 37**

has to be determined is which one is to be written first. It will obviously be the one with the smaller identification number.

If the disk number is greater than the card number the literal 'NEW MEMBER' is moved to the area assigned on the output line to MEMBER STATUS and the contents of the card moved to OUTPUT–HOLD, a 79-column field in the detail line. The reason for this is to eliminate the letter A from the output listing. Moving an 80-column alphanumeric field to a 79-column field left-adjusts the receiving field, thereby truncating the last character. After this line is printed, a new transaction card is read and this procedure repeated. If the disk number is the smaller, the disk record is written, a new disk record read, and a comparison made with the correct transaction card.

If the disk is exhausted first, the AT END condition will be activated and the current transaction card written, followed by the rest of the transaction cards, which are automatically written at the end of the updated list. If, however, the transaction list is depleted first, the AT END condition will have the effect of first printing the current transaction card, followed by the printing of the remainder of the disk records. At the completion of the updating of all the transaction cards, the end-of-job is reached, at which point the three files are closed and the program terminated. Here is the output to the run using sample data, some of which were deliberately punched incorrectly to test the program.

PROGRAM 37
Update—Add

```
00001          IDENTIFICATION DIVISION.
00002          PROGRAM-ID. UPDATE-ADD.
00003          AUTHOR. PETER M.C. MCKAY.
00004          REMARKS.    THIS PROGRAM ILLUSTRATES ADDING TO A FILE.
00005
00006
C0007          ENVIRONMENT DIVISION.
00008          CONFIGURATION SECTION.
00009          SPECIAL-NAMES.
C0010              C01 IS TO-TOP-OF-PAGE.
00011          INPUT-OUTPUT SECTION.
00012          FILE-CONTROL.
00013              SELECT CARD-FILE ASSIGN TO UT-S-READER.
00014              SELECT DISK-FILE ASSIGN TO UT-S-DISKREAD.
C0015              SELECT NEW-FILE  ASSIGN TO UT-S-PRINTER.
00016
00017
00018          DATA DIVISION.
00019          FILE SECTION.
00020
00021          FD  DISK-FILE
00022              LABEL RECORDS ARE STANDARD,
00023              RECORDING MODE IS F,
00024              RECORD CONTAINS 80 CHARACTERS,
00025              BLOCK CONTAINS 80 CHARACTERS.
00026          01  DISK-REC.
00027              05 DISK-NUMBER     PICTURE 9(9).
00028              05 FILLER          PICTURE X.
00029              05 DISK-MEMBER     PICTURE X(21).
C0030              05 FILLER          PICTURE X(03).
00031              05 DISK-ADDRESS    PICTURE X(21).
00032              05 FILLER          PICTURE X(03).
00033              05 DISK-STATE-ZIP  PICTURE X(19).
00034              05 FILLER          PICTURE X(03).
00035
00036          FD  CARD-FILE
00037              LABEL RECORDS ARE OMITTED.
00C38          01  CARD-REC.
00039              05 CARD-NUMBER     PICTURE 9(9).
C0040              05 FILLER          PICTURE X(01).
00041              05 CARD-MEMBER     PICTURE X(21).
00042              05 FILLER          PICTURE X(03).
00043              05 CARD-ADDRESS    PICTURE X(21).
```

```
00044                05 FILLER       PICTURE X(03).
00045                05 CARD-STATE-ZIP PICTURE X(19).
00046                05 FILLER       PICTURE X(02).
00047                05 TYPE-OF-CHANGE PICTURE X.
00048
00049        FD  NEW-FILE
00050            LABEL RECORDS ARE OMITTED.
00051        01  OUTPUT-REC.
00052                05 PRINT-LINE    PICTURE X(132).
00053
00054
00055        WORKING-STORAGE SECTION.
00056        01  DETAIL-LINE.
00057                05 OUTPUT-HOLD    PICTURE X(79).
00058                05 FILLER        PICTURE X(5)        VALUE SPACES.
00059                05 MEMBER-STATUS PICTURE X(12).
00060
00061        01  HEADER-1.
00062                05 FILLER        PICTURE X(09)       VALUE 'IC-NUMBER'.
00063                05 FILLER        PICTURE X(08)       VALUE SPACES.
00064                05 FILLER        PICTURE X(04)       VALUE 'NAME'.
00065                05 FILLER        PICTURE X(20)       VALUE SPACES.
00066                05 FILLER        PICTURE X(07)       VALUE 'ADDRESS'.
00067                05 FILLER        PICTURE X(13)       VALUE SPACES.
00068                05 FILLER        PICTURE X(14)       VALUE 'CITY / STATE /'.
00069                05 FILLER        PICTURE X(04)       VALUE ' ZIP'.
00070                05 FILLER        PICTURE X(07)       VALUE SPACES.
00071                05 FILLER        PICTURE X(06)       VALUE 'STATUS'.
00072
00073        01  HEADER-2.
00074                05 FILLER        PICTURE X(09)       VALUE ALL '*='.
00075                05 FILLER        PICTURE X(01)       VALUE SPACES.
00076                05 FILLER        PICTURE X(19)       VALUE ALL '*='.
00077                05 FILLER        PICTURE X(05)       VALUE SPACES.
00078                05 FILLER        PICTURE X(23)       VALUE ALL '*='.
00079                05 FILLER        PICTURE X(01)       VALUE SPACES.
00080                05 FILLER        PICTURE X(23)       VALUE ALL '*='.
00081                05 FILLER        PICTURE X(03)       VALUE SPACES.
00082                05 FILLER        PICTURE X(13)       VALUE ALL '*='.
00083
00084
00085        PROCEDURE DIVISION.
00086            OPEN  INPUT  DISK-FILE
00087                         CARD-FILE
00088                  OUTPUT NEW-FILE.
00089            WRITE OUTPUT-REC FROM HEADER-1.
00090            WRITE OUTPUT-REC FROM HEADER-2.
00091            MOVE SPACES TO OUTPUT-REC.
00092            WRITE OUTPUT-REC.
00093            DISPLAY HEADER-1.
00094            DISPLAY HEADER-2.
00095            MOVE SPACES TO OUTPUT-REC.
00096            DISPLAY OUTPUT-REC.
00097
00098        READ-THE-DISK.
00099            READ DISK-FILE AT END GO TO WRITE-REST-OF-THE-CARDS.
00100
00101        READ-A-CARD.
00102            READ CARD-FILE AT END GO TO WRITE-REST-OF-THE-DISK.
00103            IF TYPE-OF-CHANGE  IS NOT EQUAL TO 'A', THEN
00104                  DISPLAY CARD-REC, '     WRONG TYPE OF CHANGE CODE'
00105                  GO TO READ-A-CARD.
00106
00107        COMPARE-CARD-WITH-DISK.
00108            IF DISK-NUMBER IS EQUAL TO CARD-NUMBER THEN
00109                  DISPLAY CARD-REC, '    DISK NUMBER EQUALS CARD',
00110                  'NUMBER, CHECK TYPE OF CHANGE'
00111                  GO TO READ-A-CARD.
00112            IF DISK-NUMBER IS GREATER THAN CARD-NUMBER, THEN
00113                  MOVE 'NEW MEMBER' TO MEMBER-STATUS,
00114                       MOVE CARD-REC TO OUTPUT-HOLD
00115                            WRITE OUTPUT-REC FROM DETAIL-LINE
00116                            GO TO READ-A-CARD.
00117            WRITE OUTPUT-REC FROM DISK-REC.
00118            READ DISK-FILE AT END GO TO WRITE-REST-OF-THE-CARDS.
00119            GO TO COMPARE-CARD-WITH-DISK.
00120
00121        WRITE-REST-OF-THE-CARDS.
00122            MOVE '    NEW MEMBER' TO MEMBER-STATUS.
00123            MOVE CARD-REC TO OUTPUT-HOLD.
00124            WRITE OUTPUT-REC FROM DETAIL-LINE.
00125            READ CARD-FILE AT END GO TO EOJ.
00126            GO TO WRITE-REST-OF-THE-CARDS.
```

```
00127
00128          WRITE-REST-OF-THE-DISK.
00129              WRITE OUTPUT-REC FROM DISK-REC.
00130              READ DISK-FILE AT END GO TO EOJ.
00131              GO TO WRITE-REST-OF-THE-DISK.
00132
00133          EOJ.
00134              CLOSE    CARD-FILE
00135                       DISK-FILE
00136                       NEW-FILE.
00137              STOP RUN.
```

OUTPUT TO PROGRAM 37

ID-NUMBER	NAME	ADDRESS	CITY / STATE / ZIP	STATUS
002606108	DEL T. A. PHI	146 W. 4TH	N.Y. NY 10012	NEW MEMBER
012341253	MARGIE BRAND	2650 E 12 STREET	BROOKLYN, N.Y. 11235	
021879654	KOSEPH JAISER	747 CALLE CONTRAIGALIA	BALCNA, ITALY	NEW MEMBER
102035456	DAVID FIFE	5900 BALEYBRIDGE AVENUE	BROCKLYN, N.Y.10463	
103065997	LILLIA POON	505 1C STREET	BROCKLYN, 11215	
110225477	DENNIS SCHWARTZ	880 THERIDE AVENUE	BRONX N.Y. 10473	
123458975	JOE MANDELSKY	10011 BINARY ROAD	BKLYN N.Y. 13421	NEW MEMBER
127403158	PETER M C MCKAY	104 CALLE ANASCC	SANTURCE PUERTO RICO	NEW MEMBER
245799210	WENDY WONG	14 MCNTH COURT	CLIFTON, N.J. 07013	
302021475	MITCHEL RUBIN	2542 W 2 STREET	BROOKLYN, N.Y.11223	
302145785	GOOK CHIN	78 PERSIAN DRIVE	NEW ROCHELLE 10801	
410235478	ANDREA ROTH	66 GLORY STREET	IRVINGTON, N.J.07411	
442030156	PETER GARCIA	5711 YORK AVENUE	N.Y. 10021	
542003214	ALINA CHOOCHOO	71 APPLE STREET	N.Y. 10012	
552021417	ROBERT BALCOME	8312 35 STREET	J.HTS. N.Y. 11372	
558553210	BARBARA HODGIE	423 76 STREET	S.BERGEN N.J. 07047	
664012354	ELSIE SCHMIDT	78-25 84 STREET	GLENDALE N.Y. 11227	
705010665	WENDY ROTTMAN	2469 HARBOR LANE	BELLEMORE 11710	
732596315	KATIE SOMMER	81 SOMERSET STREET	GARDEN CITY 11530	
774222541	DEBBIE FELDIE	14 FLOREN PLACE	SCARSDALE 10583	
885444602	ANDREW WEISSMAN	5 UNIVERSITY PLACE	N.Y. 10003	
885446320	ANDY DAVIS	99 BLEECKER STREET	N.Y. 10012	
903335478	BARRIE LOWENDORF	6000 TOENAIL ROAD	YONKERS 10710	
999522140	CARMELLA CARNOVALI	11 CEDAR STREET	N.Y. 11570	

ID-NUMBER	NAME	ADDRESS	CITY / STATE / ZIP	STATUS	
000356878	RONALD S. PRIEVER	170-30 1130 AVE	ALANTOWN, PA	C	WRONG TYPE OF CHANGE CODE
789456123	STEWART S. KAPLAN	37 MAIN S REET	LINSCOTT L.I. 18976		WRONG TYPE OF CHANGE CODE

13.3 UPDATING A FILE WITH DELETIONS ONLY

To illustrate the technique of deleting cards from a file, the following somewhat similar program was written. It accesses the same unchanged master file on disk as was used in the previous program. The input to the program is a series of membership cards which are to be deleted. A transaction card to be deleted has the letter "D" punched in column 80. Any input card not punched with the letter "D" in column 80 is flagged as an error.

Here is the list of the cards which are to be deleted. Notice that there are three cards which are mispunched and should be flagged as errors.

```
000356878 RONALD S. PRIEVER    170-30 1130 AVE      ALANTOWN, PA            D
002606108 DEL T. A. PHI        146 W. 4TH           N.Y. NY 10012           D
110225477 DENNIS SCHWARTZ      880 THERIDE AVENUE   BRONX N.Y. 10473        D
1234589759 JOE MANDEL          CONEY ISLAND         NY                      A
127403158 PETER M C MCKAY      104 CALLE ANASCO     SANTURCE PUERTO RICO    A
245799210 WENDY WONG           14 MONTH COURT       CLIFTON, N.J. 07013     D
664012354 ELSIE SCHMIDT        78-25 84 STREET      GLENDALE N.Y. 11227     D
789456123 STEWART S. KAPLAN    37 MAIN STREET       LINSCOTT L.I. 18976
```

The logic used to update the master file is very similar to that used in the previous program. In fact, the only difference between this and the last program is that the paragraph named COMPARE–CARD–WITH–DISK causes different actions to be taken based on the result of each test. In updating for deletions only, it is normal for the disk number to be equal to the card number, whereas before equal numbers indicated an error had been detected. If a match is made, both records are discarded (not just a pun!) and a new pair of records read, one from disk and the other from the transaction card file. A printout is made for each deletion executed. If the numbers do not match, a test must be made, as before, to determine which membership number is the greater. If the disk number is greater than the card number, then the error message CARD OUT OF SEQUENCE, IGNORED is displayed and a new card read. If it is less, the disk record is written onto the printer, and a new disk record read. Unlike the addition program, when the disk file is exhausted, any cards remaining in the transaction file must be in error.

PROGRAM 38
Update—Deletions

```
00001          IDENTIFICATION DIVISION.
00002          PROGRAM-ID. UPDATE-DELETIONS.
00003          AUTHOR. PETER M.C. MCKAY.
00004          REMARKS.     THIS PROGRAM ILLUSTRATES DELETING
00005                       RECORDS FROM A FILE.
00006
00007          ENVIRONMENT DIVISION.
00008
00009          CONFIGURATION SECTION.
00010          INPUT-OUTPUT SECTION.
00011          FILE-CONTROL.
00012              SELECT CARD-FILE ASSIGN TO UT-S-READER.
00013              SELECT DISK-FILE ASSIGN TO UT-S-DISKREAD.
00014              SELECT NEW-FILE  ASSIGN TO UT-S-PRINTER.
00015
00016          DATA DIVISION.
00017          FILE SECTION.
00018
00019          FD  DISK-FILE
00020              LABEL RECORDS ARE STANDARD,
00021              RECORDING MODE IS F,
00022              RECORD CONTAINS 80 CHARACTERS,
00023              BLOCK CONTAINS 80 CHARACTERS.
00024
00025          01  DISK-REC.
00026              05 DISK-NUMBER    PICTURE 9(9).
00027              05 FILLER         PICTURE X.
00028              05 DISK-MEMBER    PICTURE X(21).
00029              05 FILLER         PICTURE X(03).
00030              05 DISK-ADDRESS   PICTURE X(21).
00031              05 FILLER         PICTURE X(03).
00032              05 DISK-STATE-ZIP PICTURE X(19).
00033              05 FILLER         PICTURE X(03).
00034
00035          FD  CARD-FILE
00036              LABEL RECORDS ARE OMITTED.
00037
00038          01  CARD-REC.
00039              05 CARD-NUMBER    PICTURE 9(9).
00040              05 FILLER         PICTURE X(01).
00041              05 CARD-MEMBER    PICTURE X(21).
00042              05 FILLER         PICTURE X(03).
00043              05 CARD-ADDRESS   PICTURE X(21).
00044              05 FILLER         PICTURE X(03).
00045              05 CARD-STATE-ZIP PICTURE X(19).
00046              05 FILLER         PICTURE X(02).
00047              05 TYPE-OF-CHANGE PICTURE X.
00048
```

```
00049          FD  NEW-FILE
00050              LABEL RECORDS ARE OMITTED.
00051
00052          01  OUTPUT-REC.
00053              05 PRINT-LINE      PICTURE X(132).
00054
00055          WORKING-STORAGE SECTION.
00056
00057          01  DETAIL-LINE.
00058              05 OUTPUT-HOLD      PICTURE X(75).
00059              05 FILLER           PICTURE X(5)      VALUE SPACES.
00060              05 MEMBER-STATUS    PICTURE X(12).
00061
00062          01  HEADER-1.
00063              05 FILLER           PICTURE X(09)     VALUE 'ID-NUMBER'.
00064              05 FILLER           PICTURE X(08)     VALUE SPACES.
00065              05 FILLER           PICTURE X(04)     VALUE 'NAME'.
00066              05 FILLER           PICTURE X(20)     VALUE SPACES.
00067              05 FILLER           PICTURE X(07)     VALUE 'ADDRESS'.
00068              05 FILLER           PICTURE X(13)     VALUE SPACES.
00069              05 FILLER           PICTURE X(14)     VALUE 'CITY / STATE /'.
00070              05 FILLER           PICTURE X(04)     VALUE ' ZIP'.
00071              05 FILLER           PICTURE X(07)     VALUE SPACES.
00072              05 FILLER           PICTURE X(06)     VALUE 'STATUS'.
00073
00074          01  HEADER-2.
00075              05 FILLER           PICTURE X(09)     VALUE ALL '*='.
00076              05 FILLER           PICTURE X(01)     VALUE SPACES.
00077              05 FILLER           PICTURE X(19)     VALUE ALL '*='.
00078              05 FILLER           PICTURE X(05)     VALUE SPACES.
00079              05 FILLER           PICTURE X(23)     VALUE ALL '*='.
00080              05 FILLER           PICTURE X(01)     VALUE SPACES.
00081              05 FILLER           PICTURE X(23)     VALUE ALL '*='.
00082              05 FILLER           PICTURE X(03)     VALUE SPACES.
00083              05 FILLER           PICTURE X(13)     VALUE ALL '*='.
00084
00085          PROCEDURE DIVISION.
00086              OPEN  INPUT  DISK-FILE
00087                           CARD-FILE
00088                    OUTPUT NEW-FILE.
00089              WRITE OUTPUT-REC FROM HEADER-1.
00090              WRITE OUTPUT-REC FROM HEADER-2.
00091              DISPLAY HEADER-1.
00092              DISPLAY HEADER-2.
00093              MOVE SPACES TO OUTPUT-REC.
00094              DISPLAY OUTPUT-REC.
00095              MOVE SPACES TO OUTPUT-REC.
00096              WRITE OUTPUT-REC.
00097
00098          READ-THE-DISK.
00099              READ DISK-FILE AT END GO TO WRITE-REST-OF-THE-CARDS.
00100
00101          READ-A-CARD.
00102              READ CARD-FILE AT END GO TO WRITE-REST-OF-THE-DISK.
00103              IF TYPE-OF-CHANGE IS NOT EQUAL TO 'D' THEN
00104                 DISPLAY CARD-REC, '   WRONG TYPE OF CHANGE CODE'
00105                 GO TO READ-A-CARD.
00106          COMPARE-CARD-WITH-DISK.
00107              IF DISK-NUMBER IS EQUAL TO CARD-NUMBER THEN
00108                 DISPLAY CARD-REC, '   HAS BEEN DELETED'
00109                 GO TO READ-THE-DISK.
00110              IF DISK-NUMBER IS GREATER THAN CARD-NUMBER, THEN
00111                 DISPLAY CARD-REC '   CARD OUT OF SEQUENCE,'
00112                    ' IGNORED'
00113                            GO TO READ-A-CARD.
00114              WRITE OUTPUT-REC FROM DISK-REC.
00115              READ DISK-FILE AT END GO TO WRITE-REST-OF-THE-CARDS.
00116              GO TO COMPARE-CARD-WITH-DISK.
00117
00118          WRITE-REST-OF-THE-CARDS.
00119              DISPLAY CARD-REC '   CARD OUT OF SEQUENCE, IGNORED'.
00120              READ CARD-FILE AT END GO TO EOJ.
00121              GO TO WRITE-REST-OF-THE-CARDS.
00122
00123          WRITE-REST-OF-THE-DISK.
00124              WRITE OUTPUT-REC FROM DISK-REC.
00125              READ DISK-FILE AT END GO TO EOJ.
00126              GO TO WRITE-REST-OF-THE-DISK.
00127
00128          EOJ.
00129              CLOSE   CARD-FILE
00130                      DISK-FILE
00131                      NEW-FILE.
00132              STOP RUN.
```

OUTPUT TO PROGRAM 38

ID-NUMBER	NAME	ADDRESS	CITY / STATE / ZIP	STATUS
012341253	MARGIE BRAND	2650 E 12 STREET	BROOKLYN, N.Y. 11235	
102035456	DAVID FIFE	5900 BALEYBRIDGE AVENUE	BROOKLYN, N.Y.10463	
103065997	LILLIA POON	505 10 STREET	BROOKLYN, 11215	
302021475	MITCHEL RUBIN	2542 W 2 STRRET	BROOKLYN, N.Y.11223	
302145785	GOOK CHIN	78 PERSIAN DRIVE	NEW ROCHELLE 10801	
410235478	ANDREA RUTH	66 GLORY STREET	IRVINGTON, N.J.07411	
442030156	PETER GARCIA	5711 YORK AVENUE	N.Y. 10021	
542003214	ALINA CHOOCHOO	71 APPLE STREET	N.Y. 10012	
552021417	RUBERT BALCOME	8312 35 STREET	J.HTS. N.Y. 11372	
558553210	BARBARA HUDGIE	423 76 STREET	S.BERGEN N.J. 07047	
705010665	WENDY ROITMAN	2469 HARBOR LANE	BELLEMORE 11710	
732596315	KATIE SOMMER	81 SOMERSET STREET	GARDEN CITY 11530	
774222541	DEBBIE FELDIE	14 FLOREN PLACE	SCARSDALE 10583	
385444602	ANDREW WEISSMAN	5 UNIVERSITY PLACE	N.Y. 10003	
885446320	ANDY DAVIS	99 BLEECKER STREET	N.Y. 10012	
903335478	BARRIE LOWENDORF	6000 TOENAIL ROAD	YONKERS 10710	
999522140	CARMELLA CARNOVALI	11 CEDAR STREET	N.Y. 11570	

ID-NUMBER	NAME	ADDRESS	CITY / STATE / ZIP		STATUS
002606108	DEL T. A. PHI	146 W. 4TH	N.Y. NY 10012	D	CARD OUT OF SEQUENCE, IGNORED
110225477	DENNIS SCHWARTZ	880 THERIDE AVENUE	BRONX N.Y. 10473	D	HAS BEEN DELETED
1234589759	JOE MANDEL	CONEY ISLAND	NY		WRONG TYPE OF CHANGE CODE
127403158	PETER M C MCKAY	104 CALLE ANASCO	SANTURCE PUERTO RICO	A	WRONG TYPE OF CHANGE CODE
245799210	WENDY WONG	14 MONTH COURT	CLIFTON, N.J. 07013	D	HAS BEEN DELETED
664012354	ELSIE SCHMIDT	78-25 84 STREET	GLENDALE N.Y. 11227	D	HAS BEEN DELETED
789456123	STEWART S. KAPLAN	37 MAIN S REET	LINSCOTT L.I. 18976		WRONG TYPE OF CHANGE CODE

13.4 UPDATING A FILE WITH CHANGES ONLY

The input cards to the next program are all intended to be change cards, indicated with a c punched in column 80. They are read in turn and matched with the unchanged master file as used in the two preceding programs. Each time a match is made, the data on the master list are to be changed to that contained in the corresponding transaction card. Once again the logic used is strikingly similar to that of the previous program. For each change made, a notation to that effect is recorded in the printed report.

Here is the list of input cards comprising the transaction file; four of them have been (deliberately) mispunched. The first two are also invalid because on both the identification numbers precede the first one on disk. It is impossible therefore to match them. They are also flagged as errors by an appropriate message.

INPUT TO PROGRAM 39

002606108	DEL T. A. PHI	146 W. 4TH	N.Y. NY 10012	C
021679654	KOSEPH JAISFF	1313 MOCKINGBIRD LANE	BALONA, ITALY	C
110225477	DENNIS SCHWARTZ	880 THERIDE AVENUE	BRONX N.Y. 10473	D
1234589759	JOE MANDEL	CONEY ISLAND	NY	A
127403158	PETER M C MCKAY	104 CALLE ANASCO	SANTURCE PUERTO RICO	A
245799210	WENDY WONG	14 MONTH COURT	SPRINGFIELD GARDENS	C
664012354	JOSE SCHMIDT	168-40 127 AVE.	GLENDALE N.Y. 11227	C
789456123	STEWART L. KAPLAN	75 CALLE DE VINO	PARIS FRANCE	

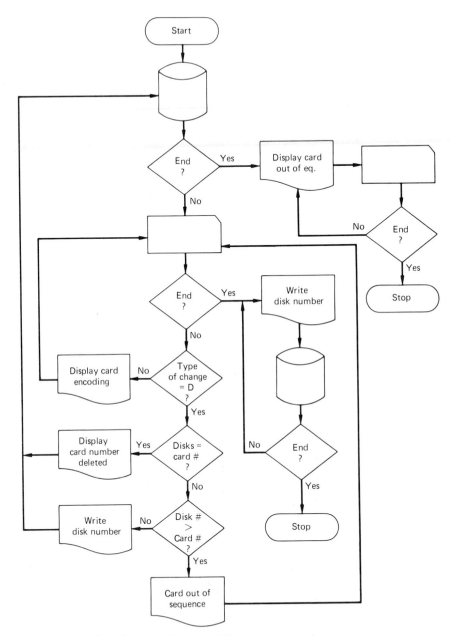

FIGURE 30 **Flowchart for Program 38**

PROGRAM 39
Update—Changes

```
00001           IDENTIFICATION DIVISION.
00002
00003           PROGRAM-ID. UPDATE-CHANGE.
00004           AUTHOR. PETER M.C. MCKAY.
00005           REMARKS.    THIS PROGRAM UPDATES A FILE BY CHANGING ITS CONTENTS.
00006
00007           ENVIRONMENT DIVISION.
00008
00009           CONFIGURATION SECTION.
00010
00011           INPUT-OUTPUT SECTION.
00012           FILE-CONTROL.
00013               SELECT CARD-FILE ASSIGN TO UT-S-READER.
00014               SELECT DISK-FILE ASSIGN TO UT-S-DISKREAD.
00015               SELECT NEW-FILE  ASSIGN TO UT-S-PRINTER.
00016
00017           DATA DIVISION.
00018           FILE SECTION.
00019
00020·          FD  DISK-FILE
00021               LABEL RECORDS ARE STANDARD,
00022               RECORDING MODE IS F,
00023               RECORD CONTAINS 80 CHARACTERS,
00024               BLOCK CONTAINS 80 CHARACTERS.
00025
00026           01  DISK-REC.
00027               05 DISK-NUMBER    PICTURE 9(9).
00028               05 FILLER         PICTURE X.
00029               05 DISK-MEMBER    PICTURE X(21).
00030               05 FILLER         PICTURE X(03).
00031               05 DISK-ADDRESS   PICTURE X(21).
00032               05 FILLER         PICTURE X(03).
00033               05 DISK-STATE-ZIP PICTURE X(19).
00034               05 FILLER         PICTURE X(03).
00035
00036           FD  CARD-FILE
00037               LABEL RECORDS ARE OMITTED.
00038
00039           01  CARD-REC.
00040               05 CARD-NUMBER    PICTURE 9(9).
00041               05 FILLER         PICTURE X(01).
00042               05 CARD-MEMBER    PICTURE X(21).
00043               05 FILLER         PICTURE X(03).
00044               05 CARD-ADDRESS   PICTURE X(21).
00045               05 FILLER         PICTURE X(03).
00046               05 CARD-STATE-ZIP PICTURE X(19).
00047               05 FILLER         PICTURE X(02).
00048               05 TYPE-OF-CHANGE PICTURE X.
00049
00050           FD  NEW-FILE
00051               LABEL RECORDS ARE OMITTED.
00052
00053           01  OUTPUT-REC.
00054               05 PRINT-LINE     PICTURE X(132).
00055
00056           WORKING-STORAGE SECTION.
00057
00058           01  DETAIL-LINE.
00059               05 OUTPUT-HOLD     PICTURE X(79).
00060               05 FILLER          PICTURE X(5)       VALUE SPACES.
00061               05 MEMBER-STATUS   PICTURE X(12).
00062
00063           01  HEADER-1.
00064               05 FILLER          PICTURE X(09)      VALUE 'ID-NUMBER'.
00065               05 FILLER          PICTURE X(08)      VALUE SPACES.
00066               05 FILLER          PICTURE X(04)      VALUE 'NAME'.
00067               05 FILLER          PICTURE X(20)      VALUE SPACES.
00068               05 FILLER          PICTURE X(07)      VALUE 'ADDRESS'.
00069               05 FILLER          PICTURE X(13)      VALUE SPACES.
00070·              05 FILLER          PICTURE X(14)      VALUE 'CITY / STATE /'.
00071               05 FILLER          PICTURE X(04)      VALUE ' ZIP'.
00072               05 FILLER          PICTURE X(07)      VALUE SPACES.
00073               05 FILLER          PICTURE X(06)      VALUE 'STATUS'.
00074
00075           01  HEADER-2.
00076               05 FILLER          PICTURE X(09)      VALUE ALL '*='.
00077               05 FILLER          PICTURE X(01)      VALUE SPACES.
00078               05 FILLER          PICTURE X(19)      VALUE ALL '*='.
00079               05 FILLER          PICTURE X(05)      VALUE SPACES.
```

```
00080          05 FILLER          PICTURE X(23)     VALUE ALL '*='.
00081          05 FILLER          PICTURE X(01)     VALUE SPACES.
00082          05 FILLER          PICTURE X(23)     VALUE ALL '*='.
00083          05 FILLER          PICTURE X(03)     VALUE SPACES.
00084          05 FILLER          PICTURE X(13)     VALUE ALL '*='.
00085
00086      PROCEDURE DIVISION.
00087
00088          OPEN  INPUT  DISK-FILE
00089                       CARD-FILE
00090                OUTPUT NEW-FILE.
00091          WRITE OUTPUT-REC FROM HEADER-1.
00092          WRITE OUTPUT-REC FROM HEADER-2.
00093          DISPLAY HEADER-1.
00094          DISPLAY HEADER-2.
00095          MOVE SPACES TO OUTPUT-REC.
00096          WRITE OUTPUT-REC.
00097          MOVE SPACES TO OUTPUT-REC.
00098          DISPLAY OUTPUT-REC.
00099
00100      READ-THE-DISK.
00101          READ DISK-FILE AT END GO TO WRITE-REST-OF-THE-CARDS.
00102
00103      READ-A-CARD.
00104          READ CARD-FILE AT END GO TO WRITE-REST-OF-THE-DISK.
00105          IF TYPE-OF-CHANGE IS NOT EQUAL TO 'C' THEN
00106                  DISPLAY CARD-REC, '  WRONG TYPE OF CHANGE CODE'
00107                  GO TO READ-A-CARD.
00108
00109      COMPARE-CARD-WITH-DISK.
00110          IF DISK-NUMBER IS EQUAL TO CARD-NUMBER THEN
00111                  MOVE 'CHANGED INFO' TO MEMBER-STATUS
00112                  MOVE CARD-REC TO OUTPUT-HOLD
00113                      WRITE OUTPUT-REC FROM DETAIL-LINE
00114                      GO TO READ-THE-DISK.
00115          IF DISK-NUMBER IS GREATER THAN CARD-NUMBER, THEN
00116              DISPLAY CARD-REC '  CARD OUT OF SEQUENCE,'
00117              ' IGNORED'
00118                      GO TO READ-A-CARD.
00119          WRITE OUTPUT-REC FROM DISK-REC.
00120          READ DISK-FILE AT END GO TO WRITE-REST-OF-THE-CARDS.
00121          GO TO COMPARE-CARD-WITH-DISK.
00122
00123      WRITE-REST-OF-THE-CARDS.
00124          DISPLAY CARD-REC '  CARD OUT OF SEQUENCE, IGNORED'.
00125          READ CARD-FILE AT END GO TO EOJ.
00126          GO TO WRITE-REST-OF-THE-CARDS.
00127
00128      WRITE-REST-OF-THE-DISK.
00129          WRITE OUTPUT-REC FROM DISK-REC.
00130          READ DISK-FILE AT END GO TO EOJ.
00131          GO TO WRITE-REST-OF-THE-DISK.
00132
00133      EOJ.
00134          CLOSE  CARD-FILE
00135                 DISK-FILE
00136                 NEW-FILE.
00137          STOP RUN.
```

OUTPUT TO PROGRAM 39

ID-NUMBER	NAME	ADDRESS	CITY / STATE / ZIP	STATUS
==*=*=*	*=*=*=*=*=*=*=*=*	*=*=*=*=*=*=*=*=*=*=*	*=*=*=*=*=*=*=*=*=*=*=*	*=*=*=*=*=*
012341253	MARGIE BRAND	2650 E 12 STREET	BROOKLYN, N.Y. 11235	
102035456	DAVID FIFE	5900 BALEYBRIDGE AVENUE	BROOKLYN, N.Y. 10463	
103065997	LILLIA POON	505 10 STREET	BROOKLYN, 11215	
110225477	DENNIS SCHWARTZ	880 THERIDE AVENUE	BRONX N.Y. 10473	
245799210	WENDY WONG	14 MONTH COURT	SPRINGFIELD GARDENS	CHANGED INFO
302021475	MITCHEL RUBIN	2542 W 2 STRRET	BROOKLYN, N.Y. 11223	
302145785	GOUK CHIN	78 PERSIAN DRIVE	NEW ROCHELLE 10801	
410235478	ANDREA ROTH	66 GLORY STREET	IRVINGTON, N.J. 07411	
442030156	PETER GARCIA	5711 YORK AVENUE	N.Y. 10021	
542003214	ALINA CHOCCHOO	71 APPLE STREET	N.Y. 10012	
552021417	ROBERT BALCOME	8312 35 STREET	J.HTS. N.Y. 11372	
558553210	BARBARA HUDGIE	423 76 STREET	S.BERGEN N.J. 07047	
664012354	JOSE SCHMIDT	168-40 127 AVE.	GLENDALE N.Y. 11227	CHANGED INFO
705010665	WENDY ROITMAN	2469 HARBOR LANE	BELLEMORE 11710	
732596315	KATIE SOMMER	81 SOMERSET STREET	GARDEN CITY 11530	
774222541	DEBBIE FELDIE	14 FLOREN PLACE	SCARSDALE 10583	
885444602	ANDREW WEISSMAN	5 UNIVERSITY PLACE	N.Y. 10003	
885446320	ANDY DAVIS	99 BLEECKER STREET	N.Y. 10012	
903335478	BARRIE LOWENDORF	6000 TOENAIL ROAD	YONKERS 10710	
999522140	CARMELLA CARNOVALI	11 CEDAR STREET	N.Y. 11570	

ID-NUMBER	NAME	ADDRESS	CITY / STATE / ZIP	STATUS
==*=*=*	*=*=*=*=*=*=*=*=*=*	*=*=*=*=*=*=*=*=*=*=*=*	*=*=*=*=*=*=*=*=*=*=*	*=*=*=*=*=*=*
002606108	DEL T. A. PHI	146 W. 4TH	N.Y. NY 10012 C	CARD OUT OF SEQUENCE, IGNORED
021879654	KOSEPH JAISER	1313 MOCKINGBIRD LANE	BALONA, ITALY C	CARD OUT OF SEQUENCE, IGNORED
110225477	DENNIS SCHWARTZ	880 THERIDE AVENUE	BRONX N.Y. 10473 D	WRONG TYPE OF CHANGE CODE
123458S759	JOE MANDEL	CCNEY ISLAND	NY	WRONG TYPE OF CHANGE CODE
127403158	PETER M C MCKAY	104 CALLE ANASCC	SANTURCE PUERTO RICO A	WRONG TYPE OF CHANGE CODE
789456123	STEWART L. KAPLAN	75 CALLE DE VINO	PARIS FRANCE	WRONG TYPE OF CHANGE CODE

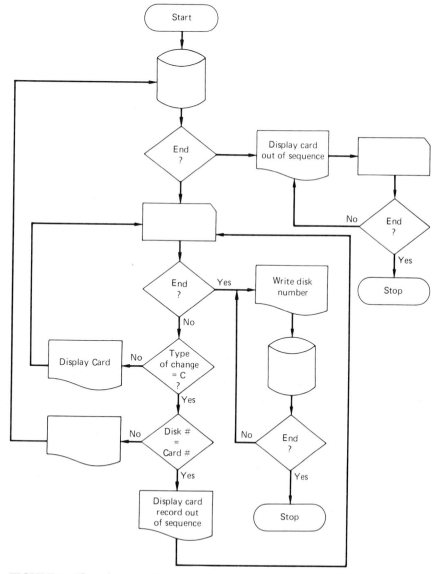

FIGURE 31 Flowchart for Program 39

13.5 UPDATING A FILE WITH ADDITIONS, DELETIONS, AND CHANGES

The usual situation is, of course, when the transaction cards consist of adds, deletions, and changes. Surprisingly, however, the logic required to update the master list in this situation is not much more involved than what we have already encountered.

The type of change on any card is indicated by a suitable punch in column 80; A for add, D for delete, and C for change. These three kinds of notation are specified by three condition-name clauses (88 levels) under the 05 level name TYPE–OF–CHANGE. This is tested for the type of transaction recorded and control is sent to the appropriate paragraph. If the punch in column 80 is not A, D, or C, an error message is printed and a new card read in.

Each paragraph of the comprehensive program will now be quite familiar and should present little problem, if any, in following the logic. Here is the input file. It will be noticed that one card is to be deleted, five are to be added, two changed, and six data cards flagged as errors.

INPUT TO PROGRAM 40

```
020305579 RONALD S. FEIFVER    1001 PARK AVENUE     N.Y. NY  10023         C
002606108 DEL TAPHI            146 W. 4TH           N.Y. NY  10012         A
021879654 KOSEPH JAISER        U. OF. BALONY        BALONA. ITALY          C
110225477 DENNIS SCHWARTZ      880 THERIDE AVENUE   BRONX N.Y. 10473       D
123458975 JOE MANDEL           111-56  CHERRY ST.   BKLYN NY  11208        A
127403158 PETER M C MCKAY      104 CALLE ANASCO     SANTURCE PUERTO RICO A
149499031 HERMAN CHINITZ       81 FUCLID AVE.       BKLYN NY    18711      A
213132486 SUE E. HASSON        246 STAUBER ST.      NY NY   11/93          D
222560379 G. C. SMITH          222 W. 113 ST.       MONTECELLO NY 13057    D
245799210 WENDY WONG           14 MONTH COURT       SPRINGFIELD GARDENS    C
542003214 ALINA CHOUCHOO       44 W. 4TH ST         N.Y. NY  10012         A
658971099 DREW V. BOXER        100 PARK PLACE       ATLANTIC CIYT NJ       A
664012354 JOSE  SCHMIDT        168-40 127 AVE.      GLENDALE N.Y. 11227    C
789456123 STEWART S. KAPLAN    37 MAIN STREET       LINSCOTT L.I. 18976
```

PROGRAM 40
Update—All

```
00001        IDENTIFICATION DIVISION.
00002        PROGRAM-ID. UPDATE-ALL.
00003        AUTHOR. PETER M.C. MCKAY.
00004        REMARKS.    THIS PROGRAM ILLUSTRATES  THE UNION OF ALL
00005                    PREVIOUS UPDATING TECHNIQUES.
00006
00007        ENVIRONMENT DIVISION.
00008        CONFIGURATION SECTION.
00009        INPUT-OUTPUT SECTION.
00010        FILE-CONTROL.
00011            SELECT CARD-FILE ASSIGN TO UT-S-READER.
00012            SELECT DISK-FILE ASSIGN TO UT-S-DISKREAD.
00013            SELECT NEW-FILE  ASSIGN TO UT-S-PRINTER.
00014
00015        DATA DIVISION.
00016
00017        FILE SECTION.
00018
00019        FD  DISK-FILE
00020            LABEL RECORDS ARE STANDARD,
00021            RECORDING MODE IS F,
00022            RECORD CONTAINS 80 CHARACTERS,
00023            BLOCK CONTAINS 80 CHARACTERS.
00024        01  DISK-REC.
00025            05 DISK-NUMBER     PICTURE 9(9).
00026            05 FILLER          PICTURE X.
```

```
00027                    05 DISK-MEMBER    PICTURE X(21).
00028                    05 FILLER         PICTURE X(03).
00029                    05 DISK-ADDRESS   PICTURE X(21).
00030                    05 FILLER         PICTURE X(03).
00031                    05 DISK-STATE-ZIP PICTURE X(19).
00032                    05 FILLER         PICTURE X(03).
00033
00034           FD  CARD-FILE
00035               LABEL RECORDS ARE OMITTED.
00036           01  CARD-REC.
00037                    05 CARD-NUMBER    PICTURE 9(9).
00038                    05 FILLER         PICTURE X(01).
00039                    05 CARD-MEMBER    PICTURE X(21).
00040                    05 FILLER         PICTURE X(03).
00041                    05 CARD-ADDRESS   PICTURE X(21).
00042                    05 FILLER         PICTURE X(03).
00043                    05 CARD-STATE-ZIP PICTURE X(19).
00044                    05 FILLER         PICTURE X(02).
00045                    05 TYPE-OF-CHANGE PICTURE X.
00046                         88 ADDITION          VALUE 'A'.
00047                         88 DELETION          VALUE 'D'.
00048                         88 CHANGE            VALUE 'C'.
00049
00050           FD  NEW-FILE
00051               LABEL RECORDS ARE OMITTED.
00052           01  OUTPUT-REC.
00053                    05 PRINT-LINE     PICTURE X(132).
00054
00055
00056           WORKING-STORAGE SECTION.
00057           01  DETAIL-LINE.
00058                    05 OUTPUT-HOLD    PICTURE X(79).
00059                    05 FILLER         PICTURE X(5)      VALUE SPACES.
00060                    05 MEMBER-STATUS  PICTURE X(12).
00061
00062           01  HEADER-1.
00063                    05 FILLER         PICTURE X(09)     VALUE 'ID-NUMBER'.
00064                    05 FILLER         PICTURE X(08)     VALUE SPACES.
00065                    05 FILLER         PICTURE X(04)     VALUE 'NAME'.
00066                    05 FILLER         PICTURE X(20)     VALUE SPACES.
00067                    05 FILLER         PICTURE X(07)     VALUE 'ADDRESS'.
00068                    05 FILLER         PICTURE X(13)     VALUE SPACES.
00069                    05 FILLER         PICTURE X(14)     VALUE 'CITY / STATE /'.
00070                    05 FILLER         PICTURE X(04)     VALUE ' ZIP'.
00071                    05 FILLER         PICTURE X(07)     VALUE SPACES.
00072                    05 FILLER         PICTURE X(06)     VALUE 'STATUS'.
00073
00074           01  HEADER-2.
00075                    05 FILLER         PICTURE X(09)     VALUE ALL '*='.
00076                    05 FILLER         PICTURE X(01)     VALUE SPACES.
00077                    05 FILLER         PICTURE X(19)     VALUE ALL '*='.
00078                    05 FILLER         PICTURE X(05)     VALUE SPACES.
00079                    05 FILLER         PICTURE X(23)     VALUE ALL '*='.
00080                    05 FILLER         PICTURE X(01)     VALUE SPACES.
00081                    05 FILLER         PICTURE X(23)     VALUE ALL '*='.
00082                    05 FILLER         PICTURE X(03)     VALUE SPACES.
00083                    05 FILLER         PICTURE X(13)     VALUE ALL '*='.
00084
00085
00086
00087           PROCEDURE DIVISION.
00088               OPEN INPUT  DISK-FILE
00089                           CARD-FILE
00090                    OUTPUT NEW-FILE.
00091               WRITE OUTPUT-REC FROM HEADER-1.
00092               WRITE OUTPUT-REC FROM HEADER-2.
00093               MOVE SPACES TO OUTPUT-REC.
00094               WRITE OUTPUT-REC.
00095               DISPLAY HEADER-1.
00096               DISPLAY HEADER-2.
00097               MOVE SPACES TO OUTPUT-REC.
00098               DISPLAY OUTPUT-REC.
00099
00100           READ-THE-DISK.
00101               READ DISK-FILE AT END GO TO WRITE-REST-OF-THE-CARDS.
00102
00103           READ-A-CARD.
00104               READ CARD-FILE AT END GO TO WRITE-REST-OF-THE-DISK.
00105
00106           ADD-DELETE-CHANGE-TESTER.
00107               IF DELETION GO TO DELETION-RTN.
00108               IF ADDITION GO TO ADDITION-RTN.
00109               IF CHANGE GO TO CHANGE-RTN.
```

```
00110              DISPLAY CARD-REC '   UNKNOWN CHANGE CODE, CARD IGNORED'
00111              GO TO READ-A-CARD.
00112
00113     ADDITION-RTN.
00114         IF DISK-NUMBER IS EQUAL TO CARD-NUMBER THEN
00115              DISPLAY CARD-REC, '   DISK=CARD-NO: CHECK TYPE'
00116              GO TO READ-A-CARD.
00117         IF DISK-NUMBER IS GREATER THAN CARD-NUMBER THEN
00118              MOVE 'NEW MEMBER' TO MEMBER-STATUS,
00119              MOVE CARD-REC TO OUTPUT-HOLD
00120              WRITE OUTPUT-REC FROM DETAIL-LINE
00121              GO TO READ-A-CARD.
00122         GO TO WRITE-THE-DISK-REC.
00123
00124     DELETION-RTN.
00125         IF DISK-NUMBER IS EQUAL TO CARD-NUMBER THEN
00126              DISPLAY CARD-REC '   HAS BEEN DELETED'
00127              GO TO READ-THE-DISK.
00128         IF DISK-NUMBER IS GREATER THAN CARD-NUMBER THEN
00129              DISPLAY CARD-REC '   CARD OUT OF SEQUENCE,'
00130              ' IGNORED'
00131              GO TO READ-A-CARD.
00132         GO TO WRITE-THE-DISK-REC.
00133
00134     CHANGE-RTN.
00135         IF DISK-NUMBER IS EQUAL TO CARD-NUMBER THEN
00136              MOVE 'CHANGED INFO' TO MEMBER-STATUS
00137              MOVE CARD-REC TO OUTPUT-HOLD
00138              WRITE OUTPUT-REC FROM DETAIL-LINE
00139              GO TO READ-THE-DISK.
00140         IF DISK-NUMBER IS GREATER THAN CARD-NUMBER THEN
00141              DISPLAY CARD-REC '   CARD OUT OF SEQUENCE,'
00142              ' IGNORED'
00143              GO TO READ-A-CARD.
00144
00145     WRITE-THE-DISK-REC.
00146         WRITE OUTPUT-REC FROM DISK-REC.
00147         READ DISK-FILE AT END GO TO WRITE-REST-OF-THE-CARDS.
00148         GO TO ADD-DELETE-CHANGE-TESTER.
00149
00150     WRITE-REST-OF-THE-CARDS.
00151         IF NOT ADDITION
00152              DISPLAY CARD-REC '   CARD OUT OF SEQUENCE, IGNORED'
00153              GO TO WRITE-REST-OF-THE-CARDS.
00154         MOVE 'NEW MEMBER' TO MEMBER-STATUS.
00155         MOVE CARD-REC TO OUTPUT-HOLD.
00156         WRITE OUTPUT-REC FROM DETAIL-LINE.
00157         READ CARD-FILE AT END GO TO EOJ.
00158         GO TO WRITE-REST-OF-THE-CARDS.
00159
00160     WRITE-REST-OF-THE-DISK.
00161         MOVE SPACES TO MEMBER-STATUS.
00162         MOVE DISK-REC TO OUTPUT-HOLD.
00163         WRITE OUTPUT-REC FROM DETAIL-LINE.
00164         READ DISK-FILE AT END GO TO EOJ.
00165         GO TO WRITE-REST-OF-THE-DISK.
00166
00167     EOJ.
00168         CLOSE   CARD-FILE
00169                 DISK-FILE
00170                 NEW-FILE.
00171         STOP RUN.
```

OUTPUT TO PROGRAM 40

ID-NUMBER	NAME	ADDRESS	CITY / STATE / ZIP	STATUS
012341253	MARGIE BRAND	2650 E 12 STREET	BROOKLYN, N.Y. 11235	
002606108	DEL TAPHI	146 W. 4TH	N.Y. NY 10012	NEW MEMBER
102035456	DAVID FIFE	5900 BALEYBRIDGE AVENUE	BROOKLYN, N.Y.10463	
103065997	LILLIA POON	505 10 STREET	BROOKLYN, 11215	
123458975	JOE MANDEL	111-56 CHERRY ST.	BKLYN NY 11208	NEW MEMBER
127403158	PETER M C MCKAY	104 CALLE ANASCO	SANTURCE PUERTO RICO	NEW MEMBER
149495031	HERMAN CHINITZ	81 EUCLID AVE.	BKLYN NY 18711	NEW MEMBER
245799210	WENDY WONG	14 MONTH COURT	SPRINGFIELD GARDENS	CHANGED INFO
302021475	MITCHEL RUBIN	2542 W 2 STREET	BROOKLYN, N.Y.11223	
302145785	GOOK CHIN	78 PERSIAN DRIVE	NEW ROCHELLE 10801	
410235478	ANDREA ROTH	66 GLORY STREET	IRVINGTON, N.J.07411	
442030156	PETER GARCIA	5711 YORK AVENUE	N.Y. 10021	
542003214	ALINA CHOOCHOO	71 APPLE STREET	N.Y. 10012	

```
552021417 ROBERT BALCOME          8312 35 STREET        J.HTS. N.Y. 11372
55855321C BARBARA HODGIE          423 76 STREET         S.BERGEN N.J. 07047
658971099 DREW V. BUXER           100 PARK PLACE        ATLANTIC CIYT NJ          NEW MEMBER
664012354 JOSE  SCHMIDT           168-40 127 AVE.       GLENDALE N.Y. 11227       CHANGED INFO
705010665 WENDY ROITMAN           2469 HARBOR LANE      BELLEMORE 11710
732596315 KATIE SOMMER            81 SOMERSET STREET    GARDEN CITY 11530
774222541 DEBBIE FELDIE           14 FLOREN PLACE       SCARSDALE 10583
885444602 ANDREW WEISSMAN         5 UNIVERSITY PLACE    N.Y.    10003
88544532C ANDY DAVIS              99 BLEECKER STREET    N.Y.    10012
903335478 BARRIE LOWENDORF        6000 TCENAIL ROAD     YONKERS 10710
99952214C CARMELLA CARNOVALI      11 CEDAR STREET       N.Y.  11570
```

```
ID-NUMBER        NAME              ADDRESS           CITY / STATE / ZIP        STATUS
*=*=*=*=*  *=*=*=*=*=*=*=*=*  *=*=*=*=*=*=*=*=*=*  *=*=*=*=*=*=*=*=*=*=*  *=*=*=*=*=*=*

020305579 RONALD S. PRIEVER       1001 PARK AVENJE      N.Y. NY  10023    C    CARD OUT OF SEQUENCE, IGNORED
021879654 KOSEPH JAISER           U. CF. BALCNY         BALOMA, ITALY     C    CARD UUT OF SEQUENCE, IGNORED
110225477 DENNIS SCHWARTZ         880 THERIDE AVENUE    BRONX N.Y. 10473  D    HAS BEEN DELETED
213132486 SUE E. HASSON           248 STAUBER ST.       NY NY  11793      D    CARD OUT OF SEQUENCE, IGNORED
222560379 G. C. SMITH             222 W. 113 ST.        MONTECELLO NY 13057 D  CARD OUT OF SEQUENCE, IGNORED
542003214 ALINA CHOUCHOO          44 W. 4TH ST          N.Y. NY  10012    A    DISK=CARD-NO: CHECK TYPE
789456123 STEWART S. KAPLAN       37 MAIN STREET        LINSCCIT L.I. 18976    UNKNOWN CHANGE CODE, CARD IGNORED
```

13.6 GENERATING A DISK FILE OF REJECTED CARDS

It is to be noticed that the output to the previous program consists of two separate parts. In the first part, an updated membership list is printed, followed by the second part, which consists of a combined list of invalid input cards and cards to be deleted. It was by means of appropriate JCL cards that the listing of rejected data cards was printed on a separate page. This approach may be criticized for two reasons. In the first place, the DISPLAY verb should be used very sparingly, if at all. Second, using machine-dependent JCL detracts from the generality of the program. In order to overcome these two criticisms, the previous program has been amended so that all rejected input cards are stored on disk. Once this rejected card file is complete, the file is then printed after the printout of the updated list, using the WRITE instead of the DISPLAY statement. The input and output to the amended program is identical to that of Program 40 and so is not shown.

Essentially Program 41 is not very different from Program 40, on which it is modelled. The first change we notice is that under FILE–CONTROL there is an additional SELECT in which REJECT–FILE is assigned to UT–S–REJECTS, where REJECTS is a temporary area on disk set up by appropriate JCL. A separate FD is, of course, set up for REJECT–FILE in the FILE–SECTION of the DATA DIVISION.

In the Procedure Division, not only is NEW–FILE OPENed as an output file, but so is REJECT–FILE. This file is opened in preparation for the writing of all the invalid input data cards to the program. Once each of the invalid data cards has been detected and written onto this disk area, REJECT–FILE is CLOSED along with CARD–FILE and DISK–FILE. It is at this point that REJECT–FILE becomes an input file, even though it was an output file in the previous operation. Therefore REJECT–FILE must be opened as an input file so its contents can be read and subsequently written onto NEW–FILE, which is assigned to the printer. Once all the invalid data cards have been printed, both REJECT–FILE and NEW–FILE are closed, and the program terminated in the normal way.

PROGRAM 41
Last Update

```
00001          IDENTIFICATION DIVISION.
C0002          PROGRAM-ID.  LAST-UPDATE.
C0003          AUTHOR. PETER M.C. MCKAY.
00004          REMARKS.THIS PROGRAM SHOWS HOW TO USE A TEMPORARY FILE TO
00005               STORE DATA THAT IS TO BE RECALLED AT A LATER TIME.
C0006
C0007          ENVIRONMENT DIVISION.
C0008          CONFIGURATION SECTION.
00009          SPECIAL-NAMES.
C0010               C01 IS NEW-PAGE.
00011          INPUT-OUTPUT SECTION.
00012          FILE-CONTROL.
00013               SELECT CARD-FILE ASSIGN TO UT-S-READER.
J0014               SELECT DISK-FILE ASSIGN TO UT-S-DISKREAD.
00015               SELECT NEW-FILE  ASSIGN TO UT-S-PRINTER.
00016               SELECT REJECT-FILE ASSIGN TO UT-S-REJECTS.
00017
00018          DATA DIVISION.
00019
C0020          FILE SECTION.
C0021
J0022          FD  DISK-FILE
00023               LABEL RECORDS ARE STANDARD,
00024               RECORDING MODE IS F,
J0025               RECORD CONTAINS 80 CHARACTERS,
00026               BLOCK CONTAINS 80 CHARACTERS.
00027          01  DISK-REC.
C0028               05 DISK-NUMBER    PICTURE 9(9).
C0029               05 FILLER         PICTURE X.
C0030               05 DISK-MEMBER    PICTURE X(21).
J0031               05 FILLER         PICTURE X(03).
00032               05 DISK-ADDRESS   PICTURE X(21).
C0033               05 FILLER         PICTURE X(03).
J0034               05 DISK-STATE-ZIP PICTURE X(19).
00035               05 FILLER         PICTURE X(03).
J0036
00037          FD  CARD-FILE
C0038               LABEL RECORDS ARE OMITTED.
00039          01  CARD-REC.
C0040               05 CARD-NUMBER    PICTURE 9(9).
00041               05 FILLER         PICTURE X(01).
C0042               05 CARD-MEMBER    PICTURE X(21).
00043               05 FILLER         PICTURE X(03).
C0044               05 CARD-ADDRESS   PICTURE X(21).
C0045               05 FILLER         PICTURE X(03).
J0046               05 CARD-STATE-ZIP PICTURE X(19).
C0047               05 FILLER         PICTURE X(02).
J0048               05 TYPE-OF-CHANGE PICTURE X.
J0049                    88 ADDITION           VALUE 'A'.
C0050                    88 DELETION           VALUE 'D'.
J0051                    88 CHANGE             VALUE 'C'.
C0052
C0053          FD  NEW-FILE
J0054               LABEL RECORDS ARE OMITTED.
J0055          01  OUTPUT-REC.
C0056               05 PRINT-LINE     PICTURE X(133).
00057
C0058          FD  REJECT-FILE
J0059               RECORD CONTAINS 132 CHARACTERS
C0060               LABEL RECORDS ARE STANDARD.
00061          01  REJECT-RECORD.
00062               05  REJECTED-MEMBER    PICTURE X(80).
C0063               05  CAUSE              PICTURE X(52).
J0064
00065          WORKING-STORAGE SECTION.
00066          01  DETAIL-LINE.
J0067               02  FILLER             PICTURE X(1)   VALUE SPACES.
00068               02  OUTPUT-LINE.
J0069               05 OUTPUT-HOLD    PICTURE X(79).
C0070               05 FILLER         PICTURE X(5)    VALUE SPACES.
C0C71               05 MEMBER-STATUS  PICTURE X(12).
J0C72               05  FILLER        PICTURE X(36)   VALUE SPACES.
```

```
00C73
00074        01   HEADER-1.
0OC75             05  FILLER           PICTURE X(01)        VALUE SPACES.
00076             05  FILLER           PICTURE X(09)        VALUE 'ID-NUMBER'.
00077             05  FILLER           PICTURE X(08)        VALUE SPACES.
00078             05  FILLER           PICTURE X(04)        VALUE 'NAME'.
00079             05  FILLER           PICTURE X(20)        VALUE SPACES.
C0C80             05  FILLER           PICTURE X(07)        VALUE 'ADDRESS'.
00081             05  FILLER           PICTURE X(13)        VALUE SPACES.
00082             05  FILLER           PICTURE X(14)        VALUE 'CITY / STATE /'.
0OC83             05  FILLER           PICTURE X(04)        VALUE ' ZIP'.
00084             05  FILLER           PICTURE X(07)        VALUE SPACES.
00085             05  FILLER           PICTURE X(06)        VALUE 'STATUS'.
00086
COC87        01   HEADER-2.
00088             05  FILLER           PICTURE X(01)        VALUE SPACES.
0OC89             05  FILLER           PICTURE X(09)        VALUE ALL '*='.
00090             05  FILLER           PICTURE X(01)        VALUE SPACES.
00091             05  FILLER           PICTURE X(19)        VALUE ALL '*='.
00092             05  FILLER           PICTURE X(05)        VALUE SPACES.
C0093             05  FILLER           PICTURE X(23)        VALUE ALL '*='.
C0094             05  FILLER           PICTURE X(01)        VALUE SPACES.
00095             05  FILLER           PICTURE X(23)        VALUE ALL '*='.
00096             05  FILLER           PICTURE X(03)        VALUE SPACES.
00097             05  FILLER           PICTURE X(13)        VALUE ALL '*='.
C0C98
C0099
C0100
00101        PROCEDURE DIVISION.
00102             OPEN  INPUT  DISK-FILE
C0103                          CARD-FILE
00104                   OUTPUT NEW-FILE
00105                          REJECT-FILE.
00106             WRITE OUTPUT-REC FROM HEADER-1 AFTER ADVANCING NEW-PAGE.
00107             WRITE OUTPUT-REC FROM HEADER-2 AFTER ADVANCING 1.
00108             MOVE SPACES TO OUTPUT-REC.
00109             WRITE OUTPUT-REC  AFTER ADVANCING 1.
C0110
00111        READ-THE-DISK.
00112             READ DISK-FILE AT END GO TO WRITE-REST-OF-THE-CARDS.
00113
00114        READ-A-CARD.
00115             READ CARD-FILE AT END GO TO WRITE-REST-OF-THE-DISK.
00116
00117        ADD-DELETE-CHANGE-TESTER.
00118             IF DELETION GO TO DELETION-RTN.
00119             IF ADDITION GO TO ADDITION-RTN.
00120             IF CHANGE GO TO CHANGE-RTN.
00121             MOVE CARD-REC TO REJECTED-MEMBER.
C0122             MOVE '   UNKNOWN CHANGE CODE, CARD IGNORED' TO  CAUSE.
00123             WRITE  REJECT-RECORD.
C0124             GO TO READ-A-CARD.
00125
00126        ADDITION-RTN.
00127             IF DISK-NUMBER IS EQUAL TO CARD-NUMBER THEN
00128                  MOVE CARD-REC TO REJECTED-MEMBER
C0129                  MOVE '   DISK = CARD-NO; CHECK TYPE' TO CAUSE
C0130                  WRITE REJECT-RECORD
00131                  GO TO READ-A-CARD.
00132             IF DISK-NUMBER IS GREATER THAN CARD-NUMBER THEN
C0133                  MOVE 'NEW MEMBER' TO MEMBER-STATUS,
00134                  MOVE CARD-REC TO OUTPUT-HOLD
00135                  WRITE OUTPUT-REC FROM DETAIL-LINE AFTER ADVANCING 1
00136                  GO TO READ-A-CARD.
00137             GO TO WRITE-THE-DISK-REC.
00138
00139        DELETION-RTN.
00140             IF DISK-NUMBER IS EQUAL TO CARD-NUMBER THEN
00141                  MOVE CARD-REC TO REJECTED-MEMBER
00142                  MOVE '   HAS BEEN DELETED' TO CAUSE
00143                  WRITE REJECT-RECORD
00144                  GO TO READ-THE-DISK.
00145             IF DISK-NUMBER IS GREATER THAN CARD-NUMBER THEN
00146                  MOVE CARD-REC TO REJECTED-MEMBER
00147                  MOVE '   CARD OUT OF SEQUENCE, IGNORED' TO CAUSE
C0148                  WRITE REJECT-RECORD
00149                  GO TO READ-A-CARD.
C0150             GO TO WRITE-THE-DISK-REC.
00151
00152        CHANGE-RTN.
00153             IF DISK-NUMBER IS EQUAL TO CARD-NUMBER THEN
00154                  MOVE 'CHANGED INFO' TO MEMBER-STATUS
00155                  MOVE CARD-REC TO OUTPUT-HOLD
00156                  WRITE OUTPUT-REC FROM DETAIL-LINE AFTER ADVANCING 1
```

```
00157              GO TO READ-THE-DISK.
00158         IF DISK-NUMBER IS GREATER THAN CARD-NUMBER THEN
00159              MOVE CARD-REC TO REJECTED-MEMBER
00160              MOVE '  CARD OUT OF SEQUENCE, IGNORED' TO CAUSE
00161              WRITE REJECT-RECORD
00162              GO TO READ-A-CARD.
00163
00164    WRITE-THE-DISK-REC.
00165         MOVE DISK-REC TO OUTPUT-LINE.
00166         WRITE OUTPUT-REC FROM DETAIL-LINE AFTER ADVANCING 1.
00167         READ DISK-FILE AT END GO TO WRITE-REST-OF-THE-CARDS.
00168         GO TO ADD-DELETE-CHANGE-TESTER.
00169
00170    WRITE-REST-OF-THE-CARDS.
00171         IF NOT ADDITION THEN
00172              DISPLAY CARD-REC '  CARD OUT OF SEQUENCE, IGNORED'
00173              GO TO WRITE-REST-OF-THE-CARDS.
00174         MOVE 'NEW MEMBER' TO MEMBER-STATUS.
00175         MOVE CARD-REC TO OUTPUT-HOLD.
00176         WRITE OUTPUT-REC FROM DETAIL-LINE AFTER ADVANCING 1.
00177         READ CARD-FILE AT END GO TO EOJ.
00178         GO TO WRITE-REST-OF-THE-CARDS.
00179
00180    WRITE-REST-OF-THE-DISK.
00181         MOVE SPACES TO MEMBER-STATUS.
00182         MOVE DISK-REC TO OUTPUT-HOLD.
00183         WRITE OUTPUT-REC FROM DETAIL-LINE AFTER ADVANCING 1.
00184         READ DISK-FILE AT END GO TO EOJ.
00185         GO TO WRITE-REST-OF-THE-DISK.
00186
00187    EOJ.
00188         CLOSE    CARD-FILE
00189                  DISK-FILE
00190                  REJECT-FILE.
00191
00192
00193         OPEN  INPUT REJECT-FILE.
00194         WRITE OUTPUT-REC FROM HEADER-1 AFTER ADVANCING NEW-PAGE.
00195         WRITE OUTPUT-REC FROM HEADER-2 AFTER ADVANCING 1.
00196         MOVE SPACES TO OUTPUT-REC.
00197         WRITE OUTPUT-REC  AFTER ADVANCING 1.
00198
00199    WRITE-THE-REJECT-FILE.
00200         READ REJECT-FILE INTO OUTPUT-LINE AT END GO TO STOP-RUN.
00201         WRITE OUTPUT-REC FROM DETAIL-LINE AFTER ADVANCING 1.
00202         GO TO  WRITE-THE-REJECT-FILE.
00203
00204    STOP-RUN.
00205         CLOSE REJECT-FILE.
00206         CLOSE NEW-FILE.
00207         STOP RUN.
```

SORTING

14.1 SORT, USING, AND GIVING.

Those readers who have had some computer programming experience in languages other than COBOL will recall that the task of sorting a series of scores or names is quite an intellectual feat. Not so in COBOL. The language provides the programmer with a tailor-made package of routines which does the job for him. As usual, however, certain careful attention to detail is imperative. Once such detail has been mastered, sorting becomes rather trivial.

The need for sorting in business applications is virtually limitless. Accounts may have to be printed and processed in order of ascending or possibly descending account number, transactions may have to be reported in ascending order of company name (as they would appear in a dictionary, for example), or according to some combination of an alphabetical and a numeric sort such as state name, branch number, and department number.

For all these different types of sorts, the key word is SORT, a COBOL word which brings into play the routines required to accomplish the desired purpose. These routines are, on most COBOL systems, part of a complex SORT/MERGE module, normally supplied by the manufacturer. This module represents a very important part of the system's *software* as opposed to the printer, card reader, disk, and so on, which make up the system's *hardware*.

14.2 A NUMERIC SORT

As a preliminary to the use of the SORT verb, an additional file must be defined in the Environment Division. Suppose, for example, we wished to sort a set of input cards punched with assorted Social Security numbers in columns 1 through 9. Let us assume that no other data are punched on the cards. The first thing to be done is to allocate some area of the disk for the sorted file. Let us call it SORT-FILE. Under the paragraph name FILE–CONTROL, a SELECT is assigned to some appropriately named area of disk, say UT–S–SORTER. This name must appear in the control cards that separate the program from the data cards, along with certain additional control cards whose role is to allocate certain so-called sort work areas of which three are necessary. These cards are indicated in the diagram of the deck which will follow shortly.

In the same manner that an input file and an output file always have their associated FD, the sort file has its special associated letters. As you may have already guessed, it is SD which stands for Sort Description, which is never spelled out in full nor do the letters SD take periods. The SD is included in the File Section of the Data Division. An important point that must be made with reference to the sort file is that one does *not* write anything about label records being omitted. To do so would be an error and the program would abort. In the 1974 version of the COBOL compiler, however, the statement

LABEL RECORDS ARE OMITTED

is treated as a simple comment and as such is ignored by the compiler. Since 1974 compilers are not yet as common as previous compilers, it is recommended that the label statement be totally omitted.

Following the SD is the name of the sort file—in our case we called it SORT–FILE. As in the case of an FD, an 01 level must follow the SD. The 05 level statement within this record defines the field to be sorted and the name to be associated with that field. We have called it SORT–SOC–SEC–NO and it has a picture of 9(9).

Now we come to the Procedure Division. Here we use the verb SORT followed by the name of the file to be sorted.

The SORT verb takes the following form:

```
SORT sort-file-name
ON {ASCENDING / DESCENDING} KEY data-name

USING    file-name-1    GIVING    file-name-2.
```

This portion of the coding is placed in the Procedure Division, where one is at liberty to create arbitrarily defined sections. Here a section is declared for the sort procedure with the name SORT–PROCEDURE SECTION. If the numeric data are to be sorted in ascending order, obviously the word ASCENDING would be used. Similarly, data to be sorted in descending order use the word DESCENDING. Now in our code the sort file has only a single data-name, namely SORT–SOC–SEC–NO. Nevertheless, this name—it really is a *key*—must be stated as the keyname.

Since the data to be sorted originate from the input file IN–FILE and once sorted will be sent for printing to the output file OUT–FILE, the Sort Section is written

```
SORT-PROCEDURE SECTION.
DO-THE-SORT.
    SORT SORT-FILE
    ON DESCENDING KEY SORT-SOC-SEC-NO
    USING IN-FILE
    GIVING OUT-FILE.
```

This virtually terminates the Procedure Division. What is conspicuous about it is its brevity. The alert reader will notice that neither the input nor the output files are opened, nor are they closed.

The USING clause opens the input file, moves the input data to the SORT module and then closes the input file. By the same token, the GIVING clause opens the output file, moves the sorted data to the output file and writes the sorted data onto disk or the printer, or whatever output device, as specified by the Job Control Language (JCL), and closes the output file.

In other words, the programmer is relieved of several chores includ-

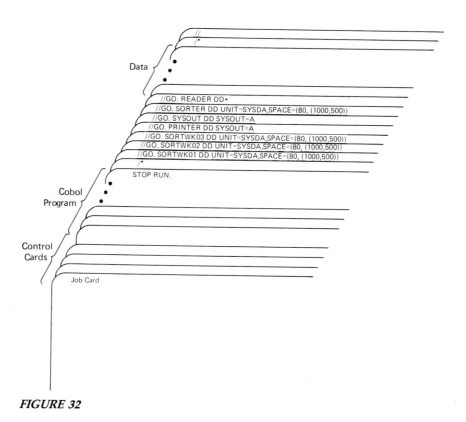

Data

```
//GO. READER DD•
//GO. SORTER DD UNIT=SYSDA,SPACE=(80, (1000,500))
//GO. SYSOUT DD SYSOUT=A
//GO. PRINTER DD SYSOUT=A
//GO. SORTWK03 DD UNIT=SYSDA,SPACE=(80, (1000,500))
//GO. SORTWK02 DD UNIT=SYSDA,SPACE=(80,500))
//GO. SORTWK01 DD UNIT=SYSDA,SPACE=(80, (1000,500))
/*
STOP RUN.
```

Cobol
Program

Control
Cards

Job Card

FIGURE 32

ing the printing out of the sorted results. Is it any wonder that programmers rather quickly learn about the SORT verb and become proficient at it in record time?

Figure 32 is a diagram of the setup of a sort program. Also following are the listing and the output of a simple program. Note that the system prints out some additional information which is not under the programmer's control.

INPUT TO PROGRAM 42

```
256421302
254638954
985647521
854789653
0C2124578
254632587
235698745
012456879
C12345678
987654321
102030654
C23145685
025647852
036985214
741258963
CCCCC0CC0
111112453
S99999999
586532147
325647852
123664785
025478541
233568957
021453698
258745632
```

PROGRAM 42
Sort 1

```
00001        IDENTIFICATICN DIVISION.
00002        PROGRAM-ID. SCRT-CNE.
00003        REMARKS. SIMPLE NUMERIC SORT WITH USING AND GIVING CLAUSES.
CC804        AUTHOR. ELI J. CPAS.
00005
00006        ENVIRONMENT DIVISICN.
C0007        INPUT-OUTPUT SECTICN.
00008        FILE-CONTROL.
00009            SELECT IN-FILE ASSIGN TC UT-S-READER.
C0010            SELECT CUT-FILE ASSIGN TO UT-S-PRINTER.
00011            SELECT SORT-FILE ASSIGN TC UT-S-SCRTER.
00012
C0013        DATA DIVISICN.
00014
00015        FILE SECTICN.
CC016
00017        FD  IN-FILE
00018            LABEL RECCRDS ARE OMITTED.
00019        01  CARD-IN.
C0020            05 SOC-SEC-NO      PICTURE 9(9).
00021            05 FILLER          PICTURE X(71).
00022
00023        FD  CUT-FILE
00024            LABEL RECCRDS ARE OMITTED.
00025        01  PRINT-LINE.
00026            05 LINE-OUT        PICTURE X(80).
00027
00028        SD  SORT-FILE.
00029        01  SORT-DATA.
00030            05 SORT-SCC-SEC-NC PICTURE 9(9).
00031
C0032        PROCEDURE DIVISION.
00033
00034            OPEN OUTPUT OUT-FILE.
```

```
00035                    MOVE '  SORTED' TO PRINT-LINE.
C0036                    WRITE PRINT-LINE.
00037                    MOVE 'SOC-SEC-NO' TO PRINT-LINE.
00038                    WRITE PRINT-LINE.
00039                    MOVE SPACES TO PRINT-LINE.
C0040                    WRITE PRINT-LINE.
00041                    CLOSE OUT-FILE.
00042
00043            SORT-PROCEDURE SECTION.
00044
00045            DO-THE-SORT.
00046                    SORT SORT-FILE
00047                    ON DESCENDING KEY SORT-SOC-SEC-NO
00048                    USING IN-FILE
00049                    GIVING ,OUT-FILE.
00050
00051            END-SORT.
00052
00053                    DISPLAY '*** END OF SOCIAL SECURITY NUMBER SORT ***'.
00054                    STOP RUN.
```

OUTPUT TO PROGRAM 42

```
    SORTED
SOC-SEC-NO

 999999999
 987654321
 985647521
 854789653
 741258963
 586532147
 325647852
 258745632
 256421302
 254638954
 254632587
 235698745
 233568957
 123564785
 111112453
 102030654
 036985214
 025647852
 025478541
 023145689
 C21453658
 012456879
 012345678
 002124578
 C00000000
```

```
WERO45I   END SORT PH
WERO55A   INSERT        25, DELETE         25
WER177I   TURNAROUND SORT PERFORMED
WERO54A   RCD IN       , OUT
WER169I   TPF'S APPLIED 123456789ABCDEF
WER052I   END SYNCSORT   OPT= M,  SORT1   ,GO
*** END OF SOCIAL SECURITY NUMBER SORT ***
```

14.3 AN ALPHABETIC SORT

In the same way that numeric data can be sorted so can alphabetic data be sorted. As we have seen, every item of data is converted within the computer to a *binary* number, whether the data item is a decimal number or an alphabetic character. Just as the number 5 is less than 6, so the binary number equivalent to the letter D is less than that for the letter E, and so on. Advantage of this fact is taken when sorting alphabetic data.

In the next program the data consists of a deck of cards, each of which is punched with a person's name, beginning in column 1. No name is greater than 10 characters. Apart from the fact that the input data name has a picture of A rather than X, there is absolutely no difference between this program, which sorts alphabetic data in ascending order, and the previous program, which sorted numeric data in descending order.

INPUT TO PROGRAM 43

```
BILL
DAVID
JACK
JILL
BARBARA
DIANE
HENRY
MOISHE
YANKLE
BEN
ADRIAN
DORIS
EUGENE
BARRY
LARRY
GEORGE
CHARLIE
NANCY
WILLIAM
ELI
```

PROGRAM 43
Sort 2

```
00001        IDENTIFICATION DIVISION.
00002        PROGRAM-ID. SORT-TWO.
00003        REMARKS. SIMPLE ALPHABETIC SORT WITH USING AND GIVING CLAUSES.
00004        AUTHOR. ELI J. OPAS.
00005
00006        ENVIRONMENT DIVISION.
00007        INPUT-OUTPUT SECTION.
00008        FILE-CONTROL.
00009            SELECT IN-FILE ASSIGN TO UT-S-READER.
00010            SELECT OUT-FILE ASSIGN TO UT-S-PRINTER.
00011            SELECT SORT-FILE ASSIGN TO UT-S-SORTER.
00012
00013        DATA DIVISION.
00014
00015        FILE SECTION.
00016
00017        FD  IN-FILE
00018            LABEL RECORDS ARE OMITTED.
00019        01  CARD-IN.
00020            05 NAME-IN         PICTURE A(10).
00021            05 FILLER          PICTURE X(70).
00022
00023        FD  OUT-FILE
00024            LABEL RECORDS ARE OMITTED.
00025        01  PRINT-LINE.
00026            05 LINE-OUT        PICTURE X(80).
00027
00028        SD  SORT-FILE.
00029        01  SORT-DATA.
00030            05 SORT-NAME       PICTURE A(10).
00031
00032        PROCEDURE DIVISION.
00033
00034            OPEN OUTPUT OUT-FILE.
00035            MOVE '  SORTED' TO PRINT-LINE.
00036            WRITE PRINT-LINE.
00037            MOVE '  NAMES' TO PRINT-LINE.
00038            WRITE PRINT-LINE.
00039            MOVE SPACES TO PRINT-LINE.
00040            WRITE PRINT-LINE.
00041            CLOSE OUT-FILE.
00042
00043        SORT-PROCEDURE SECTION.
00044
00045        DO-THE-SORT.
00046            SORT SORT-FILE
```

```
00047              ON ASCENDING KEY SORT-NAME
00048              USING IN-FILE
00049              GIVING OUT-FILE.
00050
00051     END-SORT.
00052
00053              DISPLAY '*** END OF NAME SORT ***'.
00054              STOP RUN.
```

OUTPUT TO PROGRAM 43

```
      SORTED
      NAMES

   ADRIAN
   BARBARA
   BARRY
   BEN
   BILL
   CHARLIE
   DAVID
   DIANE
   DORIS
   ELI
   EUGENE
   GEORGE
   HENRY
   JACK
   JILL
   LARRY
   MOISHE
   NANCY
   WILLIAM
   YANKLE


   WER045I   END SORT PH
   WER055A   INSERT        20, DELETE        20
   WER177I   TURNAROUND SORT PERFORMED
   WER054A   RCD IN        , OUT
   WER169I   TPF'S APPLIED 123456789ABCDEF
   WER052I   END SYNCSORT   OPT= M,  SORT2   ,GO        ,
   *** END OF NAME SORT ***
```

14.4 AN ALPHABETIC SORT WITHIN A NUMERIC SORT

Suppose we have data punched on cards in the following manner:

```
1234   NAILS
9845   SCREWS
4567   NAILS
9181   SCREWS
2102   TACKS
9220   SCREWS
```

where the four digits represent a part number and this is followed by a part name. What we would like to do is to sort the data alphabetically in descending order, that is, in a reverse dictionary fashion. However, each time a part name is repeated, that data card should be sorted in ascending order of part number.

Still using the USING and GIVING options (there are others), we can solve the problem by the usual method. A sort file is set up with an SD, appropriate names being given to the fields to be sorted. In the Procedure Division, however, after the SORT instruction we attach two separate clauses, namely

```
ON DESCENDING KEY SORT-PART-NAME
ON ASCENDING   KEY SORT-PART-NO
```

This manner of controlling the sort is reminiscent of the "most inclusive/ least inclusive" concept we discussed in the Report Writer chapter.

INPUT TO PROGRAM 44

```
1234   NAILS
9845   SCREWS
4567   NAILS
9181   SCREWS
2102   TACKS
9220   SCREWS
```

PROGRAM 44
Sort 3

```
00001          IDENTIFICATION DIVISICN.
00002          PROGRAM-ID. SCRT-THREE.
00003          AUTHOR. ELI J. OPAS.
00004          REMARKS. AN ALPHABETIC SORT WITHIN A NUMERIC SORT.
00005
00006          ENVIRONMENT DIVISICN.
00007          INPUT-OUTPUT SECTION.
00008          FILE-CONTROL.
00009              SELECT IN-FILE ASSIGN TC UT-S-READER.
00010              SELECT CUT-FILE ASSIGN TO UT-S-PRINTER.
00011              SELECT SORT-FILE ASSIGN TC UT-S-SCRTER.
00012
00013          DATA DIVISION.
00014
00015          FILE SECTION.
00016
00017          FD  IN-FILE
00018              LABEL RECCRDS ARE OMITTED.
00019          01  CARD-IN.
00020              05 PART-NO        PICTURE 9(4).
00021              05 FILLER         PICTURE X(3).
00022              05 PART-NAME      PICTURE A(10).
00023              05 FILLER         PICTURE X(63).
00024
00025          FD  OUT-FILE
00026              LABEL RECCRDS ARE OMITTED.
00027          01  PRINT-LINE.
00028              05 LINE-OUT        PICTURE X(80).
00029
00030          SD  SORT-FILE.
00031          01  SCRT-DATA.
00032              05 SORT-PART-NO    PICTURE 9(4).
00033              05 FILLER          PICTURE X(3).
00034              05 SORT-PART-NAME  PICTURE A(10).
00035              05 FILLER          PICTURE X(63).
00036
00037          PROCEDURE DIVISION.
00038
00039              OPEN CUTPUT OUT-FILE.
00040              MOVE '   SCRTED' TC PRINT-LINE.
00041              WRITE PRINT-LINE.
00042              MOVE 'PART    NAME' TC PRINT-LINE.
00043              WRITE PRINT-LINE.
00044              MOVE SPACES TO PRINT-LINE.
00045              WRITE PRINT-LINE.
00046              CLOSE OUT-FILE.
00047
00048          SORT-PROCEDURE SECTICN.
00049
00050          SORT-THE-FILE.
00051              SORT SCRT-FILE
00052              ON DESCENDING KEY SORT-PART-NAME
00053              ON ASCENDING KEY SORT-PART-NO
00054              USING IN-FILE
00055              GIVING CUT-FILE.
00056
00057          END-SORT.
00058
00059              DISPLAY '*** END CF SCRT ***'.
00060              STOP RUN.
```

```
         SORTED
PART      NAME

2102     TACKS
9181     SCREWS
9220     SCREWS
9845     SCREWS
1234     NAILS
4567     NAILS
```

OUTPUT TO PROGRAM 44

```
WER045I   END SORT PH
WER055A   INSERT        6, DELETE       6
WER177I   TURNAROUND SORT PERFORMED
WER054A   RCD IN        , OUT
WER169I   TPF'S APPLIED 123456789ABCDEF
WER052I   END SYNCSORT   OPT= M,  SCRT3   ,GO
*** END OF SORT ***
```

14.5 SORTING ON ONE OF TWO KEYS

The input to the next program has the first name punched in column 1 and the last name in column 22. The question now arises: What kind of output will be printed if only the *last* name is designated as the SORT key and the sort is to be carried out in ascending order? The point being made here is that no provision has been made in Program 45 to sort according to the first name as well.

The program shown was run; the output illustrates that although the last name is indeed sorted correctly the first name appears in some undetermined order.

INPUT TO PROGRAM 45

```
HENRY              MULLISH
ELI                OPAS
BEN                MULLISH
HENRI              OPAS
ADRIAN             MULLISH
SARAH              OPAS
DORIS              MULLISH
```

PROGRAM 45
Sort 4

```
00001          IDENTIFICATION DIVISION.
00002          PROGRAM-ID. SORT-FOUR.
00003          AUTHOR. ELI J. OPAS.
00004          REMARKS. A SORT WITH ONE KEY.
00005
00006          ENVIRONMENT DIVISION.
CG007
00008          INPUT-OUTPUT SECTION.
00009          FILE-CONTROL.
C0010              SELECT IN-FILE ASSIGN TO UT-S-READER.
00011              SELECT OUT-FILE ASSIGN TO UT-S-PRINTER.
00012              SELECT SORT-FILE ASSIGN TO UT-S-SORTER.
00013
00014          DATA DIVISION.
00015
00016          FILE SECTION.
00017
00018          FD  IN-FILE
00019              LABEL RECORDS ARE OMITTED.
00020          01  CARD-IN.
00021              05  FIRST-NAME      PICTURE X(21).
00022              05  LAST-NAME       PICTURE X(21).
00023              05  FILLER          PICTURE X(38).
00024
00025          FD  OUT-FILE
00026              LABEL RECORDS ARE OMITTED.
```

```
00027           01  PRINT-LINE.
00028               05 LINE-OUT         PICTURE X(80).
00029
00030           SD  SORT-FILE.
00031           01  SORT-DATA.
00032               05 SORT-FIRST-NAME PICTURE X(21).
00033               05 SORT-LAST-NAME  PICTURE X(21).
00034               05 FILLER          PICTURE X(38).
00035
00036           PROCEDURE DIVISION.
00037
00038               OPEN OUTPUT OUT-FILE.
00039               MOVE '         SORTED NAMES' TO PRINT-LINE.
00040               WRITE PRINT-LINE.
00041               MOVE 'FIRST NAME          LAST NAME' TO PRINT-LINE.
00042               WRITE PRINT-LINE.
00043               MOVE SPACES TC LINE-OUT.
00044               WRITE PRINT-LINE.
00045               CLOSE OUT-FILE.
00046
00047           SORT-PROCEDURE SECTION.
00048
00049           SORT-THE-NAME.
00050
00051               SORT SORT-FILE
00052               ON ASCENDING KEY SORT-LAST-NAME
00053               USING IN-FILE
00054               GIVING OUT-FILE.
00055
00056           END-SORT.
00057
00058               DISPLAY '*** END CF SORT ***'.
00059               STOP RUN.
```

OUTPUT TO PROGRAM 45

```
                SORTED NAMES
FIRST NAME              LAST NAME

DORIS                   MULLISH
ADRIAN                  MULLISH
BEN                     MULLISH
HENRY                   MULLISH
HENRI                   OPAS
ELI                     OPAS
SARAH                   OPAS


WER045I  END SORT PH
WER055A  INSERT          7, DELETE        7
WER177I  TURNAROUND SORT PERFORMED
WER054A  RCD IN        , OUT
WER169I  TPF'S APPLIED 123456789ABCDEF
WER052I  END SYNCSORT   OPT= M,  SORT4   ,GC        ,
*** END OF SORT ***
```

14.6 AN ALPHABETIC SORT WITHIN
AN ALPHABETIC SORT

In the next program, provision is made for sorting both the last name and the first name in ascending order. Otherwise, the program is identical in all respects to Program 45. The output shows that the sort has been done correctly.

INPUT TO PROGRAM 46

```
RACHEL                  OPAS
HENRY                   MULLISH
BEN                     MULLISH
SARAH                   OPAS
ADRIAN                  MULLISH
ELI                     OPAS
HENRI                   OPAS
```

PROGRAM 46

Sort 5

```
00001      IDENTIFICATION DIVISION.
00002      PROGRAM-ID. SORT-FIVE.
00003      AUTHOR. ELI J. OPAS.
00004      REMARKS. A SORT WITH TWO KEYS.
00005
00006      ENVIRONMENT DIVISION.
00007      INPUT-OUTPUT SECTION.
00008      FILE-CONTROL.
00009          SELECT IN-FILE ASSIGN TO UT-S-READER.
00010          SELECT OUT-FILE ASSIGN TO UT-S-PRINTER.
00011          SELECT SORT-FILE ASSIGN TO UT-S-SORTER.
00012
00013      DATA DIVISION.
00014
00015      FILE SECTION.
00016      FD  IN-FILE
00017          LABEL RECORDS ARE OMITTED.
00018      01  CARD-IN.
00019          05 FIRST-NAME      PICTURE X(21).
00020          05 LAST-NAME       PICTURE X(21).
00021          05 FILLER          PICTURE X(38).
00022
00023      FD  OUT-FILE
00024          LABEL RECORDS ARE OMITTED.
00025      01  PRINT-LINE.
00026          05 LINE-OUT        PICTURE X(80).
00027
00028      SD  SORT-FILE.
00029      01  SORT-DATA.
00030          05 SORT-FIRST-NAME PICTURE X(21).
00031          05 SORT-LAST-NAME  PICTURE X(21).
00032          05 FILLER          PICTURE X(38).
00033
00034      PROCEDURE DIVISION.
00035
00036          OPEN OUTPUT OUT-FILE.
00037          MOVE '         SORTED NAMES' TO PRINT-LINE.
00038          WRITE PRINT-LINE.
00039          MOVE 'FIRST NAME            LAST NAME' TO PRINT-LINE.
00040          WRITE PRINT-LINE.
00041          MOVE SPACES TO PRINT-LINE.
00042          WRITE PRINT-LINE.
00043          CLOSE OUT-FILE.
00044
00045      SORT-PROCEDURE SECTION.
00046
00047      SORT-THE-NAME.
00048
00049          SORT SORT-FILE
00050          ON ASCENDING KEY SORT-LAST-NAME
00051          ON ASCENDING KEY SORT-FIRST-NAME
00052          USING IN-FILE
00053          GIVING OUT-FILE.
00054
00055      END-SORT.
00056
00057          DISPLAY '*** END OF SORT ***'.
00058          STOP RUN.
```

OUTPUT TO PROGRAM 46

```
            SORTED NAMES
FIRST NAME            LAST NAME

ADRIAN                MULLISH
BEN                   MULLISH
HENRY                 MULLISH
ELI                   OPAS
HENRI                 OPAS
RACHEL                OPAS
SARAH                 OPAS

 WER045I  END SORT PH
 WER055A  INSERT          7, DELETE          7
 WER177I  TURNAROUND SORT PERFORMED
 WER054A  RCD IN        , OUT
 WER169I  TPF'S APPLIED 123456789ABCDEF
 WER052I  END SYNCSORT   OPT= M,  SCRT5    ,GC      ,
*** END OF SORT ***
```

14.7 AN EXAMPLE OF THREE SORT KEYS

The next program is a further illustration of the USING and the GIVING clauses associated with the SORT verb. As you will recall, these clauses open and close files and print the sorted output. In the program which follows, the data cards are punched with the name of the state in columns 1–15, the city in columns 26–40, and the zip code in columns 51–55. The input cards are in random order. The purpose of the program is to sort the cards according to state, and within each state according to city and within each city according to zip-code in ascending order. This is accomplished by

```
SORT SORT-FILE
ON ASCENDING KEY SORT-STATE
ON ASCENDING KEY SORT-CITY
ON ASCENDING KEY SORT-ZIP
USING IN-FILE
GIVING OUT-FILE.
```

A maximum of 12 ascending and/or descending keys are permitted. If there are more than one keys being sorted in the same direction (note that SORT-STATE, SORT-CITY and SORT-ZIP are all sorted in ASCENDING order), the words ON ASCENDING KEY may be omitted for each *successive* repetition.

INPUT TO PROGRAM 47

```
NEW YORK        NEW YORK          11202
CALIFORNIA      SAN FRANCISCO     94598
CALIFORNIA      IRVINE            94203
CALIFORNIA      LOS ANGELES       94789
OREGON          MUCHO             12345
NEW YORK        NEW YORK          11434
NEW YORK        POUGHKEEPSIE      11035
NEW YORK        BUFFALO           11002
NEW YORK        BUFFALO           11475
NEW YORK        NEW YORK          11235
NEW YORK        ALBANY            11467
NEW YORK        TROY              11300
CALIFORNIA      SAN FRANCISCO     94536
NEW YORK        ALBANY            11420
OREGON          TUCHAHOE          12456
CALIFORNIA      SAN FRANCISCO     94536
CALIFORNIA      IRVINE            94211
NEW YORK        TROY              11369
NEW YORK        NEW YORK          11253
NEW YORK        TROY              11378
CALIFORNIA      IRVINE            94521
CALIFORNIA      SAN FRANCISCO     94501
NEW YORK        BUFFALO           11520
OREGON          MUCHO             12348
NEW YORK        ALBANY            11487
CALIFORNIA      SAN FRANCISCO     94587
OREGON          TRAVINA           12005
CALIFORNIA      LOS ANGELES       94725
OREGON          TUCHAHOE          12402
OREGON          MUCHO             12347
OREGON          TUCHAHOE          12423
CALIFORNIA      SAN FRANCISCO     94521
CALIFORNIA      IRVINE            94251
NEW YORK        ALBANY            11489
NEW YORK        ALBANY            11458
OREGON          BILLING           12703
OREGON          BILLING           12754
```

```
CALIFORNIA          LOS ANGELES        94752
OREGON              TUCHAHOE           12485
NEW YORK            POUGHKEEPSIE       11036
NEW YORK            TROY               11352
OREGON              MUCHO              12346
NEW YORK            NEW YORK           11200
```

PROGRAM 47
Sort 6

```
00001          IDENTIFICATION DIVISION.
00002          PROGRAM-ID. SORT-SIX.
00003          AUTHOR. ELI J. OPAS.
00004          REMARKS. A SORT WITH THREE KEY FIELDS.
00005
00006          ENVIRONMENT DIVISION.
C0007          INPUT-OUTPUT SECTION.
00008          FILE-CONTROL.
00009              SELECT IN-FILE ASSIGN TO UT-S-READER.
00010              SELECT OUT-FILE ASSIGN TO UT-S-PRINTER.
00011              SELECT SORT-FILE ASSIGN TO UT-S-SORTER.
00012
00013          DATA DIVISION.
00014
C0015          FILE SECTION.
00016
00017          FD  IN-FILE
00018              LABEL RECORDS ARE OMITTED.
00019          01  STATE-CITY-ZIP.
00020              05 STATE            PICTURE X(15).
00021              05 FILLER           PICTURE X(10).
00022              05 CITY             PICTURE X(15).
00023              05 FILLER           PICTURE X(10).
00024              05 ZIP              PICTURE 9(5).
00025              05 FILLER           PICTURE X(25).
00026
00027          FD  OUT-FILE
00028              LABEL RECORDS ARE OMITTED.
00029          01  LINE-OUT.
00030              05 FILLER           PICTURE X(133).
00031
00032          SD  SORT-FILE.
00033          01  STATE-CITY-ZIP-SORT.
00034              05 SORT-STATE       PICTURE X(15).
00035              05 FILLER           PICTURE X(10).
00036              05 SORT-CITY        PICTURE X(15).
00037              05 FILLER           PICTURE X(10).
00038              05 SORT-ZIP         PICTURE 9(5).
00039              05 FILLER           PICTURE X(25).
00040
00041          PROCEDURE DIVISION.
00042
00043              OPEN OUTPUT  OUT-FILE.
00044              MOVE
00045                  '  STATE                    CITY              ZIP'
00046                  TO LINE-OUT.
00047              WRITE LINE-OUT.
00048              MOVE SPACES TO LINE-OUT.
00049              WRITE LINE-OUT.
00050              CLOSE OUT-FILE.
00051
00052          SORT-OUT SECTION.
00053
00054          SORT-IT-OUT.
00055
00056              SORT SORT-FILE
00057              ON ASCENDING KEY SORT-STATE
00058              ON ASCENDING KEY SORT-CITY
00059              ON ASCENDING KEY SORT-ZIP
00060              USING IN-FILE
00061              GIVING OUT-FILE.
00062
00063          END-OF-SORT.
00064
00065              DISPLAY '***SORT COMPLETED***'.
00066              STOP RUN.
```

OUTPUT TO PROGRAM 47

STATE	CITY	ZIP
CALIFORNIA	IRVINE	94203
CALIFORNIA	IRVINE	94211
CALIFORNIA	IRVINE	94251
CALIFORNIA	IRVINE	94521
CALIFORNIA	LOS ANGELES	94725
CALIFORNIA	LOS ANGELES	94752
CALIFORNIA	LOS ANGELES	94789
CALIFORNIA	SAN FRANCISCO	94501
CALIFORNIA	SAN FRANCISCO	94521
CALIFORNIA	SAN FRANCISCO	94536
CALIFORNIA	SAN FRANCISCO	94536
CALIFORNIA	SAN FRANCISCO	94587
CALIFORNIA	SAN FRANCISCO	94598
NEW YORK	ALBANY	11420
NEW YORK	ALBANY	11458
NEW YORK	ALBANY	11467
NEW YORK	ALBANY	11487
NEW YORK	ALBANY	11489
NEW YORK	BUFFALO	11002
NEW YORK	BUFFALO	11475
NEW YORK	BUFFALO	11520
NEW YORK	NEW YORK	11200
NEW YORK	NEW YORK	11202
NEW YORK	NEW YORK	11235
NEW YORK	NEW YORK	11253
NEW YORK	NEW YORK	11434
NEW YORK	POUGHKEEPSIE	11035
NEW YORK	POUGHKEEPSIE	11036
NEW YORK	TROY	11300
NEW YORK	TROY	11352
NEW YORK	TROY	11369
NEW YORK	TROY	11378
OREGON	BILLING	12703
OREGON	BILLING	12754
OREGON	MUCHO	12345
OREGON	MUCHO	12346
OREGON	MUCHO	12347
OREGON	MUCHO	12348
OREGON	TRAVINA	12005
OREGON	TUCHAHOE	12402
OREGON	TUCHAHOE	12423
OREGON	TUCHAHOE	12456
OREGON	TUCHAHOE	12485

```
WER045I  END SORT PH
WER055A  INSERT        43, DELETE        43
WER177I  TURNAROUND SORT PERFORMED
WER054A  RCD IN        , OUT
WER169I  TPF'S APPLIED 123456789ABCDEF
WER052I  END SYNCSORT   OPT= M,  SORT6  ,GO
***SORT COMPLETED***
```

14.8 THE INPUT PROCEDURE

Suppose now we have some alphabetic data punched on cards in a predetermined field and our purpose is not only to print out the input data but also to sort it into alphabetical order before printing the sorted data (this is the substance of Program 48, which follows). Since we plan on acting on the input data *before* it is sent to the SORT module, we can no longer take advantage of the USING option. Instead, we are forced to use the INPUT PROCEDURE option. However, if we resort to this option, it is our responsibility to code the instructions which OPEN and CLOSE the input file, and MOVE the data to the SORT area, something which the USING clause did for us automatically in each of the SORT programs illustrated so far.

The purpose of the INPUT PROCEDURE is to process the input data according to the programmer's directions and then to transfer or release the data to the SORT module for sorting. Remember that since the USING clause is not included, it is the programmer's responsibility to provide the instructions to OPEN and CLOSE the input file.

In the program which follows, the section associated with the INPUT PROCEDURE is the PRINT–THE–NAME–UNSORTED SECTION. Within this section the input file IN–FILE is opened, a header is printed, the input file is read, its contents printed; the input information is moved to the sort record and released to the SORT module for sorting. The release to the sort phase is accomplished by means of the RELEASE verb. Once a record has been RE-LEASEd it is sorted immediately. The RELEASE verb could be regarded as a WRITE instruction, in which the data being released from the sort record are written on the *sort module.*

When the AT END condition is encountered while reading the input file IN–FILE, control is sent to the paragraph CLOSE–THE–FILES. At this point the sorted data will have been written onto the area of disk called SORT–FILE, which is closed automatically as part of the sort package. The header *** SORTED NAMES *** is moved to CARD–OUT, which is immediately written. Both the input and output files are then closed. Closing the output file might seem to the reader to be an error of logic since we are closing it immediately prior to writing the sorted names, which after all is the purpose of the program. The fact of the matter is that this last portion of the Procedure Division, CLOSE–THE–FILES, represents the concluding segment of the INPUT PROCEDURE, that is, PRINT–THE–NAME–UNSORTED. The next instruction to be executed is in the SORT paragraph. This instruction is GIVING OUT–FILE. As we already know, the GIVING option automatically opens the file in question. It is mandatory for us, therefore, to close the file before executing the GIVING instruction. Since OUT–FILE is assigned to the PRINTER, the sorted names are printed in the desired manner.

INPUT TO PROGRAM 48

```
SMITH JOHN
MULLISH HENRY
OPAS ELI
HODGES BARBARA
JONES DAVID
```

PROGRAM 48
Sort 7

```
00001     IDENTIFICATION DIVISION.
00002     PROGRAM-ID. SORT-SEVEN.
00003     AUTHOR. ELI J. OPAS.
00004
00005     ENVIRONMENT DIVISION.
00006
00007     INPUT-OUTPUT SECTION.
00008     FILE-CONTROL.
00009         SELECT IN-FILE   ASSIGN TO UT-S-READER.
00010         SELECT OUT-FILE ASSIGN TO UT-S-PRINTER.
00011         SELECT SORT-FILE ASSIGN TO UT-S-SORTLIB.
00012
00013     DATA DIVISION.
00014
00015     FILE SECTION.
```

```
00016
00017          FD   IN-FILE
00018               LABEL RECORDS ARE OMITTED.
00019          01   CARD-IN.
00020               05  NAME-IN           PICTURE X(25).
00021               05  FILLER            PICTURE X(55).
00022
00023          FD   OUT-FILE
00024               LABEL RECORDS ARE OMITTED.
00025          01   CARD-OUT.
00026               05  NAME-OUT          PICTURE X(25).
00027               05  FILLER            PICTURE X(55).
00028
00029          SD   SORT-FILE.
00030          01   NAME-SORT.
00031               05  SORT-NAME         PICTURE X(25).
00032               05  FILLER            PICTURE X(55).
00033
00034          PROCEDURE DIVISION.
00035
00036          SORT-THE-NAME SECTION.
00037
00038          SORT-IT-OUT.
00039
00040              SORT SORT-FILE
00041              ASCENDING KEY SORT-NAME
00042              INPUT PROCEDURE PRINT-THE-NAME-UNSORTED
00043              GIVING OUT-FILE.
00044
00045              STOP RUN.
00046
00047          PRINT-THE-NAME-UNSORTED SECTION.
00048
00049          OPEN-THE-FILES.
00050              OPEN INPUT IN-FILE, OUTPUT OUT-FILE.
00051
00052          PRINT-UNSORTED-HEADING.
00053
00054              MOVE '*** UNSORTED NAMES ***' TO CARD-OUT.
00055              WRITE CARD-OUT.
00056
00057          READ-AND-WRITE.
00058              READ IN-FILE AT END GO TO CLOSE-THE-FILES.
00059              WRITE CARD-OUT FROM CARD-IN.
00060              MOVE CARD-IN TO NAME-SORT.
00061              RELEASE NAME-SORT.
00062              GO TO READ-AND-WRITE.
00063
00064          CLOSE-THE-FILES.
00065              MOVE SPACES TO CARD-OUT.
00066              WRITE CARD-OUT.
00067              MOVE '*** SORTED NAMES ***' TO CARD-OUT.
00068              WRITE CARD-OUT.
00069              CLOSE IN-FILE, OUT-FILE.
```

OUTPUT TO PROGRAM 48

```
*** UNSORTED NAMES ***
SMITH JOHN
MULLISH HENRY
OPAS ELI
HODGES BARBARA
JONES DAVID

*** SORTED NAMES ***
HODGES BARBARA
JONES DAVID
MULLISH HENRY
OPAS ELI
SMITH JOHN


WER045I  END SORT PH
WER055A  INSERT      5, DELETE      5
WER177I  TURNAROUND SORT PERFORMED
WER054A  RCD IN      , OUT
WER165I  TPF'S APPLIED 123456789ABCDEF
WER052I  END SYNCSORT  OPT= M,  SORT7  ,GC     ,
```

14.9 USING BOTH INPUT AND OUTPUT PROCEDURES

The last situation which we shall cover in our study of sorting techniques is the case in which the input and the output data to the SORT module are to be modified. Analogous to the INPUT PROCEDURE, which may be selected in place of the USING option, there is an OUTPUT PROCEDURE, which may replace the GIVING option.

The input data to the program which follows contains the following information:

col	1–25	name of driver
	26–30	number of miles driven
	36–37	number of recorded accidents

The purpose of the program is to select from the input file only those driver records which indicate that the driver has logged more than 25,000 miles and has had less than three accidents. These are to be transmitted to the sort file and sorted according to descending order of miles travelled and ascending order of name (that is, in alphabetical order).

Just as the RELEASE statement is analogous to the WRITE verb, so a RETURN statement functions as a READ. The general form of the RETURN statement is

```
RETURN sort-file-name RECORD [INTO identifier]
AT END imperative-statement
```

where the RETURN statement causes sorted records from the SORT module to be accessed. The INTO option behaves like an automatic MOVE and AT END indicates the action to be taken when no more sorted records are left.

A listing of the input cards to Program 49 follows in the input for the program.

INPUT TO PROGRAM 49

```
HENRY MULLISH          28000    00
ELI OPAS               25000    00
JOHN MALLON            15000    00
LORI KUKIN             29000    01
MICHAEL LEGMAN         10000    05
SUSAN MAILMAN          25000    00
MARK PEARLMUTTER       10000    04
BARBARA HODGES         32000    00
PAUL MCKAY             56000    01
ROBERT FREEMON         30000    02
PETER MCKAY            56000    02
DANNY SCHWARTZMAN      75000    02
PAULA MCKAY            56000    03
ROBERT SAWHILL         50000    03
CHARLES CHAPLIN        25555    02
CHESTER MORRIS         30000    03
RINGO STARR            42000    05
JOHN SAWHILL           50000    01
DAVID BLAUSTEIN        75000    00
```

PROGRAM 49
Sort 8

```
00001          IDENTIFICATION DIVISION.
00002          PROGRAM-ID. SCRT-EIGHT.
00003          AUTHOR. ELI J. OPAS.
00004          REMARKS. A SORT WITH BOTH AN INPUT AND OUTPUT PROCEDURE.
00005          ENVIRONMENT DIVISION.
00006          INPUT-OUTPUT SECTION.
00007          FILE-CONTROL.
00008              SELECT IN-FILE ASSIGN TO UT-S-READER.
00009              SELECT SORT-FILE ASSIGN TO UT-S-SORTER.
00010              SELECT OUT-FILE ASSIGN TO UT-S-PRINTER.
00011
00012          DATA DIVISION.
00013          FILE SECTION.
00014          FD  IN-FILE
00015              LABEL RECORDS ARE OMITTED.
00016
00017          01  DRIVER-IN.
00018              05 NAME-IN         PICTURE X(25).
00019              05 MILES-IN        PICTURE 9(5).
00020              05 FILLER          PICTURE X(5).
00021              05 ACCIDENTS-IN    PICTURE 9(02).
00022              05 FILLER          PICTURE X(43).
00023
00024          FD  OUT-FILE
00025              LABEL RECORDS ARE OMITTED.
00026
00027          01  WINNER-OUT.
00028              05 NAME-OUT         PICTURE X(25).
00029              05 MILES-OUT        PICTURE 9(5).
00030              05 FILLER           PICTURE X(5).
00031              05 ACCIDENTS-OUT    PICTURE 99.
00032              05 FILLER           PICTURE X(43).
00033
00034          SD  SORT-FILE.
00035          01  DRIVER-SORT.
00036              05 SORT-NAME       PICTURE X(25).
00037              05 SORT-MILES      PICTURE 9(5).
00038              05 FILLER          PICTURE X(5).
00039              05 SORT-ACCIDENTS  PICTURE 99.
00040              05 FILLER          PICTURE X(43).
00041
00042          PROCEDURE DIVISION.
00043          SORT-THEM-OUT.
00044              SORT SORT-FILE
00045              DESCENDING KEY SORT-MILES
00046              ASCENDING KEY SORT-ACCIDENTS
00047              ASCENDING KEY SORT-NAME
00048              INPUT PROCEDURE FIND-THE-ELIGIBLE-DRIVER
00049              OUTPUT PROCEDURE LIST-THE-WINNERS.
00050              STOP RUN.
00051
00052          FIND-THE-ELIGIBLE-DRIVER SECTION.
00053          OPEN-IN-FILE.
00054              OPEN INPUT IN-FILE.
00055
00056          SCREEN-THE-DRIVERS.
00057              READ IN-FILE AT END GO TO CLOSE-IN-FILE.
00058              IF MILES-IN > 25000 AND ACCIDENTS-IN < 3
00059              RELEASE DRIVER-SORT FROM DRIVER-IN.
00060              GO TO SCREEN-THE-DRIVERS.
00061
00062          CLOSE-IN-FILE.
00063              CLOSE IN-FILE.
00064
00065          LIST-THE-WINNERS SECTION.
00066
00067          PREPARE-TO-LIST.
00068              OPEN OUTPUT OUT-FILE.
00069              MOVE '  *** WINNING DRIVERS ***' TO WINNER-OUT.
00070              WRITE WINNER-OUT.
00071              MOVE SPACES TO WINNER-OUT.
00072
00073          LIST-WINNING-DRIVERS.
00074              RETURN SORT-FILE RECORD INTO WINNER-OUT
00075                  AT END GO TO CLOSE-OUT-FILE.
00076              WRITE WINNER-OUT.
00077              GO TO LIST-WINNING-DRIVERS.
00078          CLOSE-OUT-FILE.
```

```
00079                    CLOSE OUT-FILE.
00080
00081        EXIT-PARA.
00082            EXIT.
```

OUTPUT TO PROGRAM 49

```
    *** WINNING DRIVERS ***
DAVID BLAUSTEIN        75000     00
DANNY SCHWARTZMAN      75000     02
PAUL MCKAY             56000     01
PETER MCKAY            56000     02
JOHN SAWHILL           50000     01
BARBARA HODGES         32000     00
ROBERT FREEMON         30000     02
LORI KUKIN             29000     01
HENRY MULLISH          28000     00
CHARLES CHAPLIN        25555     02
```

14.10 REVIEW EXERCISE

1. Write a COBOL program which will sort a card file using an input procedure to select only those records for the sort which have an asterisk in column 80. The cards should be sorted in ascending order on the basis of the Social Security number, which is punched in columns 20–28. Assume that all remaining columns contain valid information. The sorted records should then be listed by means of an output procedure.

15

WRITING, RUNNING, CHECKING, AND DEBUGGING PROGRAMS

Writing a computer program to solve a particular problem represents only the middle segment of a three-phase operation. Once the problem has been defined, a method of solving it has to be developed; this is the first phase. The method then has to be translated into the instructions, operations, and options available to the COBOL programmer and the program written, punched, and run on the computer with sample data. This is the major phase, the actual writing of the program. It is only fair to say to the novice programmer that it is most unlikely that the program will run correctly the first time. In the event that the reader thinks that the programs illustrated in this text all worked the first time, or even were written originally in the way they appear in their published form, let it be said without any hesitation that this is far from the truth. Almost all of the programs required extensive amendments before they worked correctly and were regarded as acceptable for inclusion in the text. One can only imagine the author's frustration and anguish that accompanied the evolution of the programs from their original to their final states. In most cases, however, the sense of satisfaction and gratification achieved when a program does *exactly* what it is supposed to do far outweighs the irritation, even the torment, experienced along the way. The fact of the matter is that the computer is an awfully dumb machine. It does what you tell it to do, not necessarily what you intended it to do. The finding and eliminating of errors—the debugging stage—is the third phase.

Since the kinds of errors one can make are so varied, one has to adopt a kind of strategy when writing a program. After all, one may make errors of logic and syntax, and of keypunching itself; and one can misspell data names, and use reserved words in places other than in their correct places. Since there exists what amounts to an inevitability of making errors, one must reconcile oneself to this fact and program accordingly. For example, intermediate results may be seen by inserting into the program a liberal sprinkling of DISPLAY statements for the first run or two. This might help to clear up the initial mistakes, or, as they are called, *bugs*. Once the bugs have been cleared up—in official jargon, once the program has been *debugged*—the DISPLAY statements can be eliminated. In what may be termed "defensive programming" one can prepare as much as possible for many types of errors. Any effort expended in devising tricks or traps to catch bugs will pay off handsomely, for the time spent in finding a bug can far exceed the time required to anticipate it.

The compiler is geared to help the programmer as much as possible. It spends a certain amount of time checking for errors of syntax. If one is found, a *diagnostic* message is printed out matching the number of the card in violation with the description of the detected error. The different kinds of diagnostic messages run into the hundreds. In fact, if you would like to see for yourself a complete list of the diagnostics that are possible on the IBM 370, try running the following simple, five-line program. The PROGRAM-ID name ERRMSG is a special name reserved for this particular chore.

PROGRAM 50
ERRMSG

```
IDENTIFICATION DIVISION.
PROGRAM-ID. ERRMSG.
ENVIRONMENT DIVISION.
DATA DIVISION.
PROCEDURE DIVISION.
```

In essence program errors fall into two categories: those which become manifest during compilation and those which become apparent during execution of the program. Four types of errors are flagged by the system. This is done by printing out the number of the card in violation, an error code, and finally the error message itself. The four types of errors are coded w, c, e and d. Sometimes more than one will appear as the result of a single error.

15.1. w LEVEL DIAGNOSTICS

The least severe of the errors is the warning, coded with the letter w. It does not interfere with the running of the program and informs the programmer that the instruction, though not entirely in keeping with the rules, has been accepted. A typical w level diagnostic would be a warning that a data name is too long or is truncated, or an item has been moved into a field which is not big enough to contain all of it (this could easily have been intentional on the part of the programmer), or a blank space has been omitted where one should have been. Often these w-type diagnostics are ignored, but it is recommended that the errors be corrected and the program rerun. If these w level diagnostics are not corrected, anyone subsequently looking at the program will waste time checking over each diagnostic to ensure that it is not a potential source of error.

15.2 c LEVEL DIAGNOSTICS

In a c level diagnostic the compiler has detected some sort of ambiguity and has made a guess at the intended operation. If the guess is correct, all is well and the program is not in need of human intervention. The results produced will probably be fine, but only on *condition* that the right guess has been made by the compiler. It is for this reason it is called a c level diagnostic. It is strongly advised that all c level diagnostics be corrected before the program is regarded as acceptable.

15.3 e LEVEL DIAGNOSTICS

The compiler finds the two previous levels of diagnostics (w and c) during compilation, the initial phase that the program undergoes. Sometimes, however, errors do not become apparent until the program is actually in execution. Such errors are regarded with such severity that execution is terminated abruptly. These fatal execution errors are flagged with the code letter e. The omission of a required paragraph name, for example, is a primary candidate for an e level diagnostic. The violation must be corrected before the program is resubmitted.

15.4 d LEVEL DIAGNOSTICS

The d level diagnostic is the most severe kind possible in COBOL. It stands for "disaster." This is the diagnostic which is printed out in the event of a compiler error, a contingency over which the programmer has no control. It is extremely rare and ordinarily the programmer may never see a d level error during a whole career. Running a FORTRAN program on a COBOL compiler might produce a d level diagnostic!

15.5 COBOL DEBUGGING AIDS

There are various alternatives, some or even all of which may be incorporated into a COBOL program, that will make the task of debugging a program easier. As already mentioned, a liberal sprinkling of DISPLAY statements is always a good idea. But COBOL provides the programmer with other specially designed debugging features to overcome those most embarrassing moments when neither compilation nor execution bugs have been detected, yet no output is produced. Such features are used simultaneously with other elementary techniques such as using dummy data to test for all possible contingencies and real data to check out the program for the specific application under the normal prevailing conditions.

One of the most common debugging features on the IBM 370 is

what is known as the *trace*. Suppose we have a program whose Procedure
Division is composed of a series of paragraphs, each, of course, with its
own unique paragraph name. The instruction READY TRACE, when inserted
in the Procedure Division (in the B margin), causes the system to print
out during execution the names of each paragraph name executed in
the order of execution. On some systems these paragraph names are
printed along the width of the page and on others underneath each other.
To "switch off" the trace, as it were, the instruction RESET TRACE is used.
This feature is particularly helpful in isolating errors of logic. As soon
as the error has been isolated and corrected, the trace statements should
be removed from the deck.

Another useful device is to place EXHIBIT statements at key points,
or "check points," along the program. In its most elementary form the
EXHIBIT statement behaves simply as a DISPLAY statement. For example,
inserting

```
EXHIBIT RETAIL-PRICE
```

at a point of the program in the B margin, where RETAIL–PRICE is a data
name in the program, will print out its value at that pont. Similarly,
inserting

```
EXHIBIT 'REACHED RETAIL-PRICE-PARA'
```

will print out the message in quotes.
The instruction

```
EXHIBIT GROSS-PAY, ' IS THE GROSS PAY'
```

will print out first the value of the data name GROSS–PAY, which is followed
in turn on the same line by the message in quotes. In order to ensure
that there is a separation between the value printed out for GROSS-PAY
and its accompanying message a blank is deliberately included as the
first character of the quoted message.

A more interesting version of the EXHIBIT statement is the form which
prints out first the *name* of the data name, then an equal sign, a space,
and finally the actual value of the data name. For example, the instruction

```
EXHIBIT NAMED GROSS-PAY
```

will print out the data name and its value in the following form:

```
GROSS-PAY = 123456
```

where the actual data name is followed by an equals sign with a blank
on each side. By the same token the instruction

EXHIBIT NAMED GROSS–PAY 'WEEKLY WAGE ONLY'

would print out when executed

GROSS–PAY = 123456 WEEKLY WAGE ONLY

For those occasions when it is desired to print out the value of a data name only if its value *has changed from the last time the instruction was executed,* yet another form of the EXHIBIT may be used. For example, if we want to check whether GROSS–PAY had changed its value we can write

EXHIBIT CHANGED GROSS–PAY

If the value of GROSS–PAY had, in fact, changed, its present value would have been printed out preceded by an equals sign and a blank.

Finally, there is a version of the EXHIBIT which combines both the NAMED and the CHANGED options. As you might have guessed, it is the CHANGED NAME option, as in

EXHIBIT CHANGED NAME GROSS–PAY

where the value of GROSS–PAY will be printed alongside the printout GROSS–PAY = , only if its value has changed.

To conclude this chapter, we will mention another option which is usually found associated with the EXHIBIT statement—the ON option. For example,

ON 650 EXHIBIT NAMED GROSS–PAY

will print out the word GROSS–PAY = , followed by the current value of GROSS–PAY after the instruction has been executed 650 times.

15.6 JOB CONTROL LANGUAGE (JCL) FOR THE IBM 370 OS SYSTEM

In order to run any COBOL program, it is necessary to punch certain control cards which must accompany the program. The Job Control Language (JCL) cards, which we shall describe here, apply to the IBM 360/370 system, probably the most popular commercial computer system in the world today.

The COBOL program itself together with its data and associated control cards constitute a "job." In order to identify the user to the system, the very first control card (often referred to as the *job card*) contains the user's account number and the name of the user. This enables the system to ascertain that the account is valid and verifies the associated user's name. In addition to this information, the user must supply a job name composed of up to eight characters. A job name must begin with an alphabetic

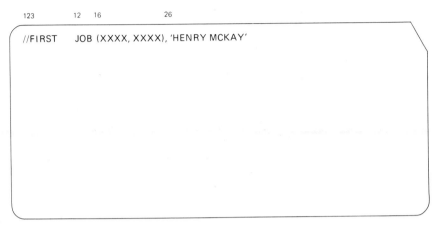

```
 123      12  16            26

//FIRST    JOB (XXXX, XXXX), 'HENRY MCKAY'
```

FIGURE 33

character but may be followed by either alphabetic or numeric characters. No special symbols such as a period, comma, or a minus sign, and so on, may be used—and this includes the blank space. The job name serves to identify the particular job to the supervisory system.

Figure 33 shows a typical job card.

The job card must begin with a slash in columns 1 and 2 and is immediately followed by the job name. The word JOB, which starts in column 12, must be preceded and followed by a space. Within the parentheses, beginning with column 16, is the account number which is supplied to authorized users by the installation. After the closing parenthesis is a comma followed immediately (that means no space!) by the name of the user, which is enclosed within apostrophes.

The second control card is generally the EXEC card, which specifies the particular compiler to be used. At NYU it is currently the version COBOLU (the ANSI compiler). Other compliers which may be available at various installations are COBOLE, COBOLF, COBUCS, and COBACG, which will all compile and execute a COBOL program.

Figure 34 shows a typical EXEC card.

The third control card is punched

```
//COB.SYSIN DD *
```

This card specifies that the COBOL program itself follows immediately. Therefore the four divisions of the program follow this //COB.SYSIN DD * card. After the program is a card punched with /* in columns 1 and 2, which indicates the end of the program. What follows after the /* card depends upon the nature of the program.

```
12 4      9
// EXEC COBOLU
```

FIGURE 34

1. If the only input/output verb used in the program is DISPLAY (as done in Program 1 in the text) the only cards necessary are:

```
//GO.SYSOUT DD SYSOUT=A
//
```

2. If the ACCEPT also is used in the program the following set-up is necessary:

```
//GO.SYSOUT DD SYSOUT=A
//GO.SYSIN DD *
    data card(s) to be read by ACCEPT
/*
//
```

3. If just WRITE's are used, as was done in Program 5, the following JCL is required:

```
//GO.mnemonic-name DD SYSOUT=A
//
```

The mnemonic-name is the programmer-selected name associated with the file in question. For an output file a common choice is PRINTER, but PAYFILE, ACCTREC, and ACCTPAY are just as acceptable. Whatever name is chosen must appear in the SELECT clause in the Environment Division.

4. For a program using READ's, WRITE's and DISPLAY's, the necessary JCL is

```
/*
//GO.SYSOUT DD SYSOUT=A
//GO.READER DD *
    data
/*
//
```

where the output file is assigned to SYSOUT and the input file to READER in the SELECT clauses.

5. If the programmer wishes any output produced by a DISPLAY instruction to be printed on a *separate* page, the JCL is

```
/*
//GO.SYSOUT DD SYSOUT=A
//GO.PRINTER DD SYSOUT=A
//GO.READER DD *
    data
/*
//
```

Almost all of the programs run and discussed in this book have the setup as indicated in 4 above. The complete deck looks as shown in Figure 35.

15.7 INTERPRETING SYSTEM TERMINATION CODES

When writing a COBOL program, one of course takes the utmost care. It often transpires (much too frequently as a matter of fact), however, that despite our valiant attempts, errors of logic or of keypunching do creep in. The system has been designed so that if it detects an error and abnormally ends (ABENDS) the program, it categorizes the source of the error according to a system code. These codes are usually prefixed by 0C (zero C) followed by a digit and are printed out before the listing of the program.

The termination code 0C1 is generally caused by an attempt to read or write a file which has not yet been opened, or one which has been closed.

Code 0C2 is caused by a missing or a misspelled DD statement in the JCL.

Code 0C4 is caused by subscripting beyond the length of the table. An uninitialized subscript or index will also cause an 0C4, as indeed will an attempt to enter a so-called "protected" area. Once again, an attempt to read an unopened file may cause an 0C4 error message.

An uninitialized subscript or index can cause an 0C5 error. Other causes include subscripts which are too large, an OPEN statement which has failed due to JCL errors, or a misspelled or missing DD statement. Still other causes are attempting to close an already closed file, making an improper exit from a PERFORM, or attempting to access an input or

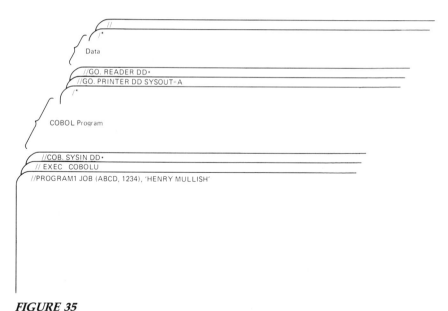

```
                                         //
                                       /*
                              Data
                          //GO. READER DD·
                          //GO. PRINTER DD SYSOUT=A
                        /*
                 COBOL Program

              //COB. SYSIN DD·
             // EXEC   COBOLU
           //PROGRAM1 JOB (ABCD, 1234), 'HENRY MULLISH'
```

FIGURE 35

output area before a READ or an OPEN instruction for the file in question is executed.

Code 0C6 may be caused by an improper exit from a PERFORM statement.

Code 0C7 is probably the most frequent execution time-error message encountered by students who are novices in the COBOL language. The most common reason for an 0C7 error message is that the data are not of the correct form. Blank spaces within a numeric field will cause an 0C7 error, as indeed will the inclusion of a decimal point, comma, dollar sign, or any other nonnumeric character.

Finally, a program which for some reason or other exceeds the allotted execution time may be terminated and the completion code 322 printed. Two possible reasons for this error are (1) that the computation actually requires a greater time period than either the user has specified in the JCL or the "default" time allows, or (2) the program is caught in an infinite loop.

MISCELLANEOUS TOPICS

16.1 SIGNED NUMBERS

In all of the programs we have encountered so far, all numeric fields have been assigned a picture of one or more 9's. For example, the data names for Social Security numbers, identification numbers, hours worked, rate per hour all have fields of 9's. When assigning a picture of all 9's, it is implied that the number in question is positive. In fact, if the result of a subtraction of two numbers were negative, and its result had a picture of all 9's only, the result would be printed as a positive number, which would be the absolute value of the correct result. In certain situations this could lead to disastrous consequences. In order to insure that the appropriate sign of a number is retained, its associated picture must be preceded by the letter S. Many professional programmers consider it good programming practice to use the letter S in the pictures of all numeric fields. For example, suppose in Working–Storage we have the two following 77 level items:

```
77 UNSIGNED-FIELD PICTURE  999.
77 SIGNED-FIELD    PICTURE S999.
```

If in the Procedure Division we then execute the following statements

```
MOVE -50 TO UNSIGNED-FIELD, SIGNED-FIELD.
DISPLAY   UNSIGNED-FIELD, SIGNED-FIELD.
```

The numbers

50   -50

will be stored internally and will be printed as shown. In the case of the unsigned field, UNSIGNED–FIELD, with the picture of 999 rather than S999, the printed result of 50 is obviously incorrect. It is important to note that the presence of an S in a numeric field does not alter the size of the field at all, and should not be counted when totalling up the characters in the record.

When reading in a negative number as a numeric data item, one might think that all one has to do is to precede the number with a negative sign. This is not so. One must first of all make sure that the associated picture is preceded by an S and that the negative sign is *multipunched* over the rightmost digit. However strange this concept appears, the correct negative value will be read in. Once again, the minus sign is not counted in the width of the data field.

16.1.1. The SIGN Clause

IBM COBOL provides the programmer with a method of reading in data which have minus signs either to the left or to the right. Normally a negative number punched on data cards is assumed to have the negative sign overpunched on the rightmost digit. Using the SIGN clause, one may specify whether the sign (usually negative) is punched to the left or to the right of the number. For example

$$-12345 \quad +12345 \quad 12345- \quad 12345+$$

would be acceptable punched data items provided the SIGN clause were used. It has the form

$$[\underline{SIGN} \text{ IS}] \left\{ \begin{matrix} \underline{LEADING} \\ \underline{TRAILING} \end{matrix} \right\} [\underline{SEPARATE} \text{ CHARACTER}]$$

This somewhat uncommonly used instruction may be part of an input record description in the Data Division. Here are some examples of how the SIGN clause may be used, indicating the effective size of the corresponding field.

DATA ITEM AS PUNCHED ON CARD	ENTRY DESCRIPTION	SIZE OF PUNCHED FIELD
1̄23	PICTURE S999	3
123̄	PICTURE S999 SIGN IS TRAILING	3
123+	PICTURE S999 SIGN TRAILING SEPARATE	4
−123	PICTURE S999 SIGN IS LEADING SEPARATE CHARACTER	4

If the SIGN clause is omitted, it is assumed to be SIGN IS TRAILING. Only if the SEPARATE option is used is the character S in the PICTURE clause included in the size of the field.

16.1.2. The STOP Statement

Throughout this text we have terminated each program by execution of the statement STOP RUN. Since this instruction permanently stops execution of the program, it cannot be restarted short of reading it in again. However, this is not the only form of the STOP; it is possible to instruct the computer to both pause and print a message by means of the following form of the instruction:

STOP literal

This statement also causes the computer to stop executing. The literal in question may be either a numeric or a non-numeric literal. For example, we might have

STOP 'OUT OF DATA'.

or

STOP 1234.

In both these cases the execution of the STOP instruction causes a pause in execution. This time, however, the program may be restarted by the intervention of the operator. The literal specified in the STOP instruction is printed on the printer before the computer comes a halt.

In the case of a numeric literal, a list of numeric error codes might be established and given to the operator; when one of these errors is encountered, he will be able to consult his list of error codes and determine what action to take to rectify the matter. The operator can then restart the job.

16.2 THE USAGE CLAUSE

As the reader is well aware, all COBOL instructions are ultimately converted to the language the computer really understands, namely the binary language. If one were to pry open the cover of the computer memory, one would be confronted by a dazzling array of switches represented only by zeroes and ones, and nothing else. Nevertheless, for various purposes the formats of certain data are stored differently depending upon their intended usage. The informed programmer is at liberty to state the intended usage of his data. By doing so, he can optimize the efficiency of his program. The clause

USAGE IS

may be used for describing data which may be one of the following types:

```
DISPLAY
⎰COMPUTATIONAL-3
⎱COMP-3
⎰COMPUTATIONAL
⎱COMP
```

where COMPUTATIONAL-3 may be abbreviated to COMP-3, and likewise COMPUTATIONAL to COMP. However, the clause USAGE IS may always be omitted entirely.

DISPLAY is the term used to describe the manner in which both input and output information is stored internally. Assembly language programmers, those programmers who code programs in a language much closer to that of the computer, refer to this mode of representation as *zoned decimal* or *unpacked* format. If there is no usage clause specified in the record description, USAGE is assumed to be DISPLAY. DISPLAY is therefore said to be the default option. In the first of the next two examples, the USAGE clause is explicitly stated whereas in the second it is implied. Nevertheless, both examples are treated in an equivalent manner by the COBOL compiler:

```
05 WAGES PICTURE 999V99 USAGE IS DISPLAY.
05 WAGES PICTURE 999V99.
```

Computational data (data which will be used for arithmetic purposes) may be efficiently stored in its so-called packed form. COBOL programmers can specify this format by writing

```
USAGE IS COMPUTATIONAL-3.
```

or

```
USAGE IS COMP-3.
```

or

```
COMPUTATION-3.
```

or simply

```
COMP-3.
```

If a number is stored in DISPLAY format, and used in a calculation, it first has to be converted from DISPLAY format (unpacked) to COMP-3 (packed), the calculation done in COMP-3, and, finally, the result converted to DISPLAY (unpacked) for printing the result. Each of these conversions, of course, takes precious computer time. When COMP-3 is used, all these conversions to and from packed format are avoided and the execution of the program made much more efficient. COMP-3 format is specified for numeric fields only, and is never used for reading cards or for printing.

The COMPUTATIONAL form (binary), or COMP as it is usually written, is invariably used for storing data in strict binary form. There are many purposes for which binary arithmetic is considered both more efficient and desirable. Counting operations are often specified to be COMPUTATIONAL. If one attempts to display data stored in COMPUTATIONAL form, the output will be printed in binary, a form which we human beings have much trouble in deciphering. If, however, such data are DISPLAYed or EXHIBITed, they will be printed in display form, leaving them in their original form internally. Many professional programmers use COMP for counters, subscripts, table values, and data names used strictly for computation.

16.3 HARDWARE

The computing environment is generally divided up into *hardware* and *software*. The main frame of the computer, for example, is generally the most conspicuous part of the hardware. Other hardware elements are the disks, the operating panel, the card reader, the line printer, and drum. The picture below shows an IBM 370/145 computer center with its various hardware members. The disk storage unit is in the far right corner, while the card punch is in the far left. The card reader is front left and the high-speed printer is front right. All the way to the left are the tape drives and in the back left is the operator's console.

The keypunch machine is often the standard hardware device for punching input cards. A trained keypunch operator is capable of keypunching cards rapidly and accurately by means of the so-called "drumcard." It is beyond the scope of this book to describe in detail how the

drum may be exploited, but it is nonetheless recommended that an intro-duction to its use be requested of the keypunch operator.

There is also another machine (not illustrated) which is called a *verifier*. Once a program deck has been punched, it may then be checked with a verifier machine, preferably by an operator other than the one who punched the deck initially. Each card is treated as if it were to be repunched. No holes are punched this time; instead, spring-loaded plung-ers take the place of the punch mechanism. If holes actually appear where they are supposed to, the plungers penetrate the holes and the column is considered to be correctly keypunched. If, however, there is a dis-crepancy between the punched card and what the verifier operator has keyed in, a red light is actuated to alert the operator to the discrepancy. Either the card has been initially punched incorrectly, or an error has been made during the verification process. Either way, the appropriate action must be taken. In effect, therefore, verifying a deck is tantamount to repunching the whole deck again, a time-consuming luxury not every-one can afford.

16.3.1. Magnetic Tapes

Some commercial installations record all of their business transactions on magnetic tape. Some of them have libraries consisting literally of hun-dreds of magnetic tape reels. In early computers, magnetic tape was actu-ally made of a long strip of paper-thin steel. Modern computers, however,

use continuous strips of plastic tape, coated on one side with a metallic oxide. Usually the tape is one-half inch wide and can be in any of the standard lengths of 250, 600, 1200, or 2400 feet securely wound around plastic reels. This is the same type of tape as used in tape recorders, where audio signals are recorded on the tape. With a computer, however, data are recorded by a system of magnetized spots conforming to a specific pattern for each specific character. These "bits," as they are called, correspond to the form in which the information is actually stored in the internal memory of the computer. Notice the mounted tape on the right hand side of the picture below, just above the video screen.

16.3.2. Disk Storage

Despite the considerable advantages that magnetic tapes offer for storing masses of information, they suffer from the disadvantage that in order to get from one item of information to another the entire length of tape between the two items must be scanned. In other words, to access the seven hundred and fiftieth record on the tape, 749 records must first be processed before the desired record can be accessed. Obviously for many situations, this method of accessing information can be extremely inefficient and expensive.

In order to provide a much faster method of accessing mass data, *disk* drives were invented and today are one of the most common means of storing voluminous data. A disk pack rotates at a constant speed much like a phonograph record. Instead of only one platter, the disk pack usually contains eleven metal disks permanently attached to a central spindle

as shown in Figure 36. No information may be written on either the top surface of the uppermost disk nor on the undersurface of the lowermost disk. On each of the surfaces are a specific number of concentric circles called *tracks*. In the Model 2316 disk pack, for example, there are 200 concentric circles (tracks) on each of the 20 usable surfaces. There are therefore 20×200 tracks per disk pack, making for a total of 4000 tracks on which data can be either written or accessed. Although these concentric circles get smaller towards the center of the disk, each of the tracks, regardless of position, has the same data capacity.

As in the case of magnetic tape, data are recorded on disk as magnetic spots called bits, corresponding to the manner in which the data are stored internally.

When data are either written on the disk or read from the disk, movable read/write heads move in and out to the appropriate track. Even though only one track may be accessed at any given moment, whenever the access mechanism moves, all 20 read/write heads move simultaneously. For any position therefore, 20 tracks can be accessed without moving the head mechanism. Each set of these 20 tracks is regarded as a *cylinder*. Unlike magnetic tape, information on disk may be directly accessed. It is for this reason that disk is the kind of device referred to as a DASD (pronounced *das-dee*), which stands for Direct Access Storage Device.

16.4 SOFTWARE

No computer is of any value if it does not come equipped with the system routines to control it. These system routines contain the supervisory routine, the library routines, the compilers, and the utility routines. The software may be viewed in a manner analogous to the automobile, which requires fuel for it to function at all. Writing the programs for the software packages can range in complexity from a simple COBOL program to a highly sophisticated assembler (binary) program. The overall computer system

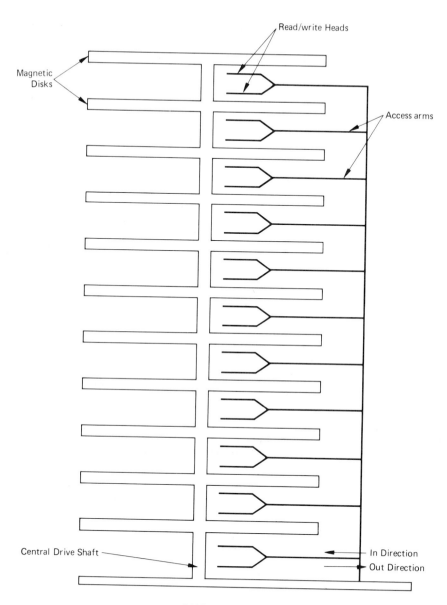

DIAGRAM OF DISK DEVICE

FIGURE 36

therefore is a very intimate marriage of both hardware and software, each one requiring the other for success.

16.5 FILE STRUCTURE

Although it has not as yet been specifically stated, the FILE SECTION defines all those data areas that are part of the input or the output files. These files will also have been defined in the ENVIRONMENT DIVISION, where by means of a SELECT clause the particular files are defined and assigned to input output devices. For every SELECT clause contained in the ENVIRONMENT DIVISION, a file name is declared.

When a READ instruction is executed in the PROCEDURE DIVISION, data are transmitted to the input area reserved for that input file. Similarly, whenever a WRITE statement is executed, all the information stored in an output area is transmitted to the specified output device.

As you will have noticed in each of the programs, each file mentioned in the file section is described with an FD entry. FD, in fact, stands for File Description. Each file may be a card file, tape file, or disk file.

A file invariably consists of many individual records, each of which may be recorded in one of three different modes. One of the standard entries refers to the mode in which the data is recorded. It is the recording mode clause which has the generalized format

$$\underline{\text{RECORDING}} \text{ MODE IS } \begin{Bmatrix} \text{F} \\ \text{V} \\ \text{U} \end{Bmatrix}$$

where F stands for fixed, V for variable, and U for unspecified. If all the records within a file are of the same length, such as is the case with a card file (every card must contain 80 characters), the RECORDING MODE IS F.

For those situations in which record lengths are not fixed, they may be designated as variable or unspecified. In the following diagram (Figure 37), reading from left to right the file is composed of five records made up of 20, 50, 100, 150, 20, and 200 characters respectively.

In such a situation, the RECORDING MODE IS V, for *variable*. It is only fair to say that for records of variable length additional programming burdens are encountered and therefore variable-length records are discouraged.

If the records are of neither variable nor fixed length, the clause RECORDING MODE IS U (for *unspecified*) is used. Again, files with unspecified

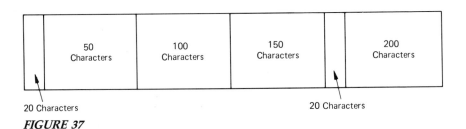

FIGURE 37

recording modes are seldom encountered except in more sophisticated situations.

Since the RECORDING MODE clause is optional, it may of course be omitted. In such cases, the computer itself determines whether the file is variable or fixed.

A required clause under the FD is LABEL RECORDS, which has the following generalized format

$$\underline{\text{LABEL RECORDS}} \text{ ARE } \left\{ \begin{array}{l} \underline{\text{STANDARD}} \\ \underline{\text{OMITTED}} \\ \text{non-standard entry} \end{array} \right\}$$

Label records are created as the first and last records of a magnetic tape or disk, and supply important identifying information to the system. These are *created* on output files and are *checked* on input files. LABEL RECORDS ARE STANDARD has the effect of triggering the COBOL routines for writing the labels on output files or for checking the labels on input files.

The writing of header and trailer records does not apply to unit-record devices such as the card reader or line printer. For unit-record files, therefore, we write

LABEL RECORDS ARE OMITTED.

A third optional clause under the FD is the RECORD CONTAINS clause, which has the following format:

RECORD CONTAINS integer CHARACTERS.

As the clause suggests, the RECORD CONTAINS clause indicates the number of characters that it contains. For example, RECORD CONTAINS 133 CHARACTERS would describe a print file with 133-position records. The usual size of a printed line is 132 characters. We write 133 however because the first position is reserved for carriage control purposes. It is positions 2 through 133 of the records that are actually printed. An input card file may have an entry which reads RECORD CONTAINS 80 CHARACTERS.

When tapes or disk are used, a BLOCK CONTAINS clause may be included. It has the general form

$$\underline{\text{BLOCK CONTAINS}} \text{ integer } \left\{ \begin{array}{l} \underline{\text{RECORDS}} \\ \underline{\text{CHARACTERS}} \end{array} \right\}$$

Tape or disk files are often blocked for reasons of expediency. If many logical records are contained within a block, more efficient use of the file is accomplished since less time is consumed in accessing the recorded information. Usually the COBOL programmer is not expected to know the most efficient block size (or the *blocking factor,* as it is called) but is informed of this by a systems expert. If an FD does in fact include a BLOCK CONTAINS clause, no further entry is required to perform the operations on that blocked data. This clause is never used when unit record devices are designated. In such cases the entire clause is omitted.

The last optional entry permitted in the file description is the DATA RECORD clause, which is of the form:

$$\text{DATA} \begin{Bmatrix} \underline{\text{RECORD}} \text{ IS} \\ \underline{\text{RECORDS}} \text{ ARE} \end{Bmatrix} \text{record-name-1 [record-name-2] . . .}$$

The DATA RECORD(S) clause defines the names of the record or records within the file. Naturally if there is only one record in the file DATA RECORD is used. These assigned record names, it is pointed out, must be unique to the program, and must conform to the rules for constructing user-supplied names. It would be reasonable to suppose that if more than one data record is specified, additional core is required. This is in fact *not* the case since a single input or output area, as the case may be, is merely redefined by subsequent record definitions.

Since the DATA RECORD(S) clause is the last optional entry for all file descriptions, it is always followed by a period to designate the end of the FD.

Here are some typical examples of file descriptions:

```
1. FD  IN-FILE
        LABEL RECORDS ARE OMITTED
        RECORD CONTAINS 80 CHARACTERS
        DATA RECORD IS SALES-RECORD.

2. FD  MASTER-FILE
        RECORDING MODE IS F
        LABEL RECORDS ARE STANDARD
        RECORD CONTAINS 65 CHARACTERS
        BLOCK CONTAINS 10 RECORDS
        DATA RECORDS ARE ACCTS-RECEIVABLE, ACCTS-PAYABLE.
```

16.6 THE WATBOL COMPILER

The tendency nowadays is for COBOL programmers to get their training at educational institutions, either under the auspices of a particular computer manufacturer or in one of the various colleges. There are even high schools where COBOL is now taught as a regular part of the curriculum. One of the glaring realities in an educational environment is that novices make unlimited errors. This is perfectly natural and is to be expected. After all, part of the educational process is to purge oneself of the incorrect thinking which causes these errors.

In the University of Waterloo in Ontario, Canada, is a Computer Systems Group which has succeeded in writing a special COBOL compiler geared for the student. It permits many if not most of the options available on the full COBOL compiler and is particularly useful in that detected errors are more explicitly documented. Usually a dollar sign, for example, is printed out on the program listing immediately beneath the area of the violation, thereby directing the programmer's attention to the part of the statement which has created the diagnostic. Not only is the compiler rich in its diagnostic capability but it is also "fast and dirty."

A "fast and dirty" compiler is one which is fast during compilation, the phase during which most if not all of a student's program errors will be found. Such a compiler is not suited for commercial purposes because the generated code is not optimized and would result in unduly long execution times. Since student problems are generally short, running them in inefficient machine code is not particularly disturbing. Furthermore, the operating system assigns a very high priority to jobs running under WATBOL. The net result is that a student can obtain a fast turn-around, which is always a treasured asset.

In naming the compiler produced by this group at the University of Waterloo, the first three letters of Waterloo were attached to the last three letters of COBOL, giving us WATBOL.

At New York University, where WATBOL is routinely used as the student compiler, turn-around time is about 10 minutes compared to at least an hour using the regular COBOL compiler. What is more, all the time used running WATBOL (as distinct from COBOL) is gratis whereas regular COBOL time is strictly budgeted. No greater inducement is necessary to encourage students to run their programs on the WATBOL compiler.

Instead of the four levels of diagnostics recognized by the standard COBOL compiler, namely, W, C, E, and D, the WATBOL compiler issues compile-time diagnostics at five levels of severity. They are MESSAGE, WARNING, EXTENSION, ERROR, and TERMINATION.

A nonfatal MESSAGE is issued for minor infractions of the rules, such as omitting a space after a period or a comma. Execution of the program, however, continues.

More severe violations of COBOL rules are flagged by a WARNING. Using a program name greater in length than eight characters or including a minus sign in it (invariably referred to as a hyphen) would cause a WARNING. A WARNING is also not fatal.

Since WATBOL allows for various nonstandard instructions known as "extensions," WATBOL prints out the word EXTENSION for each statement which incorporates such an extension. The purpose of the diagnostic is to alert the user that if the program is to be run subsequently on another computer which does not allow for that particular extension, the program will have to be amended accordingly.

A more severe violation is flagged by the word ERROR. In this case, execution of the program is usually halted since to continue might result in incorrect output.

An even more severe violation is flagged by the word TERMINATION. As its name suggests, it terminates execution of the program.

A typical example of a WATBOL diagnostic is shown below. An attempt is made to execute the instruction.

```
DIVIDE A1 BY A2.
```

As you may recall, when the preposition BY is used in the DIVIDE statement, the GIVING clause must also be used. Here is the way in which the diagnostic is printed.

```
61              DIVIDE A1 BY A2.
                              $
******ERROR 537 MISSING KEYWORD GIVING.
```

In the above case, instruction 61 is in violation of the rules of syntax. A dollar sign is printed beneath the period, indicating the point where the violation has been detected. On the next line, after the five asterisks, is printed the error number (in this case, ERROR 537) and a description of the nature of the error.

You may recall earlier on in the text, when we discussed the MULTIPLY verb, we made the point that one cannot say

```
MULTIPLY A1 TIMES A2
```

however acceptable this may be in conversational English. One has to write, of course,

```
MULTIPLY A1 BY A2.
```

Here is what happens if this error is attempted in WATBOL. It gives not one diagnostic but two. Error 532 points out that instead of the word TIMES the preposition BY has been assumed. But then immediately afterwards, error 850 announces that it has detected a missing or invalid operand. Presumably the data-name A2 is lost or ignored because of the first diagnostic.

```
67              MULTIPLY A1 TIMES A2.
                              $
*****ERROR 532 MISSING KEYWORD—BY ASSUMED.
*****ERROR 850 MISSING OR INVALID OPERAND.
```

To obtain a list of all of the possible diagnostics available on the WATBOL compiler, all one need do is to run the following short program. The program name is a special eight-character word, namely COBERMSG, for COBOL error messages.

PROGRAM 51
COBERMSG

```
IDENTIFICATION DIVISION.
PROGRAM-ID. COBERMSG.
ENVIRONMENT DIVISION.
DATA DIVISION.
PROCEDURE DIVISION.
    STOP RUN.
```

The output to this program is quite voluminous but will be of great interest to the novice programmer. Of even greater interest and usefulness is a list of the complete set of reserved, key words recognized by the WATBOL compiler. This may be obtained by running the identical program to that above for producing the error messages. The only change that has to be made is that the program name has to be COBKEYWD instead of COBERMSG. It is recommended that when writing programs in WATBOL the list of reserved words be kept close by for ready reference.

There are, however, some incompatibilities between WATBOL and IBM COBOL. They include the following:

1. Whereas in COBOL no spaces may appear before the separators comma, semicolon, and period, spaces are optional in WATBOL.
2. Non-numeric literals may be enclosed within either single or double quotes but not a combination of them. In other words, the literals 'GROSS-PAY' and "WAGES" are both acceptable but 'NET-INCOME" is not. HOWEVER, the inclusion of either of the quote signs is permitted provided that it is enclosed by a pair of the other quote signs. FOR example, 'FICA"S-AMOUNT' and "FICA'S-AMOUNT" are both valid nonnumeric literals in WATBOL.
3. In COBOL a comment card is specified by punching an asterisk in column 7. Unlike COBOL, in WATBOL a comment card cannot immediately precede a continuation card.
4. Some program text is allowed on the same line as Division or Section headers in WATBOL, but this is not a recommended practice.
5. Multiple receiving fields are permitted in ADD, SUBTRACT, MULTIPLY, DIVIDE and COMPUTE statements. For example,

```
ADD A B GIVING C D.
```

In this case the sum of A and B will be stored in both C and D. By the same token

```
COMPUTE W X = Y + Z
```

will store the sum of Y and Z in both W and X.

6. The debugging aids READY TRACE and RESET TRACE are permitted. Instead of the paragraph names of the executed program being printed out, their internally stored statement numbers are printed. What appears on the output is a succession of statement numbers.

7. The input file must be assigned to SYSIN and the output file to SYSOUT.

8. The simple WRITE statement on SYSOUT is treated equivalently as the COBOL statement WRITE AFTER ADVANCING. In other words, they both cause the printer to space before printing. Since the WRITE AFTER ADVANCING option necessitates a blank in column 1 for carriage control, the simple WRITE in WATBOL should have 133 characters per line, or on some systems, 121 characters.

9. Output produced by the WATBOL compiler prints immediately after the program listing. Therefore it may be desirable to resort to SPECIAL–NAMES to go to the top of a new page before printing.

10. Uncleared areas of output are printed with double quotation marks.

A typical WATBOL program control card set-up is now shown:

```
//JOB      JOB(xxxx,xxxx),'your name',CLASS=C
$JOB      WATBOL anyname

          {COBOL Program}

$ENTRY    (whether data is used or not)
          {data cards (if used)}

$EOF
/*.
//
```

At different installations, minor changes may be necessary.

16.7 STRUCTURED PROGRAMMING

In recent years, programmers have been criticized for writing programs which are aesthetically unpleasing to the eye, and lacking in structural integrity. The whole purpose of writing a program in the COBOL language is to enable another programmer to understand it with the maximum of ease and to amend it, if necessary, with a minimum of effort. If a program is so designed that GO TO statements are liberally sprinkled throughout, it makes the job of following the logic of that program extremely difficult, and at best nerve-racking.

Ideally speaking, a program should be written so that the statements of the program are executed sequentially in the order in which they appear, with a minimum of GO TO's. By discreet use of the IF . . . THEN . . . ELSE

. . . statement, conditional branching can be made effectively between the existing alternatives. And lastly, looping should be effected by means of the PERFORM statement, perhaps with the UNTIL clause in given situations. Each of these considerations will influence the manner in which a programmer solves a particular problem, and will inevitably reflect upon his or her style of programming. What is implied also is a need for "egoless" programming. There seems little point in resorting to a short but esoteric technique which only the original programmer understands rather than adding one or two more steps to make the program completely comprehensible, not only to the original programmer but also to the individual who has to maintain the program long after the original programmer has left for greener pastures. In short, the method to be recommended is the so-called KISS method–an acronym for Keep It Simple Stupid.

16.8 THE TELEPHONE PROBLEM

It is customary for the standard seven-digit telephone number to be composed of a two-letter exchange code, followed by a digit, followed by a four-digit number. For example, some typical telephone numbers are AC–2–1234, SU–5–9801, and MU–4–4444. The tendency of late is to replace the letter codes with numerics. The result is that almost all newly assigned telephone numbers are composed of seven numerics. For some people, remembering a seven-digit telephone number is far more difficult than one composed of two letters followed by five numeric digits. In order to assist such people, the following program has been devised.

It will be noticed that in the standard telephone dial (see Figure 38) there are 10 finger positions for the digits 0 through 9 (the program is equally applicable to push-button instruments). Associated with the digit 2, for example, are the letters ABC. Digits 3 through 9 on the dial also have letters associated with them, as shown in the diagram. The digits 0 and 1 do *not* have corresponding alphabetics.

The purpose of this program is to read a given seven-digit telephone number and to print out every possible alphabetic combination corresponding to that telephone number. Within the 2,187 combinations it is hoped at least one word or name will be included which somehow describes the individual who has the telephone number, thereby avoiding the difficulty of having to remember the seven digits. One could then simply dial the seven lettered word or name.

Since the digits 0 and 1 do not have corresponding letters, some kind of decision has to be made if the telephone number in question contains one or both of these two digits. Either the telephone number can be rejected outright or a substitution can be made. For example, the zero can be replaced by the letter z, which incidentally does not appear on the telephone dial. As for the digit 1, this could be substituted with, say, a minus sign. This version of the program rejects any telephone number which contains a zero or a 1.

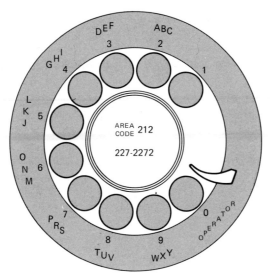

FIGURE 38

The input to the program is a seven-digit telephone number punched in columns 1 through 7. Each digit is assigned an 05 level data name DIGIT–1 through DIGIT–7. The output consists of a printout of the telephone number to be converted, followed by the 2,187 possible alphabetic combinations corresponding to that telephone number printed in 11 columns on each page.

In order to come to an understanding of how the program works, we will consider first the simple case of a 3-digit telephone number, 247. The letters associated with these three digits are

2	4	7
ABC	GHI	PRS

The idea is to select systematically each of the letters in turn until all combinations are exhausted. The first combination, taking the first letter from each group of three, is AGP. Next is AGR followed by AGS, taking the second two letters in turn from the third group. At this point, the third trio, PRS, is "exhausted." Next we take the first letter of the first group, A, followed by the second letter of the second group, H, followed in turn by each of the letters of the third group. We therefore arrive at the combinations AHP AHR AHS. Next we combine A with the third letter of the second group I, matching it up successively with PRS of the third group to obtain the combinations AIP AIR and AIS. This exhausts both the third and the second groups. At this point, we begin with the second letter of the first group, combining it in turn with each letter of the second and third group, exactly as before. This gives us the combinations

```
BGP   BGR   BGS
BHP   BHR   BHS
BIP   BIR   BIS
```

Finally, the letter c of the first group is combined with each letter of the second and third groups, creating the combinations

```
CGP   CGR   CGS
CHP   CHR   CHS
CIP   CIR   CIS
```

Thus we have arrived at each of the possible combinations using the digits 2, 4, and 7. In essence, we have accessed each of the letters associated with these three digits in the following manner

```
1   1   1
1   1   2
1   1   3
1   2   1
1   2   2
1   2   3
1   3   1
1   3   2
1   3   3
2   1   1
    ⋮
3   2   3
3   3   3
```

In the program where we deal with seven digits rather than three digits, this scheme is accomplished by exploiting the advanced version of the PERFORM instruction in which counter-1 through counter-7 are varied from one by one until they each become greater than three. Counter-1 through counter-7 play the role of pointers which progressively point to a single letter in each of the seven groups.

The 24 letters ABCDEFGHIJKLMNOPRSTUVWXY are listed as entries to the 01 level entry name NUMBER–CONVERSION–DATA. These entries are redefined by LETTER–TABLE in which each of the valid digits, EACH–DIGIT, occurs 8 times and LETTERS occurs three times. These 24 entries constitute a 2-dimensional table in which each of the elements has a picture of X.

After the telephone number is read, it is tested to insure that it is not non-numeric. If it passes this test, it is then checked to determine whether it contains a zero or a 1. If either of these tests fails, an appropriate error message is printed out, the card is rejected, and a new telephone number is read.

If the telephone number is valid for conversion purposes, 1 is subtracted from digit-1 through digit-7 successively in order that the 2-dimensional table may be set up as shown.

TELEPHONE DIGIT	CORRESPONDING LETTERS		
2	A	B	C
3	D	E	F
4	G	H	I
5	J	K	L
6	M	N	O
7	P	R	S
8	T	U	V
9	W	X	Y

That is to say, the letters corresponding to the digit 2 are located in the first row and similarly the letters corresponding to the digit 3 are in the second row, and so on.

It will be noticed that MAKE–A–WORD is a section header which encompasses paragraphs FIND–POSITION–ON–PRINT–LINE through MOVE–EACH–LETTER–TO–WORD. We may therefore PERFORM this section by utilizing the section name instead of using the THRU option of the PERFORM instruction. The purpose of this section is to select each of the 2187 combinations of letters which are then printed out in three and one-half pages, eleven columns per page. The reader's attention is drawn to the fact that the PERFORM instruction does not officially accept more than two AFTER phrases. Nevertheless, on both the regular IBM COBOL compiler and the WATBOL compiler a warning only is printed and the computation carried out exactly as written.

A perusal of the output on the second page will show that the name BARBARA is included as one of the possibilities. If the person with the telephone number 227–2272 happens to have the name Barbara, dialing her name will of course be the right number and there will be no need for any mental gymnastics to remember her telephone number. Of course, if her last name happens by chance to be Cascara, (a name which appears in the middle of the fourth page) dialing either her first or last name will reach the correct number!

In any case, here is a program designed to print out all possible combinations of letters for any seven-digit telephone number which does not contain a zero or a one. To test the program, two invalid input data cards have been read in; this accounts for the first two printouts. Following these two printouts is that for the acceptable telephone number 227–2272.

PROGRAM 52
Telefone

```
00001          IDENTIFICATION DIVISICN.
00002          PROGRAM-ID.  TELEFCNE.
00003          AUTHOR. PETER MICHAEL CHRISTOPHER MCKAY.
00004
00005          ENVIRONMENT DIVISICN.
00006          CONFIGURATION SECTICN.
CCC07          SOURCE-COMPUTER. IBM-370-145.
00008          OBJECT-COMPUTER. IBM-370-145.
CC009          SPECIAL-NAMES.
C0010              C01 IS NEWPAGE.
00011          INPUT-OUTPUT SECTICN.
C0012          FILE-CCNTRCL.
C0013              SELECT  INFILE ASSIGN TC UR-S-REACER.
00014              SELECT  CUTFILE ASSIGN TC UR-S-PRINTER.
00015          DATA DIVISICN.
00016          FILE SECTICN.
00017          FD  INFILE
00018              LABEL RECCRDS ARE CMITTED.
00019          01  TELEPHONE-NUMBER.
00020              02  PHONE-NUMBER.
00021                  05  DIGIT-1          PICTURE 9.
00022                  05  DIGIT-2          PICTURE 9.
00023                  05  DIGIT-3          PICTURE 9.
00024                  05  DIGIT-4          PICTURE 9.
00025                  05  DIGIT-5          PICTURE 9.
C0026                  05  DIGIT-6          PICTURE 9.
00027                  05  DIGIT-7          PICTURE 9.
00028              02  FILLER               PICTURE X(73).
00029
00030          FD  OUTFILE
00031              LABEL RECCRDS ARE CMITTED.
00032
00033
00034          01  OUTLINE.
00035              05 FILLER       PICTURE X(133).
00036
00037          WORKING-STCRAGE SECTICN.
00038          77 POSITIONER       PICTURE 99          VALUE ZERC.
00039
00040          01  HEADER-1.
C0041              05 FILLER              PICTURE X(26)
00042              VALUE ' THE TELEPHCNE NUMBER IS: '.
00043              05 PHCNE-NUMBER-CUT    PICTURE 99989999.
00044          01  WORDS-CUT.
00045              03 FILLER      PICTURE X           VALUE SPACE.
00046              03 WCRD-CUT CCCURS 11 TIMES.
00047                  05 FILLER PICTURE X(12).
C0048
00C49          01  COUNTER-RECCRD.
00050              05  COUNTER-1   PICTURE 9.
00051              05  COUNTER-2   PICTURE 9.
00052              05  COUNTER-3   PICTURE 9.
00053              05  COUNTER-4   PICTURE 9.
00054              05  COUNTER-5   PICTURE 9.
00055              05  COUNTER-6   PICTURE 9.
00056              05  COUNTER-7   PICTURE 9.
00057
00058          01  NUMBER-CCNVERSICN-DATA.
00059              05  FILLER      PICTURE X(12)    VALUE 'ABCDEFGHIJKL'.
00060              05  FILLER      PICTURE X(12)    VALUE 'MNOPRSTUVWXY'.
00061
00062          01  LETTER-TABLE REDEFINES NUMBER-CONVERSION-DATA.
00063              02  EACH-CIGIT CCCURS  8 TIMES.
00064                  03  LETTERS CCCURS 3 TIMES.
00065                      05  FILLER PICTURE X.
00066
00067          01  COMPLETED-WCRD.
00068              05  LETTER-1    PICTURE X.
00069              05  LETTER-2    PICTURE X.
C0070              05  LETTER-3    PICTURE X.
C0071              05  LETTER-4    PICTURE X.
00072              05  LETTER-5    PICTURE X.
00073              05  LETTER-6    PICTURE X.
00074              05  LETTER-7    PICTURE X.
00075
00076
00077          PROCEDURE DIVISICN.
00078
00079              OPEN INPUT INFILE, OUTPUT CUTFILE.
```

```
00080
00081           READ-A-PHONE-NUMBER.
00082               MOVE SPACES TO OUTLINE.
00083               WRITE OUTLINE AFTER ADVANCING NEWPAGE.
00084               MOVE SPACES TO WORDS-OUT.
00085               READ INFILE AT END GO TO CLOSE-IT-UP.
00086               MOVE PHONE-NUMBER TO PHONE-NUMBER-OUT.
00087               WRITE  OUTLINE FROM HEADER-1 AFTER 5.
00088
00089               IF PHONE-NUMBER IS NOT NUMERIC THEN
00090                   MOVE ' THIS PHONE NUMBER  IS REJECTED BECAUSE IT CONTAIN
00091                   'S NON-NUMERIC CHARACTERS' TO OUTLINE
00092                   WRITE OUTLINE AFTER ADVANCING 10 LINES
00093                   GO TO READ-A-PHONE-NUMBER.
00094
00095               IF DIGIT-1 EQUAL  ZERO OR DIGIT-1 EQUAL  1
00096                   OR DIGIT-2 EQUAL ZERO OR DIGIT-2 EQUAL 1
00097                   OR DIGIT-3 EQUAL ZERO OR DIGIT-3 EQUAL 1
00098                   OR DIGIT-4 EQUAL ZERO OR DIGIT-4 EQUAL 1
00099                   OR DIGIT-5 EQUAL ZERO OR DIGIT-5 EQUAL 1
00100                   OR DIGIT-6 EQUAL ZERO OR DIGIT-6 EQUAL 1
00101                   OR DIGIT-7 EQUAL ZERO OR DIGIT-7 EQUAL 1
00102               THEN
00103                   MOVE '            THE PHONE NUMBER HAS ONES OR ZEROS, THE
00104                   'REFORE IT WAS REJECTED' TO OUTLINE
00105                   WRITE OUTLINE AFTER ADVANCING 10
00106                   GO TO READ-A-PHONE-NUMBER.
00107
00108
00109               SUBTRACT 1 FROM DIGIT-1, DIGIT-2, DIGIT-3, DIGIT-4,
00110                   DIGIT-5, DIGIT-6, DIGIT-7.
00111
00112               PERFORM MAKE-A-WORD
00113                   VARYING COUNTER-1 FROM 1 BY 1 UNTIL COUNTER-1 > 3,
00114                   AFTER COUNTER-2 FROM 1 BY 1 UNTIL COUNTER-2 > 3,
00115                   AFTER COUNTER-3 FROM 1 BY 1 UNTIL COUNTER-3 > 3,
00116                   AFTER COUNTER-4 FROM 1 BY 1 UNTIL COUNTER-4 > 3,
00117                   AFTER COUNTER-5 FROM 1 BY 1 UNTIL COUNTER-5 > 3,
00118                   AFTER COUNTER-6 FROM 1 BY 1 UNTIL COUNTER-6 > 3,
00119                   AFTER COUNTER-7 FROM 1 BY 1 UNTIL COUNTER-7 > 3.
00120               WRITE OUTLINE FROM WORDS-OUT AFTER ADVANCING 1.
00121               GO TO READ-A-PHONE-NUMBER.
00122
00123           CLOSE-IT-UP.
00124               MOVE SPACES TO OUTLINE.
00125               WRITE OUTLINE BEFORE ADVANCING NEWPAGE.
00126               CLOSE INFILE, OUTFILE.
00127               STOP RUN.
00128
00129
00130           MAKE-A-WORD SECTION.
00131
00132           FIND-POSITION-ON-PRINT-LINE.
00133               IF POSITIONER IS LESS THAN 11 THEN
00134                           ADD 1 TO POSITIONER
00135                   ELSE
00136                           WRITE OUTLINE FROM WORDS-OUT AFTER 1,
00137                           MOVE 1 TO POSITIONER,
00138                           MOVE SPACES TO WORDS-OUT.
00139
00140           MOVE-EACH-LETTER-TO-WORD.
00141               MOVE LETTERS (DIGIT-1, COUNTER-1) TO LETTER-1.
00142               MOVE LETTERS (DIGIT-2, COUNTER-2) TO LETTER-2.
00143               MOVE LETTERS (DIGIT-3, COUNTER-3) TO LETTER-3.
00144               MOVE LETTERS (DIGIT-4, COUNTER-4) TO LETTER-4.
00145               MOVE LETTERS (DIGIT-5, COUNTER-5) TO LETTER-5.
00146               MOVE LETTERS (DIGIT-6, COUNTER-6) TO LETTER-6.
00147               MOVE LETTERS (DIGIT-7, COUNTER-7) TO LETTER-7.
00148               MOVE COMPLETED-WORD TO WORD-OUT (POSITIONER).
```

OUTPUT TO PROGRAM 52

THE TELEPHONE NUMBER IS: AR66679

THIS PHONE NUMBER IS REJECTED BECAUSE IT CONTAINS NON-NUMERIC CHARACTERS

THE TELEPHONE NUMBER IS: 2606789

THE PHONE NUMBER HAS ONES OR ZEROS, THEREFORE IT WAS REJECTED

THE TELEPHONE NUMBER IS: 2212272

```
AAPAAPA   AAPAARA   AAPAAHC   AAPAASA   AAPAASB   AAPAASC   AAPABPA   AAPABPB
AAPAAPB   AAPAARC   AAPABSB   AAPABPA   AAPACPA   AAPASB    AAPACPC   AAPACRA
AAPAAPC   AAPAASB   AAPABPA   AAPABPB   AAPACPB   AAPABPC   AAPBAPC   AAPBARC
AAPABRA   AAPACSB   AAPABPB   AAPACPA   AAPBAPC   AAPBBRC   AAPBBSA   AAPBBSB
AAPABPC   AAPABPB   AAPBCRB   AAPBCSA   AAPBCSA   AAPBBPC   AAPBCSC   AAPCAPA
AAPBASB   AAPBASB   AAPBCPB   AAPBCRC   AAPBCSB   AAPBCRB   AAPCASC   AAPCAPB
AAPBSC    AAPCPA    AAPDCRA   AAPBCRB   AAPCASA   AAPBCRA   AAPBCSB   AAPCCRB
AAPCAPB   AAPBCPB   AAPCARC   AAPCPC    AAPCASB   AAPCASA   AAPCCPB   AAPCCRC
AAPCAPC   AAPCARC   AAPCBSC   AAPCBRC   AAPCCPB   AAPCCPA   AARAARA   AARAASA
AAPCCSB   AAPCBKB   AAPCBESE  AAPCBSC   AARAARA   AARAAPC   AARAARC   AARAASC
AARAARA   AAPCCSB   AARAAPA   AAPCCPA   AARABRC   AARABSA   AARABSC   AARBARC
AARAASC   AARAARA   AARAAPB   AARAAPB   AARACSB   AARABRR   AARAPPA   AARBAPB
AAKABPB   AARAASC   AAKABPB   AARACPB   AAR BBPA  AARACSC   AARACRC   AARBBRA
AARACPB   AARACPA   AARACRA   AARACRC   AARBBPB   AARBBPA   AAKBBPB   AARBCRC
AARHARB   AARACPB   AARACRA   AARBHPA   AARBCPC   AARBCPA   AAR BBPA  AARCARA
AARBBSB   AARHARB   AARBBSB   AARBCRB   AARBCRA   AARBBPB   AARBCRA   AARCARC
AARBRC    AARBBSB   AARBBPC   AARCPB    AARCPA    AARBCPC   AARBCPC   AARCCPA
AARBCSC   AARBRC    AARCAPB   AARHCPA   AARCPB    AARCPA    AARCARB   AARCCSA
AARCBPA   AARBCSB   AARCAPB   AARCARB   AARCBSA   AARCBRB   AARCBPA   AASAAPB
AARCCPB   AARCBPA   AARCCPB   AARCCSA   AARCCSC   AARCCSA   AARCBSC   AASACSA
AASAARB   AARCCPB   AASAARC   AASAAPC   AASAAPC   AASAAPA   AASABPA   AASACSC
AASAASB   AASAARB   AASABSC   AASACPA   AASACPB   AASACPC   AASABSB   AASBCPB
AASACSC   AASAASB   AASACPA   AASACPB   AASACRB   AASACRB   AASBCPA   AASCAPC
AASBCPC   AASACSC   AASABPC   AASBBRR   AASBBSB   AASBBSB   AASBCPB   AASCBRC
AASBBPB   AASBCPC   AASBBRC   AASBBRR   AASBSA    AASBSBA   AASCAPC   AASCCSA
AASBCRB   AASBBPB   AASBCRC   AASBCSA   AASCBPC   AASCAPB   AASCBRC   AASCCSB
AASCARB   AASBCRB   AASBCRB   AASCRC    AASCBRA   AASCBRB   AASCBRA   ABPABPA
AASCBSA   AASCARB   AASCASC   AASCBSA   AASCBPC   AASCBPC   AASCCSA   ABPACPC
AASCCSC   AASCBSA   AASCCSC   AASCCPB   AASCCRB   AASCCPC   ABPABSC   ABPABPB
ABPAAPB   AASCCSC   ABPAARA   ABPAARB   ABPAASB   ABPAASA   AbPAASA   ABPARB
ABPA3PC   ABPAAPB   ABPAARB   ABPARRH   ABPABSA   ABP ABSC  ABP ABSC  ABPACPC
ABPACRA   ABPA3PC   ABPAARC   ABPACSA   ABPACSC   ABPABSB   ABPBARP   ABPBBSA
ABPARC    ABPACRA   ABPACSC   ABPACRC   AEPBPPB   ABPBBPA   ABPPBRC   ABPPBSA
ABPPBSB   ABPARC    ABPBPSA   ABP CASB  ABPBPB    ABPBBPC   ABPCBSB   ABPCBPB
ABPBBSC   ABPPBSB   ABP BCPB  ABPBCPA   ABPBCRR   ABPBCRC   ABPCBPA   ABPCCRA
ABPCAPA   ABPBBSC   ABPBCPA   ABPBCRC   ABPCCPA   ABPCBSC   ABPCCPC   ABRAABS
ABPCAPB   ABPCAPA   ABPCBRC   ABP CBSA  ABPCBSC   ABPCCPB   ABRAARB   ABRAABSB
ABPCCRC   ABPCAPB   ABPCCSB   ABPCBRC   ABRAAPA   ABRAAPB   ABRABSA   ABRBBPC
ABRABBC   ABPCCRC   ABRAABPB  ABRARPB   ABRACRB   ABRACSC   ABRACSC   ABRBCRB
ABRAASC   ABRABBC   ABRACPA   ABRACPB   ABRACRB   ABRACSB   ABRBBPA   ABRCARC
ABRBAPC   ABRAASC   ABRACPB   ABKBARC   ABHBBSC   ABRBCPA   ABRBCPC   ABRCBSC
ABRBBRC   ABRBAPC   ABRBARA   ABRRBBSB  ABRLAPB   ABRBCRB   ABRCARC   ABSAABSB
ABRBCRC   ABRBBRC   ABRBBRC   ABRBCSA   ABRCAPA   ABSACPB   ABSACRA   ABSABRA
ABRCARA   ABRBCRC   ABRBCSB   ABRCBPC   ABRCCRC   ABSAASC   ABSACRB   ABSACRC
ABSACSR   ABRCARA   ABRCCPB   ABRCCRA   ABSAASB   ABSAPB    ABSACRB   ABSBCPA
ABSAARC   ABSACSR   ABSAARC   ABSAASB   ABSACPA   ABSACPD   ABSBASC   ABSCBRB
ABSACSR   ABSAARC   ABSABSA   ABSABSB   ABSBBRC   ABSBBSB   ABSBBSB   ABSCCSA
ABSBCPC   ABSACSR   ABSBBSC   ABSBBPB   ABSBBRB   ABSBRRC   ABSCAPB   ABSCCSB
ABSBCPC   ABSBCPC   ABSBCRB   ABSBCRC   ABSCCSA   ABSCBSC   ABSCAPC   ACPAASB
ABSCARA   ABSBCPC   ABSCARC   ABSBCRC   ABSCCPB   ABSCCRB   ABSCBRC   ACPACPB
ABSCBPC   ABSCARA   ABSCBCR   ABSCBRC   ABSCCPA   ABSCCRA   ABSCCRC   ACPBARA
ABSCRC    ABSCBPC   ABSCRB    ABSCRA    ACPAACPA  ACPAAPC   ACPAASA   ACPBARC
ABSCCSB   ABSCRC    ABSCCSB   A3SCBSC   ACPABRC   ACPABRK   ACPABSB   ACPBCSB
ACPABPA   ABSCCSB   ACPAAPA   A3SCBSB   ACPACSB   ACPACSA   ACPABSC   ACPCCPC
ACPBPA    ACPABPA   ACPAAPB   ACPAAPB   ACPBBPB   ACPACPC   ACPACPA   ACPCPCC
ACPACPC   ACPBPA    ACPACRC   ACPAPRC   ACPBCRB   ACPBCPC   ACPBARA   ACRAARB
ACPACRA   ACPACPC   ACPACRH   ACPACSB   ACPBCPC   ACPBCPB   ACPBCSA   ACRABSA
ACPBSA    ACPACRA   ACPACPC   ACPBBSB   ACPCARC   ACPCARC   ACPBCSB   ACRACSB
ACPBBSA   ACPBSA    ACPBBSC   ACPCPA    ACPCBPB   ACPBCRB   ACPCASC   ACRBBPA
ACPBCSC   ACPBBSA   ACPCAPB   ACPCPA    ACPCARC   ACPCARC   ACPCCPA   ACRBBPB
ACPCBPC   ACPBCSC   ACPCAPA   ACPCARB   ACPCBSC   ACPCBRC   ACRAAPB
ACPCRC    ACPCBPC   ACPCCSA   ACPCCSB   ACPCCSC   ACPCCSB   ACRABRC
ACRAARA   ACPCRC    ACRACRA   ACRABPC   ACRABPC   ACRACRB   ACRACSA
ACRAASB   ACRAARA   ACRACPE   ACRACPC   ACRACRA   ACRACPC   ACRACSB
ACRBAPA   ACRAASB   ACRARA    ACRBARE   ACRBASC   ACRBASA   ACRBBPA
ACRBAPC   ACRBAPA                                 ACRBAPC
```

ACRBBPC	ACRBBRA	ACRBBRB	ACRBBRC	ACRBBSA	ACRBBSB	ACRBBSC	ACRBCPA	ACRBCPB	ACRBCPC	ACRBCRA
ACRBCRB	ACRBCRC	ACRBCSA	ACRBCSB	ACRBCSC	ACRCAPA	ACRCAPB	ACRCAPC	ACRCARA	ACRCARB	ACRCARC
ACRCASA	ACRCASB	ACRCASC	ACRCBPA	ACRCBPB	ACRCBPC	ACRCBRA	ACRCBRB	ACRCBRC	ACRCBSA	ACRCBSB
ACRCBSC	ACRCCPA	ACRCCPB	ACRCCPC	ACRCCRA	ACRCCRB	ACRCCRC	ACRCCSA	ACRCCSB	ACRCCSC	ACSAAPA
ACSAAPB	ACSAAPC	ACSAARA	ACSAARB	ACSAARC	ACSAASA	ACSAASB	ACSAASC	ACSABPA	ACSABPB	ACSABPC
ACSABRA	ACSABRB	ACSABRC	ACSABSA	ACSABSB	ACSABSC	ACSACPA	ACSACPB	ACSACPC	ACSACRA	ACSACRB
ACSACRC	ACSACSA	ACSACSB	ACSACSC	ACSBAPA	ACSBAPB	ACSBAPC	ACSBARA	ACSBARB	ACSBARC	ACSBASA
ACSBASB	ACSBASC	ACSBBPA	ACSBBPB	ACSBBPC	ACSBBRA	ACSBBRB	ACSBBRC	ACSBBSA	ACSBBSB	ACSBBSC
ACSBCPA	ACSBCPB	ACSBCPC	ACSBCRA	ACSBCRB	ACSBCRC	ACSBCSA	ACSBCSB	ACSBCSC	ACSCAPA	ACSCAPB
ACSCAPC	ACSCARA	ACSCARB	ACSCARC	ACSCASA	ACSCASB	ACSCASC	ACSCBPA	ACSCBPB	ACSCBPC	ACSCBRA
ACSCBRB	ACSCBRC	ACSCBSA	ACSCBSB	ACSCBSC	ACSCCPA	ACSCCPB	ACSCCPC	ACSCCRA	ACSCCRB	ACSCCRC
ACSCCSA	ACSCCSB	ACSCCSC	BAPAAPA	BAPAAPB	BAPAAPC	BAPAARA	BAPAARB	BAPAARC	BAPAASA	BAPAASB
BAPAASC	BAPABPA	BAPABPB	BAPABPC	BAPABRA	BAPABRB	BAPABRC	BAPABSA	BAPABSB	BAPABSC	BAPACPA
BAPACPB	BAPACPC	BAPACRA	BAPACRB	BAPACRC	BAPACSA	BAPACSB	BAPACSC	BAPBAPA	BAPBAPB	BAPBAPC
BAPBARA	BAPBARB	BAPBARC	BAPBASA	BAPBASB	BAPBASC	BAPBBPA	BAPBBPB	BAPBBPC	BAPBBRA	BAPBBRB
BAPBBRC	BAPBBSA	BAPBBSB	BAPBBSC	BAPBCPA	BAPBCPB	BAPBCPC	BAPBCRA	BAPBCRB	BAPBCRC	BAPBCSA
BAPBCSB	BAPBCSC	BAPCAPA	BAPCAPB	BAPCAPC	BAPCARA	BAPCARB	BAPCARC	BAPCASA	BAPCASB	BAPCASC
BAPCBPA	BAPCBPB	BAPCBPC	BAPCBRA	BAPCBRB	BAPCBRC	BAPCBSA	BAPCBSB	BAPCBSC	BAPCCPA	BAPCCPB
BAPCCPC	BAPCCRA	BAPCCRB	BAPCCRC	BAPCCSA	BAPCCSB	BAPCCSC	BARAAPA	BARAAPB	BARAAPC	BARAARA
BARAARB	BARAARC	BARAASA	BARAASB	BARAASC	BARABPA	BARABPB	BARABPC	BARABRA	BARABRB	BARABRC
BARABSA	BARABSB	BARABSC	BARACPA	BARACPB	BARACPC	BARACRA	BARACRB	BARACRC	BARACSA	BARACSB
BARACSC	BARBAPA	BARBAPB	BARBAPC	BARBARA	BARBARB	BARBARC	BARBASA	BARBASB	BARBASC	BARBBPA
BARBBPB	BARBBPC	BARBBRA	BARBBRB	BARBBRC	BARBBSA	BARBBSB	BARBBSC	BARBCPA	BARBCPB	BARBCPC
BARBCRA	BARBCRB	BARBCRC	BARBCSA	BARBCSB	BARBCSC	BARCAPA	BARCAPB	BARCAPC	BARCARA	BARCARB
BARCARC	BARCASA	BARCASB	BARCASC	BARCBPA	BARCBPB	BARCBPC	BARCBRA	BARCBRB	BARCBRC	BARCBSA
BARCBSB	BARCBSC	BARCCPA	BARCCPB	BARCCPC	BARCCRA	BARCCRB	BARCCRC	BARCCSA	BARCCSB	BARCCSC
BASAAPA	BASAAPB	BASAAPC	BASAARA	BASAARB	BASAARC	BASAASA	BASAASB	BASAASC	BASABPA	BASABPB
BASABPC	BASABRA	BASABRB	BASABRC	BASABSA	BASABSB	BASABSC	BASACPA	BASACPB	BASACPC	BASACRA
BASACRB	BASACRC	BASACSA	BASACSB	BASACSC	BASBAPA	BASBAPB	BASBAPC	BASBARA	BASBARB	BASBARC
BASBASA	BASBASB	BASBASC	BASBBPA	BASBBPB	BASBBPC	BASBBRA	BASBBRB	BASBBRC	BASBBSA	BASBBSB
BASBBSC	BASBCPA	BASBCPB	BASBCPC	BASBCRA	BASBCRB	BASBCRC	BASBCSA	BASBCSB	BASBCSC	BASCAPA
BASCAPB	BASCAPC	BASCARA	BASCARB	BASCARC	BASCASA	BASCASB	BASCASC	BASCBPA	BASCBPB	BASCBPC
BASCBRA	BASCBRB	BASCBRC	BASCBSA	BASCBSB	BASCBSC	BASCCPA	BASCCPB	BASCCPC	BASCCRA	BASCCRB
BASCCRC	BASCCSA	BASCCSB	BASCCSC	BBPAAPA	BBPAAPB	BBPAAPC	BBPAARA	BBPAARB	BBPAARC	BBPAASA
BBPAASB	BBPAASC	BBPABPA	BBPABPB	BBPABPC	BBPABRA	BBPABRB	BBPABRC	BBPABSA	BBPABSB	BBPABSC
BBPACPA	BBPACPB	BBPACPC	BBPACRA	BBPACRB	BBPACRC	BBPACSA	BBPACSB	BBPACSC	BBPBAPA	BBPBAPB
BBPBAPC	BBPBARA	BBPBARB	BBPBARC	BBPBASA	BBPBASB	BBPBASC	BBPBBPA	BBPBBPB	BBPBBPC	BBPBBRA
BBPBBRB	BBPBBRC	BBPBBSA	BBPBBSB	BBPBBSC	BBPBCPA	BBPBCPB	BBPBCPC	BBPBCRA	BBPBCRB	BBPBCRC
BBPBCSA	BBPBCSB	BBPBCSC	BBPCAPA	BBPCAPB	BBPCAPC	BBPCARA	BBPCARB	BBPCARC	BBPCASA	BBPCASB
BBPCASC	BBPCBPA	BBPCBPB	BBPCBPC	BBPCBRA	BBPCBRB	BBPCBRC	BBPCBSA	BBPCBSB	BBPCBSC	BBPCCPA
BBPCCPB	BBPCCPC	BBPCCRA	BBPCCRB	BBPCCRC	BBPCCSA	BBPCCSB	BBPCCSC	BBRAAPA	BBRAAPB	BBRAAPC
BBRAARA	BBRAARB	BBRAARC	BBRAASA	BBRAASB	BBRAASC	BBRABPA	BBRABPB	BBRABPC	BBRABRA	BBRABRB
BBRABRC	BBRABSA	BBRABSB	BBRABSC	BBRACPA	BBRACPB	BBRACPC	BBRACRA	BBRACRB	BBRACRC	BBRACSA
BBRACSB	BBRACSC	BBRBAPA	BBRBAPB	BBRBAPC	BBRBARA	BBRBARB	BBRBARC	BBRBASA	BBRBASB	BBRBASC
BBRBBPA	BBRBBPB	BBRBBPC	BBRBBRA	BBRBBRB	BBRBBRC	BBRBBSA	BBRBBSB	BBRBBSC	BBRBCPA	BBRBCPB
BBRBCPC	BBRBCRA	BBRBCRB	BBRBCRC	BBRBCSA	BBRBCSB	BBRBCSC	BBRCAPA	BBRCAPB	BBRCAPC	BBRCARA
BBRCARB	BBRCARC	BBRCASA	BBRCASB	BBRCASC	BBRCBPA	BBRCBPB	BBRCBPC	BBRCBRA	BBRCBRB	BBRCBRC
BBRCBSA	BBRCBSB	BBRCBSC	BBRCCPA	BBRCCPB	BBRCCPC	BBRCCRA	BBRCCRB	BBRCCRC	BBRCCSA	BBRCCSB
BBRCCSC	BBSAAPA	BBSAAPB	BBSAAPC	BBSAARA	BBSAARB	BBSAARC	BBSAASA	BBSAASB	BBSAASC	BBSABPA
BBSABPB	BBSABPC	BBSABRA	BBSABRB	BBSABRC	BBSABSA	BBSABSB	BBSABSC	BBSACPA	BBSACPB	BBSACPC
BBSACRA	BBSACRB	BBSACRC	BBSACSA	BBSACSB	BBSACSC	BBSBAPA	BBSBAPB	BBSBAPC	BBSBARA	BBSBARB
BBSBARC	BBSBASA	BBSBASB	BBSBASC	BBSBBPA	BBSBBPB	BBSBBPC	BBSBBRA	BBSBBRB	BBSBBRC	BBSBBSA
BBSBBSB	BBSBBSC	BBSBCPA	BBSBCPB	BBSBCPC	BBSBCRA	BBSBCRB	BBSBCRC	BBSBCSA	BBSBCSB	BBSBCSC
BBSCAPA	BBSCAPB	BBSCAPC	BBSCARA	BBSCARB	BBSCARC	BBSCASA	BBSCASB	BBSCASC	BBSCBPA	BBSCBPB
BBSCBPC	BBSCBRA	BBSCBRB	BBSCBRC	BBSCBSA	BBSCBSB	BBSCBSC	BBSCCPA	BBSCCPB	BBSCCPC	BBSCCRA
BBSCCRB	BBSCCRC	BBSCCSA	BBSCCSB	BBSCCSC	BCPAAPA	BCPAAPB	BCPAAPC	BCPAARA	BCPAARB	BCPAARC
BCPAASA	BCPAASB	BCPAASC	BCPABPA	BCPABPB	BCPABPC	BCPABRA	BCPABRB	BCPABRC	BCPABSA	BCPABSB
BCPABSC	BCPACPA	BCPACPB	BCPACPC	BCPACRA	BCPACRB	BCPACRC	BCPACSA	BCPACSB	BCPACSC	BCPBAPA
BCPBAPB	BCPBAPC	BCPBARA	BCPBARB	BCPBARC	BCPBASA	BCPBASB	BCPBASC	BCPBBPA	BCPBBPB	BCPBBPC
BCPBBRA	BCPBBRB	BCPBBRC	BCPBBSA	BCPBBSB	BCPBBSC	BCPBCPA	BCPBCPB	BCPBCPC	BCPBCRA	BCPBCRB
BCPBCRC	BCPBCSA	BCPBCSB	BCPBCSC	BCPCAPA	BCPCAPB	BCPCAPC	BCPCARA	BCPCARB	BCPCARC	BCPCASA

```
CCPABRB   CCPABRA   CCPABPC   CCPABPB   CCPAASC   CCPAASB   CCPAASA   CCPAARC   CCPAARB   CCPAARA
CCPACSA   CCPACRC   CCPACRB   CCPACRA   CCPACPB   CCPACPA   CCPABSC   CCPABSB   CCPABSA   CCPABRC
CCPBASC   CCPBASB   CCPBASA   CCPBARC   CCPBARA   CCPBAPC   CCPBAPB   CCPBAPA   CCPBBPB   CCPACSB
CCPBCPA   CCPBCPA   CCPBBSC   CCPBBSB   CCPBBRC   CCPBBRB   CCPBBKA   CCPBBPC   CCPBBPB   CCPBBPA
CCPCARA   CCPCAPC   CCPCAPB   CCPCAPA   CCPBCSB   CCPBCSA   CCPCASB   CCPCASA   CCPCARC   CCPBCPC
CCPCBRC   CCPCBRB   CCPCBPC   CCPCBPB   CCPCBPA   CCPCBSC   CCPCASB   CCPCBSC   CCPCBSB   CCPCARB
CCPCCSB   CCPCCSA   CCPCCRC   CCPCCRB   CCPCCPC   CCPCCPB   CCPCCPA   CCRAAPB   CCRAAPA   CCPCBSA
CCRABPA   CCRAASC   CCRAASB   CCRAASA   CCRAARC   CCRAARB   CCRAAPC   CCRABRA   CCRABPC   CCPCCSC
CCRACPC   CCRACPB   CCRACPA   CCRABSC   CCRABSA   CCRABRC   CCRABRB   CCRACRC   CCRACRB   CCRABPB
CCRBARB   CCRBARA   CCRBAPC   CCRBAPB   CCRABSA   CCRACSC   CCRABSC   CCRBASB   CCRBASA   CCRACRA
CCRBBSA   CCRBBRC   CCRBBRB   CCRBBRA   CCRACSC   CCRABPC   CCRABRC   CCRBCPA   CCRBASB   CCRBARC
CCRBCSC   CCRBCSB   CCRBCSA   CCRBCRC   CCRBBPB   CCRBBPA   CCRBASC   CCRCAPC   CCRBCPA   CCRBBSB
CCRCBPB   CCRCBPA   CCRCBCSA  CCRCASB   CCRBCRB   CCRBCPC   CCRBCPB   CCRCBRB   CCRCBPC   CCRBCSC
CCRCCRA   CCRCCPC   CCRCCPB   CCRCRCPA  CCRCARC   CCRCARB   CCRCBRC   CCSAASC   CCRCCRC   CCRCAPA
CCSAARC   CCSAARB   CCSAARA   CCRCRCSC  CCRCESB   CCRCCSC   CCRCBRC   CCSABRA   CCSAASB   CCRCBPC
CCSABSB   CCSABSA   CCSACSB   CCSAAPC   CCSAAPA   CCSABPC   CCSARPA   CCSBBRC   CCSACPA   CCRCCRB
CCSBAPA   CCSACSC   CCSACSB   CCSACSA   CCSABRA   CCSACRA   CCSACPC   CCSCCRA   CCSBAPC   CCSAASA
CCSBBPC   CCSBBPB   CCSBASB   CCSBASA   CCSBARC   CCSBARB   CCSBARB             CCSBBRB   CCSABPB
CCSBCRB   CCSBCRA   CCSBCPB   CCSBCPB   CCSBBSB   CCSBBSB   CCSBBSA             CCSBCSA   CCSBBRA
CCSCASA   CCSCARC   CCSCARB   CCSCARA   CCSCAPB   CCSCAPA   CCSCBSC             CCSCASC   CCSBCRC
CCSCBSC   CCSCBSB   CCSCBSA   CCSCBRC   CCSCBRA   CCSCBPC   CCSCCRA             CCSCCPB   CCSCASB
          CCSCESB             CCSCCSB   CCSCCRC                                          CCSCCPA
```

16.9 THE 1974 COBOL COMPILER

All the programs illustrated in this book have been run on the 1968 ANSI compiler, which is by far the COBOL compiler most commonly used today. It should be pointed out, however, that there is a tendency in several installations to upgrade the COBOL compiler from the 1968 version to the more recent 1974 standard. The difference between the two compilers is not very great, and at most some minor adjustments may be necessary when running programs on the 1974 standard. The major differences are the following:

1. The punctuation rules regarding spaces are relaxed in the 1974 standard. A comma, semicolon, or a period may be preceded by a space, and a left parenthesis may be followed by a space.
2. In the WRITE statement, the word LINE is equivalent to LINES.
3. The REMARKS paragraph in the IDENTIFICATION DIVISION has been replaced by a regular comment card, characterized by an asterisk in column 7.

16.10 THE UNWRITTEN MURPHY'S LAW

There is a most pervasive law that programmers the world over soon learn to respect even though no legislative body ever passed it nor does it appear on any nation's constitution. It is universally spoken of simply as Murphy's Law. Its origin is rather obscure, but it is an axiom that unfortunately proves its validity time and time again. It may be stated in various ways; here are some of the most common versions.

1. In any field of detailed endeavor, anything that can go wrong *will* go wrong.
2. If left to themselves, things always go from bad to worse.
3. If there is a possibility of several things going wrong, the one that will, in fact, go wrong is the one that will do the most damage.
4. Nature invariably sides with the hidden flaw.
5. (This is really Chisholm's Law, a variant of Murphy's Law.) If everything seems to be going well, it is clear that something important has been overlooked.
6. (This is actually Gumperson's Law, another variant of Murphy's Law.) If anything can go wrong, it will, and what's more, it will go wrong at precisely the worst possible moment.

A
STANDARD COBOL NOTATION

Throughout this text the reader will have been exposed to a rather extensive repertoire of the COBOL language. These elements of the language may be used only where they are appropriate, and only when they are in strict conformity with the syntactical rules of the COBOL language. Often certain optional features are permitted, or may be omitted at the discretion of the programmer. In order that the reader may know at a glance precisely what is mandatory and what is optional with any specific instruction, each one in this appendix is written in a universally accepted notation which conforms to the following conventions:

1. All words written in uppercase are COBOL keywords. If they are underlined, they are a keyword that *must* be used for a particular feature. If the word is not underlined, the keyword is optional but is generally included for ease of comprehension, greater clarity, and improved readability.
2. All words written in lowercase represent entries which must be supplied by the programmer.
3. Any part of an instruction which is enclosed in brackets [ ] is optional.
4. If there are alternatives for a given instruction, these will be included in braces { }. One of the stated alternatives must be selected by the programmer.
5. If a clause is to be repeated as many times as a programmer desires, this is indicated by an ellipsis (. . .), which, as you can see, is a succession of three dots.

What follow are some elementary formal COBOL notations together with applied examples.

COBOL INSTRUCTION FORMATS

(a) GO TO procedure-name-1

    GO TO   DISCOUNT-PARA

(b) ADD data-name-1 TO data-name-2

    ADD   BONUS TO WAGES

(c) DIVIDE data-name-1 INTO data-name-2 [ROUNDED] [ON SIZE ERROR imperative-statement]

DIVIDE MONTHS INTO YEAR.

DIVIDE   5 INTO WORK-WEEK ROUNDED.

DIVIDE TOTAL-DEPENDENTS INTO NET-INCOME

    ON SIZE ERROR DISPLAY 'ERROR ON DIVIDE'.

DIVIDE AMT INTO CREDITS ROUNDED

    SIZE ERROR STOP RUN.

IDENTIFICATION DIVISION FORMATS

IDENTIFICATION DIVISION.

(ID DIVISION.*)

PROGRAM-ID. program-name.

AUTHOR. [comment-entry] . . .

INSTALLATION. [comment-entry] . . .

DATE-WRITTEN. [comment-entry] . . .

DATE COMPILED. [comment-entry] . . .

SECURITY. [comment-entry] . . .

REMARKS. [comment-entry] . . .

ENVIRONMENT DIVISION—FORMATS

ENVIRONMENT DIVISION.

CONFIGURATION SECTION.

SOURCE–COMPUTER. computer-name.

OBJECT–COMPUTER. computer-name.

SPECIAL–NAMES. [channel-name IS mnemonic-name]

INPUT–OUTPUT SECTION.

FILE–CONTROL. SELECT file-name ASSIGN TO system-name

DATA DIVISION.

FILE SECTION.

FD file-name.

$$\left[\text{BLOCK CONTAINS integer} \left\{ \begin{matrix} \text{RECORDS} \\ \text{CHARACTERS} \end{matrix} \right\} \right]$$

[RECORDING MODE IS mode]

$$\text{LABEL} \left\{ \begin{matrix} \text{RECORD IS} \\ \text{RECORDS ARE} \end{matrix} \right\} \left\{ \begin{matrix} \text{OMITTED} \\ \text{STANDARD} \end{matrix} \right\}$$

$$\left[\text{DATA} \left\{ \begin{matrix} \text{RECORD IS} \\ \text{RECORDS ARE} \end{matrix} \right\} \text{data-name-1 [data-name-2]} \ . \ . \ . \right]$$

77   data-name

             01–49 $\left\{ \begin{matrix} \text{data-name-1} \\ \text{FILLER} \end{matrix} \right\}$

* For IBM versions only. [This sequence of options may be remembered by the initials of the paragraph names: I PAID DSR.]

[REDEFINES data-name-2]
[BLANK WHEN ZERO]

$\left\{ \begin{array}{l} \text{JUSTIFIED} \\ \text{JUST} \end{array} \right\}$ RIGHT

$\left\{ \begin{array}{l} \text{PICTURE} \\ \text{PIC} \end{array} \right\}$ IS character-string

$\left[\text{[SIGN IS]} \left\{ \begin{array}{l} \text{LEADING} \\ \text{TRAILING} \end{array} \right\} \text{[SEPARATE CHARACTER]} \right]$

[OCCURS integer TIMES [DEPENDING ON data-name INDEXED BY index-name-1 [index-name-2] . . .]
[USAGE IS usage-type]
[VALUE IS literal]

$\left[\text{88 condition-name} \left\{ \begin{array}{l} \text{VALUE IS} \\ \text{VALUES ARE} \end{array} \right\} \text{literal-1 [THRU literal-2] [literal-3} \right.$

[THRU literal-4]] . . .]

[WORKING-STORAGE SECTION.]
[77 level-description] . . .
[01 record-description] . . .

BASIC FORMATS FOR
TABLE HANDLING

Format 1

OCCURS integer TIMES

$\left[\left[\left\{ \begin{array}{l} \text{ASCENDING} \\ \text{DESCENDING} \end{array} \right\} \text{KEY IS data-name-1 [data-name-2 . . .] . . .} \right] \right.$ . . .
[INDEXED BY index-name-1 [index-name-2] . . .]

Format 2

OCCURS integer-2 TO integer-2 TIMES [DEPENDING ON data-name-1]

$\left[\left\{ \begin{array}{l} \text{ASCENDING} \\ \text{DESCENDING} \end{array} \right\} \text{KEY IS data-name-2 [data-name-3] . . .} \right]$ . . .

[INDEXED BY index-name-1 [index-name-2] . . .]

Format 3 [IBM version]

OCCURS integer-2 TIMES [DEPENDING ON data-name-1]

$\left[\left\{ \begin{array}{l} \text{ASCENDING} \\ \text{DESCENDING} \end{array} \right\} \text{KEY IS data-name-2 [data-name-3] . . .} \right]$ . . .
[INDEXED BY index-name-1 [index-name-2] . . .]

THE REDEFINES CLAUSE

Level-number data-name-1 REDEFINES [data-name-2] . . .

PROCEDURE DIVISION INSTRUCTIONS

The ACCEPT Instruction

$\text{ACCEPT data-name} \left[\text{FROM} \left\{ \begin{array}{l} \text{SYSIN} \\ \text{CONSOLE} \\ \text{mnemonic-name} \end{array} \right\} \right]$

THE ADD INSTRUCTION

Format 1

$$\text{\underline{ADD}} \begin{Bmatrix} \text{data-name-1} \\ \text{constant-1} \end{Bmatrix} \begin{bmatrix} \text{data-name-2} \\ \text{constant-2} \end{bmatrix} \ldots \text{\underline{TO}} \text{ data-name-m [ROUNDED]}$$

[data-name-n [ROUNDED]] . . . [ON SIZE ERROR imperative-statement]

Format 2

$$\text{\underline{ADD}} \begin{Bmatrix} \text{data-name-1} \\ \text{constant-1} \end{Bmatrix} \begin{Bmatrix} \text{data-name-2} \\ \text{constant-2} \end{Bmatrix} \begin{bmatrix} \text{data-name-3} \\ \text{constant-3} \end{bmatrix} \ldots \text{\underline{GIVING}} \text{ identifier-m}$$

[ROUNDED] [ON SIZE ERROR imperative statement]

Format 3

$$\text{\underline{ADD}} \begin{Bmatrix} \text{\underline{CORRESPONDING}} \\ \text{\underline{CORR}} \end{Bmatrix} \text{data-name-1 \underline{TO} data-name-2 [ROUNDED] [ON \underline{SIZE ERROR}}$$

imperative statement]

CLOSE file-name-1 [file-name-2] . . .

$$\text{\underline{COMPUTE}} \text{ data-name-1 [ROUNDED]} = \begin{Bmatrix} \text{data-name-2} \\ \text{constant} \\ \text{arithmetic-expression} \end{Bmatrix}$$

[ON SIZE ERROR imperative statement(s)]

THE DISPLAY INSTRUCTION

$$\text{\underline{DISPLAY}} \begin{Bmatrix} \text{data-name-1} \\ \text{literal-1} \end{Bmatrix} \begin{bmatrix} \text{data-name-2} \\ \text{literal-2} \end{bmatrix} \ldots$$

$$\begin{bmatrix} \text{UPON} \begin{Bmatrix} \text{\underline{CONSOLE}} \\ \text{\underline{SYSPUNCH}} \\ \text{\underline{SYSOUT}} \\ \text{mnemonic-name} \end{Bmatrix} \end{bmatrix}$$

Format 1

$$\text{\underline{DIVIDE}} \begin{Bmatrix} \text{data-name-1} \\ \text{constant} \end{Bmatrix} \text{\underline{INTO}} \text{ data-name-2 [ROUNDED]}$$

[ON SIZE ERROR imperative-statement(s)]

Format 2

$$\text{\underline{DIVIDE}} \begin{Bmatrix} \text{data-name-1} \\ \text{constant-1} \end{Bmatrix} \begin{Bmatrix} \text{\underline{INTO}} \\ \text{\underline{BY}} \end{Bmatrix} \begin{Bmatrix} \text{data-name-2} \\ \text{constant-2} \end{Bmatrix}$$

GIVING data-name-3 [ROUNDED] [REMAINDER data-name-4]
[ON SIZE ERROR imperative-statement(s)]

THE EXIT STATEMENT

paragraph-name, EXIT

THE GO TO STATEMENT
Format 1
GO TO procedure-name

Format 2
GO TO procedure-name-1 [procedure-name-2] . . . DEPENDING ON data-name

IF data-name IS [NOT] $\begin{Bmatrix} \text{POSITIVE} \\ \text{NEGATIVE} \\ \text{ZERO} \end{Bmatrix}$ THEN $\begin{Bmatrix} \text{imperative statement(s)} \\ \text{NEXT SENTENCE} \end{Bmatrix}$

$\left[\begin{Bmatrix} \text{ELSE} \\ \text{OTHERWISE} \end{Bmatrix} \begin{Bmatrix} \text{imperative statement(s)} \\ \text{NEXT SENTENCE} \end{Bmatrix}\right]$

IF data-name IS [NOT] $\begin{Bmatrix} \text{NUMERIC} \\ \text{ALPHABETIC} \end{Bmatrix}$ THEN $\begin{Bmatrix} \text{imperative statement(s)} \\ \text{NEXT SENTENCE} \end{Bmatrix}$

$\left[\begin{Bmatrix} \text{ELSE} \\ \text{OTHERWISE} \end{Bmatrix} \begin{Bmatrix} \text{imperative statement(s)} \\ \text{NEXT SENTENCE} \end{Bmatrix}\right]$

IF [NOT] condition-name THEN $\begin{Bmatrix} \text{imperative statement(s)} \\ \text{NEXT SENTENCE} \end{Bmatrix}$ $\left[\begin{Bmatrix} \text{ELSE} \\ \text{OTHERWISE} \end{Bmatrix}\right.$

$\left.\begin{Bmatrix} \text{imperative statement(s)} \\ \text{NEXT SENTENCE} \end{Bmatrix}\right]$

THE MOVE INSTRUCTION
Format 1
MOVE $\begin{Bmatrix} \text{data-name-1} \\ \text{literal-1} \end{Bmatrix}$ TO data-name-2 [data-name-3] . . .

Format 2
MOVE $\begin{Bmatrix} \text{CORRESPONDING} \\ \text{CORR} \end{Bmatrix}$ record-name-1 TO record-name-2

THE OPEN STATEMENT
OPEN [INPUT file-name(s)]
     [OUTPUT file-name(s)]

THE PERFORM INSTRUCTION
Format 1
PERFORM para-name-1 [THRU para-name-2] $\left[\begin{Bmatrix} \text{data-name} \\ \text{integer} \end{Bmatrix} \text{TIMES}\right]$

Format 2
PERFORM para-name-1 [THRU para-name-2] UNTIL condition

Format 3
PERFORM para-name-1 [THRU para-name-2]

                    VARYING data-name-1 FROM $\begin{Bmatrix} \text{data-name-2} \\ \text{constant-2} \end{Bmatrix}$

$$\text{BY} \begin{Bmatrix} \text{data-name-3} \\ \text{constant-3} \end{Bmatrix} \underline{\text{UNTIL}} \text{ condition-1}$$

$$\left[\underline{\text{AFTER}} \text{ data-name-4} \underline{\text{FROM}} \begin{Bmatrix} \text{data-name-5} \\ \text{constant-5} \end{Bmatrix} \right.$$

$$\left. \underline{\text{BY}} \begin{Bmatrix} \text{data-name-6} \\ \text{constant-6} \end{Bmatrix} \underline{\text{UNTIL}} \text{ condition-2} \right]$$

$$\left[\underline{\text{AFTER}} \text{ data-name-7} \underline{\text{FROM}} \begin{Bmatrix} \text{data-name-8} \\ \text{constant-8} \end{Bmatrix} \right.$$

$$\left. \underline{\text{BY}} \begin{Bmatrix} \text{data-name-9} \\ \text{constant-6} \end{Bmatrix} \underline{\text{UNTIL}} \text{ condition-3} \right]$$

The programmer is at liberty to define a series of paragraphs by a SECTION name in the Procedure Division. This alternative avoids having to use the THRU option. One can therefore select a suitable SECTION name, say PARA–1–TO–PARA–10 SECTION, and write the instruction

    PERFORM PARA–1–TO–PARA–10.

rather than the instruction

    PERFORM PARA–1 THRU PARA–10.

Many professional programmers prefer to PERFORM sections.

THE READ STATEMENT

    READ file-name RECORD [INTO record-name]

$$\begin{Bmatrix} \text{AT} \underline{\text{END}} \\ \underline{\text{INVALID}} \text{ KEY} \end{Bmatrix} \text{ imperative-statement(s)}$$

SEARCH STATEMENT
Format 1

    SEARCH data-name-1 [VARYING {index-name-1 / data-name-2}]

    [AT END imperative-statement(s)]

$$\underline{\text{WHEN}} \text{ condition-1} \begin{Bmatrix} \text{imperative-statement(s)} \\ \underline{\text{NEXT SENTENCE}} \end{Bmatrix}$$

$$\left[\underline{\text{WHEN}} \text{ condition-2} \begin{Bmatrix} \text{imperative-statement(s)} \\ \underline{\text{NEXT SENTENCE}} \end{Bmatrix} \right] \cdots$$

Format 2

    SEARCH ALL data-name [AT END imperative-statement(s)]

$$\underline{\text{WHEN}} \text{ condition} \begin{Bmatrix} \text{imperative-statement(s)} \\ \underline{\text{NEXT SENTENCE}} \end{Bmatrix}$$

THE SET INSTRUCTION

$$\underline{SET} \text{ index-name } \left\{ \begin{array}{l} \underline{TO} \left\{ \begin{array}{l} \text{integer-1} \\ \text{data-name-1} \end{array} \right\} \\ \left\{ \begin{array}{l} \underline{UP\ BY} \\ \underline{DOWN\ BY} \end{array} \right\} \left\{ \begin{array}{l} \text{integer-1} \\ \text{data-name-1} \end{array} \right\} \end{array} \right\}$$

STOP INSTRUCTION

$$\underline{STOP} \left\{ \begin{array}{l} \underline{RUN} \\ \text{literal} \end{array} \right\}$$

THE SUBTRACT STATEMENT
Format 1

$$\underline{SUBTRACT} \left\{ \begin{array}{l} \text{data-name-1} \\ \text{constant-1} \end{array} \right\} \left[\begin{array}{l} \text{data-name-2} \\ \text{constant-2} \end{array} \right] \ldots$$

[FROM data-name-3 [ROUNDED]]
[data-name-4 [ROUNDED]] . . .
[ON SIZE ERROR imperative-statement(s)]

Format 2

$$\underline{SUBTRACT} \left\{ \begin{array}{l} \text{data-name-1} \\ \text{constant-1} \end{array} \right\} \begin{array}{l} \text{data-name-2} \\ \text{constant-2} \end{array} \ldots$$

$$\left[\underline{FROM} \left\{ \begin{array}{l} \text{data-name-3} \\ \text{constant-3} \end{array} \right\} \right.$$

GIVING data-name-4 [ROUNDED]

[ON SIZE ERROR imperative-statement(s)]

Format 3

$$\underline{SUBTRACT} \left\{ \begin{array}{l} \underline{CORRESPONDING} \\ \underline{CORR} \end{array} \right\} \text{ record-name-1}$$

FROM record-name-2 [ROUNDED]

[ON SIZE ERROR imperative-statement(s)]

THE WRITE INSTRUCTION

WRITE record-name-1 [FROM record-name-2]

$$\left[\left\{ \begin{array}{l} \underline{BEFORE} \\ \underline{AFTER} \end{array} \right\} \underline{ADVANCING} \left\{ \begin{array}{l} \text{integer LINES} \\ \text{data-name LINES} \\ \text{mnemonic-name} \end{array} \right\} \right]$$

THE SORT MODULE INSTRUCTIONS
DATA DIVISION

SD sort-file-name
RECORDING MODE IS mode

DATA {RECORD IS / RECORDS ARE} record-name-1 [record-name-2] . . .

RECORD CONTAINS integer CHARACTERS

[LABEL {RECORD IS / RECORDS ARE} {STANDARD / OMITTED}]

PROCEDURE DIVISION

RELEASE sort-record-name [FROM record-name]

RETURN sort-file-name RECORD

[INTO record-name] AT END imperative-statement(s)

SORT file-name-1 ON {ASCENDING / DESCENDING} KEY

data-name-1 [data-name-2] . . . ON {ASCENDING / DESCENDING} KEY

data-name-3 [data-name-4 . . .] . . .

{INPUT PROCEDURE IS procedure-name-1 [THRU procedure-name-2] / USING   file-name-2 }

{OUTPUT PROCEDURE   procedure-name-3 [THRU procedure-name-4] / GIVING   file-name-3 }

REPORT WRITER—BASIC FORMATS

FILE-SECTION—REPORT clause

{REPORT IS / REPORTS ARE} report-name-1 [report-name-2] . . .

REPORT SECTION

REPORT SECTION.

RD   report-name.

{CONTROL IS / CONTROLS ARE} {FINAL / data-name-1 [data-name-2] . . . / FINAL [data-name-1] . . .}

PAGE {LIMIT IS / LIMITS ARE} integer-1 {LINE / LINES}

[HEADING integer-2]
[FIRST DETAIL integer-3]
[LAST DETAIL integer-4]
[FOOTING integer-5]

REPORT WRITER DESCRIPTION ENTRIES

Format 1

01   [data-name-1]
LINE NUMBER IS   {integer-1 / PLUS integer-2 / NEXT PAGE}

NEXT GROUP IS   {integer-1 / PLUS integer-2 / NEXT PAGE}

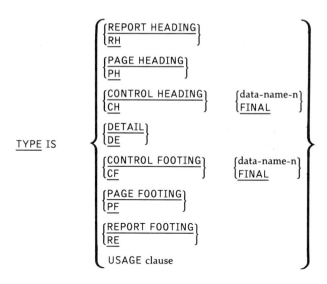

$$\text{\underline{TYPE} IS} \begin{cases} \begin{Bmatrix} \underline{\text{REPORT HEADING}} \\ \underline{\text{RH}} \end{Bmatrix} \\ \begin{Bmatrix} \underline{\text{PAGE HEADING}} \\ \underline{\text{PH}} \end{Bmatrix} \\ \begin{Bmatrix} \underline{\text{CONTROL HEADING}} \\ \underline{\text{CH}} \end{Bmatrix} \begin{Bmatrix} \text{data-name-n} \\ \underline{\text{FINAL}} \end{Bmatrix} \\ \begin{Bmatrix} \underline{\text{DETAIL}} \\ \underline{\text{DE}} \end{Bmatrix} \\ \begin{Bmatrix} \underline{\text{CONTROL FOOTING}} \\ \underline{\text{CF}} \end{Bmatrix} \begin{Bmatrix} \text{data-name-n} \\ \underline{\text{FINAL}} \end{Bmatrix} \\ \begin{Bmatrix} \underline{\text{PAGE FOOTING}} \\ \underline{\text{PF}} \end{Bmatrix} \\ \begin{Bmatrix} \underline{\text{REPORT FOOTING}} \\ \underline{\text{RE}} \end{Bmatrix} \\ \text{USAGE clause} \end{cases}$$

Format 2

> level-number   [date-name-1]
> > LINE   clause—see format 2
> > USAGE   clause

Format 3

> level-number [data-name-1]
> > <u>COLUMN</u> NUMBER IS integer-1
> > <u>GROUP</u> INDICATE
> > JUSTIFIED clause
> > LINE   clause—see format 1
> > PICTURE   clause
> > <u>RESET</u> ON $\begin{Bmatrix} \text{data-name-1} \\ \underline{\text{FINAL}} \end{Bmatrix}$
> > BLANK WHEN ZERO   clause
> > <u>SOURCE</u> is data-name-3 data-name-4 . . .
> > <u>SUM</u> data-name-3 [data-name-4] . . . [<u>UPON</u> data-name-5]
> > <u>VALUE</u> IS literal-1
> > USAGE clause

Format 4

> 01   data-name-1
> > BLANK WHEN ZERO clause
> > COLUMN clause—see format 3
> > GROUP clause—see format 3
> > JUSTIFIED clause
> > LINE clause see format 1
> > PICTURE clause
> >
> > RESET clause—see format 3
> >
> > $\begin{cases} \text{SOURCE clause} \\ \text{SUM} \quad \text{clause} \\ \text{VALUE} \quad \text{clause} \end{cases}$ —see format 3

TYPE clause—see format 1
USAGE clause

REPORT WRITER FORMATS FOR THE
PROCEDURE DIVISION

GENERATE   data-name
INITIATE   report-name-1   [report-name-2] . . .
TERMINATE report-name-1   [report-name-2] . . .
USE BEFORE REPORTING   data-name

FLOWCHARTING

Flowcharts are the blueprints from which the logic employed in a program can be represented diagrammatically. As such, they perform an extremely useful role both for the writer of the program and for anyone else who has to assume responsibility for the maintenance of the program. Flowcharts provide additional documentation for programs and are usually drawn before the actual programs are written. To paraphrase a well-known proverb, a flowchart is worth a thousand words.

Since the early days of computer programming, a convention has developed regarding the symbols customarily used in flowcharts. These symbols, standarized by the American National Standards Institute, are listed below. Each of the symbols represents a particular function such as reading, writing, processing, and decision-making.

The basic concepts within a program are usually written within the appropriate flowchart symbols. Upon looking at the flowchart, one can usually get a sense of the overall logic used within the program at a single glance. Once a flowchart has been written and carefully checked, the programmer can be confident that all of the logical paths are consistent and that there are no undetermined paths—"loose ends" so to speak.

Programs in which the logic is straightforward may not, in fact, require flowcharts since the programs can be written directly from the statement of the problem. However, for those programs in which the logic is fairly complicated, and the decisions that have to be made are quite numerous, a prewritten flowchart is invariably worth the time and effort spent in writing it.

Flowcharting Symbols	Meaning
	Input or output by means of punched cards
	Input or output in which a printed document is used
	An unspecified input-output medium
	Input-output in which magnetic disk is used for storage
	Any computational process within the computer
	The beginning or end of a program segment
	A decision box which shows the paths to be taken upon the presence or absence of a given condition

IBM AMERICAN NATIONAL STANDARD COBOL RESERVED WORDS

No word in the following list should appear as a programmer-defined name. The keys that appear before some of the words, and their meanings, are:

(aa) before a word means that the word is an IBM extension to American National Standard COBOL.

(aac) before a word means that the word is an IBM extension to both American National Standard COBOL and CODASYL COBOL.

(ca) before a word means that the word is in CODASYL COBOL, reserved word not incorporated in American National Standard COBOL, or in IBM American National Standard COBOL.

(sp) before a word means that the word is an IBM function-name established in support of the SPECIAL-NAMES function.

(spn) before a word means that the word is used by an IBM American National Standard COBOL compiler, but not this compiler.

(aam) before a word means that the word is defined by American National Standard COBOL, but is not used by this compiler.

ACCEPT
ACCESS
(aa) ACTUAL
ADD
(aa) ADDRESS
ADVANCING
AFTER
ALL
ALPHABETIC
ALPHANUMERIC
ALPHANUMERIC-EDITED
ALTER
ALTERNATE
(aa) AND
APPLY
ARE
AREA
AREAS
ASCENDING
(aa) ASSIGN
(sp) AT
AUTHOR

(aac) BASIS
BEFORE
(aa) BEGINNING
BLANK
BLOCK
(ca) BOTTOM
BY

(aa) CALL
(aa) CANCEL
(aac) CBL
(aa) CD
CF
CH
(aa) CHANGED
CHARACTER
CHARACTERS
(aam) CLOCK-UNITS
CLOSE
(aam) COBOL
(aam) CODE
COLUMN
(sp) COM-REG
COMMA
(spn) COMMUNICATION
(aa) COMP
(aa) COMP-1
(aa) COMP-2

(aa) COMP-3
(aa) COMP-4
COMPUTATIONAL
(aa) COMPUTATIONAL-1
(aa) COMPUTATIONAL-2
(aa) COMPUTATIONAL-3
(aa) COMPUTATIONAL-4
COMPUTE
CONFIGURATION
(sp) CONSOLE
CONTAINS
CONTROL
CONTROLS
COPY
(aa) CORE-INDEX
CORR
CORRESPONDING
COUNT
(sp) CSP
CURRENCY
(aac) CURRENT-DATE
(spn) CYL-INDEX
(spn) CYL-OVERFLOW

(sp) C01
(sp) C02
(sp) C03
(sp) C04
(sp) C05
(sp) C06
(sp) C07
(sp) C08
(sp) C09
(sp) C10
(sp) C11
(sp) C12

DATA
(aa) DATE
DATE-COMPILED
DATE-WRITTEN
(ca) DAY
DAY-OF-WEEK
DE
(aac) DEBUG
DEBUG-CONTENTS
(ca) DEBUG-ITEM
(ca) DEBUG-LINE
(ca) DEBUG-NAME
(ca) DEBUG-SUB-1
(ca) DEBUG-SUB-2
(ca) DEBUG-SUB-3
(ca) DEBUGGING

(aac) DELETE
(aa) DELIMITED
(aa) DELIMITER
DEPENDING
DESCENDING
DESTINATION
DETAIL
(aac) DISABLE
(aa) DISP
DISPLAY
(aa) DISPLAY-ST
(aa) DISPLAY-n
DIVIDE
DIVISION
DOWN

EGI
(aa) EJECT
ELSE
EMI
(aac) ENABLE
(aa) END
END-OF-PAGE
(aa) ENDING
ENTER
(aa) ENTRY
ENVIRONMENT
EOP
EQUAL
(aac) EQUALS
ERROR
ESI
EVERY
(aa) EXAMINE
(aac) EXCEEDS
(aa) EXHIBIT
EXIT
(spn) EXTENDED-SEARCH

FD
FILE
FILE-CONTROL
FILE-LIMIT
FILE-LIMITS
FILLER
FINAL
FIRST
FOOTING
FOR
FROM

GENERATE
GIVING
GO
(aac) GOBACK
GREATER
GROUP

HEADING
HIGH-VALUE
HIGH-VALUES
(aa) HOLD

I-O
I-O-CONTROL
IDENTIFICATION
(aac) IF
IN
INDEX
INDEXED
INDICATE
(aa) INITIAL
INITIATE
INPUT
INPUT-OUTPUT
(aac) INSERT
INSPECT
INSTALLATION
INTO
INVALID
IS

(ca) JUST
JUSTIFIED

KEY
KEYS

(aac) LABEL
(aa) LABEL-RETURN
LAST
LEADING
(aa) LEAVE
(aa) LENGTH
LESS
(aa) LIBRARY
LIMIT
LIMITS
(ca) LINAGE
(ca) LINAGE-COUNTER
LINE
LINE-COUNTER
LINES
LINKAGE
LOCK
LOW-VALUE
LOW-VALUES
(ca) LOWER-BOUND
(ca) LOWER-BOUNDS

(aa) MASTER-INDEX
MEMORY
(ca) MERGE
(aac) MESSAGE
MODE
MODES
MODULES
MOVE
MULTIPLE
MULTIPLY

(aac) NAMED
NEGATIVE
NEXT
NO
(aa) NOMINAL
NOT
NOTE
(aa) NSTD-REELS
NUMBER
NUMERIC
NUMERIC-EDITED

OBJECT-COMPUTER
(aa) OBJECT-PROGRAM
OCCURS
OF
OFF
(ca) OH
OMITTED
ON
OPTIONAL
OR
(aa) OTHERWISE
OUTPUT
OV
OVERFLOW

PAGE
PAGE-COUNTER
PERFORM
PF
PH
PIC
PICTURE
PLUS
(aac) POINTER
POSITION
(aa) POSITIONING
POSITIVE
(aac) PREPARED
(aac) PRINT-SWITCH
(ca) PRINTING
(ca) PRIORITY
PROCEDURE
(ca) PROCEDURES

(ca) PROCEED
PROCESS
PROCESSING
PROGRAM
PROGRAM-ID

(aac) QUEUE
QUOTE
QUOTES

(aa) RANDOM
RANGE
RD
READ
(aac) READY
(aac) RECEIVE
RECORD
RECORD-OVERFLOW
RECORDING
RECORDS
REDEFINES
REEL
(ca) REFERENCES
RELEASE
(aa) RELOAD
REMAINDER
REMARKS
RENAMES
(aa) REORG-CRITERIA
REPLACING
REPORT
REPORTING
REPORTS
(aac) REREAD
RERUN
RESERVE
RESET
RETURN
RETURN-CODE
REVERSED
REWIND
REWRITE
RF
RH
RIGHT
ROUNDED
(ca) RUN

(ca) SA
SD
SEARCH
SECTION
SECURITY
(aa) SEEK
SEGMENT
SEGMENT-LIMIT
SELECT
(ca) SELECTED
SEND
SENTENCE
SEPARATE
SEQUENTIAL
(aac) SERVICE
SET
SIGN
SIZE
(aac) SKIP1
(aa) SKIP2
SKIP3
(aac) SORT
(aa) SORT-CORE-SIZE
SORT-FILE-SIZE
SORT-MERGE
SORT-MESSAGE
SORT-MODE-SIZE
SORT-RETURN
SOURCE
SOURCE-COMPUTER
SPACE
SPACES
SPECIAL-NAMES
STANDARD
(aac) START

STATUS
STOP
(aa) STRING
(aa) SUB-QUEUE-1
(aa) SUB-QUEUE-2
(aa) SUB-QUEUE-3
SUBTRACT
SUM
SUPERVISOR
SUPPRESS
SUSPEND
SYMBOLIC
SYNC
SYNCHRONIZED
(sp) SYSIN
(sp) SYSIPT
(sp) SYSLST
(sp) SYSOUT
(sp) SYSPUNCH
(sp) S01
(sp) S02

TABLE
(aa) TALLY
TALLYING
TAPE
(aac) TERMINAL
TERMINATE
(aac) TEXT
THAN
THEN
THROUGH
THRU
(aac) TIME
TIME-OF-DAY
TIMES
TO
(aac) TOTALED
TOTALING
TRACE
(aac) TRACK
TRACK-AREA
TRACK-LIMIT
(aa) TRACKS
TRAILING
TRANSFORM
(spn) TYPE

(ca) UNEQUAL
UNIT
UNSTRING
UNTIL
UP
(sp) UPON
(spn) UPPER-BOUND
(spn) UPPER-BOUNDS
(spn) UPSI-0
(spn) UPSI-1
(spn) UPSI-2
(spn) UPSI-3
(spn) UPSI-4
(spn) UPSI-5
(spn) UPSI-6
(spn) UPSI-7
USAGE
USE
USING

VALUE
VALUES
VARYING

WHEN
WITH
WORDS
WORKING-STORAGE
WRITE
(aa) WRITE-ONLY
(aa) WRITE-VERIFY

ZERO
ZEROES
ZEROS

WATBOL KEYWORD LIST

ACCEPT	COMP-2	DEBUG-NAME
ACCESS	COMP-3	DEBUG-SUB-1
ACTUAL	COMP-4	DEBUG-SUB-2
ADD	COMPUTATIONAL	DEBUG-SUB-3
ADDRESS	COMPUTATIONAL-1	DEBUGGING
ADVANCING	COMPUTATIONAL-2	DECIMAL-POINT
AFTER	COMPUTATIONAL-3	DECLARATIVES
ALL	COMPUTATIONAL-4	DELETE
ALPHABETIC	COMPUTE	DELIMITED
ALPHANUMERIC	CONFIGURATION	DELIMITER
ALPHANUMERIC-EDITED	CONSOLE	DEPENDING
ALTER	CONSTANT	DEPTH
ALTERNATE	CONTAINS	DESCENDING
AND	CONTROL	DESTINATION
APPLY	CONTROLS	DETAIL
ARE	COPY	DISABLE
AREA	CORE-INDEX	DISP
AREAS	CORR	DISPLAY
ASCENDING	CORRESPONDING	DISPLAY-ST
ASSIGN	COUNT	DIVIDE
AT	CSP	DIVISION
AUTHOR	CURRENCY	DOWN
BASIS	CURRENT-DATE	DUPLICATES
BEFORE	CYL-INDEX	DYNAMIC
BEGINNING	CYL-OVERFLOW	EGI
BLANK	C01	EJECT
BLOCK	C02	ELSE
BOTTOM	C03	EMI
BY	C04	ENABLE
CALL	C05	END
CANCEL	C06	END-OF-PAGE
CBL	C07	ENDING
CD	C08	ENTER
CF	C09	ENTRY
CH	C10	ENVIRONMENT
CHANGED	C11	EOP
CHARACTER	C12	EQUAL
CHARACTERS	DATA	EQUALS
CLOCK-UNITS	DATE	ERROR
CLOSE	DATE-COMPILED	ESI
COBOL	DATE-WRITTEN	ETI
CODE	DAY	EVERY
COLUMN	DAY-OF-WEEK	EXAMINE
COM-REG	DE	EXCEEDS
COMMA	DEBUG	EXCEPTION
COMMUNICATION	DEBUG-CONTENTS	EXHIBIT
COMP	DEBUG-ITEM	EXIT
COMP-1	DEBUG-LINE	EXTEND

EXTENDED-SEARCH
FILE
FILE-CONTROL
FILE-LIMIT
FILE-LIMITS
FILLER
FIRST
FOOTING
FOR
FROM
GENERATE
GOBACK
GREATER
GROUP
HEADING
HIGH-VALUE
HIGH-VALUES
HOLD
I-O
I-O-CONTROL
IDENTIFICATION
INDEX
INDEXED
INDICATE
INITIAL
INITIALIZE
INITIATE
INPUT
INPUT-OUTPUT
INSERT
INSPECT
INSTALLATION
INTO
INVALID
JUST
JUSTIFIED
KEY
KEYS
LABEL
LABEL-RETURN
LAST
LEADING

LEAVE
LEFT
LENGTH
LESS
LIBRARY
LIMIT
LIMITS
LINAGE
LINAGE-COUNTER
LINE
LINE-COUNTER
LINES
LINKAGE
LOCK
LOW-VALUE
LOW-VALUES
LOWER-BOUND
LOWER-BOUNDS
MASTER-INDEX
MEMORY
MERGE
MESSAGE
MODE
MODULES
MORE-LABELS
MOVE
MULTIPLE
MULTIPLY
NAMED
NEGATIVE
NEXT
NOMINAL
NOT
NOTE
NSTD-REELS
NUMBER
NUMERIC
NUMERIC-EDITED
OBJECT-COMPUTER
OBJECT-PROGRAM
OCCURS
OMITTED
OPEN
OPTIONAL

ORGANIZATION
OTHERWISE
OV
OVERFLOW
PAGE
PAGE-COUNTER
PERFORM
PF
PH
PIC
PICTURE
PLUS
POINTER
POSITION
POSITIONING
POSITIVE
PREPARED
PRINT-SWITCH
PRINTING
PRIORITY
PROCEDURE
PROCEDURES
PROCEED
PROCESS
PROCESSING
PROGRAM
PROGRAM-ID
QUEUE
QUOTE
QUOTES
RANDOM
RANGE
RD
READ
READY
RECEIVE
RECORD
RECORD-OVERFLOW
RECORDING
RECORDS
REDEFINES
REEL
REFERENCES
RELATIVE
RELEASE
RELOAD
REMAINDER
REMARKS
REMOVAL

RENAMES	SORT-MESSAGE	TO
REORG-CRITERIA	SORT-MODE-SIZE	TOP
REPLACING	SORT-RETURN	TOTALED
REPORT	SOURCE	TOTALING
REPORTING	SOURCE-COMPUTER	TRACE
REPORTS	SPACE	TRACK
REREAD	SPACES	TRACK-AREA
RERUN	SPECIAL-NAMES	TRACK-LIMIT
RESERVE	STANDARD	TRACKS
RESET	START	TRAILING
RETURN	STATUS	TRANSFORM
RETURN-CODE	STOP	TYPE
REVERSED	STRING	UNEQUAL
REWIND	SUB-QUEUE-1	UNIT
REWRITE'	SUB-QUEUE-2	UNSTRING
RF	SUB-QUEUE-3	UNTIL
RH	SUBTRACT	UP
RIGHT	SUM	UPON
ROUNDED	SUPERVISOR	UPPER-BOUND
RUN	SUPPRESS	UPPER-BOUNDS
SA	SUSPEND	UPSI-0
SAME	SYMBOLIC	UPSI-1
SD	SYNC	UPSI-2
SEARCH	SYNCHRONIZED	UPSI-3
SECTION	SYSIN	UPSI-4
SECURITY	SYSIPT	UPSI-5
SEEK	SYSLST	UPSI-6
SEGMENT	SYSOUT	UPSI-7
SEGMENT-LIMIT	SYSPCH	USAGE
SELECT	SYSPUNCH	USE
SELECTED	S01	USING
SEND	S02	VALUE
SENTENCE	TABLE	VALUES
SEPARATE	TALLY	VARYING
SEQUENTIAL	TALLYING	WHEN
SERVICE	TAPE	WITH
SET	TERMINAL	WORDS
SIGN	TERMINATE	WORKING-STORAGE
SIZE	TEXT	WRITE
SKIP1	THAN	WRITE-ONLY
SKIP2	THEN	WRITE-VERIFY
SKIP3	THROUGH	ZERO
SORT	THRU	ZEROES
SORT-CORE-SIZE	TIME	ZEROS
SORT-FILE-SIZE	TIME-OF-DAY	
SORT-MERGE	TIMES	

COBOL CODING SHEET

PRINTER LAYOUT WORKSHEET

DATE _____ PAGE _____
REFERENCE # _____
PREPARED BY _____
REVIEWED BY _____

INDEX